COMPUTATIONAL
INTELLIGENCE
for
DECISION
SUPPORT

The CRC Press

International Series on
Computational Intelligence

Series Editor
L.C. Jain, Ph.D., M.E., B.E., (Hons), Fellow I.E. (Australia)

L.C. Jain, R.P. Johnson, Y. Takefuji, and L.A. Zadeh
Knowledge-Based Intelligent Techniques in Industry

L.C. Jain and C.W. de Silva
Intelligent Adaptive Control: Industrial Applications in the Applied Computational Intelligence Set

L.C. Jain and N.M. Martin
Fusion of Neural Networks, Fuzzy Systems, and Genetic Algorithms: Industrial Applications

H.-N. Teodorescu, A. Kandel, and L.C. Jain
Fuzzy and Neuro-Fuzzy Systems in Medicine

C.L. Karr and L.M. Freeman
Industrial Applications of Genetic Algorithms

L.C. Jain and B. Lazzerini
Knowledge-Based Intelligent Techniques in Character Recognition

L.C. Jain and V. Vemuri
Industrial Applications of Neural Networks

H.-N. Teodorescu, A. Kandel, and L.C. Jain
Soft Computing in Human-Related Sciences

B. Lazzerini, D. Dumitrescu, L.C. Jain, and A. Dumitrescu
Evolutionary Computing and Applications

B. Lazzerini, D. Dumitrescu, and L.C. Jain
Fuzzy Sets and Their Application to Clustering and Training

L.C. Jain, U. Halici, I. Hayashi, S.B. Lee, and S. Tsutsui
Intelligent Biometric Techniques in Fingerprint and Face Recognition

Z. Chen
Computational Intelligence for Decision Support

L.C. Jain
Evolution of Engineering and Information Systems and Their Applications

H.-N. Teodorescu and A. Kandel
Dynamic Fuzzy Systems and Chaos Applications

L. Medsker and L.C. Jain
Recurrent Neural Networks: Design and Applications

L.C. Jain and A.M. Fanelli
Recent Advances in Artifical Neural Networks: Design and Applications

M. Russo and L.C. Jain
Fuzzy Learning and Applications

J. Liu
Multiagent Robotic Systems

M. Kennedy, R. Rovatti, and G. Setti
Chaotic Electronics in Telecommunications

H.-N. Teodorescu and L.C. Jain
Intelligent Systems and Techniques in Rehabilitation Engineering

I. Baturone, A. Barriga, C. Jimenez-Fernandez, D. Lopez, and S. Sanchez
Microelectronics Design of Fuzzy Logic-Based Systems

T. Nishida
Dynamic Knowledge Interaction

C.L. Karr
Practical Applications of Computational Intelligence for Adaptive Control

COMPUTATIONAL INTELLIGENCE
for
DECISION SUPPORT

Zhengxin Chen
University of Nebraska, Omaha

CRC Press
Taylor & Francis Group
Boca Raton London New York

CRC Press is an imprint of the
Taylor & Francis Group, an **informa** business

CRC Press
Taylor & Francis Group
6000 Broken Sound Parkway NW, Suite 300
Boca Raton, FL 33487-2742

First issued in paperback 2019

© 2000 by Taylor & Francis Group, LLC
CRC Press is an imprint of Taylor & Francis Group, an Informa business

No claim to original U.S. Government works

ISBN-13: 978-0-8493-1799-6 (hbk)
ISBN-13: 978-0-367-39923-8 (pbk)

Library of Congress Card Number 99-049863

Library of Congress Cataloging-in-Publication Data

Chen, Zhengxin
    Computational intelligence for decision support / Zhengxin Chen.
        p. cm.—(International series on computational intelligence)
    Includes bibliographical references.
    ISBN 0-8493-1799-1 (alk. paper)
        1. Decision support systems. 2. Computational intelligence. I. Title. II. CRC Press
    international series on computational intelligence.

T58.62 .C33 1999
658.4'03—dc21

                                                                                    99-049863

**Visit the Taylor & Francis Web site at
http://www.taylorandfrancis.com**

**and the CRC Press Web site at
http://www.crcpress.com**

Table of Contents

Part II

Preface

WHY THIS BOOK IS NEEDED

Decision support refers to applications involving comprehensive analysis and exploration of current and historical data in organizations to support high-level decision making. Intelligent decision support relies on many techniques provided by various disciplines such as computational intelligence (or artificial intelligence, AI) and database management systems (DBMS). Artificial intelligence is the science of building intelligent agents (an agent is a system which acts intelligently). Recently an alternative term *computational intelligence* has gained popularity. By emphasizing specific computational mechanisms underlying (or behind) symbolic reasoning process rather than focusing on controversial issues around symbolic reasoning itself (as in AI), computational intelligence provides a solid approach to effectively achieve many goals of artificial intelligence. (In this preface, we will use the terms AI and computational intelligence interchangeably.)

Although there are excellent books on AI, DBMS and decision support systems, few (if any exist at all) of these books address their relationship in a holistic manner. The conventional view on the role of AI and DBMS in decision support is that decision support can be assisted by these techniques. Although this perspective is not wrong, it does not reflect the intrinsic connection between AI and DBMS on the one hand and decision support on the other.

In contrast to the conventional perspective, we view computational intelligence as the science developed *for* decision support (as well as for other applications). This perspective will not only allow a more active (thus more accurate) role of computational intelligence in decision support, but also provide a natural bridge to connect computational intelligence with DBMS. Note that the key aspect contributed by computational intelligence to decision support is the concept of reasoning, while the key aspect contributed by DBMS (and in other information retrieval systems) to decision support is the concept of retrieval. By viewing *reasoning as extended retrieval*, we can effectively integrate computational intelligence and DBMS for intelligent decision support. This book will explore this unique perspective.

WHAT READERS CAN EXPECT FROM THIS BOOK

The book is written as a concise textbook with some noticeable features.

(a) The book presents an integrated approach that can quickly push the interested scholars to the frontier of intelligent decision support. Readers who do not have enough background can take advantage of the first six chapters of this book which provide a necessary foundation for the entire book. Readers with sufficient background may skip over some sections in early chapters (see organization of the book below). However, in order to follow the integrated treatment of the materials, it is recommended for the reader to read the whole book, but with emphasis on certain chapters of greatest interest.

(b) The book may benefit readers from different disciplines and can be used at different levels (to be explained in "How to use the book"). Note that this treatment is not intended to blur the boundaries of different computer science disciplines; our purpose is just to encourage an integrated way of thinking which is a critical element of decision making. There are materials taken from existing books because they are nice, but there are more materials not found in any individual book. We cover some selected, matured computational intelligence techniques useful for decision support; we should not only correctly apply these techniques, but also analyze the indications (such as similarities or differences) behind these techniques, and identify invariants shared by various techniques. With emphasis on applications, we have made a compromise between theoretical rigorous and practical concerns. We cover some most recent developments in data mining and data warehousing, yet we still stick with the most important principles of intelligent decision making. In addition, we are interested in using folk psychology to implement systems to assist human intelligence (that is, we will include materials from "sidetrack AI").

(c) Readers can easily follow the book because it is written in a concise manner. Many chapters contain plenty of examples to illustrate well-selected materials. This can help the reader to focus on the materials of particular interest. Although intended for real-world applications, examples in this book are made simple so that readers can follow the various basic ideas discussed. The author has tried to make each chapter independent (although chapters or sections may cite each other).

(d) A list of self-examination questions is attached with each chapter. In addition, in most summary sections (at the end of chapters) we provide bibliographical remarks for further readings. The reading list contains a small set of well-selected research papers (or monographs) and extends the materials covered in that chapter. Thus the book can also be used as a reference book.

HOW THIS BOOK IS ORGANIZED

The contents of this book can be roughly divided into four parts. The organization of the book is sketched below.

Six chapters in Part I provide an overview for necessary background information. These chapters can be used together as an introductory textbook covering parts of these fields.

Part II (Chapters 7-9) further explores the notion of inference as extended retrieval. Starting from an overview of conceptual modeling, we discuss several aspects usually not covered in AI or DBMS textbooks, such as computational creativity. We also pay attention to conceptual queries and intensional answers, as well as their relationships. Part II will help the reader to understand the intrinsic relationship between computational intelligence and decision support, namely, why computational intelligence is important to decision support.

Part III (Chapters 10-13) presents some most important techniques of computational intelligence which are useful for decision support. Materials are selected to be representative in this field. Rather than a miscellaneous collection of a "technique show," materials are presented in a manner to foster an integrated way of scientific thinking. In order to provide a common ground for various techniques to be discussed, we start with a discussion on data warehousing environments which have been used as a popular platform for decision support. Various data mining techniques are discussed, with the focus on the unique features of each technique. In addition, fuzzy set theory, rough sets, and genetic algorithms are selected to illustrate different but complementary techniques needed for decision support. We encourage readers to compare these techniques as well as different perspectives behind these techniques.

To understand where these approaches are from is important to reveal some "technical invariant" behind scientific thinking. Although it is difficult to predict where future techniques will go, an in-depth study of existing techniques will help readers be prepared to deal with technical challenges to be encountered in the future. Some techniques may fade away (or be absorbed into newer techniques), but many key ideas will still last. Due to these considerations, in the last part of this book (Chapter 14), we wrap up by discussing common features of methods, as well as providing high-level heuristics for integrated problem solving.

HOW TO USE THIS BOOK: INSTRUCTORS, STUDENTS, SCIENTISTS, LEISURE READERS

For instructors:

Although this book is intended as a coherent whole, expected to be covered by following the sequence of chapter numbers, each chapter is written in a self-contained manner. The writing of the book follows a module design principle so that different components (parts or chapters) can be grouped in a flexible manner.

For instructors, the book can be adopted for several different courses. It can be used at the junior/senior level as an introductory AI textbook in computer science (CS) or information technology (IT). The instructor should elaborate certain chapters including Chapter 2, covering materials such as state space search, knowledge representation and reasoning, and expert systems. On the other hand, certain chapters in Part II should be skipped. The instructor should also provide programming assignments for students to practice basic concepts in computational intelligence. Alternatively, the book can serve a junior/senior level DBMS course with emphasis on conceptual modeling. If the book is used this way, certain chapters such as Chapters 7 and 12 should be skipped.

The book may also be applied to a course of decision support systems in information technology (IT) or management information sciences (MIS). If it is so used, the instructor may skip some technical detail but put more emphasis on integration of related tools, emphasizing data warehousing, data mining and soft computing. Additional materials (including case studies) should be provided to illustrate how these computational techniques can be used in decision support, assisted with case studies. Due to the comprehensive nature of this course, materials not emphasized in lectures can be assigned as reading materials for the students. The book does not cover any detail in query processing and transaction processing in DBMS. However, if you are interested in the approach presented in this book and want to extend it to DBMS, please contact the author at the email address listed at the end of preface.

This text is also suitable for a first year graduate course focusing on intelligent decision support. If the book is used in this manner, it should be accompanied by recent research papers organized by the instructor. For example, if this book is used as the starting point for studying data mining, a detailed reading list available in Chapter 10 can be used for this purpose.

For students:

Since this book is intended not to be too technical, students will find that most of this book is not difficult to read. You should read the chapters assigned by the instructor, and feel free to read the rest. However, you should not stop at "I understand the sentences presented in the text." Unless you have practiced the knowledge, you will not be able to master it. You should make a serious effort to answer the self-examination questions and do other assignments given by the instructor. Do not be satisfied with what these techniques are, but always ask yourself how and why these techniques are useful for decision support.

For graduate students, this book serves as a road map for your own research. With the advice of your instructor, you should read a small number of technical papers as indicated in the reading list, present your comments, and consider how to apply the theory or how to improve/extend the work. You may not be able do much in a regular semester, but you may elaborate on your findings for your thesis or graduate project (if you are so interested).

For scientists and leisure readers:

Although I recommend that you read from the first chapter to the last chapter, you can pick whatever you like to read. For scientists from disciplines other than computer science, information technology and management information systems, I encourage you to compare the way of scientific thinking as described in this book with your own discipline. For leisure readers, you will find that the information superhighway is not just full of traffic of techniques, but traffic of scientific thinking as well. You will find philosophical thoughts behind techniques may be different from those provided by professional philosophers. Whether you are a casual reader or a sophisticated thinker/practitioner, the book may present a novel way for you to understand computational intelligence for decision making. Comments, criticism and suggestions are welcome.

Comments, criticisms and suggestions are welcome. Please contact me at zchen@unomaha.edu.

Chapter 1

DECISION SUPPORT AND COMPUTATIONAL INTELLIGENCE

1.1 OVERVIEW

In this chapter we provide a brief overview on the notion of decision support, and the role of computational intelligence in decision support. Starting with the notion of decision support as problem solving, we elaborate the need for decision support agents. The role of computational intelligence for decision support is then briefly examined, and several remarks on computational intelligence are given. Since decision support is concerned with integrated management of data and knowledge, a comparative discussion on data and knowledge is also provided. This discussion is followed by a remark on the importance of a holistic, retrospective, cross-domain analysis for integrated data and knowledge management. Some important issues to be covered in this book are briefly discussed.

1.2 THE NEED FOR DECISION SUPPORT AGENTS

The need for computerized mechanism for decision support comes from well-known limits of human knowledge-processing: Studies suggest that a person's capacity for processing the contents of his or her immediate field of awareness is limited to manipulating up to about seven pieces of knowledge at any one time. The stress, errors and oversights that can result from being overloaded with knowledge can be just as detrimental as not having enough knowledge. In addition, a person may not be especially skilled at some kinds of knowledge manipulations (e.g., mathematical ones). It has been noticed that the need for support for human decision makers is due to four kinds of limits: cognitive limits, economic limits, time limits and competitive demands [Holsapple and Whinston 1996]. Various kinds of support can be provided, such as

- *User alert* (alerting the user to a decision-making opportunity or challenge);
- *Problem recognition* (recognizing problems that need to be solved as part of the decision making process);
- *Problem solving*;
- *Facilitating/extending the user's ability to process knowledge* (e.g., acquire, transform, explore the knowledge);

- *Stimulation* (stimulating the user's perception, imagination, or creative insight);
- *Coordinating/facilitating interactions* (among participants in multi-participant decision makers); and
- *Others*.

The task of decision support can be carried out by constructing *intelligent agents*. The term *agent* is used to refer to any person, program, or device capable of reasoning and decision making. It is often useful for an agent to be aware of what it knows or believes or what some other agent believes. An *intelligent agent* can perceive the environment and act rationally based on reasoning (a discussion on intelligent agent can be found in Chapter 2).

In order to understand how decision support agents can provide help, we now take a brief look at different forms of computerized decision support.

1.3 COMPUTERIZED DECISION SUPPORT MECHANISMS

The task of decision support can be carried out by decision support systems. A *decision support system* (*DSS*) refers to a computerized system which assists management decision making by combining data, sophisticated analytical models and tools, and user-friendly software into a powerful system than can support semi-structured or unstructured decision making in organizations. DSSs are computer-mediated tools that assist managerial decision making by presenting information and interpretations for various alternatives. Such systems can help the decision makers to make more effective and efficient choices [Radermacher 1994]. DSS provides users with a flexible set of tools and capabilities for analyzing important blocks of data. A DSS must be simple, robust, easy to control, adaptive, complete on important issues, and easy to communicate with. A DSS emphasizes change, flexibility and a quick response. A DSS can also *evolve* as the decision maker learns more about the problem. In many cases, managers cannot specify in advance what they want from computer programmers and model builders.

However, the concept of decision support is not restricted to decision support systems as briefly summarized above. For example, recently, *decision support queries* have drawn more and more attention from organizations. Such queries comprehensively analyze/explore current and historical data, identify useful trends and create summaries of data to support high-level decision making for *knowledge workers*, which refers to executives, managers, as well as analysts. On-Line Analytical Processing (OLAP) [Chaudhuri and Dayal 1997] and data mining [Chen, Han and Yu 1996] are useful tools for answering users' *ad hoc* decision support queries.

In this book we use the term *decision support* in a broad sense. It could be decision support for business management, decision support for management of engineering, as well as others.

1.4 COMPUTATIONAL INTELLIGENCE FOR DECISION SUPPORT

Computational intelligence is the field of studying how to build intelligent agents. To see why computational intelligence is important to decision support, we can take a look at the decision support process.

Decision making is a process of choosing among alternative courses of action for the purpose of attaining a goal or goals, and decision support shares many important concerns with decision making. Managerial decision making is synonymous with the whole process of management. The decision-making process is basically identical with the problem-solving process. Computational intelligence provides useful theories and applicable techniques needed by decision support problem solving as identified in [Holsapple and Whinston 1996]. Reasoning has been shown to be a critical aspect of decision making. It forms the basis for evaluation and judging information that has been received. Perception and cognition are being recognized increasingly as critical elements of effective decision making. Intelligent information systems will incorporate these elements along with expert systems that act as decision advisors. Human reasoning underlies intelligent information systems because such systems will have to be sensitive to the manger's cognitive ability.

A decision depends on the information perceived and how well it is understood. Knowledge workers rely on their perceptions and cognitive abilities when using information. Where perception or cognition limits their effectiveness, an intelligent information system can supplement their abilities. An effective manager is one who perceives problems correctly and knows how to respond to a situation using analytic techniques, when required, and exercising judgment to find good solutions. In addition, the task of decision support also demands other desirable features, such as imagination and creativity. Computational creativity and computer-assisted human intelligence can provide valuable help for decision makers in this regard.

1.5 A REMARK ON TERMINOLOGY

The term *artificial intelligence* (AI) was coined by John McCarthy in 1954 and has been widely used in United States and many other parts of the world. This may not be a perfect term, because the word "artificial" is somewhat controversial. Since then, several other competing terms have also been proposed, such as machine intelligence, computational intelligence, and more recently, soft computing. Unfortunately, these alternative terms also caused some confusion by themselves. Since the term machine intelligence has been mainly used as an alias of artificial intelligence in early history of AI and is no longer a major contender, here we will give brief comments on the other two terms. This discussion will also be helpful in defining the scope of this book.

For many researchers in Canada, the term computational intelligence is just the Canadian brand of artificial intelligence. In this sense, computational intelligence has existed for several decades. However, a more popular understanding of the term "computational intelligence" refers to different research interests existing under the umbrella of artificial intelligence. This caused a *de facto* split and eventually, in the late 1980s and early 1990s, the term "computational intelligence" emerged as a discipline different from AI. According to [Bezdek 1992], in the strictest sense, computational intelligence depends on numerical data supplied by manufacturers and does not rely on knowledge. Therefore, artificial neural networks should be called as computational intelligence. It is interesting to note that several well-known publication databases (including INSPEC) categorize publications using *both* terms of computational intelligence and artificial intelligence, with only 14-33% of overlap (for articles published up to 1992).

Another popular term is *soft computing*. According to [Zadeh 1994], it refers to the discipline situated at the confluence of distinct methodologies: fuzzy logic, neural network and probabilistic reasoning, the latter including evolutionary algorithms, chaos theory, causal networks, and so on. According to the contents listed here, soft computing is almost like an alias of computational intelligence defined by Bezdek. One thing we want to emphasize is that the term soft computing indicates a paradigm shift away from the original interest of artificial intelligence. To understand this, we just need to remember where the word "soft" is from: Soft computing differs from conventional (hard) computing in that, unlike hard computing, it is tolerant of imprecision, uncertainty and partial truth. Although in effect, the role model for soft computing is the human mind [Zadeh 1994], it puts emphasis on the underlying computational tools. Note that soft computing methods themselves (such as fuzzy set theory, rough set theory, neural networks, genetic algorithms, etc.) are just computational tools. (A recent discussion on quantum computational intelligence has also put emphasis on quantum computing [Hirsh 1999].) For this reason in this book we will not use this term, but we remind the reader to remember the close relationship between computational intelligence and soft computing.

We have chosen materials developed under either the umbrella of artificial intelligence or computational intelligence, so long as they can contribute to decision support. Our viewpoint about these two terms can be explained as follows. We believe these two fields largely overlap, but each does have a different emphasis. Artificial intelligence has a discipline of science, whereas computational intelligence has a stronger flavor of engineering. Computational intelligence seemingly has more fruitful results in business and engineering applications. Nevertheless, artificial intelligence was the original motive of studying computerized intelligence, and still sets the tone for such kind of studies.

To avoid confusion caused by terminology, in this book we will stay with the term "computational intelligence." We will emphasize the materials which have important applications to decision support, including features of some soft computing techniques, various machine learning methods, as well as others. However, we do not restrict ourselves to applications alone, because we believe that without a good understanding of the basic underlying theories related to these applications, we will not have a comprehensive understanding on the role of computational intelligence to decision making. That is why this book starts with a discussion on the basics of computational intelligence (such as issues related to symbolic reasoning). Since our main interests are on the use of computerized intelligence for decision making, we will take a practical approach to deal with materials that may involve sophisticated theoretical work in computational intelligence.

1.6   DATA, INFORMATION AND KNOWLEDGE

In order to understand the role of intelligent agents for decision support, we need a holistic view on the tasks to be carried out for decision support. Typically, decision support in organizations requires the following two kinds of management:

- Data management. The data management includes the database, which contains relevant data for the situation and is managed by a database management system.
- Knowledge management. It handles various tasks involved in reasoning.

An important notion discussed throughout this book is knowledge, which consists of facts and *inference rules* used for *reasoning*. Knowledge could be *procedural*, which refers to knowing how to do something, or *declarative*, which refers to knowing that something is true or false. *Commonsense knowledge* refers to the knowledge a normal child possesses and has played an important role in computational intelligence. In addition, we can talk about *tacit knowledge* (or *unconscious knowledge*), which refers to knowledge cannot be expressed in language (for example, nodding). The study of knowledge is referred to as *epistemology*. (Another useful philosophical term is *ontology*, which refers to systematic study of being. Knowledge management, to be discussed in Chapter 5, is concerned with ontology.)

In order to better understand the importance of knowledge, it would be beneficial to take a look at the hierarchy of knowledge (see Figure 1.1, which is revised from [Giarratano and Riley 1998]. At the bottom of this hierarchy is the *data*, which is filtered from *noise*. Processed data is referred to as *information*, indicating or measuring how much we know from the underlying data. (In a loose sense, data can be viewed as the primitive form of information.) Information used by agents to solve a problem will be referred to as *knowledge*. We say we can *access* information, but only an agent *possesses* the knowledge. Traditionally, knowledge has been associated with the concept of *belief*, which refers to statements that are inside the mind of an agent or can be inferred by the agent. These statements do not have to be true, and can be believed to varying degrees [Delgrande and Mylopoulos 1987, Poole, Mackworth and Goebel 1998]. Belief is thus concerned with the mental status of the agents. Without considering the mental status of the agents, it would be difficult to distinguish knowledge from information. Despite the differences between data and knowledge, however, both are useful in problem solving for decision support. In fact, a successful integration of management of both data and knowledge is the focal concern of this book. Finally, at the top of the hierarchy, we have *meta-knowledge*. Just like knowledge can be used to manipulate the data, knowledge itself can be manipulated by meta-knowledge, which refers to knowledge about knowledge (more discussion on meta-knowledge can be found in Chapter 14).

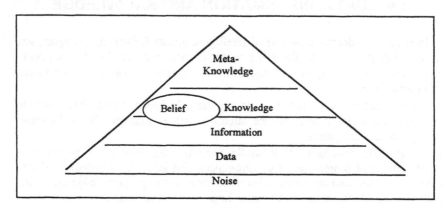

Figure 1.1 Hierarchy of abstraction

1.7 ISSUES TO BE DISCUSSED IN THIS BOOK

Computational intelligence for decision support is interdisciplinary in nature. In this book, we will examine important issues related to decision support, particularly those related to management of databases and knowledge bases. In order to study these issues to some depth, we will examine selected fundamental aspects in computational intelligence. Studying these aspects will help us to understand why computational intelligence is important to decision making, where the challenges are from, and how to integrate them.

Several features of this book have already been discussed in the Preface and will not be repeated here. Some additional remarks follow. One remark is on agents. An agent-based perspective can thread various research directions within computational intelligence in a holistic manner. In addition, this perspective allows us to extend our discussion to the materials which do not fall in computational intelligence proper, such as integrity constraints in relational databases and agent-based data mining. Throughout this book, agent-based considerations will be emphasized. We take a simple but useful idea to thread the materials together, namely, reasoning as involved in intelligence is viewed as extended retrieval. This perspective helps us to bridge the gap between these two types of information systems, such as the different scales between them. An agent-based approach makes this unified perspective possible.

Next, a remark on integration itself. There are many aspects of integration: Integration of systems, integrated use of problem solving methods, integrated use of tools, and, most importantly, an integrated way of thinking for problem solving. We will focus on most of these aspects throughout this book (except for integrated use of tools, which is not within the scope of this book). Since management of data has been a focal concern in decision support, we will also pay much attention on database management as well, even though it is not part of computational intelligence. A holistic view of data and knowledge will help us to understand the similarity as well as the difference between them (such as scaling-up problems of computational intelligence to match database management) and reduce the hurdle of integration of different types of systems. This allows a unified treatment of various topics, such as the role of agent in DBMS, and unified treatment of machine learning and data mining (this is only possible when data and knowledge are discussed in the same, rather than separate, context).

Successful decision support requires integration of data management and knowledge management. To achieve such integration, a cross-domain analysis is needed to combine the studies previous carried out in different disciplines. As noted by [Klir 1985], traditional science, such as mathematics, chemistry or physics, is one-dimension in nature. Scientific studies have passed the one-dimensional science into a two-dimensional science period. The two-dimensional science is characterized by a cross-domain study, that is, it focuses on the relational rather than individual aspects of isolated domains, and its integration with the traditional disciplines of science. Systems theory has been developed for this purpose. This kind of study continues the vein of cybernetics, which is based on the recognition that information-related problems can be meaningfully and beneficially studied, at least to some extent, independently of any specific context. In addition, due to the nature of cross-domain analysis, the interdisciplinary examination should be carried out as a retrospective analysis. Although the task of intelligent decision support does not require us to pay attention to systems theory itself, a holistic view of the problem solving process and an integrated treatment of data and knowledge management are among the most important things we should keep in mind.

Computational intelligence has achieved tremendous success, but there have been many hypes as well as critics about computational intelligence. Starting from the next chapter, we will discuss the basics of computational intelligence, which serves as the starting point of studying intelligent decision support. A good understanding on the nature of computational intelligence will help us to establish a realistic attitude toward computational intelligence for decision making.

SUMMARY

In this chapter we provided an overview of computational support for decision making. In this summary section we provide some references related to general aspects of this topic. [Brodie et al. 1984, Brodie and Mylopoulos 1986, Delgrande and Mylopoulos 1987] discuss important issues related to integrated database and knowledge base management. They were published in 1980s, but many important points made there are still valid. A nice reference source is the four volume handbook [Barr and Feigenbaum1981].

Some recent computational intelligence textbooks include [Russell and Norvig, 1995, Poole, Mackworth and Goebel, 1998, Luger and Stubblefield 1998]. Other textbooks include [Winston 1992; Rich and Knight 1991]. A discussion on intelligent agent-assisted decision support systems can be found in [Wang 1997]. Discussion on the term "computational intelligence" can be found in [Bezdek 1992, Bezdek 1994, Marks 1993, Zurada, Marks II and Robinson, 1994]. A recent textbook covering several major branches of computational intelligence (in the sense of [Bezdek 1994] is [Pedrycz 1996].

Decision support systems and the role of computational intelligence are widely discussed in literature, including [Radermacher 1994, Holsapple and Whinston 1996].

SELF-EXAMINATION QUESTIONS

1. Why is computational intelligence important to decision support? Answer this question by collecting two or three case studies from your own organization, newspapers or magazines.
2. Make your own examples to compare data versus information, and data versus knowledge.
3. Make your own example to illustrate why interdisciplinary problem solving is important.

REFERENCES

Bezdek, J. C., On the relationship between neural networks, pattern recognition and intelligence, *The International Journal of Approximate Reasoning*, 6, 85-107, 1992.

Bezdek, J. C., What is computational intelligence? *Computational Intelligence Imitating Life* (Zurada, J. M., Marks II, R. J. and Robinson, C. J. eds.), pp. 1-12, IEEE Press, 1994.

Brodie, M., L., Mylopoulos, J. and Schmidt, J. W., *On Conceptual Modelling: Perspectives from Artificial Intelligence, Databases, and Programming Languages*, Springer-Verlag, New York, 1984.

Brodie, M. L., and Mylopoulos, J. (eds.), *On Knowledge Base Management Systems: Integrating Artificial Intelligence and Database Technologies*, Springer-Verlag, New York, 1986.

Chaudhuri, S. and U. Dayal, An overview of data warehousing and OLAP Technology, *SIGMOD Record*, 26(1), 65-74, 1997.

Chen, M. S., Han, J. and Yu, P. S., Data mining: An overview from a database perspective, *IEEE Transactions on Knowledge and Data Engineering*, 8(6), 866-883, 1996.

Delgrande, J. P. and Mylopoulos, J., Knowledge representation: Features of knowledge, in *Fundamentals of Artificial Intelligence: An Advanced Course* (Bibel , W. and Jorrand, Ph. eds.), pp. 3-38, 1987.

Giarratano, J. and Riley, G., *Expert Systems: Principles and Programming (3rd ed.)*, PWS Publishing, Boston, 1998.

Hirsh, H., A quantum leap for AI (Trends & Controversies column), *IEEE Intelligent Systems & Their Applications*, 14(4), 9-18, 1999.

Holsapple, C. W. and Whinston, A. B., *Decision Support Systems: A Knowledge-Based Approach*, West Publishing Company, Minneapolis/St. Paul, 1996.

Klir, C. J., *Architecture of Systems Problem Solving*, Plenum Press, New York, 1985.

Marks II, R. J., Intelligence: Computational versus artificial, *IEEE Transactions on Neural Networks*, 4 (5), 1993.

Pedrycz, W., *Computational Intelligence*, CRC Press, Boca Raton, 1996.

Poole, C., Mackworth, A. and Goebel. R., *Computational Intelligence: A Logical Approach*, Oxford University Press, New York, 1998.

Radermacher, F. J., Decision support systems: Scope and potential. *Decision Support Systems*, 12, 257-265, 1994.

Rich, E. and Knight, K., *Artificial Intelligence* (2nd ed.), McGraw-Hill, New York, 1991.

Russell, S. and Norvig, P., *Artificial Intelligence: A Modern Approach*, Prentice Hall, Englewood Cliffs, NJ, 1995.

Wang, H., Intelligent agent-assisted decision support systems: Integration of knowledge discovery, knowledge analysis, and group decision support, *Expert Systems with Applications,* 12(3), 323-335, 1997.

Winston, P. H., *Artificial Intelligence* (3rd ed.), Addison Wesley, Reading, MA, 1992.

Zadeh, L., Fuzzy Logic, Neural Networks, and Soft Computing. *Communications of the ACM,* 37(3), 77-86, 1994.

Zurada, J. M., Marks II, R. J. and Robinson, C. J., Introduction, *Computational Intelligence Imitating Life* (J. M. Zurada, R. J. Marks II and C. J. Robinson eds.), pp. v - xi, IEEE Press, 1994.

Chapter 2

SEARCH AND REPRESENTATION

2.1 OVERVIEW

In this chapter we provide an overview on computational intelligence. Starting with some sample problems studied by computational intelligence, we define computational intelligence as construction of intelligent agents and examine some underlying assumptions of computational intelligence. Since agents solve problems through searching, the emphasis of this chapter is on search methods. The first half of this chapter (Sections 2.2 to 2.4) provides a general discussion on computational intelligence. The second half (Section 2.5 to 2.10) is devoted to two key ideas in symbol-based computational intelligence: search and representation. We first discuss some data structures needed for data search and space state search. Basic algorithms for blind search and heuristic search are then studied. We also discuss basic issues related to representing knowledge for search. Therefore, this chapter provides a roadmap of the entire book.

2.2 SAMPLE PROBLEMS AND APPLICATIONS OF COMPUTATIONAL INTELLIGENCE

2.2.1 SOME SIMPLE EXAMPLES

We use the following examples to illustrate what kinds of problems are handled in computational intelligence.

Example 1. Consider the following simple puzzle (which will be referred to as the *FWGC puzzle*).

> A farmer with his wolf, goat, and cabbage come to the edge of a river they wish to cross. There is a boat at the river's edge (west bank or east bank). The boat can only carry two things (including the only rower, the farmer) at a time. If the wolf is ever left alone with the goat, the wolf will eat the goat. If the goat is left alone with the cabbage, the goat will eat the cabbage. How will you solve the problem by devising a sequence of crossings of the river?

In order to explain the problem and solve it, in Figure 2.1 we first use an intuitive representation (part (a) of the figure) to illustrate the problem solving process, and in part (b) we indicate a more abstract way to solve the same problem.

West bank		East bank	[FWGC]
FWGC			[wwww] (initial state)
W C	FG→	F G	[wewe]
FW C	←F	G	[wwew
C	FW→	FWG	[eeew]
F GC	←FG	W	[weww]
G	FC→	FW C	[eewe]
F G	←F	W C	[wewe]
	FG→	FWGC	[eeee] (goal state)
(a) Intuitive representation			(b) State representation

Figure 2.1 FWGC Puzzle

Figure 2.1(a) shows how the problem can be solved step by step on a piece of paper. For example, the first step indicates the action of "farmer takes cabbage" (a legal move) cross the river. Figure 2.1(a) thus illustrates the important role of *state space search* in problem solving. A *state* is a configuration that is described by a set of variables along with their values. The set of states involved in the problem solving is referred to as the *state space*. Problem solving can thus be conducted as searching in this space. If we can find a *path* (which consists of various states involved in the problem solving process) from the *initial* state (the state we start with the problem solving) to the *goal* state (the state we want to reach), then the problem is solved. In order to make such a search feasible, an appropriate representation of a state is important. In the FWGC puzzle, a state can be represented as an ordered list of four variables, with each variable representing the current location (east bank, e, or west bank, w) of one of the objects (farmer, wolf, goat and cabbage -- in this order). So if farmer and goat are at the west bank while wolf and cabbage are at the east bank, that state is represented as [wewe]. The initial state in this problem can be represented as [wwww] while the goal state can be represented as [eeee]. You may check the following path

[wwww] → [wewe] → [wwew] → [eeew] → [weww] → [eewe]
→ [wewe] → [eeee]

is indeed a solution. How to find this solution path? Various search algorithms (such as depth first search) can be used and will be summarized in a later section.

Example 2. *The eight puzzle (8-puzzle).* Consider the following board configuration. Eight ($8 = 3^2 - 1$) differently numbered tiles are fitted into 3^2 spaces on a grid. One space is left blank so that tiles can be moved around to form different patterns. For example, Figures 2.2 (a) and (b) represent an initial state and a goal state, respectively. We are looking for a solution path from (a) to (b). Notice that the regulation requires that any legal change of the state must involve the move of the blank. For example, we may shift tile 8 down; this move can also be viewed as moving the blank up (so that 8 is shifted down). Note also that we cannot directly swap two tiles (for example, swap tiles 8 and 3) because no tile can be lifted up from the plain where it is positioned. Therefore, for the state shown in (a), only four moves are allowed: move the blank up, down, left, or right. Restrictions like these will be referred to as legal move rules or *mandatory rules* (to be distinguished from *heuristic rules* discussed later).

(a) ...... (b)

Initial state   Goal state

Figure 2.2 8-Puzzle

From the initial state we move to the following states; each is referred to as the *child* of the original state (notice they are constructed following the mandatory rules), as shown in Figure 2.3.

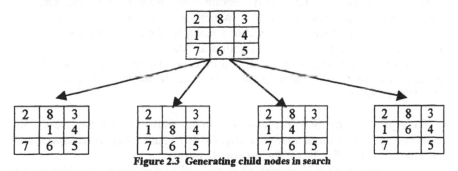

Figure 2.3 Generating child nodes in search

So which child state should be taken? We may try one of them, using a well-known search algorithm (such as breadth first or depth first, see Section 2.8). To improve the efficiency, however, we may also use some criterion to select the "best" state (instead of doing a "blind" search.) Figure 2.4 depicts an example of a solution path which can be obtained on a piece of paper.

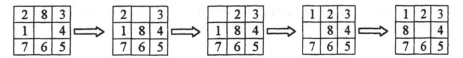

Figure 2.4 A solution path

How to solve this problem using a computer? We can represent the board as a two-dimensional array, and represent each tile accordingly (see Figure 2.5).

For example, in the initial state, tile 2 is in position X = 1 and Y = 3, or simply (1, 3). Similarly, tile 8 is in position (2,3) while tile 6 is in position (2, 1).

Y

2	8	3
1		4
7	6	5

X

Figure 2.5 Representing a state in 8-puzzle probelm

Alternatively, we can represent the board using a 1-dimensional array (or list). The following is an example of how to define positions:

$$\{1\}\{2\}\{3\}$$
$$\{4\}\{5\}\{6\}$$
$$\{7\}\{8\}\{9\}$$

The initial state can now be represented as an ordered list [2, 8, 3, 1, 0, 4, 7, 6, 5] (here 0 represents the blank). This is to say position {1} holds tile 2, position {2} holds tile 8, etc.

Up to this point you may think we have just talked about computerized problem solving. Indeed we have. However, the problems we just discussed share some basic features. Both require "intelligence," but this kind of intelligence is different from that which is used to solve many other computational problems, such as those using mathematical equations. Both require representimg the current situation as "states," and problem solving is carried out as state space search. In addition, we may also notice that there is a need for a criterion so that a "good" choice can be made to more effectively solve the problem.

Example 3. The previous two examples illustrate the importance of constructing spaces for problem solving. However, other important aspects are also needed. Consider the following simple puzzle.

> Mozart visited Vienna three times, and he died there. On which of the three visits did he die?

This puzzle is somewhat different from those seen earlier, and you know the answer -- it is seemingly quite straightforward. But how could you get the answer? How would you write a computer program to produce the answer? In order to solve this problem, you have to start with some assumptions, which are used as background knowledge, and then represent the knowledge in a form so that state space search can be conducted. You should be able to answer these questions after you finish reading this and next chapters.

2.2.2 APPLICATIONS

So far we have only discussed toy problems. However, computational intelligence problems go far beyond those. The following are some real-world applications.

Application 1. *Expert systems.* Expert systems are computer programs for problem solving in some specific domains (such as medicine, car troubleshooting, etc.) in a manner similar to human experts. Expert systems have been one of the most successful application areas in computational intelligence. As an example, consider a simple expert system concerning personal finance state, which is revised from [Dunken 1995]. A portion of the *And/Or tree* is shown in Figure 2.6. Note that Case 2 in this figure illustrates an *and node* where conditions "client is middle age," "job is steady" and "client has children" should be satisfied at the same time. It is preferable to use an arc to connect the branches involved in an and node. Note also that in this figure, only a portion of the structure is shown, and each box indicates a subtree which is not shown. Expert systems will be examined in Chapter 5.

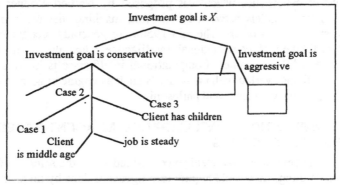

Figure 2.6 A portion of an and/or tree used by an expert system

Application 2. *Robotics.* Robotics is the science and engineering for building *robots* that are capable of performing certain atomicic actions. For example, the PEBBLES robot being developed at the MIT AI lab is a prototype microrover for the 2003 mission to Mars. PEBBLES' exploration tasks, which include navigation, visual exploration, and sample rock collection, are selected and performed in the complete absence of human teleoperation.

Application 3. *Computer chess.* The Deep Blue chess machine became the first computer program to beat a reigning world chess champion (Gary Kasparov) in May 1997. It is a parallel supercomputer that processes an average of 200 million chess positions per second.

Additional examples can be found in game playing, perception (receiving information from sensors and acting), natural language understanding, as well as many others. As we will see later in this book, computational intelligence has many important contributions to various aspects of decision support.

2.3 DEFINITION OF COMPUTATIONAL INTELLIGENCE

2.3.1 HISTORICAL DEVELOPMENT OF COMPUTATIONAL INTELLIGENCE

The field of computational intelligence (or artificial intelligence) began to emerge as a separate field of study during the mid-20th century when the computer became a commercial reality. Prior to that time, a number of pioneer works were beginning to mature. Among the developments were the work of logicians such as Alonzo Church, Kurt Godel, Emil Post and Alan Turing; the new field of cybernetics which was proposed by Norbert Wiener to bring together many parallels between human and machine; the work in formal grammars; as well as others. The mid-1950s are generally recognized as the official birth date of computational intelligence when the term "artificial intelligence" (AI) was coined. Computational intelligence is interdisciplinary in nature, and has overlap with many fields such as engineering, mathematics, linguistics, cognitive science and philosophy.

2.3.2 COMPUTATIONAL INTELLIGENCE AS AGENT-BASED PROBLEM SOVLING

Pioneers in computational intelligence defined it as "the science of making machines do things that would require intelligence if done by men." Since this definition is too general, many efforts have been made to make it more concrete. Several popular definitions can be found in [Russell and Norvig 1995]. As already mentioned, computational intelligence is now defined as the study and construction of intelligent *agents*. An agent is something that perceives and acts [Russell and Norvig 1995]. The following important aspects of the concept of agent should be emphasized:

- *Agents are (semi)autonomous*: Each agent has certain responsibilities in problem solving with little or no knowledge of either what other agents do or how they do it.
- *Agents are "situated"*: Each agent is sensitive to its own surrounding environments and usually has no knowledge of the full domain of all agents.
- *Agents are interactional* and the society of agents is structured: Agents cooperate on a particular task.
- *The phenomenon of intelligence in this environment is "emergent"*: The overall cooperative result of the society of agents can be viewed as greater than the sum of its individual contributors.
- *Agents versus objects:* It would be beneficial to compare agents with objects as discussed in the object-oriented paradigm. There are many similarities between these two, including the fact that both of them support *anthropomorphism* (namely, demonstrate human-like behavior).

However, there are also important differences; particularly, agents are more active than objects.

Features described above indicate that the concept of agent is very powerful. Because of this, agent-based approaches are rapidly gaining popularity. As a result, many venders have labeled their products as "agent-based," or have included agent-based components in their products. In order to prevent misuse of the "agent" concept, it is important to check the definition (or required features) of agent to verify these claims.

As a simple example of how intelligent agents can benefit human beings, consider the following scenario [Chen 1999a]. Suppose you are a researcher or an upper-level college student working on a research paper for a course project. To fulfill your research need, you ask intelligent agents for help. Your specific task is:

> Give me a hard copy of the recent article "MoneyExpress: An inventive agent for fast money-making" in *Journal of Intelligent Agents* by J. Robertson, K. Chen and M. Williams.

Later in the day, you may receive several follow-up messages. The following is from agent A:

> The article is not found in the specified journal. Do you want me to send a memo to my friend (also an intelligent agent) J to conduct a Web search for relevant materials on intelligent money-making?

Another message was sent by agent B:

> The article is not found in the specified journal (probably yet to appear). However, I found a article with the same title on last year's Conference Proceedings on Intelligent Agents, written by K. Cohen, R. Robertson and M. Williams. Assuming "Chen" is a misspelling of "Cohen," these two articles were written by the same group of authors, and may be very similar in contents. I have asked my friend T (an intelligent agent) to produce a photocopy for you.

Of course you are impressed by agent B because (among other things) she is able to correct possible human errors. But even agent A has demonstrated some admirable traits, because he is able to communicate with other agents and is able to take an initiative, rather than passively execute human instructions (just as agent A did).

Various search algorithms used by agents have been developed. Some of them will be discussed later in this chapter. The role of agents in intelligent decision making will be discussed throughout this book. Discussion on intelligent agents can also be found in [[Bienkowski 1998, Hayes 1999].

2.3.3 MEASURING THE INTELLIGENCE: TURING TEST

The Turing test measures the performance of an allegedly intelligent machine against that of a human being, arguably the best and only standard for intelligent behavior. The test places the machine and a human counterpart in rooms apart from another human, the interrogator. The interrogator is not able to see or speak directly to either of them, does not know their identity, and can only communicate with them by using a textual device such as a terminal. The interrogator is asked to distinguish the computer from the human being solely on the basis of their answers to questions asked over this device. Note that although the Turing test has been a well-known concept, it is not without controversies. A rich literature exists on the topic of measuring intelligence. However, in this book we will not get into more detail about this debate.

2.4 BASIC ASSUMPTIONS OF COMPUTATIONAL INTELLIGENCE

Computational intelligence is considered as an empirical inquiry due to its exploratory nature. The complex tasks involved in computational intelligence require us to make reasonable assumptions, and carry out research based on these assumptions. We should notice that different assumptions have been made due to concerns from various perspectives (such as philosophy, psychology, as well as others). Debates have been carried out around these assumptions. In the following, we briefly examine some important assumptions used in computational intelligence (but we will not get involved into these debates).

2.4.1 SYMBOLISM

2.4.1.1 Physical symbolism and representation
This assumption states that intelligent actions are demonstrated based on physical symbols. A symbol is just a token to denote a thing which has a well-defined meaning. For example, "student" is a symbol denoting a concrete thing (an object), "thought" is a simple denoting an abstract object, and "take" is also a symbol denoting an activity. Symbolism serves as the foundation for state space search and knowledge representation, two of the most fundamental issues discussed in artificial intelligence literature.

2.4.1.2 Physically grounded
The physical-ground hypothesis assumes that in order to build a system that is intelligent, it is necessary to have representations grounded in the physical world. This assumption challenges the physical-symbol system hypothesis in computational intelligence. The hope is that the physical-ground hypothesis obviates the need for symbolic representations or models because the world becomes its own best model. This assumption has been adopted by some researchers in computational intelligence, but is not widely accepted. We will not pursue this direction further.

2.4.1.3 Subsymbolism

The basic feature of subsymbolism is to de-emphasize the use of symbols to denote objects and relations; intelligence is viewed as arising from the collective behavior of large numbers of simple, interacting components. A well-known example of subsymbolism is *neural networks* (NNs). Unlike symbol-based computational intelligence, a neural network system assumes no correspondence between the units of computation and objects or relations in the world. There is a distributed representation: represent knowledge implicitly in patterns of interactions between components (weights). For this reason, the term *connectionism* has been used to describe neural networks. In this book, although we do not locate any chapter or section to discuss neural networks, from time to time we will compare this approach with other approaches.

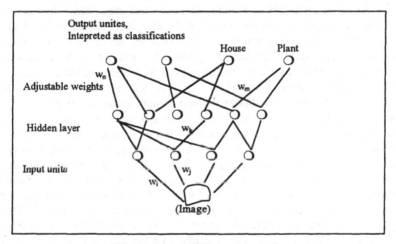

Figure 2.7 A simple neural network

2.4.1.4 Other approaches

Other approaches also exist. For example, Copycat's architecture is claimed as neither symbolic nor connectionist, nor as a hybrid of these two (although it can be thought as this way). [Hofstadter 1995] argued that the program has a novel type of architecture somewhere in between these extremes. It is an emergent architecture, in the sense that the program's top-level behavior emerges as a statistical consequence of myriad small computational actions, and concepts in creating analogies can be considered by realization of "statistically emergent active symbols." Since approaches like this are not popular, we will not pursue this direction further.

2.4.2 SEQUENTIAL OR PARALLEL

The concept of artificial neural network goes beyond subsymbolism. In fact, the distributed nature of neural network (as discussed above) makes it a perfect example of massive parallel processing. Each artificial neuron can be considered as an extremely simple processing element, and these processing elements can process information in parallel. In this sense, neural networks are at odds with sequential models as exemplified by Newell's "Unified theories of cognition"[Newell 1990].

The UTC presents a cognitive architecture rooted in conceptually serial register-transfer level of computer architecture (so little adapted to the needs of cognitive neuroscience). Newell emphasizes a serial symbol-computation perspective throughout. Most parts of this book will follow this tradition.

2.4.3 LOGIC-BASED APPROACH

An influential viewpoint in traditional computational intelligence community is that computational intelligence urgently needs mathematical and logical theory. As a founder of computational intelligence, John McCarthy [Lifschitz 1991] argued that we will not reach human level intelligence by more algorithms reducing the complexity of a problem from n^2 to $n \log n$. The more common sense we formalize, the more we will need to develop logic, exactly as has happened for physics and mathematics. However, the choice of a logic-based approach to computational intelligence has been very controversial. The main problem is that logic has been developed with goals quite different from computational intelligence, e.g., to prove the consistency of mathematical reasoning, or to provide semantics to (parts of) natural language. Although logic is a very good starting point which allows formalizing many forms of common sense, it is far from having the expressibility needed to represent basic notations in computational intelligence. Nevertheless, a logic-based approach provides a standard for studying various useful forms of reasoning. For example, production systems model (to be discussed in Chapter 5) can be considered as a "loose" form of logic, and conceptual graphs (Chapter 6) can be converted into logic by following certain steps. In addition, conceptual and logical data modeling can also benefit from logic (Chapters 4 and 6). Therefore, logic can be considered as the starting point of an integrated approach for decision making, and will be discussed in the next chapter.

2.4.4 HUMAN INTELLIGENCE AS METAPHOR

Computational intelligence is exploratory in nature and is thus an empirical science [Simon 1995]. Since the natural intelligence (particularly, human intelligence) is the only model we are familiar with, it is natural to use human intelligence as the model to develop computational intelligence systems. However, this does not mean computational intelligence must follow the exact ways human beings approach reasoning.

In addition, there may be many different ways to use human intelligence as a metaphor. In fact, symbolism and subsymbolism can be considered as two different ways of modeling intelligence -- at the cognition level or at the brain level. We should note, however, using human intelligence as a metaphor is not the only option. In fact, recent studies in artificial life (AL) and adaptive behavior have tried to re-situate computational intelligence-related research within the context of an artificial biology and zoology, respectively. The bottom line of these directions is that we need much more understanding of the animal substrates of human behavior before we can fulfil the dreams of computational intelligence [Humphrys 1999].

2.4.5 SUMMARY

In summary, the assumptions used by "mainstream" computational intelligence can be illustrated through Newell's United Theories of Cognition (UTC) framework [Newell 1990], which has three principal themes:

(1) Psychology has arrived at the possibility of unified theories of cognition;

(2) There is a common foundation underlying cognitive science;

(3) An architecture called Soar developed by Newell and his research group is a candidate unified theory of cognition that is useful as an exemplar of the concepts.

Fundamental knowledge system functions of UTC include the following:

- symbol (as already discussed);
- representation: symbol structures act as representations as they obey. Newell's basic representation law can be expressed as

$$\text{Decode } [\text{Encode}[T](\text{Encode}[S])] = T(S),$$

where T stands for transformation while S stands for situation. So this formula says that transforming a situation is done by encoding both the transformation and situation and then decoding them.

In the remaining part of this chapter, we will examine the two most important issues of computational intelligence under the UTC framework, namely, search and representation.

2.5 BASIC STORAGE AND SEARCH STRUCTURES

2.5.1 ABSTRACT DATA TYPES AND DATA STRUCTURES

The remaining part of this chapter is devoted to basics of search. We start with an informal review for some important abstract data types. The purpose of this review is to make our discussion somewhat self-contained. *Abstract data types* (ADTs) are conceptual description of data elements, including a set of operations. For example, the ADT stack has a "last-in-first-out" feature, and is characterized by operations such as push and pop. An ADT can be considered as a primitive form of the concept "object" (in the context of object-oriented paradigm). The implemented form of ADTs is usually referred to as data structures. For example, stacks can be implemented using arrays or linked lists. Examples of using these data structures can be found later in this chapter.

2.5.2 LINEAR STRUCTURES: LISTS, STACKS, QUEUES AND PRIORITY QUEUES

In linear data structures, a strict order is defined for all elements: one element is followed by another (except for the first and the last elements). The most popular linear structure is a list. Two restricted formats of linear structures are *stacks* (featured by last-in-first-out) and *queues* (featured by first-in-first-out). Although linear structures are simple, they are useful in modeling real-world problems. For example, the rate at which fund managers buy and sell stocks -- known as the turnover rate -- can be high, generating substantial capital gains and taxes. To combat this, tax-managed mutual funds often employ the old "buy and hold" strategy, lowering the number of transactions until a later date. Under most circumstances, a fund manager will sell the earliest-bought shares of a stock first, since they probably had the lowest purchase price and will bring the greatest profit. This is generally known on Wall Street as "first in, first out." However, managers of tax-managed funds do something more like "last in, first out." They're often careful to trade shares they purchased more recently, which will tend to sell for less capital gains.

A special kind of queue is called *priority queue*, where the order is not determined by time of each element entering the queue, but rather, by the priority associated with each element. The use of a priority queue will be illustrated in solving the 8-puzzle problem (Section 2.8.2).

2.5.3 TREES

A *tree* can be considered as a generalization of a list. A list is like a chain, while a tree allows branches. In fact, a *tree* is a hierarchical structure consisting of nodes (where data are stored) connected by edges. There is a designated node called the root of the tree. It would be beneficial if we view a tree as a root connected to several subtrees (each subtree is itself a tree). This perspective allows us to define a tree recursively. Of all kinds of trees, binary trees are of particular interest, where at most two subtrees (left subtree and right subtree) are allowed for each node. The nodes in a binary tree can be visited using various ways, including preorder (the root of a tree is visited first, followed by left and right subtrees), inorder (the root of a tree is visited after left subtree but before the right subtree) and postorder (the root of a tree is visited after left and right subtrees). There is also a lever-order traversal, where the nodes can be reached from the root (called the children of the root) are visited after the root itself. The children of these nodes are then visited in turn. Tree structures used for storage and search purpose are called *search trees*. In reality, *binary search trees* are a popular search structure. A binary search tree has an *order* property: for any node, keys stored in the left subtree are smaller than the key stored in the node itself and the keys stored the right subtree are larger than the key stored in the node itself (note that the term *key* refers to search key which is a variable whose value is used to guide the search). Another useful tree structure is *heap*. A *binary heap* is a binary tree which has a balanced structure and has a heap order property: the key of the parent is always smaller than its children. There is an interesting relationship between a priority queue (which is usually conceived as a linear structure) and a heap (which is a tree). This is because in a priority queue, so long as we can always easily find the element with the highest priority, we do not have to worry about the exact order of other elements. This way of thinking leads to the heap implementation of the priority queue [Weiss 1998].

2.5.4 INDEX STRUCTURES FOR DATA ACCESS

For huge amounts of data, data structures for external storage are needed so that we can efficiently access data stored in secondary memory. A *database* stores structured data (usually in secondary memory) such as student information records, course information records, as well as others. Indexing techniques are needed to assist the search of the data. There are two basic kinds of indices: *Ordered indices* (based on a sorted ordering of the values) and *hash indices* (based on the values being distributed uniformly across a range of buckets. The bucket to which a value is assigned is determined by a *hash function*, which is a content-to-address mapping.) *Extendible hashing* is a technique used to guarantee a find operation is performed in two disk accesses for database input/output processing. A useful index structure is B tree, which has many variations [Weiss 1998, Silberschatz, Korth and Sudarshan 1998].

2.5.5 DISCRIMINATION TREES FOR INFORMATION RETRIEVAL

Search structures would become much more complex if what to be accessed is not structured data. Accessing such kind of data is studied in the field of *information retrieval (IR)*. A *discrimination tree* (or network) is a data structure used for storing and retrieving large numbers of symbolic objects. The basic idea behind discrimination networks is to recursively partition a set of objects. Each partition divides the set of objects into subsets based on some simple rule. In a problem solving approach called *case-based reasoning* [Kolodner 1993], previously acquired cases are stored in a discrimination network for convenience of later retrieval.

2.5.6 GRAPHS

A *graph* $G = (V, E)$ consists of a set of vertices (or nodes), V, and a set of edges (or arcs), E. Each edge is a pair (v, w), where v, w $\in$ V. Various graph search algorithms have been developed. A path through a graph connects a sequence of nodes through successive arcs. Graphs serve as a useful vehicle to model many real-world problems. State space search (to be discussed later in this chapter) can usually be conducted through graph search algorithms, where the states form the vertices of a graph. Among the most fundamental graph search algorithms are depth-first and breadth-first search, which will be briefly reviewed in Section 2.8. The graph is a very general concept and many other data structures can be considered as special cases of a graph. For example, a tree can be viewed as a graph in which two nodes have at most one path between them. A network can also be considered as a graph. Graphs play an important role in computational intelligence problem solving. Various problem solving constructs to be introduced in the next few chapters are all variations of graphs, such as entity-relationship diagrams for conceptual data modeling (Chapter 6), conceptual graphs and frame systems for knowledge representation (Chapter 6), as well as others.

2.5.7 REMARKS ON SEARCH OPERATION

One of the very important operations in many data structures is search, which is the operation of looking for a specific item in a data structure. It is interesting to note the relationship between search operation and operations under other names. For example, a "find" operation frequently means searching the data structure. Retrieval of information usually involves search, but may also involve some additional operations (for example, perform reasoning based on the result of search). Searching a tree or a graph may require visiting all the elements in that data structure (if the target of search is not there), in this case the search operation actually has the same effect of the traversal operation. For example, the *depth first search* (DFS) algorithm in graphs is an extension of the preorder traversal in trees. It can be considered as an extension of pre-order traversal for (ordered) trees. The search follows a particular direction (usually the leftmost), going as far as possible, until a dead end is reached. A backtrack then occurs and search continues in the same fashion until all the vertices have been visited. *Breadth first search* (BFS) in a graph can be considered as an extension of level order traversal for the trees. One thing we should keep in mind about graph search algorithms is that we should avoid visiting the same node more than once.

2.6   PROBLEM SOLVING USING SEARCH

In the previous section we discussed storage and search structures. In this section we further discuss issues related to using these structures for problem solving.

2.6.1 MEANINGS OF SEARCH

In order to understand the role of search in problem solving, let us briefly discuss the different meanings of search based on a comments given by [Mitchell 1998]. Search is not necessarily restricted to physical symbolism, although physical symbolism has some impact on the form of search. It has been noted that there are at least three (somewhat overlapping) meanings of search:

- *Search for stored data*: For example, we can use binary search in a binary search tree as outlined in Section 2.5.3.

- *Search for paths to goals*: These are typical graph search algorithms. The problem is to efficiently find a set of actions that move from a given initial state to a given goal. This is central to symbol-based computational intelligence. Search algorithms to be described later in this chapter belong to this category.
- *Search for solutions*: It is a more general class of search. The idea is to efficiently find a solution to a problem in a large space of candidate solutions. The rationale to study this kind of search is that graph search as discussed in (b) does not always apply and not all problems require finding a path from initial state to a goal. An example would be the task of determining protein structure. Genetic algorithms belong to this category (as to be briefly discussed in Chapter 16). It subsumes (b), because a path through a search tree can be encoded as a candidate solution.
- *Extended meaning of search*: The discussion given above has been mainly from the traditional computational intelligence perspective. The topic to be examined in this book, namely, computational intelligence for decision support, has widened the contents covered by the notion of search. In fact, various kinds of retrieval (as to be discussed in Chapter 5) can be considered as generalized search. The notion of viewing reasoning as extended retrieval has further extended the notion of search, and will be discussed in Chapter 7.

In this chapter, we mainly focus on state space search for symbolic reasoning. Nevertheless, we will take a brief look at other search mechanisms, because management of data should be integrated into the process of management of knowledge.

2.6.2 STATE SPACE SEARCH

We can now take a brief look at an important notion in symbol-based computational intelligence: state space search. A good understanding of tree traversals can help us understand graph search algorithms. Graph search algorithms are particularly important for state space search, because a state space can be viewed as a graph and a state in the state space can be viewed as a vertex in the graph. However, unlike the graph search where the graph is presented in a static fashion, the states and their connections considered in a state space search are usually constructed in a dynamic manner on a need basis. This is to prevent the huge number of states to be presented. Nevertheless, the actual search process remains the same. Various search algorithms have been developed. In Section 2.8 we will review blind search algorithms, and study heuristic search algorithms. Search can also be carried out along different directions, such as data-driven and goal-driven search (to be studied in Chapter 4).

2.6.3 REMARKS ON SCALING UP

The huge number of states involved in state space search posed a severe restriction on the application of search methods in real-world problem solving. Use of heuristics and knowledge-intensive approaches may reduce the difficulties. Nevertheless, manipulating huge amounts of data that mainly reside in the secondary memory and manipulating knowledge in the main memory still pose a big challenge for the integrated use of data and knowledge-based systems. Various issues related to this synergy (many of them beyond the search task proper) will be addressed in this book. An interesting example is the relationship between machine learning (conducted in computational intelligence community) and data mining (largely originated from business analysis of huge amount of data), as to be discussed in Chapter 10.

Search is the common underlying function of database management systems and knowledge-based systems (both kinds of systems will be further discussed in Chapter 4 and Chapter 5). The inappropriate combination of two powerful search mechanisms can lead to a multiplicative explosion in computation time. Performance is thus a key challenge in the development of integrated systems which involving manipulation of both data and knowledge.

2.7 REPRESENTING KNOWLEDGE FOR SEARCH

In the last two sections we discussed general issues related to search. In order to use search to solve problems in computational intelligence, however, usually we should first represent the knowledge in an appropriate manner so that search process can be conducted on the represented knowledge. In this section, we give a brief preview on the issue of knowledge representation. More detailed discussions on knowledge representation will be provided in Chapter 3 (where we discuss predicate logic), Chapter 5 (where we discuss production rules) and Chapter 6 (where we discuss structured representations).

2.7.1 LEVELS OF ABSTRACTION IN COMPUTATIONAL INTELLIGENCE PROBLEM SOLVING

Let us first take a look at levels of abstraction involved in building computerized systems for problem solving as shown in Figure 2.8.

Knowledge level
Symbol level
Algorithm and data structure level
Programming language level
Computer architecture and operating system levels

Figure 2.8   Hierarchy of abstraction in computer problem solving

We examine these levels first from a bottom-up manner:

- *Computing architecture and operating system levels*: These are most fundamental levels considered within a computing system.
- *Programming language level*: At this level, computer programs will be written in specific programming languages and executed by underlying operating systems.
- *Algorithm and data structure level*: Algorithms developed for problem solving applications should be described in terms of abstract data types (ADT) and further implemented using various data structures. These computer programs are then handled at the programming language level.

Computational intelligence problem solving is concerned with application programs carried out on the algorithm and data structure level. In particular, when symbolic reasoning is used, we can distinguish the following levels:

- *Subsymbolic level:* Although this level is not included in Figure 2.8, as discussed in Chapter 1, problems can be solved at a level below symbolic reasoning (for example, using neural networks).
- *Symbol level* (and other forms of information levels): The symbol level is concerned with the particular *knowledge representation* (KR) formalisms used to represent problem-solving knowledge; for example, using predicate logic, production rules, or frames. In symbolic computational intelligence, states in the state space search are formed using various KR formalisms. For example, when predicate logic is used, a state could be formed by a predicate statement (see Chapter 3 for more detail).
- *Knowledge level*: The knowledge level defines the capabilities of an intelligent system. It refers to the knowledge *content* that is independent of the formalisms used to represent it (so long as the representation language is sufficiently expressive). The process of capturing knowledge at the knowledge level is referred to as *knowledge modeling*. The separation of knowledge level and symbol level resembles the concept of abstract data type (ADT) and its actual implementation using various data structures. The separation of knowledge level and symbol level is also echoed in the separation of knowledge base and its control structure, as can be found in expert systems (see Chapter 5). A direct application of knowledge level is knowledge modeling (to be discussed in Chapter 6).

2.7.2 USING ABSTRACT LEVELS

We now examine these abstract levels in a top-down manner. The hierarchical structure indicates that we should start from the most abstract level (i.e., the knowledge level). In order to support this kind of problem solving, a wide range of languages for knowledge representation (KR) should be developed at the symbol level. Note that these languages are not just used for representing knowledge, but more importantly, are based on the representation to perform reasoning (which involves searching in the state space). Therefore, the term knowledge representation (KR) actually refers to *knowledge representation and reasoning* (KR&R). These languages are usually referred to as *knowledge representation schemes*. Note also that it is possible for us to discuss the relationship between these schemes as well as the mapping between them. Knowledge representation and related search process form the core of symbol-based computational intelligence. Various KRR schemes will be discussed in Chapter 3 and Chapter 6. The represented knowledge and its reasoning is implemented through an appropriate programming language, as to be discussed next.

2.7.3 PROGRAMMING LANGUAGES FOR COMPUTATIONAL INTELLIGENCE

2.7.3.1 Desirable features of programming languages for symbolic reasoning

There are many desirable features for languages used in symbolic reasoning [Luger and Stubblefield 1998]. Among them are the following:

- support of symbolic computation;
- flexibility of control, because it is difficult to imagine that intelligence could be achieved through the step-by-step execution of fixed instruction sequences exhibited by traditional computer programs;
- support of exploratory programming methodologies (computational intelligence programming is inherently exploratory);
- and others.

2.7.3.2 Remarks on LISP, Prolog and C++

Two important languages for computational intelligence programming are LISP and Prolog. Like most traditional programming languages, LISP is procedural, because it specifies how to perform the algorithm. The syntactic elements of the LISP programming language are *symbolic expressions* (or *s-expressions* for short). An s-expression could be an atom or a list (which is a sequence of either atoms or other lists separated by blanks and enclosed in parentheses). An important feature of LISP is that both programs and data are represented as s-expressions. The power of LISP is based on the use of lists to construct arbitrarily complex data structures of symbolic and numeric atoms, along with the *forms* (i.e., LISP expressions that may be meaningfully evaluated) needed for manipulating them. Lists in LISP are recursive structures. In contrast, Prolog can be considered as an implementation of logic as a programming language. Prolog programs have a declarative reading as well as a procedural reading. Later we will summarize some most important aspects of Prolog, which are related to computational intelligence (rather than all features of being a programming language).

Object-oriented programming provides an excellent structure for solving computational intelligence problems. Through the use of classes computational intelligence programs can be written around the data types to the problem. However, we should keep in mind that C++ is not as directly suited to symbolic computation as other programming languages, such as LISP or Prolog. Nevertheless, class libraries that simulate Prolog can quickly be built. A strong motivation for using C++ for computational intelligence programs is its suitability for use in large software systems [Tracy and Bourthoorn 1996].

2.8 STATE SPACE SEARCH

We are now ready to discuss basics of state space search. A node in a graph denotes a state in a search process. Usually a path consisting of the nodes which are used as intermediate steps to reach this goal (called the *solution path*) is returned along with the goal state. We start with uniformed search.

2.8.1 UNINFORMED SEARCH (BLIND SEARCH)

2.8.1.1 Depth-first search

A well-known method for graph search is depth-first search (DFS). When this method is used, we start with any node. We keep on visiting the descendents of a node until a dead end is reached. In case a node has more than one child, the convention is to visit the left-most unvisited child first. In case a dead end is encountered, we backtrack to the parent of that node. In order to remember the nodes visited, we use a stack data structure: when we visit the descendents of a node, descendents are pushed onto the stack. After descendent nodes are visited, they are popped out from the stack. Search is continued in this manner until all the nodes in the graph are visited. As an example, consider the graph in Figure 2.9(a). Suppose we start from node A. The order of DFS traversal is indicated as 1, 2, ...9 indicated in Figure 2.9 (b).

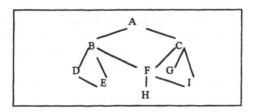

Figure 2.9 (a) A graph

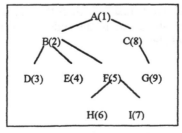

Figure 2.9 (b) An example of depth first search

2.8.1.2 Breadth-first search

An alternative method is breadth-first search (BFS), where the children of the visited node will be visited, then the children's children will be visited. Search is continued in this manner, until all the nodes are visited. In order to remember the order of children to be visited, a queue structure is used. BFS for graphs can be considered as an extension of level-order traversal for trees. For example, when BFS is applied to the example in Figure 2.9(a), we will have the following as the result: *A, B, C, D, E, F, G, H, I.*

2.8.1.3 Iterative deepening search

Comparing BFS with DFS, we note that a drawback of DFS is that it may fail to find a specified node (the goal). This case could happen, for example, when we are visiting a subtree whose depth is infinitive; in this case, we may never be able to get a chance to visit the goal node. BFS does not have this problem. In addition, in case there is more than one way to find the goal, BFS guarantees the shortest path will be returned. Better search methods should be developed. In the following, we briefly discuss an improvement of DFS, called *iterative deepening depth first search (IDDFS)*, and use an example to illustrate the basic idea.

Skeleton of the IDDFS:

---

search the tree using DFS as the tree had only one level;
repeat
    if not found, try one more level
       (revisit all the nodes visited in the previous round);
until found or there is no way to continue.

Note that in IDDFS, most work is done at the last round, but we need to perform most of the work in search anyway. (If we can find the goal earlier, we are lucky.) The idea is to perform recomputation rather than storing the previous result. Each recomputation is a depth-first search which will use less space. Since the number of nodes in a given level of the tree grows exponentially with depth, almost all the time is spent in the deepest level, even though shallower levels are generated an arithmetically increasing number of times.

As a simple example, let us take a look at the tree in Figure 2.10(a). Figure 2.10 (b) depicts the numbers denote the order of visit; they are not the data elements (which are not shown).

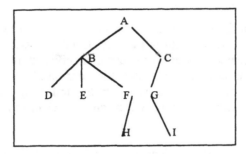

Figure 2.10 (a) A tree

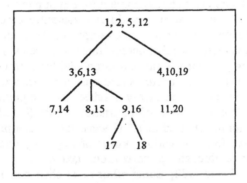

Figure 2.10 (b) Order of visit

2.8.1.4 Comparison of uninformed search algorithms

We now give a brief comparison for the uninformed search algorithms discussed. We use the following notations: b is the branching factor; d is the depth of solution; and m is the maximum depth of the search tree. (Note: usually $d < m$.) In addition to time and space complexity, we also use the following *evaluation criteria:*

- *Completeness*: Is the strategy guaranteed to find a solution when there is one?
- *Optimality*: Does the strategy find the highest-quality solution when there are several different solutions?

The result of comparison is shown in Table 2.1. Comparing BFS versus DFS, DFS is more space efficient while BFS is guaranteed to get the optimal solution and is complete. The table also clearly indicates that IDDFS combines the merits of both BFS and DFS.

Table 2.1 Comparison of uninformed search algorithms

Criterion	BFS	DFS	IDDFS
Time	b^d	b^m	b^d
Space	b^d	bm	bd
Complete?	Y	N	Y
Optimal?	Y	N	Y

2.8.2 HEURISTIC SEARCH

The search methods discussed so far all perform blind search, because none of these methods would evaluate the "goodness" of a state to be explored. In order to make search more effective and more efficient, it would be beneficial to develop some criteria to evaluate the "goodness" of each state. This is where heuristic search comes from. In the following, we first provide a discussion on heuristics, then we will discuss search methods using heuristics.

2.8.2.1 Heuristics

A heuristic is a rule of thumb which can be used to help us to solve the problem. For example, if you are looking for your friend, and if you see his car in front of the library, you may expect to find him in the library. However, heuristics are fallible, because they do not guarantee a solution (or a good solution) will be found. In our current example, the heuristic rule you used ("if somebody's car is there, then that person must be close by") is fallible because you do not know your friend's car is broken, and his roommate has given him a ride home. Nevertheless, in many situations, heuristics are useful.

Heuristics have been extensively studied by computational intelligence researchers. As for the nature of heuristics, Lenat (based on his AM and EURISKO programs) claimed that " (h)euristics are compiled hindsight, and draw their power from the various kinds of regularity and continuity in the world; they arise through specialization, generalization, and--surprisingly often--analogy" [Lenat 1982]. Some other researchers noted that "(t)he history of artificial intelligence shows us that heuristics are difficult to delineate in a clear-cut manner and that the convergence of ideas about their nature is very slow" [Groner, Groner and Bischof 1983]. A comprehensive discussion on heuristics in computational intelligence can be found in [Pearl 1984]. Heuristics have also been studied in knowledge-based systems, particularly in knowledge acquisition.

It is important to understand what heuristics are: they are *rules of thumb* (rather than mandatory rules) because although they are useful, they are also fallible. Heuristics are useful in problem solving and can be incorporated into algorithms. However, heuristics themselves are not algorithms nor solutions. Rather, they serve as a smart guide for problem solving. There are pros and cons of using heuristics: they can help to identify better (more promising) states and find shorter paths (optimal or suboptimal solutions). However, we should also remember that heuristics themselves become a kind of overhead and there is a need to limit the amount of time spent computing the heuristic values used in selecting a node for expansion. For example, many mutual funds allow investors to purchase shares through automatic investment plans, with the advantage to the investor of dollar cost averaging. Many of the funds also allow investors to pick a specific date in the month for money transfer from the bank. So how to select the best date for largest gain? The heuristic is "buying on the next-to-last market day of the month." The reason is that the market generally performs better-than-average late in the month and early in the month, so this timing puts your money into funds just before the bullish period (*Mutual Fund* Magazine, May 1999, p. 33). Note heuristics need to be measured to reflect their effect. In this mutual fund example, the heuristics used can be measured by its impact on the rate of return.

As a more concrete example, we can talk about heuristic functions for the 8-puzzle problem. One heuristic is tiles out of place. We can simply count how many tiles are out of place when it is compared with the goal and take the sum. In Figure 2.11(a), such tile is marked by an asterisk (*). The total number of tiles out of place is 5. Do this to all states that need to be evaluated. The state with the smallest sum will be selected.

State to be evaluated: Goal state:

2 *	8 *	3
1 *	6*	4
0	7	5

1	2	3
8		4
7	6	5

Figure 2.11 (a) An example

Another heuristic is *sum of distances out of place*: Unlike the previous heuristic which only considers how many tiles are out of place, we now count how far away for each tile. For example, in the state shown in the left of Figure 2.11 (b), the tile numbered 8 need at least two steps to get to the position it should be. Note that in reality, to make 8 to arrive at its destination may require more than 2 steps. As we will soon see, this is a very important property of heuristics. The least number of steps needed to reach the goal position is shown in parentheses in corresponding cells. The sum of all tiles is 1 (for tile 2) + 2 (for tile 8) + 1 (for tile 1) + 1 (for tile 6) + 1 (for tile 7) = 5. This sum is then compared with all the other sums of competing states.

2 (1)	8 (2)	3 (0)
1 (1)	6 (1)	4 (0)
0	7 (1)	5 (0)

1	2	3
8		4
7	6	5

Figure 2.11 (b)

2.8.2.2 Best first search

As an example of best first search, let us consider *hill climbing*. It is a heuristic problem-solving method that works by choosing a value for each variable and iteratively improving its assignment. It requires a heuristic value for each total assignment. Hill climbing can be viewed as a graph-searching procedure where a node in a graph corresponds to an assignment of a value to each variable as a node. The neighbors of a node correspond to an assignment of a value to each variable as a node. The neighbors of a node correspond to the assignments that are close to the assignment represented by the node. Initially a single node is selected to start. Maintaining a single node at each state, the algorithm selects the neighbor of the node with the highest heuristic value, and use that as the next node to search from. The algorithm stops when no neighbor has a higher value than the current node. A general description of the best first search algorithm is shown below.

Best first search algorithm

```
open = [start];
closed = [];
while open <> []
   {remove the state with the highest priority, denote it as d;
    if d = goal then return the path from start to d;
    else
         {generate children of d;
          for each child of d do
                {if the child is not found in open or closed
                        {assign the child a heuristic value;
                         add the child to open};
                 if the child is found in open
                         {if the child was reached by a shorter path this time
                          re-assign the child a heuristic value using shorter path}
                 if the child is found in closed
                         {if the child was  reached by a shorter path this time
                          remove the state from closed;
                          add the child to open}
           move the state to closed;
           determine the state with the highest priority to be examined next;}
   return failure (open is empty)}
```

A specific version of this algorithm is generally referred to the *A* algorithm* (pronounced as A-Star algorithm). This algorithm requires the evaluation function must take a specific form. The A* algorithm is listed below.

A* algorithm

In best first search algorithm with evaluation function
$$f(n) = g(n) + h(n)$$
where
   n is any state encountered in the search,
   $g(n)$ is the cost of n from the start state,
   $h(n)$ is the heuristic estimate of the cost of going from n to a goal and
        $h(n)$ is less than or equal to the cost of the minimal path from n
   to the goal.

To implement the A* algorithm, it is convenient to use two data structures to keep on tracing the states which have already have generated children, and the states to be examined. The former is termed as CLOSED and can be held in a stack, while the latter is termed as OPEN and can be treated as a priority queue (ordered according to estimation function values), and can be implemented as a minimum heap [Weiss 1998]. Note also in a minimum heap, although we can always find the minimum element (namely, the state with highest priority) efficiently, a sorted order does not exist. Nevertheless, for convenience of discussion, in the following, we treat the priority queue as a fully sorted list.

We use the 8-puzzle problem to illustrate how this algorithm works. For simplicity, we use the tile-out-of-place heuristic. The problem-solving process using A* algorithm is shown in Figure 2.12.

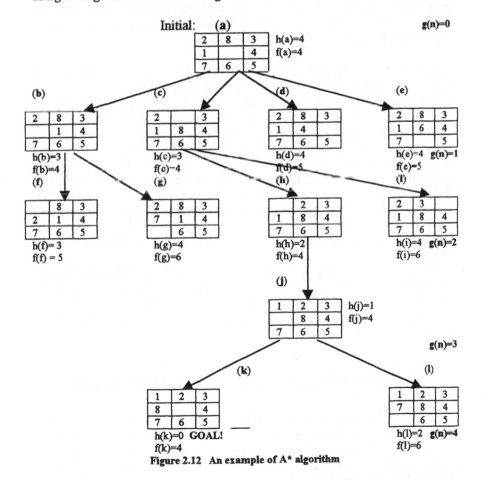

Figure 2.12 An example of A* algorithm

The elements in the Open and Closed lists are listed below, where each state is denoted by the name of the state attached by the f function value. (For a more detailed discussion of this example, see [Luger and Stubblefield, 1998]).

Open = [a4]	Closed = []
Open = [b4, c4, d5, e5]	Closed = [a4]
Open = [c4, d5, f5, e5, g6]	Closed = [b4, a4]
Open = [h4, d5, f5, e5, g6, i6]	Closed = [c4, b4, a4]
Open = [j4, d5, f5, e5, g6, i6]	Closed = [h4, c4, b4, a4]
Open = [k4, d5, f5, e5, g6, i6, l6]	Closed = [j4, h4, c4, b4, a4]
	Success (k is the goal state).

Earlier in Section 2.6.1 we discussed several different meanings of search. Apparently our current problem is to efficiently find a set of actions that move from a given initial state to a given goal. The involved actions form a *solution path*. The solution path consists of states needed to reach the goal from the initial state. One way to maintain such information is to attach additional information of parent-child relationship for all states visited. In our example, the solution path consists of the following states:

$$a \rightarrow c \rightarrow h \rightarrow j \rightarrow k.$$

In general, a solution path is a chain of states (s_1, s_2, ... s_n), with s_1 as the initial state, s_n as the goal state, and s_{j-1} as a parent of s_j, for $j \geq 2$.

Some important definitions are now in order. Heuristics that find the shortest path to a goal whenever it exists are said to be *admissible*. An admissible heuristic expresses an optimistic estimation which never overestimates. In the 8-puzzle example, counting tiles out of place is apparently an optimistic heuristic, because if a tile is two positions away from the final position, usually it takes more than two steps to actually to arrive at that position. In addition to admissibility, we can also discuss the *informedness* of a heuristic (concerned with determining which heuristic is more informed than another) and *monotonicity* (which is concerned with consistently finding the minimal path to each state they encounter in the search).

We can further extend the definition of admissibility from heuristics to algorithms. A *search algorithm is admissible* if, for any graph, it always terminates in the optimal solution path whenever a path from the initial to goal state exists. In general, we have the following important result: *All A* algorithms are admissible.*

2.9 REMARK ON CONSTRAINT-BASED SEARCH

As a special remark on the general notion of search, we give the following comment. Many problems in computational intelligence are concerned with constraints. For example, the well-known Waltz labeling algorithm applied the idea of constraint propagation to identify a three-dimensional object from a two-dimensional figure (for a brief discussion of this algorithm, see [Rich and Knight 1991]). More generally, in *constraint satisfaction problems* (CSPs), we are given a set of variables, a domain for each variable, and a set of constraints or an evaluation function. These problems involve choosing a value for each variable so that the total assignment satisfies the constraints or optimizes the evaluation function. The multidimensional aspect of these problems, where each variable can be seen as a separate dimension, makes them difficult but also provides structure that can be exploited.

CSPs can be divided into two main classes:

- *Satisfiability problems*: the goal is to find an assignment of values to variables that satisfies some constraints. These constraints are hard constraints because they have to be met.
- *Optimization problems*: each assignment of a value to each variable has a cost or an objective value associated with it; the goal is to find an assignment with the least objective value. The constraints are specified preferences and are referred to as soft constraints.

CSPs can be considered as graph-searching problems in at least two ways. One way can be summarized as follows. A node corresponds to an assignment of a value to all of the variables, and the neighbors of a node correspond to changing one variable value to a local value. These problems differ from the conventional graph-searching problems in that we are not interested in the path, there is no starting node, and one can easily generate an arbitrary node (by choosing an assignment of values to variables), so that any node can be used as a starting point [Poole, Mackworth and Goebel, 1998]. Hill climbing (as briefly discussed in Section 2.8) can be considered an example of constraint-based reasoning.

2.10 PLANNING AND MACHINE LEARNING AS SEARCH

The concept of search is pervasive in computational intelligence problem solving. To illustrate this, we briefly examine two areas of computational intelligence from the perspective of problem solving as search.

2.10.1 PLANNING AS SEARCH

Intuitively, a *plan* is a strategy for acting. Planning involves choosing a plan by considering alternative plans and reasoning about their consequences. A planner is a problem solver that can produce plans (which are sequences of actions) to achieve some goal. Planning is an important form of decision making. A typical example used to illustrate the key ideas of planning is the block world. Figure 2.13 depicts a simple task of planning. The mandatory rules used in a block world usually follow the operations of stacks. In the initial state of Figure 2.13, we have two stacks of blocks, and we want to put C on the top of E.

At the most abstract level, the task of planning is the same as problem solving. Planning can be viewed as a type of problem solving in which the agent uses beliefs about actions and their consequences to search for a solution over the most abstract space of plans, rather than over the space of situations. Planning algorithms can also be viewed as special-purpose theorem provers that reason efficiently with axioms describing actions [Russell and Norvig 1995].

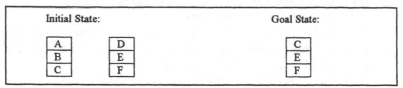

Figure 2.13 An example of planning

In a planner, operators correspond to actions that transform one state into another. As an alternative formulation of planning as search, we might use a search space consisting of all possible plans. In this case, operators transform one plan into another, by adding or reordering plan steps that correspond to actions. The advantage of this alternative formulation is that we can think of plans as something other than simple sequences of actions.

A solution to the problem depicted in Fig. 2.12 is a sequence of actions:

Move A on top of floor.
Move B on top of floor.
Move D on top of floor.
Move C on top of E.

Note the first three move operations are actually stack pop operations while the last one is a push. An example of a CLIPS program (see Chapter 5) for this simple planner can be found in [Giarratano and Riley 1998].

2.10.2 SYMBOL-BASED MACHINE LEARNING AS SEARCH

Another interesting field within computational intelligence is *machine learning*. According to [Simon 1983], leaning refers to "any change in a system that allows it to perform better the second time on repetition of the same task or on another task drawn from the same population." Various algorithms have been developed for machine learning. A simple example of learning using induction has been given in Section 3.6. Later in Chapter 10 we will discuss several different approaches of machine learning. In the following, we will only consider symbolic approaches for machine learning which are built on the assumptions of a knowledge-based system. In these approaches, the primary influence on the behavior of the learning program is its base of explicitly represented domain knowledge. The elements involved in a framework for symbol-based learning include the following [Luger and Stubblefield 1998]:

• The *data* and *goals* of the learning task;

- The *representation of knowledge* (for knowledge used as background as well as learned knowledge);
- A set of *operations* to manipulate the background knowledge;
- The *concept space* consisting of potential concept definitions; and
- Heuristics for search.

The last two elements are closely related. The learner must search the concept space to find the desired concept. Learning programs must commit to a direction and order of search, as well as to the use of available training data and heuristics to search efficiently. A discussion on some useful machine learning techniques will be provided in Chapter 10.

SUMMARY

In this chapter we discussed the most important concepts in computational intelligence. It sets the tone for all the remaining chapters, where a more detailed discussion on these concepts will be continued, particularly in Chapter 3. Search methods discussed in this chapter reflect the philosophy of *general problem solving*, which dominates the early history of computational intelligence. This philosophy has put emphasis on generic algorithms for solving all kinds of problems, and has been proven to be too ambitious (or too naïve). Later development of computational intelligence has taken more pragmatic concerns, such as domain-specific knowledge (see Chapter 5 for a discussion).

The concept of intelligent agent is very important. In this chapter we described some very basic features of agents. More discussion on intelligent agents can be found in [Bienkowski 1998]. Some recent development on intelligent agents can be found in [Hendler 1999].

There are many issues not discussed in this chapter. Here we point out two of them. One is related to games. In this chapter we discussed several puzzles. Games differ from puzzles in that usually it requires two or more parties to participate. Tic-tac-toe and chess playing are examples of games. The concept of state space search is important in game playing, and is more complex. One frequently used strategy is called *Minimax*, which is a recursive strategy. Alpha-beta pruning is used to reduce the number of positions that are evaluated in a minimax search. Alpha is the value that the human has to refute and beta is the value that the computer has to refute. For more discussion on Minimax, see [Luger and Stubblefield 1998, Winston 1992]. Another development is the concept of *co-state search*, which extended the classical concept of state in state space search [Chen 1999b].

SELF-EXAMINATION QUESTIONS

1. Give an example to illustrate how state space search can be used to solve the problem (clearly indicate how to represent the states).

2. Explain the results of three methods discussed in blind search as shown in Table 2.1.

3. In this chapter we have emphasized how to reach the goal. Another important issue is to find the solution path. How will you extend the best search algorithm so that the solution path will be returned?

4. Consider the water jug problem. You are given two jugs, a 4-gallon one and a 3-gallon one. How can you get exactly 2 gallons of water into the 4-gallon jug? Note that neither jug has any measuring markers on it, and you are not allowed to add markers or make any assumptions based on measuring. The only thing you can use is a pump that can be used to fill the jugs with water. Please answer the following:

    (a) Represent the states in an appropriate way.
    (b) What is the initial state and the goal state?
    (c) Represent all the mandatory rules used in solving this puzzle.
    (d) Find a solution path and indicate all the mandatory rules used.
    (e) Are there any heuristics which can be used to improve finding the solution path?

5. Consider the sliding-tile puzzle. Three white tiles and three black tiles are separated by an empty space in the configuration shown in Figure 2.14. Mandatory rules include the following two legal moves; each has an associated cost:

    (i)   A tile may move into an adjacent empty location with cost of 1.
    (ii)   A tile can hop over one or two other times into the empty location. This move has a cost equal to the number of tiles jumped over.

The goal is to have all the white tiles to the left of all the black tiles.

W	W	W		B	B	B

Figure 2.14 Configuration of sliding-tile puzzle

Now answer the following questions.

    (a) Propose a way to represent the states, and indicate the initial state and all the goal state(s).
    (b) Manually find a solution path.
    (c) Propose one or more heuristics, as well as corresponding evaluation functions. Which factors should be considered in designing such a function?
    (d) Use examples to illustrate how the heuristics you proposed are used in the problem solving process.

REFERENCES

Bienkowski, M.A., A reader's guide to agent literacy, *SIGART Bulletin*, 23-28, Fall 1998.

Chen, Z., Intelligent agents, in *The IEBM Handbook of Information Technology in Business*, 1999a.

Chen, Z., Searching in dual worlds, *J. Intelligent Systems*, 9(1), 55-74, 1999b.

Dunken, J., *Expert Systems: Design and Development*, Macmillan, New York, 1995.

Giarratano, J. and Riley, G., *Expert Systems: Principles and Programing* (3rd ed.), PWS Publishing, Boston, 1998.

Groner, R., Groner, M., and Bischof, W. F. (eds.), *Methods of heuristics*, L. Erlbaum Associates, Hillsdale, NJ, 1983.

Hayes, C. C., Agents in a nutshell -- a very brief introduction, *IEEE Transactions on Knowledge and Data Engineering*, 11(1), 127-132, 1999.

Hendler, J., Special issue on intelligent agents, *IEEE Intelligent Systems & Their Applications*, 14(2), 32-37, 1999.

Hofstadter, D (and the Fluid Analogies Research Group), *Fluid Concepts & Creative Analogies: Computer Models of the Fundamental Mechanisms of thought*, BasicBooks, New York, 1995.

Humphrys, M., The future of artificial intelligence, 1999. Available at: http://www.robotbooks.com/artificial-intelligence-future.htm

Kolodner, J. L., *Case-Based Reasoning*, Morgan Kaufman, San Mateo, CA, 1993.

Lenat, D. B., The nature of heuristics, *Artificial Intelligence*, 19, 189-249, 1982.

Lifschitz, V. (ed.), *Artificial Intelligence and Mathematical Theory of Computation: Papers in Honor of John McCarthy*, Academic Press, Boston, 1991.

Luger, G. and Stubblefield, W. A., *Artificial Intelligence*, (3rd ed.), Addison Wesley Longman, Harlow, England, 1998.

Mitchell, M., *An Introduction to Genetic Algorithms*, MIT Press, Cambridge, MA, 1998.

Newell, A., *Unified Theories of Cognition*, Harvard University Press, MA, 1990.

Pearl, J., *Heuristics: Intelligent Search Strategies for Computer Problem Solving*, Addison-Wesley, Reading, MA, 1984.

Poole, D., Mackworth, A. and Goebel, R., *Computational Intelligence*, Oxford University Press, New York, 1998.

Rich, E. and Knight, K., Artificial Intelligence (2nd ed.), McGraw Hill, New York, 1991.

Russell, S. J. and Norvig, P., *Artificial Intelligence: A Modern Approach*, Prentice Hall, Englewood Cliffs, NJ, 1995.

Simon, H. A., Why should machine learn? In Michalski, R. S., Carbonell, J. G., and Mitchell, T. M. (eds.), *Machine Learning: An Artificial Intelligence Approach*, Vol. 1, Tioga, Palo Alto, CA, 1983.

Simon, H. A., Artificial intelligence: an empirical science, *Artificial Intelligence*, 77, 95-127, 1995.

Tracy, K. W. and Bouthoorn, P., *Object-Oriented Artificial Intelligence Using C++*, Computer Science Press, New York, 1996.

Weiss, M. A., *Data Structures and Algorithm Analysis in C++* (2nd ed.), Benjamin/Cummings, Redwood City, CA, 1998.

Winston, H. P., *Artificial Intelligence* (3rd ed.), Addison-Wesley, Reading, MA, 1992.

Chapter 3

PREDICATE LOGIC

3.1 OVERVIEW

Continuing our discussion on key notions of search and representation, this chapter covers a specific form of knowledge representation: predicate logic. Starting with a discussion on propositional logic or zero order logic, we present basics of first order predicate logic. Prolog is used as a working language to illustrate how the reasoning process can be computationally supported. The Prolog code can also be viewed as the pseudocode for implementing the solutions in other programming languages. Although few real world systems are built based on predicate logic, predicate logic serves as a logical foundation for many other approaches. In this sense, predicate logic can be considered as a universal language. At the end of chapter, a brief overview for other forms of logic will also be provided.

3.2 FIRST ORDER PREDICATE LOGIC

3.2.1 BASICS

In this section our discussion will be focused on logic. Our discussion will be around the following two related themes:

- *First order predicate logic (FOPL) as knowledge representation scheme*: We will take a practical approach to cover the materials related to logic. Since our main interest lies in applying logic to aid decision making rather than studying logic itself, we will try to use intuitive ways to describe concepts in logic, so long as this will not sacrifice its application.
- *Prolog as a computational programming Language*: When we discuss first order predicate logic, we will use notations consistent with Prolog. For example, by Prolog convention, the use of character strings starting with a capital letter is reserved to variables. Therefore, if we want to represent a constant, such as a person's name "John," we have to write it as "john." This may look a little odd, but will make it easy for us to integrate Prolog into our discussion. Note that our purpose is to take advantage of the reasoning power of Prolog. Therefore, this chapter only covers some important aspects of Prolog (and should not be considered as an introduction to the Prolog *language*).

Our discussion of logic will be an interplay between these two themes.

3.2.2 PROPOSITIONAL CALCULUS

We start with zero-order predicate logic, usually referred to as propositional calculus (also called propositional logic). In propositional calculus, each sentence is represented by a token, referred to as a propositional symbol. For example, the sentences "John is a good student," "Mary is an excellent student," and "Kim's father is Tom" can be represented as J, M, and K, respectively. Here J, M, K are all propositional symbols; each has a *truth value* T (true) or F(false). Note although this representation is simple, its expressive power is limited. For example, the first two sentences apparently are closely related to each other, while the third one is not. However, propositional logic does not indicate this difference.

Every propositional symbol and truth symbol is a *sentence* in propositional logic. Propositional symbols can be connected together by *connectives*; they serve as operators on the propositional symbols. There are five connectives: ¬ ("not," which negates the true value), ∧ ("and," the result is true only when both of the two sentences are true; the result is referred to as the *conjunction* of two sentences, these two sentences are called *conjuncts*), ∨ ("or," the result is true if at least one of the two sentences is true; the result is the disjunction of the two sentences referred to as disjuncts), → (imply) and = (equal). Sentences constructed using these connectives and paired parentheses are referred to as *well-formed formulas* (or *WFFs*). For example, if P, Q, R are propositinal symbols, then ¬P ∨ Q, ¬ (P ∧ Q) → R.. Notice in logic we will only consider WFFs. An expression is considered as *atomic* if it cannot be decomposed into smaller ones. A literal is an atomic expression or its negation. For example, P is atomic and a literal, ¬P is a literal, and P ∨ ¬P is not an atomic expression.

Note that a WFF refers to a syntactically correct expression, and has nothing to say about its truth value. A useful form is to use *truth table*; for example, using truth table we are able to prove

"p → q" = "¬p ∨ q",

as shown in Table 3.1.

Table 3.1   A truth table

p	q	¬ p	¬ p ∨ q	p → q
T	T	F	T	T
T	F	F	F	F
F	T	T	T	T
F	F	T	T	T

A truth value assignment to sentences is called an *interpretation*. In the truth table above, each row is an interpretation. A true interpretation is called a *model* in logic. In the above table, except the second row, each row represents a model. If we can find an interpretation to make a proposition expression true, then we say this propositional expression is *satisfiable*. Determining if an arbitrary expression in propositional logic is satisfiable is in the class of NP-complete problems.

When several propositional symbols are connected together through the connective $\land$ ("and"), we say the result is a *conjunction*, and each involved propositional symbol is a *conjunct*. Similarly, when several propositional symbols are connected together through the connective $\lor$ ("or"), we say the result is a *disjunction*, and each involved propositional symbol is a *disjunct*.

The following are some important laws, which can be proved using truth tables:

The contrapositive law:
$$(P \to Q) = (\neg Q \lor P)$$
$$P \lor Q = (\neg P \to Q)$$

de Morgan's law:
$$\neg(P \lor Q) = \neg P \land \neg Q$$
$$\neg(P \land Q) = \neg P \lor \neg Q$$

Commutative law:
$$P \land Q = Q \land P$$
$$P \lor Q = Q \lor P$$

Associative law:
$$P \lor Q \lor R = (P \lor Q) \lor R = P \lor (Q \lor R)$$
$$P \land Q \land R = (P \land Q) \land R = P \land (Q \land R)$$

Distributive law:
$$P \lor (Q \land R) = (P \lor Q) \land (P \lor R)$$
$$P \land (Q \lor R) = (P \land Q) \lor (Q \land R)$$

These laws can be used in combination. For example, by applying distributive law and deMorgan's law, we have
$$\neg(P \lor (Q \land (\neg P)))$$
$$= \neg P \land (\neg Q \lor P)$$
$$= (\neg P \land \neg Q) \lor (\neg P \land P)$$
$$= \neg P \land \neg Q.$$
(The last step is because $(\neg P \land P)$ always produces a false.)

3.2.3 PREDICATES

Unlike propositional logic, predicate calculus reveals "internal structure" of a sentence. Just like a propositional symbol, a predicate symbol has a truth value. In the simplest case, a *predicate* of arity n consists of a predicate name and followed by n ordered *arguments* (also referred to as *terms*) which are enclosed in parentheses and separated by commas. For example, "John is a good student" and "Mary is an excellent student" can be represented as "student(john, good)" and "student(mary, excellent)," respectively. (Here we follow the Prolog convention: a character string starting with an uppercase letter always denotes a variable.) More generally, we can write a predicate like "student(X, Y)", which can be used to denote any student (which is represented by the first term, a variable X) with any quality (which is represented by the second term, a variable Y). On the other hand, "Kim's father is Tom" can be represented as "is_father(kim, tom)" or simply "father(kim, tom)." Notice that the order or terms is important, but the exact use of the order is up to you (the person who writes the predicate). You can represent the same English sentence by writing "father(tom, kim)," so long as you use this order in a consistent manner.

As another simple example, suppose we want to express the sentence "John is a good student" in predicate logic. We have at least the following two ways:

good-student (john).

is-student (john, good). (or simply: student(john, good).)

Both answers are correct, but the second one is a little more flexible. If we want to express Mary is an excellent student, we can use the same predicate with same number of arguments: is-student(mary, excellent). If we stay with the first answer, then we have to introduce a new predicate, such as excellent-student(mary).

We can now point out that logic has an interesting feature: after you translate English sentences into logic, the rest can be handled in a strict manner which has a strong flavor of mathematics. The irony is, however, the process of translation itself is somewhat like an art.

Note in the above example "is-student" or "good-student" is the name of the predicate (namely, the predicate symbol). This brings the question of how to name a predicate. Usually the name of the predicate could be a noun or adjective to denote the property of the arguments (such as in "student(john))", a noun to denote the *relationship* among the arguments (such as in "father(tom, kim))", or a verb to denote the *activity* participated in by the arguments (such as in "eat(tom, pizza)," which expresses the activity ("eat") involving Tom and pizza). The number of arguments of a predicate is referred to as the *arity* of the predicate.

The arguments used by a predicate are also referred to as *terms*; they can be constants, variables, or functions. A function looks like a predicate in that it may also take several arguments, but a function usually has a value other than true or false. In fact, the value of the function is determined by the arguments; in this sense, it resembles a function as used in mathematics. It is important to distinguish functions from predicates. For example, if we want to represent "Paul's father and Tom's father are friends," we can write

friend(father(paul), father(tom)).

Note here that "friend" is a predicate which has a truth value while "father" is a function which has a value of a person's name (rather than the value of true or false). Note also in predicate logic, only the predicates are first order citizens, while functions are not. That is, a sentence in predicate logic can only consist of predicates and connectives, and functions can only be used as components of predicates.

Finally, we point out that as an extension of the propositional logic, important concepts defined for propositional logic can also be extended to predicate logic. For example, an interpretation in predicate logic is a truth value assignment to sentences with all the variables substituted by values.

3.2.4 QUANTIFIERS

The use of variables has extended the power of expression. Variables are used with *quantifiers*, which indicate the role of the variables in the expression. There are two quantifiers used in predicate logic: universal $\forall$ ("for all") and existential $\exists$ ("there exists"). First order predicate calculus (also called *first order predicate logic*, or *FOPL*) allows quantified variables and not to predicates or functions. (This explains why propositional logic is also called zero-order predicate logic, because it does not use variables at all.) The following example illustrates translating English sentences into logic, using quantifiers: "For every product, there are at least two brand names competing to each other."

$\forall$Product $\exists$S1 $\exists$S2 competitor(C1, Product) $\land$ competitor(C2, Product) $\land \neg$ equal (C1, C2). (The last predicate can be written in infix format: C1 $\neq$ C2).

Each quantifier has its *scope*. In this example, all the quantifiers have the scope of entire statement. But this is not always the case. For example, it is legal to write $\forall X$ person(X) $\rightarrow$ $\exists Y$ father(X, Y) (which says everybody has his or her own father). A predicate statement like this is called a *rule*, because it contains an implication.

The following are important laws involving quantifiers:

$$\neg \exists X \, p(X) = \forall X \, \neg p(X)$$
$$\neg \forall X \, p(X) = \exists X \, \neg p(X)$$
$$\exists X \, p(X) = \exists Y \, p(Y)$$
$$\forall X \, q(X) = \forall Y \, q(Y)$$
$$\forall X \, (p(X) \land q(X)) = \forall X \, p(X) \land \forall Y \, q(Y)$$
$$\exists X \, (p(X) \lor q(X)) = \exists X \, p(X) \lor \exists Y \, q(Y)$$

3.2.5 KNOWLEDGE BASE

So far we have introduced most important concepts used by predicate logic. Now we will put these things together. Predicate logic provides a flexible way to represent knowledge. A piece of knowledge in predicate logic (referred to as a predicate expression, a predicate statement or a predicate sentence) could be either a rule or a fact. For example, "$\forall X$ goodGPA(X) $\rightarrow$ goodjob(X)" is a rule while "goodGPA(john)" is a fact. Note that a fact does not use implication, and usually does not use variables. When a predicate expression does not involve any variable, it is said to be *ground*.

A *knowledge base* consists of all the predicates (facts and rules) which are all true at the same time. Sometimes a knowledge base is also referred to as a database, but we would reserve that term for a different use (see Chapter 4). More discussion on knowledge bases will be provided later in this chapter, as well as in Chapter 5.

3.2.6 INFERENCE RULES

The semantics of predicate calculus provide a basis for a formal theory of logical inference so that new expressions can be derived. Inference rules (or laws) have been developed to derive new expressions. In order to guarantee the quality of the inference, certain properties are desired. The following terminology is directly related to this concern.

*   A predicate calculus expression X *logically follows* from a set S of predicate calculus expressions if every interpretation and variable assignment that satisfies S also satisfies X.
*   An inference rule is *sound* with respect to semantics if everything that can be derived from a knowledge base is a logical consequence of the knowledge base. Intuitively, soundness requires the derived expression is "correct," and does not generate any dependencies which should not be generated.
*   An inference rule is *complete* with respect to semantics if there is a proof of each logical consequence of the knowledge base. Informally, this is to say using what should be derived will be derived (nothing is left out).

Of course we hope inference rules are both sound and complete. For examples of unsound inference rules, see Section 3.6, where abduction and induction are discussed.

One of the most important inference rules (or laws) in propositional logic and in predicate logic is modus ponens (which is written in propositional logic):

$$Modus\ ponens: \{\ (P{\rightarrow}Q) \wedge P\ \} \Rightarrow Q$$

This law is to indicate: given $p{\rightarrow}q$ and p, we can infer q. Note that the double arrow $\Rightarrow$ works above the content level and denotes "to derive." It should be distinguished from single arrow $\rightarrow$, which denotes "imply" (at the content level). The law stated here is in the form of propositional logic. It can also be stated in predicate logic: if $\forall X\ p(X) \rightarrow q(X)$ and p(a), we can infer $q(a)$.

Some other important rules are listed below (again in the form of propositional logic, but also applicable in predicate logic).

$$Modus\ tolens: \{(P{\rightarrow}Q) \wedge \neg Q\} \Rightarrow \neg P$$

Chain rule (also called *transitivity*, or *law of the syllogism*): $(P \rightarrow Q)$
$\wedge\ (Q{\rightarrow}R) \Rightarrow P \rightarrow R$

These laws can be used in combination to perform *deductive inference* (or simply *deduction*). For example, given $P{\rightarrow}Q$, $\neg Q$, and $\neg P \rightarrow R$, we can first use modus tolens to derive $\neg P$, and then use modus ponens to derive R. This is an example of simple (*deductive*) *reasoning*.

3.2.7 SUBSTITUTION, UNIFICATION, MOST GENERAL UNIFIER

Although predicate logic shares many important properties (such as Modus ponens) with propositional logic, the use of variables makes reasoning process more complicated. We now introduce two important concepts related to this problem. *Substitution* is the process of determining two expressions (formulas) are same. *Unification* is the process for determining the substitutions needed to make two predicate calculus expressions match. Consider the following example:

$p(X,a,b)$.
$p(c, Y, Z)$.
$p(X,Y)$.
$p(Z,W,d)$.

Here is another example:

father(john, mary).
father(john, tom).
father(tom, sue).

We are looking for a unifier for :

father(X, Y).
father(U, V).

In fact, {john/X, mary/Y, john/U, mary/$\underline{V}$} is a *unifier* (the set of substitution which makes two predicates same), because we can make these two predicates same by substituting X and U by a constant "john," and by substituting Y and V by a constant "mary". However, we should also point out that there is a more powerful unifier, {X/U, Y/V} (or {U/X, V/Y}) , which is called the *most general unifier* (*MGU*), because all the possible unifiers for these two predicates are just special cases of the most general unifier.

In general, substitution may be carried out between two variables, between a constant and a variable, but cannot happen between two constants. In addition, a constant can be unified with a function, so can a variable be unified with a function, *if the function does not contain that variable as an argument*. The test of this restriction is referred to as *occurs check*. For example, a variable Y cannot be replaced by p(Y) as this creates an infinite expression: $p(p(p(p...p(Y)...)))$.

3.2.8 RESOLUTION – THE BASIC IDEA

We are now ready to discuss the issue of reasoning using resolution. The key idea for the resolution method is that it is a *refutation proof* -- use the knowledge base and the *negated* goal to obtain null clause (which indicates contradiction). Since the knowledge base by itself is consistent, the contradiction must be introduced by the negated goal. As a result, we have to conclude that the original goal is true. The resolution proof can be considered as a generalization of modus ponens, because it can do more things than modus ponens does. The knowledge base used in resolution proof takes the so called *clause form*, which is a form of conjunction of disjuncts: each individual clause is expressed with disjunction as the connective and no conjunction is allowed within each disjunct. For example, $(a \land b) \lor c$ is not in clause form, but it can be converted to clause form, because it can be rewritten as $(a \lor c) \land (b \lor c)$, which is in clause form, because both $(a \lor c)$ and $(b \lor c)$ are disjuncts. The advantage of restricting to clause form is to make the proof process an automated one.

In general, there are several steps for resolution refutation proofs: change to clause form; negate the goal; resolve clauses using substitution; and produce contradiction. The following are nine steps needed to convert a predicate into its equivalent clause form.

1.   Eliminate the $\rightarrow$ by using the inference laws introduced earlier.
2.   Push $\neg$ inside to reduce the scope of negation as much as possible.
3.   Standardize variable names by renaming all variables so that variables bound by different quantifies have unique names.
4.   Move all quantifiers to the left without changing their order.
5.   Eliminate all existential quantifiers through *skolemization*, which is illustrated by the following examples. $\exists X \forall Y\ p(X,Y)$ can be rewritten as $p(X_0,\ Y)$. $\forall X \forall Y \exists Z\ q(Z)$ can be written as $q(f(X,Y))$; here X_0 is a *Skolem constant* and f is called a *Skolem function*. Note that in both cases the existentially quantified variable was replaced by a function which has all the universally quantified variables appearing before this variable as its arguments. In the first example, there is no variable appearing before X, so X becomes a constant (we can name it in any way, because we just want to denote it as a constant, the exact content is not of our concern). In the second example, universally quantified variables X and Y are the arguments of the new function, because it depends on the actual values of X and Y (again, we do not care about the exact name of this function).
6.   Drop all universal quantification.
7.   Convert the expression to the conjunct of disjuncts form.
8.   Make each conjunct a separate clause.
9.   In each clause generated by Step 8 give the variables different names.

Note that these nine steps should be applied to each predicate statement in the knowledge base; so if the knowledge base is quite large, this conversion could be quite tedious. Fortunately it is not necessarily to do something in some steps (because the requirement is already satisfied). For a detailed discussion of these steps involved in conversion to clause form, the reader is referred to [Luger and Stubblefiled 1998]. In the following, we illustrate the general steps of resolution proof using a very simple example, which also includes the conversion of clause form.

> Given: A man is a person.
>   All persons will die.
>   Socrates is a person.
> Goal: We want to prove that Socrates will die.

The proof can be done by invoking modus ponens twice (try it!). If we use resolution proof instead, we first do the conversion. The result of conversion for each predicate statement (left) is shown in the right.

Predicate form	**Clause form**
From what is given:	
1. $\forall X$ man(X) $\rightarrow$ person(X)	¬man(X) $\vee$ person(X)
2. man(scorates)	man(scorates)
3. $\forall Y$ (person(Y) $\rightarrow$die(Y))	¬person(Y) $\vee$ die(Y)
Negated goal:	
4. ¬die(socrates)	¬die(socrates)

The process of the resolution proof is shown in Figure 3.1. The two clauses, "¬man(X) $\vee$ person(X)" and "¬person(Y) $\vee$ die(Y)" are resolved to form a *resolvant* "¬man(Y) $\vee$ die(Y)." These two clauses can be resolved because they are opposite literals. (Since resolvants are produced by two clauses, the resolution method discussed here is called *binary resolution*.) The resolvant is constructed by take the disjunction of all the other atoms appearing in these two parent clauses. Also note the role of unification in this process. The entire proof is done as the construction of the resolution tree (the root is at bottom, an empty clause as the root indicates a contradiction has been found).

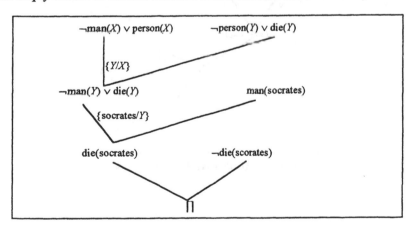

Figure 3.1 A resolution proof tree

The following are some important properties of resolution proof:

- *Refutation completeness*: The empty or null clause can always be generated whenever contradiction in the set of clauses exists.
- *Soundness:* It produces only expressions that logically follow.

Here is another example of resolution proof:

    Given: $\forall X\ p(X) \rightarrow q(X)$.

            $\forall Y\ q(Y) \rightarrow r(Y)$.

    Goal: $\forall Z\ p(Z) \rightarrow r(Z)$.

We first convert to clause form (without connectives like $\neg$, $\rightarrow$ and in disjunct form):

    (i) $\neg p(X) \vee q(X)$

    (ii) $\neg q(Y) \vee r(Y)$

To convert the negated goal to clause form, we have the following steps:

$$\neg(\forall Z\ p(Z) \rightarrow r(Z))$$
$$= \neg(\forall Z\ \neg p(Z) \vee r(Z))$$
$$= \exists Z\ p(Z) \wedge \neg r(Z)$$
$$= p(z_0) \wedge \neg r(z_0)\ \text{(The step illustrates skolmization.)}$$

Since the pieces used in resolution proof should be in disjunct form (these disjuntions are conjuncted), the negated goal is split into two clauses:

    (iii) $p(Z_0)$

    (iv) $\neg r(Z_0)$

The steps of the resolution is shown in Figure 3.2.

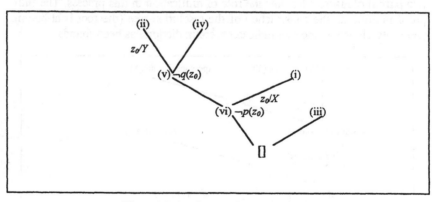

Figure 3.2 Another resolution proof tree

3.3 PROLOG FOR COMPUTATIONAL INTELLIGENCE

We are now ready to introduce Prolog and use Prolog to continue our discussion on FOPL. This treatment will allow us to take advantage of Prolog's representation and reasoning power. In fact, the Prolog programs can be viewed as pseudo codes and can be implemented in various languages, including C++.

3.3.1 BASICS OF PROLOG

PROLOG stands for programming for logic. It is a general purpose programming language, but is particularly suitable for reasoning in computational intelligence programming.

3.3.1.1 A sample Prolog program
Consider the following Prolog program.

```
father(john, tom).        % john is tom's father.
father(tom, mary).
father(tom, dave).
grandfather(larry, kim).
grandfather(X,Y) :- father(X,Z), father(Z,Y).
```

(Note: "%" denotes the rest of the line contains comments.)

This program allows us to submit queries such as to find who is who's father or who is who's grandfather. In addition, it also allows us who is who's child or grandchild by taking the advantage of unification (see Section 3.3.1.8).

3.3.1.2 Structure of a Prolog statement
In general, a Prolog program implements connectives in first order predicate logic: "and" is implemented as (,), "or" is implemented as (;), "only if" is implemented a ($\leftarrow$ or :-), and the built-in predicate "not" denotes $\neg$.

A Prolog statement (called *Horn clause*) is of the form

$$\underline{A} \qquad :- \qquad \underline{B_1, B_2, ..., B_n}$$
$$\text{Head} \qquad\qquad\qquad \text{body}$$

Note that there is at most *one* symbol in left hand side (LHS), which is referred to as the *positive* symbol. The reason of calling it the positive symbol can be understood by examining the following relationship between the conversion of the expressions:

$$A :- B_1, B_2, ..., B_n$$
$$\equiv A \leftarrow B_1, B_2, ..., B_n$$
$$\equiv B_1, B_2, ... B_n \rightarrow A$$
$$\equiv \neg (B_1 \wedge B_2 \wedge ... B_n) \vee A$$

It is important to note that there are two readings for a Prolog statement:
- *Declarative reading*: A if B_1 and... and B_n.
- *Procedural reading*: to do A, do B_1, then... then do B_n.

For example, consider the following:

grandfather(X,Z) :- father(X,Y), father(Y, Z)

This statement defines the concept of grandfather: X is the grandfather of Y if there is a person Z so that X is Z's father and Z is Y's father. This is the declarative reading. The same statement also has a procedural reading: In order to make X the grandfather of Y, X should first become the father of a person Z, and Z should become the father of Y. Which reading is more appropriate? In this particular example, probably the declarative one, but in some other cases, procedural reading may be more appropriate.

An important note should be given here that Horn clause calculus is equivalent to the full FOPL for proofs by refutation. Another note is that in Prolog terminology, a fact can be considered as a rule without body (such as "father(john, tom)" in the above example). As a further note, we point out that the following two rules:

a:-b.

a:-c.

are equal to one rule:

a :-b; c.

This is because by using distributive law and de Morgan's law, we have

$$(b \to a) \land (c \to a)$$
$$= (\neg b \lor a) \land (\neg c \lor a)$$
$$= (\neg b \land \neg c) \lor a$$
$$= \neg (b \lor c) \lor a$$
$$= (b \lor c) \to a$$

3.3.1.3 Remarks on structure of a Prolog program

We now give some remarks on how a Prolog program is structured. For more detail on Prolog language and its use in computational intelligence, please refer to references [Clocksin and Mellish 1987, Covington, Nute and Vellino 1988, Shoham 1994, Sterling and Shapiro 1994, Deransart, Ed-Dbali and Cervoni 1996].

(a) All rules are true in the "knowledge base" at the same time, so they form a conjunction.

(b) Predicates with the same predicate name are grouped together. For example, the two statements on "grandfather" can be considered as a procedure "father." Earlier we introduced the perspective of viewing a predicate as denoting a relationship. What is being discussed here denotes another perspective.

(c) Different order of clauses (rules) or different order of predicates may affect the behavior of the program (this is due to implementation-related considerations, not from logic).

(d) Predicates with the same predicate symbol may have a different number of arguments (but predicates with a different number of arguments will not unify). For example, it is legal to write $p(X,Y)$ and $p(a,Z,b)$, but they will not unify.

(e) The head of a predicate with the same predicate name in different rules may have different names for arguments (but with same arity). For example, in one rule we may have $p(X,Y)$:- ... while in another rule we may have p(Z,[]) :-... and in a third one we may have $p(\_,W)$. (Note the underscore represents an unnamed variable in Prolog.)

(f) Prolog answers queries by unification. In unification, positions of arguments are important, while names of variables are not. Section 3.3.1.8 provides a little more detail on unification.

(g) Quantifiers in Prolog: You can think of variables appearing *only in body* ("local") as being existentially quantified, and parameter variables as universally quantified. For example, consider the following rule:

grandfather(X,Z) :- father(X,Y), father(Y, Z).

both variables X and Z are universally quantified, while Z is local to the body. The corresponding FOPL statement is:

$\forall X \, \forall Y$ grandfather$(X,Y) \leftarrow \exists Z$ father(X,Z), father(Z,Y).

(h) Remark on "global" variables: There are no global variables in the sense of conventional languages. "Global" information is passed around through arguments.

3.3.1.4 Two kinds of queries (retrieval and confirmation)

In an information system such as a knowledge base system, a query is a statement requesting the retrieval of a specific piece of information. In Prolog, we can retrieve a stored fact or a fact which can be derived from the existing rules and facts. There are two ways to submit queries for retrieval:

?- grandfather(john,Y).
%find John's (one or all) grandchildren.

?- grandfather(X, mary).   %find Mary's grandfather.

?- grandfather(john, mary). % confirm or disconfirm.

Consider the following simple example:

takes(george, cs101). %George takes CS101 course.
takes(george, math201).
takes(george, mis201).
takes(sue, cs101).
takes(sue, math202).
takes(kim,cs101).
friends (X,Y) :- takes(X,Z), takes(Y,Z).
%X and Y are friends if they take the same course.

The following two queries illustrate two different types of query, namely, *confirmation* or *retrieval:*

?- takes(george, cs101). %confirmation type

?- takes(george, X).   %retrieval type, X will be substituted by a
% constant if such substitution exists.

There are some basic things we should know about Prolog:

(a) For a retrieval type query, if a user enters a semicolon(;) after an answer is retrieved, that means the user is looking for other answers. By this way, a user can ask for all answers.
(b) There are two cases when the system returns a "yes": success for a confirmation type query; more answers for retrieval type query.
(c) There are also two cases when the system returns a "no": fail (for confirmation type queries) or no more answers (for retrieval type queries).

3.3.1.5 Closed world assumption

Closed world assumption (CWA) refers to the assumption that nothing else exists outside the closed world of the knowledge base. It is closely related to another notion, *negation as failure*. Prolog answers queries using this assumption. For example, if we submit a query "likes(tom, wine)," the answer would be no, because it is not in the knowledge base nor can it be derived. The search was limited to a small world.

3.3.1.6 Answering query through depth first search

In either case of query answering, Prolog tries to prove a goal (in case of retrieval type, a guess may be made first; order of predicates may make a difference.) A depth-first search tree (DFS) with necessary backtracks will be constructed dynamically. This is an And/Or tree because some nodes (the "and" nodes) denote conditions which must be satisfied together while other nodes (the "or" nodes) denote conditions which must be satisfied separately.

As a concrete example, consider the following knowledge base in Prolog:

```
q(a)                              %(1)
r(c).                             %(2)
s(b).                             %(3)
p(X) :- q(X),write('r4'), nl.     %(4)
p(X) :- write('r5'), nl, q(X).    %(5)
p(X) :- s(X), r(Y).               %(6)
```

Consider the query "p(b)." We want to determine the output produced by this program, and draw depth first search trees to explain the results obtained. Since this is confirmation type, at the vary beginning, X is bound to b. Rule (4) is first tried, and since it is not successful, rule (5) is then tired, which failes again. Finally, Rule 6 is used and the query is eventually confirmed. Note that both node (5) and node (6) are "and" nodes. Note also that each time after a dead-end is reached, a new subtree is constructed.

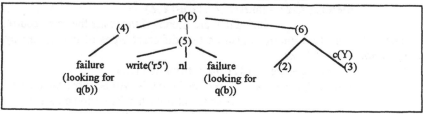

Figure 3. 3 A Prolog search tree

3.3.1.7 Relationship with resolution proof

It is the time to give an important remark on the semantics of Prolog, particularly the relationship between Prolog and resolution proof: The set of Horn clause expressions is a subset of the resolution clause space in logic programming and the resolution theorem prover is acting as a Prolog interpreter. The role of resolution theorem prover described here is not quite accurate, but we will not pursue this further, since our main interest is in applied aspects of Prolog. A little more detailed discussion on this issue can be found in [Luger and Stubblefield 1998].

3.3.1.8 Unification through recursion

Recursion plays an important role in Prolog; in fact, looping is performed by recursion. Recursion is natural for a language for reasoning. Just think about retrieving all of a person's ancestors. Using recursion is much appropriate than using iteration, and one major reason is that usually we don't know how many generations away from the considered person there are. In general, recursion refers to what a program module (for example a procedure or a function) calls itself. In Prolog, recursion occurs when a predicate refers to itself (namely, the same predicate symbol appears in both the head and the body). In fact, even the search process is recursion-based. Just like in a conventional programming language, recursion requires a general case and a base case.

The list data structure is a good example of learning recursion-based search in Prolog. An example of Prolog list is [a, b, c]. A list can be viewed as consisting of a head and a tail: the *head* of a list is simply the first element of the list (caution: there is no relationship between the head of a list and the head of a Prolog rule!), while the *tail* is the rest of the entire list (so *it is still a list!*). We can write a list using the notation of [H|T] (here H stands for the head while T stands for the tail) is not same as [H, T]). Note this is different from writing it as [H,T]. For example, [a, b, c] can be unified with [H|T], here H = a, T = [b, c]

We can now study how recursion is done on Prolog list. Consider the following predicate which checks the membership of a list (Note member is actually a built-in predicate):

```
member(X,[X|T]).                    %base case
member(X,[Y|T]) :- member(X,T).    %general case
```

These two predicates actually form a procedure. Its meaning can be explained as:

If X is identical with the head of a list

Then X is a member of this list

Else we have to check whether X is a member of the tail of the list.

Here are some sample queries:

```
?- member(a,[a,b,c]).              %confirmation
?- member(X,[a,b,c]).              %retrieval
```

Now consider another example:

```
length([], 0).
```

```
length([H|T], N) :- length(T, M), N is M + 1.
```
The meaning of this program can be explained as follows:
>   To find the length N of a list L do
>>   if L is empty then let N = 0
>>   else find the length M of the tail of L,
>>>   then add 1 to M giving N.

As one more example, consider the algorithm for merging two sorted lists (used in merge sort as well as in many external sorting methods). You may compare a recursive program in C or Pascal.

```
merge([],L2,L2).
merge(L1,[],L1).
merge([H1|T1], [H2|T2], [H1|Rslt]) :-
          H1<H2,!, merge(T1, [H2|T2], Result).
merge([H1|T1], [H2|T2], [H2|Rslt]) :-
merge([H1|T1], T2, Result).
```

3.3.1.9 More remarks on unification

Continuing our previous example, how would Prolog answer the query of p(X)? Even though this is a retrieval type of query, Prolog still uses pretty much the same way as illustrated in the above. One important difference is that instead of trying to confirm p(b) directly, the search engine has to start from a guess. Rule (4) will be tried first as before, but the variable X in p(X) will not be unified with any constant until fact (1) is used to satisfy Rule 4. Unlike the previous query, this time executing rule (4) results in success. Another important remark about retrieval type of query is that if the user is interested in additional answers, then the construction of search tree continues. Different from the case of confirmation type of query, a new subtree could be constructed not because of the failure, but because of looking for more answers. The reader is advised to complete the search tree for answering query p(X).

3.3.1.10 Using built-in predicates

The following are some built-in predicates in Prolog:
- *not:* a predicate introduced as a logical connective;
- *cut* (written as !): a goal with no arguments; it always succeeds and prevents backtracking;
- *fail:* a predicate introduced due to some language consideration,
- *nl:* new line.

For other built-in predicates in Prolog, please consult a Prolog book, such as [Clocksin and Mellish 1987, Covington *et al.* 1988].

3.3.2 SAMPLE PROLOG PROGRAMS

3.3.2.1 "I am my own grandfather" puzzle

The following is taken from N. Wirth's 1976 book with some simplification:

I married a widow (w) who has a grown-up daughter (d). My father (f) fell in love with my step-daughter and married her. Some months later, my wife gave birth to a son (s1).

Form the queries and get the answers for each of the following:

(a) Form a query to find who is my grandfather;

(b) Form a query to find all grandfather/grandchild relationship;

(c) Form a query to find who is who's brother-in-law;

(d) Form a query to find who is who's uncle;

(e) Form your own query (indicate its English meaning).

In order to answer these queries, you may need to include additional knowledge (e.g., the grandfather is father's father). You should also try to keep this kind of information as minimal as possible. For example, if there is a predicate is-father(X,Y) (which means X is Y's father), then there is no need to keep a predicate is-son , because is-son(A,B) can be expressed as is-father(B,A). The skeleton of the code is given below. A portion of this program is to be completed by the reader.

```
husband(i,w).
husband(f,d).
mother(w,d).
mother(w,s1).
father(f,i).
father(i,s1).
No more facts needed; the following are rules.

father(X,Y) :- f_in_law(X,Y).
 %This is to say f_in_law is considered as father.
father(X,Y) :- husband(X,Z), mother(Z,Y).
                    %Can you explain the meaning of
                    %this rule in English?
f_in_law(X,Y) :-   %How to define father in law?
b_in_law(X,Y) :- ...
brother(X,Y) :- b_in_law(X,Y).
            %b_in_law is considered as brother.
uncle(X,Y) :- ...
            % X is Y's uncle if Z is Y's father and
      X is Z's brother.
grandfather(X,Y) :- ...
            % Define grandfather in terms of father.
```

3.3.2.2 Farmer, wolf, goat and cabbage puzzle revisited

Our next example is to implement the farmer, wolf, goat and cabbage puzzle in Prolog. First, we should define the *mandatory rules* required for solving the problem. These rules are mandatory (and thus are distinguished from heuristic rules) because they must be followed. For example, each mandatory rule must respect the fact that the farmer is the only rower and he can only carry at most one item (other than himself). It should also respect the fact that the wolf and the goat cannot be left alone, and that the goat and cabbage cannot be left alone. There are several ways to express the mandatory rules in this puzzle. One easy way is to form a rule for each item that can be carried by the farmer: the wolf, the goat, the cabbage, and himself. The following program is adopted and revised from [Luger and Stubblefield 1998].The readers should note the parameter B in the move statements. Since Prolog does not have the concept equivalent to global variable in many conventional languages, the effect of global variable has to be achieved through parameter passing. Here B is passed around to keep track of the visited states stored in the stack.

Prolog program for the FWGC puzzle

```
unsafe([X,Y,Y,_]):-opp(X,Y).
unsafe([X,_,Y,Y]):-opp(X,Y).

opp(w,e).
opp(e,w).

move([X,X,G,C], [Y,Y,G,C], B) :-
   opp(X, Y),
   not(unsafe([Y,Y,G,C])),
   not(member_stack([Y,Y,G,C], B)),
   writelist(['try farmer takes wolf: ',Y, Y, G, C]).

move([X,W,X,C], [Y,W,Y,C], B) :-
   opp(X, Y),
   not(unsafe([Y,W,Y,C])),
   not(member_stack([Y,W,Y,C], B)),
   writelist(['try farmer takes goat: ',Y, W, Y, C]).

move([X,W,G,X], [Y,W,G,Y], B) :-
   opp(X, Y),
   not(unsafe([Y,W,G,Y])),
   not(member_stack([Y,W,G,Y], B)),
   writelist(['try farmer takes cabbage:',Y,W,G,Y]).

move([X,W,G,C], [Y,W,G,C], B) :-
   opp(X, Y),
   not(unsafe([Y,W,G,C])),
   not(member_stack([Y,W,G,C], B)),
   writelist(['try farmer takes himself:',Y,W,G,C]).
```

```
move([F,W,G,C], [F,W,G,C], _)
   :- writelist(['     BACKTRACK from:', F,W,G,C]),
      fail.

path(Z,Z,L):-write('Solution Path is:'), nl,
             reserveprint(L).
path(X,Y,L):-move(X,Z,L),
             stack(Z,L,N), path(Z,Y,N).


%The following are stack ops
empty_stack([]).

stack(T, S, [T|S]).

member_stack(E,S):-member(E,S).

add_list_to_stack(L,S,R) :- append(L,S,R).

%end stack operations

%writelist and reserveprint are writing routines.
writelist([]):- nl.
writelist([H|T]):-print(H),tab(1),writelist(T).

%reserveprint is used to check the contents of the
%stack. Not a good operation for defining a stack.
reserveprint(S):-empty_stack(S).
reserveprint(S):-stack(E,R,S),reserveprint(R),
                 write(E), nl.

%The following are driving and testing routines.
go(S,G):- not(unsafe(S)), not(unsafe(G)),
          empty_stack(E), stack(S, E, B),
          path(S, G, B).
go(S,_):- unsafe(S), write('Start unsafe!!'), nl.
go(_,G):- unsafe(G), write('Goal unsafe!!'), nl.

test :-go([w,w,w,w], [e,e,e,e]).
                  %Other tests may be added.
```

The following is a sample execution:
```
?- test.
try farmer takes goat:  e w e w
try farmer takes himself: w w e w
try farmer takes wolf:  e e e w
```

```
try farmer takes goat:   w e w w
try farmer takes cabbage: e e w e
try farmer takes wolf:   w w w e
try farmer takes goat:   e w e e
    BACKTRACK from: e w e e
    BACKTRACK from: w w w e
try farmer takes himself: w e w e
try farmer takes goat:   e e e e
Solution Path is:
[w,w,w,w]
[e,w,e,w]
[w,w,e,w]
[e,e,e,w]
[w,e,w,w]
[e,e,w,e]
[w,e,w,e]
[e,e,e,e]
yes
```

The depth first search tree constructed from execution is shown in Figure 3.4.

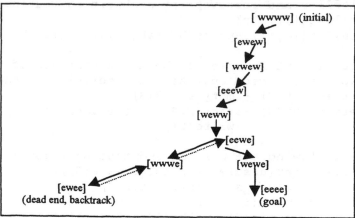

Figure 3. 4   Depth first search tree for FWGC puzzle

3.3.3 SUMMARY OF IMPORTANT THINGS ABOUT PROLOG

In summary, the following are important things to know about Prolog; they also illustrate important factors used to support reasoning:

- Recursion,
- Unification,
- Closed world assumption,
- Depth first search, and
- Resolution proof.

3.4 ABDUCTION AND INDUCTION

3.4.1 OTHER FORMS OF REASONING

As already briefly mentioned, *deduction* (or deductive reasoning) refers to logical reasoning in which conclusions must follow from their premises. Materials presented so far in this paper have been devoted to deductive reasoning using first order predicate logic. In the remaining part of this section, we provide a brief discussion on other forms of inference. Particularly, we will give a brief introduction on abduction and induction. There are two important remarks on these two reasoning methods. First, unlike deduction, both abduction and induction are not sound. Intuitively, this is to say both of these two methods do not guarantee the result of reasoning is "correct." We will explain the reason when we introduce these two methods. From the first remark comes the second remark: If a reasoning method is not sound, why do we study it at all? In fact, although abduction and induction are not sound, they are still closely related to deduction (see additional reading). Studying abduction and induction (as well as other forms of reasoning) will help us to understand the nature of reasoning. In addition, abduction and induction are very useful, because they allow us to derive conclusions which cannot be done using deduction. For example, abduction and induction can play an important role in creativity. This gives us a chance to discuss abduction and induction in other chapters of this book. For example, we will review the concept of abduction in Chapter 5 when we discuss the explanation facility in expert systems, and we will get back to the issue of induction when we discuss machine learning (Chapter 10). In addition, the discussion on computerized creativity, as presented in Chapters 7 and 8, are also related to induction and abduction.

3.4.2 INDUCTION

Induction refers to the inference from the specific case to the general. The following is a simple example of induction. Suppose we have observed facts:

        fastcar(toyota, 2000).
        fastcar(chevy, 2000).
        fastcar(dodge, 2000).
        ...
        fastcar(..., 2000).

From what we have observed above, we may want to draw the conclusion:

        fastcar(Any-model, New).

More generally, if we have observed

   $p(a) \rightarrow q(a)$,
   $p(b) \rightarrow q(b)$,

we may attempt to conclude $\forall X$, $p(X) \rightarrow q(X)$. This is actually a generalization process. Although this seems to be reasonable, we cannot take it for granted, because we may not be able to check *every* individual value of X; and so long as there is one possible value of X which makes the conclusion false, then the conclusion is not true. Apparently, inductive reasoning is not sound, but it is very useful, because it is pervasive in our daily thinking.

3.4.3 ABDUCTION

Note that in a sense, inductive reasoning can be considered as the "inverse" of modus ponens as used in deduction, because if we know $\forall X$, $p(X) \rightarrow q(X)$, then we can conclude $p(a) \rightarrow q(a)$, $p(b) \rightarrow q(b)$, etc. using modus ponens.

Abduction can be considered as another "inverse" of modus ponens. The basic idea of abduction can be described by comparing it with modus ponens:

Modus ponens: $(p \rightarrow q) \wedge p \Rightarrow q$

Abduction: $(p \rightarrow q) \wedge q \Rightarrow p$

Abduction is not sound because although p implies q, the existence of q does not necessarily imply p is true, because there may be some other reason to make q true. Nevertheless, abduction is useful because it provides a clue for the possible cause. Therefore, abduction is sometimes referred to as reasoning from observed facts to the best *explanation*.

It has been shown that abduction can be reduced to deduction on a transformed (completed) domain theory that explicitly contains the assumption that all the direct explanations of an event have been represented; under such an assumption, an event implies the disjunction of its explanations. This provides further intuition for abduction. Detail is discussed in [Torasso, Console, Portinale and Theseider 1995].

3.5 NONMONOTONIC REASONING

First order predicate logic is very basic, and its reasoning power is still limited. Non-standard logic has been developed to enhance the reasoning power. There have been various proposals. In this section we give a brief discussion about this issue. The materials presented here are important, but for those readers who are not interested in pursuing any theoretical studies, most of this section (except subsection 3.5.1) can be skipped.

3.5.1 MEANING OF NONMONOTONIC REASONING

The standard logical formalisms of reasoning are mostly monotonic: discovering new information can only increase the set of conclusions to be reached. In other words, the more you know, the more conclusions you can draw. Note that the reasoning based on a monotonic formalism has very limited ability in the exploration of the coherent relations between the data sets and their real world implications, and is inadequate in handling the incompleteness and imprecision of the data sets. In reality, much of human reasoning is *nonmonotonic*, bceasue learning new facts may actually cause retraction of previously held beliefs. If you heard WhiteTiger is a tiger, you will say WhiteTiger eats animals. But if we have learned that WhiteTiger is just a paper-tiger, we have to *retract* our previous conclusion. Nonmonotonic reasoning aims to capture the notion of commonsense reasoning and to reveal the attribute coherence under uncertainty and incompleteness [Ginsberg 1987]. In particular, knowledge resulting from nonmonotonic reasoning is often not in the form of iron clad rules, but consists of defaults subject to exceptions that are valuable to real-world applications.

Nonmonotonic reasoning was first proposed in the late 1970s. Since then, it has received much attention from the research community in computational intelligence. As indicated by McCarthy in the earlier age of nonmonotonic reasoning, when probabilistic reasoning (and not just the axiomatic basis of probability theory) has been fully formalized, it will be formally nonmonotonic [McCarthy 1980]). Recently, an update procedure was proposed to handle nonmonotonic change of knowledge. In addition, the use of default representations in incremental learning has been proposed, where a belief can be retracted. (A little more discussion on nonmonotonic reasoning can be found in Chapter 11.)

3.5.2 COMMONSENSE REASONING

As a concrete approach of nonmonotonic reasoning, let us take a look at how to use logic to model human commonsense using commonsense reasoning [McCarthy 1981]. A *program* is said to have *commonsense* if it automatically deduces for itself a sufficiently wide class of immediate consequences of anything it is told and what it already knows. Commonsense reasoning can thus serve as a tool for building intelligent agents.

A program or person has common sense if the following properties hold:

Property 1: It knows a sufficiently large set of facts of the environment where it lives;

Property 2: It can increment what it knows by automatically deducing a sufficiently large set of immediate consequences;

Property 3: It can increment what it knows by being told (concerned with natural language processing).

Properties 1 and 2 distinguish between what the program knows and what allows it to deduce new facts from what it knows -- a distinction between common sense knowledge and common sense reasoning. A very similar distinction is a distinction between the epistemological and the heuristic part of intelligence. These three properties are at the core of McCarthy's research. McCarthy was more concerned with establishing logical and mathematical foundations for reasoning, while some other well-known researchers (such as M. Minsky) were more involved with theories of how we human beings actually reason using pattern recognition and analogy, as well as the fragility of contemporary expert systems (as he observed, "some expert systems need common sense"). (A discussion on expert systems is given in Chapter 5.)

In order to study commonsense reasoning, the following three kinds of adequacy has been defined:

 a. A representation is called *metaphysically adequate* if the world could have that form without contradicting the facts of the aspect of reality that interests us.

 b. A representation is called *epistemologically adequate* for a person or machine if it can be used practically to express the facts that one actually has about the aspect of the world.

 c. A representation is called *heuristically adequate* if the reasoning processes actually gone through in solving a problem are expressible in the language.

The word epistemology is used as many philosophers use it, but with a different emphasis. Philosophers emphasize what is potentially knowable with maximal opportunities to observe compute, whereas computational intelligence researchers must take into account what is knowable with available observational and computational facilities. It can be argued that the requirement of heuristic adequacy really amounts to requiring epistemologically adequate representations of reasoning. It is a derived notion, and therefore less important than the notion of epistemological adequacy.

However, though logic is a very good starting point which allows formalizing many forms of common sense, it is far from having the expressibility needed to represent commonsense. Nevertheless, formalizing commonsense reasoning using a logic-based approach reveals many important aspects of commonsense reasoning which may not be obtained otherwise.

3.5.3 CIRCUMSCRIPTION

A specific technique in commonsense reasoning is called *circumscription*. According to McCarthy, we can confirm part of the intuition by describing a previously un-formalized mode of reasoning called circumscription, which we can show does not correspond to deduction in a mathematical systems. The conclusions it yields are just conjectures and sometimes even introduce inconsistency. We will argue that humans often use circumscription and so do robots. Informally, circumscription is a rule of conjecture that allows a person or program to jump to the conclusion that the objects which can be shown to have a certain property P by reasoning on a given set of facts are all the objects that satisfy P. More formally, let P be a predicate symbol and S a first order sentence. Let $S(\Phi)$ be the result of replacing all occurrences of P in S with Φ. Then the circumscription of P in Φ is the sentence schema

$$S(\Phi) \wedge \forall \bar{x}. (\Phi(\bar{x}) \rightarrow P(\bar{x})) \rightarrow \forall \bar{x}.(P(\bar{x}) \rightarrow \Phi(\bar{x}))$$

where $\bar{x}$ stands for the tuple $x1, \ldots, xn$. Intuitively, this formula says that if $S(\Phi)$ holds, and Φ if has a smaller extension of P, then P and Φ have the same extension. In other words, the set of objects which satisfy P is made as small as that satisfying Φ.

Reasoning schemes such as default logic, monomontonic logic and circumscription are designed to handle reasoning with default rules and retraction of beliefs. There are a series of difficult issues encountered by these approaches, and so far no default reasoning system has successfully addressed all of these issues. In addition, most logical systems are formally undecidable, and very slow in practice [Russell and Norvig 1995].

3.5.4 SUMMARY OF NONMONOTONIC REASONING

In summary, nonmonotonic approaches have shared such assumptions as: classical logic is insufficient, there is a need for a declarative solution, and the solution should be symbolic as opposed to numeric. Proof based approaches include default logic (by Reiter) and Modal approaches (by McDermott and Doyle). Minimization approaches are exemplified by McCarthy's circumscription. Connections have been found among these various approaches. The work on *truth maintenance* has a strange relationship to research in nonmonotonic reasoning [Ginsberg 1987]. Although the discussion on nonmontonic reasoning as discussed in this section falls in the context of logic, it does not have to be so. In fact, nonmonotonic reasoning has a close relationship with knowledge based systems (Chapter 5) as well as reasoning under uncertainty (Chapter 10).

As a final remark, we point out that many other approaches have been developed for logic-based problem solving, such as fuzzy logic, temporal logic, as well as others. In Chapter 12, we will take a look at some aspects of fuzzy logic. A discussion on some other approaches can be found in [Turner 1984].

SUMMARY

In this chapter we provided a discussion on deductive reasoning using first order predicate logic. We also introduced Prolog as a language for learning first order predicate logic (although strictly speaking they are not equivalent to each other). The advantage of learning Prolog is due to its reasoning power. Prolog code provides a high level description of problem solving process and can be viewed as pseudo code which can be implemented using other programming languages (such as C++).

Predicate logic plays an important role for decision support problem solving. In the next chapter we will discuss relational database in the context of predicate logic. Although in this chapter we have emphasized deductive reasoning, we have also briefly introduced other reasoning methods. Other related discussions will be provided in later chapters (including Chapter 6).

SELF-EXAMINATION QUESTIONS

1. Is this true: $\exists X\ (p(X) \land q(X)) = \exists X\ p(X) \land \exists Y\ q(Y)$? Why or why not?
2. Why use stack in solving the FWGC problem?
3. Consider the chain rule, which was presented in propositional logic. How to write it in predicate logic? How to prove it using binary resolution?
4. In Chapter 2 we considered the following simple puzzle:

> Mozart visited Vienna three times, and he died there. On which of the three visits did he die?

How will you solve this puzzle by writing a simple Prolog program?
5. Consider ADTs stack operations using Prolog implementation. Note that the same predicate "stack(Top, Stack, [Top|Stack])" can be used for *both* push and pop operation. Explain the role of unification in performing these two operations, and give several queries to illustrate how to use this predicate.

REFERENCES

Clocksin, W. F. and Mellish, C. S., Programming in Prolog (3rd ed.), Springer-Verlag, Berlin and New York, 1987.
Covington, M. A., Nute, D. and Vellino, A., *Prolog programming in depth,* Prentice Hall, Upper Saddle River, NJ, 1988.
Deransart, P., Ed-Dbali, A. and Cervoni, L., *Prolog: The Standard Reference Manual,* Spring-Verlag, Berlin, 1996.
Ginsberg, M. L., Introduction, in *Readings in Nonmonotonic reasoning* (M. L. Ginsberg ed.), pp. 1-24, 1987.
Luger, G. and Stubblefield, W., *Artificial Intelligence,* 3rd ed., Addison-Wesley Longman, Harlow, England, 1998.
McCarthy, J., Circumscription - A form of nonmonotonic reasoning, *Artificial Intelligence,* 13 (1 & 2), 1980.
Russell, S. and Norvig, P., *Artificial Intelligence: A Modern Approach,* Englewood Clliffs, NJ.: Prentice Hall, 1995.
Shoham, Y., *Artificial intelligence techniques in Prolog,* Morgan Kaufmann Publishers, San Mateo, CA, 1994.
Sterling, L. and Shapiro, E., *The Art of Prolog: Advanced Programming Techniques* (2nd ed.), MIT Press, Cambridge, MA, 1994.
Torasso, P., Console, L., Portinale, L. and Theseider, D., On the role of abduction, *ACM Computing Surveys,* 27(3), 353-355, 1995.
Turner, R., *Logic for Artifiical Intelligence,* Ellis Horwood, New York, 1984.

Chapter 4

RELATIONS AS PREDICATES

4.1 OVERVIEW

In this chapter we extend the concept of predicates to relations. We first introduce the concept of relation, then explain why a relation can be viewed as a predicate. This will provide a unified perspective toward data and knowledge retrieval. This examination leads to the discussion of formal languages (declarative and procedural) for manipulating data represented through relations; in particular, relational algebra is discussed in some detail. We further discuss integrity constraints and issues related to relational database design. The basics of Datalog, a variation of Prolog suitable for database management, are also briefly discussed.

4.2 THE CONCEPT OF RELATION

A *relational database* consists of structured data stored in a set of relations. By structured data we mean each relation has a *schema* which consists of a set of attributes. For example, a company database may have a relation to hold employee information such as employee ID, name, salary, etc. (which form a schema), a relation to hold department information, as well as other relations. Intuitively, a relation is just a table. Although this concept seems to be far away from a collection of predicates, the concepts of relation and predicate are closely related. Recall the following predicates discussed in Chapter 3:

Father(john, tom).
Father(tom, mary).
Father(tom, dave).

We can rewrite these predicates into a table form with the name of "father" consisting of two columns; each is an argument in the predicate "father," as shown in Table 4.1.

Table 4.1 A table rewritten from predicates

Father_name	Child_name
John	Tom
Tom	Mary
Tom	Dave

More formally, a *relation* is defined as a subset of a Cartesian product of a list of domains. For example, the father relation is a subset of the Cartesian products of all possible names of fathers and all possible names of children. Here the *domain* of an attribute refers to all possible values that attribute can take. Conversely, each row in the relation (usually referred to as a tuple) can be viewed as a predicate. For example, consider the relation shown in Table 4.2 (let us call it *r*):

Table 4.2 A relation

A	B	C
a1	b1	c1
a1	b2	c2
a2	b3	c1

This relation can be represented as a collection of predicates: r(a1, b1, c1), r(a1, b2, c2) and r(a2, b3, c1). It can also be expressed using set notation: r = {(a1, b1, c1), (a1, b2, c2), (a2, b3, c1)}. In this book, we will mainly use the table format, but in order to save space, occasionally the set format may also be used.

Viewing relations as predicates has the advantage of integrated treatment of data management and knowledge management, because relations can be conveniently used to represent data (as to be discussed in this chapter). However, viewing relations as predicates and viewing relations as subsets of Cartesian product may not always be consistent to each other. One such difference is the order of columns (arguments or attributes) and order of tuples (rows). If we take a strict set-theoretic perspective, both columns and rows are not ordered in a relation. However, as we have learned from predicate calculus, the order of arguments does make sense. For convenience of our discussion, we will assume the order of column is important, while the order of tuples is not important.

4.3   OVERVIEW OF RELATIONAL DATA MODEL

4.3.1 SCHEMA AND INSTANCE

We introduce the following basic terminology.

A *relation schema* comprises a list of attributes and their corresponding domains ("top layer" of the table), similar to a variable type definition. For example, in the father relation, the schema consists of attributes Father_name and Child_name.

A *relation instance* is a value of a variable (e.g. an array); it refers to the contents of a relation (consists of all tuples).

We use the notation: r(R), here the little r stands for the relation (the instances) while the big R stands for the schema. For example, we can write father(Father), where "father" stands for the actual tuples while "Father" stands for the schema.

4.3.2 DECLARATIVE AND PROCEDURAL LANGUAGES

Data are stored in a relational database to satisfy users' information needs. Users submit queries to retrieve information. The language used for submitting queries falls in one of the two categories: *declarative* (users specify *what* they want) or procedural (users specify *how* to get the needed information). Query languages can also be categorized as either *formal* (which are used for theoretical studies) or *commercial* (which are supported by commercial products and have syntactical "sugar" added). In this chapter, we study formal languages, focusing on *relational algebra (RA)*, which is a procedural language. A popular commercial language, SQL, which is based on relational algebra but with some declarative flavor, will be discussed in the next chapter.

To write a query in relational algebra, a user should specify the information needs in terms of relational operators. More detail will be given in the next section.

The formal declarative language in relational databases is called relational calculus (RC). RC is in fact a form of first order predicate calculus (introduced in Chapter 3). There are two kinds of RC: *Tuple relational calculus (TRC)* and *domain relational calculus (DRC)*.

In TRC, *tuple variables* are used. The range of a tuple variable is the whole relation. The general format to write a query in TRC is to specify the set consisting of tuples with desirable properties. If we use t to denote a tuple variable t which ranges over the entire resulting relation, we have

$$\{t \mid \text{what you want (properties)}\},$$

To be more specific, we have

$$\{ t \mid \text{condition}_1 \wedge \text{condition}_2 \wedge ... \wedge \text{condition}_n \}.$$

Each condition in the above query is a predicate. For example, consider a loan relation in a banking database with schema Loan = (loan-no., amount). A query for retrieving all tuples with loan amount greater than \$1,200 can be written as

$$\{t \mid t \in \text{ loan } \wedge \ t \text{ [amount]} > 1200\}$$

Intuitively, the philosophy of TRC is to view each table consisting of rows (tuples). Alternatively, we may think that each table consists of columns. Therefore, in domain relational calculus (DRC), we need one domain variable per column. Each tuple is constructed from domain variables, and a query in DRC has the following format:

$$\{d_1, d_2, d_3, ... d_n \mid \text{cond}(d_1, d_2, ..d_n)\}$$

Conceptually DRC is similar to TRC, but technically it is a little more difficult (because in TRC a tuple can be directly represented by a variable, while in DRC, each tuple should be constructed from domain variables).

An important notion in relational calculus is *safety*. To understand what is a safe query, we just need to know what is *unsafe*: a query may result in an infinite relation. For example, the following query is unsafe, because it asks for all tuples not satisfying a certain property, and this could result in an infinite number of tuples to be retrieved:

$$\{t \mid \neg(t \in \text{loan})\}$$

How to deal with this problem? Note that in the above query the infinite relation is caused by the negative condition "not in". To guarantee a safe query, we can impose restrictions by using some positive conditions.

The reason to study relational calculus is partly due to its theoretical importance. It has been established that the following three are equivalent in expressive power (here equivalence means they can be converted to each other): relational algebra (RA, to be discussed below), safe TRC, and safe DRC.

4.4 RELATIONAL ALGEBRA

4.4.1 PREVIEW OF RELATIONAL ALGEBRA

In order to write RA queries, we should first understand RA operators. We start with some simple examples. Table 4.3(a), (b) and (c) depict three relations respectively: relation u (U) for undergraduate student information, relation g (G) for graduate student information, and relation a (A) for address information.

Table 4.3 Three relations

(a)

Sname	Major	GPA
Sue K. Fung	CS	3.3
David M. Wilson	Math	2.2
...	...	...

(b)

Sname	Major	GPA
Mary K. Fox	IT	3.1
Ken S. Robertson	CS	3.5
...		...

(c)

Sname	Address
Mary K. Fox	12435 Dodge
David M. Wilson	1600 Farnam
...	...

The following are some examples of English queries:
- Find names and addresses of all students.
- Find names and addresses of all grad students.
- Find names of grad students.

The following are some simple examples of using relational operators. A discussion on these operations (including syntax) will be given in the next subsection.
- Union: $u \cup g$. This is to find student name, major and GPA of all students.
- Set difference: $u - g$. This is to find student name, major and GPA of undergraduate students who are not graduate students -- assuming an undergraduate student in one major could be a graduate student in another major.
- Project: $\pi_{\text{major}}(u)$. This is to find all undergraduate majors.

- Select: $\sigma_{major='CS'}$ (g). This is to find student name, major and GPA of graduate students majored in computer science.
- Cartesian product: $u \times a$. This is to establish all possible combinations of undergraduate student information and address information. This operation can be followed by a select operation to find addresses for undergraduate students as shown in the following query: $\pi_{u.Sname, a.Address}$ ($\sigma_{u.Sname=a.Sname}$ $u \times a$). Cartesian product can be used to carry out *join* operation (see below).

It is important to note that relational database can be considered as a knowledge base of ground facts. One can use Prolog rules to define the relational algebra operations. (Actually there is a version of Prolog called Datalog which is used for database. A brief discussion on Datalog can be found at the end of this chapter.) In the following we rewrite the above queries in Prolog rules.

- Union: student(S-name, Major, GPA) :-
                        undergraduate (S-name, Major, GPA).
             student(S-name, Major, GPA) :-
                        graduate (S-name, Major, GPA).
- Set difference: non-grad(S-name, Major, GPA) :-
                        undergraduate (S-name, Major, GPA),
                        not graduate (S-name, Major, GPA).
- Project: under-major(Major) :- undergraduate(S-name, Major, GPA).
- Select: cs_graduate(S-name) :- graduate(S-name, comp-science, G).
- Join: under-addr(S-name, Major, GPA) :-
             undergraduate(S-name, Major, GPA), address(S-name, Address).

Note that the join operation can be considered as performing Cartesian product followed by a selection. More discussion on join operation will be provided later.

4.4.2 HOW TO FORM A RELATIONAL ALGEBRA QUERY FROM A GIVEN ENGLISH QUERY

It is important to be able to form an SQL query for a given English query. Informally, the following are some important things which should be considered in SQL query construction:

- Study the database schema as well as the schema for each relation;
- From the interested attributes identify relevant relations;
- From the attributes, find relations, find other attributes in same relation;
- Be aware that same attribute may have different names in different relations;
- Decide appropriate RA operators (such as connecting two relations using join);
- Form the conditions in the where statement (such as SSN = ...).

Note that the result of a query is a relation (which has a schema).

Overall, the following are basic issues involved in relational database retrieval:

- Form the English query;
- Form the RA query from the English query;
- Explain RA query in English;
- Tell what is the result (i.e., the actual tuples retrieved) given actual relations.

4.4.3 RELATIONAL ALGEBRA: FUNDAMENTAL OPERATORS

4.4.3.1 Unary operators (Within same relation)

Select: Find tuples satisfying condition C from relation (r) is expressed as $\sigma_C(r)$. Note: C is a predicate, for example, (sname = 'J. Dole') and (GPA = 2.5).

Project: Find a specific attribute or set of attributes with name A from relation r, is expressed as $\pi_A(r)$.

Rename: $\rho_x(E)$ returns the result of expression E under the name x . For example, $\rho_{good\text{-}student}(\sigma_{gpa>3.0}$ (undergraduate)) renames undergraduate students with GPA greater than 3.0 as good-students.

4.4.3.2 Binary operators

We have the following set-theoretic operations:

Union: The results include all tuples in r or s: $r \cup s$ (remove duplicates). A requirement for the union operation is that both relations involved should be *union compatible,* meaning that the two relations should have same arity and the corresponding attributes should be in the same domain. The union operation has the following features:

  Commutative: $r \cup s = s \cup r$

  Associative: $(r \cup s) \cup p = r \cup (s \cup p)$

Set Difference: The result includes tuples in r but not in s : r - s. Just like the union operation, it requires union compatibility. Note that set difference operation is not commutative: $r - s \neq s - r$

Cartesian Product: $r \times s$, it combines information from two relations.

4.4.4 RELATIONAL ALGEBRA: ADDITIONAL OPERATORS

In general, additional operators can be expressed in terms of fundamental operators or just for the convenience.

- *Assignment* (used in a way similar to intermediate variable):

  $$temp \leftarrow \pi_{R\text{-}S}(r)$$

The next five operators are very useful ones.

- *Set intersection:* This is a set-theoretic binary operation. The result should return tuples in both relations r and s. Using Venn diagram we can easily verify $r \cap s = r - (r - s)$. Therefore, a set intersection can be replaced by two consecutive set differences.

- *Join:* This is a binary operation based on Cartesian product. We first consider the general theta join, then consider the natural join (which is usually used in queries).
- *Theta join* (in general form): $r \bowtie_\theta = \sigma_\theta (r \times s)$. The condition may involve attributes with same name but in two different relations. To avoid confusion, attribute A_1 (such as S-name in relation r may be denoted as $r._{A1}$.) An example of Theta join with condition $B < D$ on the following two given relations r and s is shown in Table 4.4.

Table 4.4 An example of Theta join

(a) Relation $r(R)$

A	B	C
1	2	3
4	5	6
7	8	9

(b) Relation $s(S)$

D	E
3	1
6	2

(c) Result of $r \bowtie_{B<D} s$

A	B	C	D	E
1	2	3	3	1
1	2	3	6	2
4	5	6	6	2

- *Natural join:* Join condition satisfies only equality comparison, with duplicated attributes removed. Natural join uses exact same notation as theta join, except the subscript (which indicates the join condition) is dropped. A simple example is given in Table 4.5.

Table 4.5 An example of natural join

(a) Relation $r(R)$

A	B	C
4	9	8
5	16	7
2	12	7

(b) Relation $s(S)$

C	D
7	12
4	18
8	10

(c) Relation $r \bowtie s$

A	B	C	D
4	9	8	10
5	16	7	12
2	12	7	12

- *Division:* Among all the RA operators, this one may be the most difficult one. There are two questions related to division operator: (a) when to use it, and (b) what is the result. To answer both questions, we need to consider the following. Roughly speaking, division is "almost" the inverse operation of Cartesian product. Therefore, in order to answer (a), a division $r \div s$ should be carried out to obtain the result which should hold all the features of s. For example, if we want to identify students who have received all awards in a university, we may need a division operation to carry out the job. A correct understanding of the meaning of the division will prevent writing syntactically incorrect queries involving division.

The second question in regard to division, namely, what is the result of division, can also be answered by considering division as the inverse of Cartesian product. It can also be answered by take a look at the actual process as indicated in the following definition. Formally, suppose r(R) and s(S) are relations and S ⊆ R, then division is defined as

$$r \div s = \pi_{R-S}(r) - \pi_{R-S}((\pi_{R-S} \times s) - \pi_{R-S,S}(r))$$

This formal definition is a little scary. Fortunately, in order to get the result of division, you don't have to follow these steps. Since division is "almost" the inverse operator of Cartesian product, a simple way is to start by considering ("guessing") possible answers and constructing Cartesian product (as to be explained in the class). Table 4.6 provides an example. Given r(Award, SID) and s(Award), we want to know which students have received all awards. The query requires us to compute t = r ÷ s. Note that a simple select operation does not do the job, because although it can find students who have received at least one award, it cannot find students receiving *all* awards. Note also that this division is legal because the schema of *s* is contained in the schema of *r*. The resulting table should contain only one column SID.

Table 4.6 An example of division
(a) Relation r(Awards,SID)

Award	SID
a1	b1
a2	b1
a3	b1
a4	b1
a1	b2
a3	b2
a2	b3
a3	b3
a4	b3
a1	b4
a2	b4
a3	b4

(b) Relation s(Awards)

Award
a1
a2
a3

(c) Result t(SID)

SID
b1
b4

How to calculate t(SID)? Since t(SID) may at most contain four values (b1, b2, b3, b4), for each of them, we form a Cartesian product with tuples in s(SID), and check whether the result is in r(Award, SID). If for the same value of SID, *all* the possible Cartesian products are found in r(Award, SID), then the value of B should be in the result. For example, for b2, the Cartesian product (a2, b2) is not in r(Award, SID), so b2 is not included in the result.

4.4.5 COMBINED USE OF OPERATORS

In reality, many queries can be expressed by combined use of select (σ), project (π), and join (⋈) operations. The basic structure of the commercial language SQL (to be discussed in Chapter 5) resembles these operations. Therefore, a good understanding of RA would help us to write SQL queries.

4.4.6 EXTENDED RA OPERATIONS

RA operations can be considered at different levels: fundamental, additional, and extended. Extended RA operators include generalized projection, outer join, and aggregation functions. Here we take a look at aggregation functions. *Aggregation functions* take a collection of values and return a single value as a result. There are five aggregation functions: count, sum, avg, max, min. Aggregation functions play a very important role of On-Line Analytical Processing (OLAP) for decision support queries. More discussion will be provided in Chapter 5 when we discuss the commercial language SQL.

4.5 RELATIONAL VIEWS AND INTEGRITY CONSTRAINTS

In this section, we discuss two important and related issues: relational views and integrity constraints.

4.5.1 VIRTUAL VIEWS AND MATERIALIZED VIEWS

Relational views are personalized collections of relations. They are constructed through queries. For example, in the student database, one user may be interested in all students who have good GPAs and their addresses, while another user may be interested in GPAs of undergraduate students majored in sciences. One or more views can be constructed for each user's information need. Furthermore, a view can be defined by other views and relations and can be used as a relation. Note that relation views are *virtual* tables because they are usually not stored. Views are typically implemented as follows: When a view is defined, the database system stores the definition of the view itself, rather than the result of evaluation of the RA expression that defines the view. When a view relation is used in a query, it is replaced by the stored query expression. Therefore, whenever the query is evaluated, the view relation is *recomputed*. Views are a useful tool for queries, and additional views can be further defined using previous views, or a combination of previously defined views and stored relations.

However, in some applications, in order to avoid recomputation, it would be desirable to store view relations. Stored views are referred to as *materialized views*. Recent development in data warehousing and On-Line Analytical Processing (OLAP) has made the study of materialized views an active research area. More discussion on materialized views will be in Chapter 11.

4.5.2 INTEGRITY CONSTRAINTS

Note that although views are a useful tool for queries, they present significant problems if we allow updates, insertions or deletions to be performed on views. The difficulty comes from the fact that a modification to the database expressed in terms of a view must be translated to a modification to the actual relations in the logical model of the database. As a simplest example, let us consider a view involving one relation only. Consider a relational schema S_info = (SID, major, GPA) with F = {SID $\rightarrow$ major, SID $\rightarrow$ GPA}. Apparently SID is the key. A view is constructed with schema S1 = {major, GPA}, which is a virtual relation with SID removed from S_info. Suppose S1 consists of two tuples: {(CS, 3.5), (MIS, 3.6)}. (Here we use the predicate format to represent a relation.) Now assume a user wants to insert a tuple (Math, 2.8) into S1. This request should be translated into an insert of tuple (?, Math, 2.8) into S_info. Note the question mark ? stands for a null value, because SID is not specified in the user's request. If we do allow this insert operation to occur, we will end up with a new tuple in S_info which does not have the primary key. Apparently this is a scenario we should avoid. For this reason, modification through views should be carried out carefully. Commercial products may disallow modification through views entirely (or only provide mechanism to allow modification through only one view).

The above discussion is concerned with a more general topic, namely, the consideration of integrity constraints. In fact, integrity constraints are an important concern for stored relations as well. In general, *integrity constraints* (ICs) provide a means of ensuring that changes made to the database by authorized users do not result in a loss of data consistency. There are several forms of ICs. One important form of IC is called referential integrity, and will be discussed in the next section. Other forms include domain constraints, assertions, triggers, functional and other forms of dependencies.

- *Functional dependencies* are a very important form of IC and are a very important factor which affects relational database design. Among other things, functional dependencies can be used to determine the primary key of a relation. A *key* (or *superkey*) in a relation is a set of attributes which uniquely determine the values of all attributes. As a simple intuitive example, in a student relation with schema (name, ID, major, GPA), the name or ID of a student should determine all the attributes (assuming names and IDs are all unique). Therefore, student name is a key, and ID is another key. Note also that a key combined with any other attributes is still a key. For example, name combined with major is a key. Therefore, it makes sense to define the concept of *candidate key*, which refers to a set of attributes which uniquely determine the value of other attributes, and if any attribute is removed from the candidate key, it will no longer be a key. Apparently, candidate key may not be unique; for example, student name and ID are two candidate keys. Therefore, there is a need to define the concept of *primary key*, which is the designated candidate key actually used by the database designer. In our example either student name or ID can be designated as the primary key. Concepts related to keys and functional dependencies play important roles in relational database design, and will be discussed in the next section.

- *Referential integrity* refers to a particular kind of integrity constraint to ensure data consistency. It is concerned with the situations in which change in a relation may affect other relations; it usually involves foreign keys. For example, consider a relation for course registration in a university database. If a previously planned course is to be dropped, all the tuples in the registration relation referring that course should be dropped as well. It is therefore important to preserve the referential-integrity constraint. We will revisit this issue in Section 4.6.6.
- An *assertion* is a predicate expressing a condition that we wish the database to always satisfy; it may involve several relations.
- *Triggers* (active rules): A trigger is a statement that is executed automatically by the system as a side effect of a modification to the database. An active rule consists of condition and action. An active database is equipped with active rules, and can be considered as a special form of knowledge-based system.

In general, an integrity constraint is a clause of the form

$$\text{false} :\text{-} \ a_1, \ldots \ a_k,$$

where commas denote "and," the a_i's are atoms and false is a special atom that is false in all interpretations.

At first sight, one may think ICs may have very limited usefulness; they turn out to be a very powerful tool. In databases, there are often constraints that the designer of a database knows should never be violated. If a database ever violates an IC, an error message should be displayed, and the offending clauses should be identified. In a relational database, integrity constraints are assertions database instances that are compelled to obey. Therefore, ICs play an important role in agent-based database problem solving. To illustrate, we consider the following two types of integrity constraints.

(a) An IC specifies that some conjunction of conditions should never be true of a database; for example, that no instructor should have taught a graduate-only course and a freshman course in the same semester at the same time slot 4:00pm - 5:15pm, Monday and Wednesday.

(b) An IC specifies that some condition should always be provable when another is; for example, a payment should be made to an employee at the end of each month.

4.6 FUNCTIONAL DEPENDENCIES

Integrity constraints play an important role in relational database design. Although this book is not intended for a theoretical study of this topic, we will study several important forms of integrity constraints, including functional dependencies.

4.6.1 DEFINITION OF FUNCTIONAL DEPENDENCY

Let $\alpha \subseteq R$ and $\beta \subseteq R$ be two sets of attributes. The functional dependency (FD) $\alpha \rightarrow \beta$ holds on R if, in any legal relation $r(R)$, for all pairs of tuples t_1 and t_2 in r such that if $t_1[\alpha] = t_2[\alpha]$ then $t_1[\beta] = t_1[\beta]$. Intuitively, this is to say that if two tuples agree on α, they should also agree on β. For example, in the backing relation, we have "a-no $\rightarrow$ balance" and "a-no $\rightarrow$ bname." Of course we can also write "a-no $\rightarrow$ a-no," but such kind of functional dependencies are only of theoretical importance. In general, we say a functional dependency $\alpha \rightarrow \beta$ is trivial if $\beta \subseteq \alpha$. Note that functional dependencies can be considered as a special case of implication as discussed in first order predicate logic. Note also $\{A, B\} \rightarrow C \equiv AB \rightarrow C$, and for convenience we will always write $AB \rightarrow C$ instead of $\{A, B\} \rightarrow C$.

It is important to know how to identify functional dependencies. In general, functional dependencies (and other forms of dependencies, as to be discussed later) are determined by the semantic relationship among the attributes. The database designer should collect the information among the attributes during the analysis stage. For example, we know that the student ID should uniquely determine the student GPA and major from reality, before we have retrieve the actual student data. In general, it is not a good idea to write functional dependencies by scanning a small set of data. However, in some cases, the dependency information is not available and we may have to identify functional dependencies through observation from given data. In this case, functional dependencies may be obtained using machine learning techniques (a discussion on machine learning is given in Chapters 10 and 11).

4.6.2 KEYS AND FUNCTIONAL DEPENDENCIES

The notion of functional dependency shares some common concerns with primary keys or candidate keys. For example, consider the account relation in a banking database consisting of attributes a-no (which stands for account number), balance and bname (which stands for branch name). Note that a-no functionally determines balance and bname, and a-no is the key of the account relation. However, in general, if $\alpha \rightarrow \beta$, α does not have to be the (candidate) key. For example, if we consider relation $R = (ABC)$ with the set of functional dependencies F: $\{A \rightarrow B, B \rightarrow C\}$, then apparently B is not the key. Therefore, functional dependencies have extended the notion of (candidate) key. Examples will be provided in Section 4.6.5 when key-finding algorithms are discussed.

The relationship between keys and functional dependencies can be examined from two directions:

(a) From superkeys to functional dependencies. We should understand the following two issues:

- Functional dependencies are a generalization of superkeys;
- Functional dependencies allow us to express constraints that cannot be expressed by superkeys.

(b) From functional dependencies to candidate keys. We can find candidate keys from functional dependencies as illustrated from the following example [Elmasri and Navathe 1994]. Suppose we have R=(*ABCD*): with *F*: {*A* → *BCD*, *BC* → *AD*, *D*→*B*}; we can find the candidate keys are *A*, or *BC* or *DC* At this time, we are only able to *verify* this by applying the definition of the candidate key. In addition, after we discuss inference rules in Section 4.6.3, several key-finding methods will be introduced. At that time, we will be able to *find* these keys as well.

4.6.3 INFERENCE RULES: ARMSTRONG AXIOMS

The inference rules, usually referred to as *Armstrong axioms*, are important inference laws used to manipulate functional dependencies. They work on the top of functional dependencies. Note that functional dependencies may cross relation borders within a database. To determine candidate keys for a specific relation, all the functional dependencies concerning the attributes in the schema of this relation should be considered.

Armstrong axioms--basic (α and β are two sets of attributes):

$\quad$ *Reflective rule:* $\alpha\beta \Rightarrow \alpha$

$\quad$ *Augmentation rule:* $\{\alpha\to\beta\} \Rightarrow \{\alpha\gamma\to\beta\gamma\}$

$\quad$ *Transitivity rule:* $\{\alpha\to\gamma, \gamma \to\delta\} \Rightarrow \{\alpha\to\delta\}$

The following are additional rules. They can be proved using the basic rules, but it would be more convenient if we use them as rules.

$\quad$ *Union rule:* $\{\alpha\to\beta, \alpha\to\gamma\} \Rightarrow \alpha\to\beta\gamma$

$\quad$ *Decomposition:* $\{\alpha\to\beta\gamma\} \Rightarrow \alpha\to\beta$ and $\alpha\to\gamma$.

$\quad$ *Pseudotransitivity:* $\{\alpha\to\beta, \gamma\beta\to\delta\} \Rightarrow \alpha\gamma\to\delta$

Armstrong axioms are sound and complete rules, in the sense introduced in Chapter 2.

As a simple example of applying Armstrong axioms, let us reconsider R=(*ABCD*) with *F*: {*A* → *BCD*, *BC* → *AD*, *D*→*B*}. We can derive *DC*→*A*. This is because from *D*→*B* (given) we have *DC*→*BC* (using augmentation rule), by applying transitivity rule on *DC*→*BC* and *BC* → *AD* (given), we derive *DC*→*AD*. Then by decomposition rule, we get *DC*→*A*.

4.6.4 CLOSURES AND CANONICAL COVER

In order to develop useful algorithms related to relational database design, we need the following concepts based on the set of functional dependencies F.

- *Closure of α (attributes) under F*, denoted as α^+ is a set of attributes that can be determined by (or reached from) α (a set of attributes) by repeatedly applying Armstrong axioms on FDs. This definition also indicates the basic algorithm for calculating α^+.
- *Closure of F* (denoted as F^+): The set of all functional dependencies logically implied by F. This definition also implies the basic algorithm of calculating F^+.

As a simple example, consider $R=(ABC)$ with $F: \{A \rightarrow B, B \rightarrow C\}$; we can identify the elements in F^+ and in A^+:

$$F^+: \{A \rightarrow B, B \rightarrow C, A \rightarrow C, A \rightarrow AB, AB \rightarrow C, ...\}$$
$$A^+ = ABC$$

Canonical cover F_c of F provides a sort of "standard" of F: A canonical cover F_c is a rewriting of F which meets three conditions:

- F_c is *equivalent* to F in that $F_c^+ = F^+$; this is to say that Fc and F can derive exactly the same sets of attributes.

- No FD in F_c contains an *extraneous* attribute; for example, if we know $A \rightarrow C$, then B in $AB \rightarrow C$ is extraneous.

- Each left side of a function dependency is unique; for example, if we have $F = \{A \rightarrow B, A \rightarrow C, B \rightarrow D\}$, then we should use the union rule to combine these functional dependencies to form $F = \{A \rightarrow BC, B \rightarrow D\}$, to guarantee the uniqueness of A.

4.6.5 ALGORITHMS FOR FINDING KEYS FROM FUNCTIONAL DEPENDENCIES

The following are two important aspects related to finding (candidate) keys:

    (a) determine whether a given set of attributes is a key or not.

    (b) find candidate keys from a given set of FDs.

All given functional dependencies as well as trivial functional dependencies should be considered.

Usually relational database textbooks do not provide key-finding algorithms. For convenience, in the following we provide an informal description of several algorithms. Note that in some cases one algorithm may be more appropriate than the others.

Let us use the following example to illustrate these methods: $S = (ABCDEF)$ with $F: \{AD \rightarrow B, AB \rightarrow E, C \rightarrow D, B \rightarrow C, AC \rightarrow F\}$.

- *Method 1. Attributes elimination to find a key*: Starting from all attributes, remove any attributes that can be derived from any other attributes (or their combinations). In our example, one possible elimination order is: B, E, D, F. So we find a key AC. Using different elimination order B, E, C, F, we may find another key AB. Note that we cannot remove C and D at the same time. (Why?)

- *Method 2. Attribute inclusion to find a key*: Starting from one attribute, see whether it can determine all other attributes. If not, include one more attribute. Continue until all attributes can be determined. In our example, we have $A+ = A$; if we try to add D, we have $AD+ = ABCDE$ (please verify by yourself). So AD is a key.

- *Method 3. Selected inclusion of attributes*: This can be considered as an improvement of method 2, but should start from F_c. Start from all attributes which appear only in the left-hand side of any FD. If they cannot determine all other attributes, consider the inclusion of any other attributes which appear in *both* left and right-hand side of all FDs. Continue until all attributes can be determined. In our example, we have:

L (Left only): *A*

B (Both Left and Right): *BCD*

R (Right only): *EF* (not in any key)

Considering all the combinations, we have obtained the following keys: *AB, AC, AD*.

4.6.6 REFERENTIAL INTEGRITY

The concept of primary key allows us to re-examine referential integrity in more detail. As an example, consider the following relation schemas in a banking database (primary keys are underlined):

account(<u>a-no</u>, balance, branch-name)

branch(<u>branch-name</u>, branch-city, assets)

(a) Insert a tuple into a referencing relation: A *referencing relation* is characterized by having foreign key(s). When we insert a tuple into such a relation, we should check referenced relation. In the banking example, the account relation is a referencing relation because it references the branch-name. In order to insert a new tuple into the account relation, we should first make sure that the branch name referenced in that tuple exists in the branch relation.

(b) Delete a tuple from a referenced relation: A *referenced relation* has its primary key used as foreign key by some other relation. To delete a tuple from such a relation, we should check whether this tuple is used by a referencing relation r ; if yes, we reject the delete command, or the tuples in r which reference this tuple themselves must be deleted. In the banking example, the branch relation is a referenced relation. If we want to delete a tuple in a branch relation, we should make sure no more accounts reference this branch. Note that deletion may lead to cascading deletions.

(c) Update: The content of a tuple is changed. There are two cases.

- Case 1: updating referencing relation (a relation has a foreign key): It is handled in a way similar to insert.
- Case 2: updating referenced relation (the primary key of the relation is referenced by another relation): It is handled in a way similar to delete.

4.7 BASICS OF RELATIONAL DATABASE DESIGN

4.7.1 WHAT IS THE MEANING OF A GOOD DESIGN AND WHY STUDY IT?

It is important to keep in mind that functional dependencies are defined in the entire relational database. A relational database may consists of one or more relations. One may wonder why we use just one relation for a database. If the schema of a relation consists of all the attributes of a relational database, it is referred to as the *universal relation schema*. In reality, however, instead of having one large relation in a database, usually we have a database with multiple relations. So how to determine the number of relations needed, and how to determine which attributes should go to each relation? This is a question of *relational database design*, and functional dependencies play an important role in this design process.

In order to understand what is a good design, it is important to understand what are undesirable features and anomalies of a bad design. To illustrate this, consider a student database schema consists of SID, courseID, section, instructorID, as well as other attributes. As for functional dependencies, we know course ID and section together can determine the instructorID. Suppose the database consists of a relation with schema (SID, courseID, section, instructorID). Is this a good design? Or, are there any undesirable features in this relation? Since each relation can be viewed as an abstract data type consisting of operations such as adding a tuple, deleting a tuple, and changing values within a tuple, in the following we briefly examine each of these operations.

- *Insert*: Each time a student registers for a course with a particular section, the InstructorID will be repeated. This kind of redundancy does not only waste memory, but may also cause inconsistency.

- *Delete*: If one section so far has only one student registered for the course, and that student has decided to change to some other courses, then this only tuple should be withdrawn. Note that when this tuple is deleted, the information about the course instructor is also deleted. If this is the only place to store the information about the instructor, then the instructor information for this section will no longer be available. (On the other hand, if the instructor information is also stored somewhere else, then the redundant information may cause problems similar to what happened in the insert operation as discussed above).

- *Update*: Suppose a student wants to change to another section; then what should be changed is not the section number alone, but the instructorID as well. Otherwise, inconsistency may occur.

The problems cited above are usually referred to as anomalies. How to deal with these anomalies? One solution is through decomposition: If a relation has some undesirable features, then we decompose it into smaller relations to remove these undesirable features. Consequently, two questions should be answered: A convenient way of checking undesirable features, as well as a set of algorithms to perform needed decomposition. Actually, these two questions are closely related. Both questions can be answered by considering two criteria: One is concerned with the "goodness" of individual relation, which is usually referred to as *normal forms*, and the process of obtaining relations with certain normal forms is usually referred to as *normalization*. However, a set of normalized relations may not necessarily guarantee that when they work well *as a whole*. In other words, a different criterion should be developed to reflect the *global* quality of a relational database design.

Based on the above discussion, the remaining part of this section will be organized based on the two criteria just mentioned:

- Desirable features for individual relation: Normal forms. In particular, we discuss the following normal forms:
  - ♦ Boyce-Codd Normal Form (BCNF); and
  - ♦ Third Normal Form (3NF).
- Desirable features for decomposition -- "Global" design criteria. We will discuss two of them:
  - ♦ Lossless-join decomposition; and
  - ♦ Dependency preservation.

Combining these two sets of criteria, we will introduce two decomposition algorithms:

- Lossless-join decomposition into BCNF; and
- Dependency-preserving, lossless-join decomposition into 3NF.

4.7.2 BOYCE-CODD NORMAL FORM (BCNF) AND THIRD NORMAL FORM (3NF)

We introduce the following terminology. A relation schema R is in *Boyce-Codd normal form (BCNF)* with respect to a set F of functional dependencies if for *all* functional dependencies in F^+ of the form $\alpha \rightarrow \beta$, where $\alpha \subseteq R$ and $\beta \subseteq R$, at least one of the following (a) or (b) holds. (Note: The definition actually says: The LHS of any nontrivial functional dependencies must be a super key.)

A relation schema R is in *Third normal form (3NF)* with respect to a set F of functional dependencies if for *all* functional dependencies in F^+ of the form $\alpha \rightarrow \beta$, where $\alpha \subseteq R$ and $\beta \subseteq R$, at least one of the following (a), (b) or (c) holds. Note that because of (c), the definition allows transitivity dependency in one relation.

(a) $\alpha \rightarrow \beta$ is a trivial functional dependency (i.e., $\beta \subseteq \alpha$)

(b) α is a superkey for schema R.

(c) β is a *prime* attribute of R -- namely, β is a member of any candidate key in R.

The above definitions can be extended from individual relations to the whole relational database. A *database design is in BCNF* (or *3NF*) if each member of the set of relation schema that constitutes the design is in BCNF (or 3NF).

As an example of BCNF and 3NF, consider $R=(ABCD)$ with F consisting of

(1) $A \rightarrow BCD$,

(2) $BC \rightarrow AD$,

(3) $D \rightarrow B$.

This relation is in 3NF, because we can check each functional dependency:

(1): A is a superkey, so it satisfies (b).

(2): BC is a superkey, so it satisfies (b).

(3): B is a member of candidate key BC, so it satisfies (c).

You may also verify that all functional dependencies satisfy (c) -- just to verify RHS of each functional dependency is a member of a candidate key:

In (1): B and C are members of candidate key BC, D is a member of candidate key CD.

In (2): A is a candidate key by itself, D is a member of candidate key CD.

In (3): B is a member of candidate key BC.

Note that to verify (a) or (b) or (c) is hold, you do not have to compute all candidate keys or superkeys in advance; just do some verification as needed.

However, this relation is not in BCNF , because in (3), D is not a superkey of R (note that (1) and (2) do not violate BCNF requirement).

4.7.3 REMARKS ON NORMAL FORMS AND DENORMALIZATION

Note that the difference between BCNF and 3NF lies in condition (c) as discussed in the previous section. Because of this difference, BCNF has more restrictions than 3NF, and is thus considered as a normal form higher than 3NF. Note that the condition (c) allows the transitive dependencies (as shown in $BC \rightarrow AD, D \rightarrow B$ in the above example). The consequence of transitive dependencies is that it may demonstrate some anomaly due to repetition. However, an advantage of 3NF is that it is always possible to obtain a 3NF design without sacrificing a lossless join or dependency preservation (as to be discussed in the next section).

Various normal forms have been developed, both for theoretical studies and different practical needs of relational database design. At the lowest end of the normal form hierarchy is *first normal form* (1NF), which requires that all attributes have atomic domains. A domain is atomic if elements of the domain are considered to be indivisible units. Intuitively, 1NF just requires a relation be a flat table. For example, a relation with schema (S_name, Course-taking) containing a tuple "(john, {CS1, CS2})" is not flat, because the value in "course-taking" is a set, rather than an indivisible unit. But this tuple can be rewritten as two tuples (john, CS1) and (john, CS2), which satisfy the requirement of 1NF. Although 1NF has been used as a very basic assumption in the practice of relational databases, the concept of non-first normal form (NFNF or NF^2) has also drawn much attention since the mid-1980s, partly due to its relationship with object-oriented databases. We will examine this issue in Section 4.8.

A higher normal form is called *second normal form (2NF)*. In order to define what 2NF is, we need the definition of partial dependency. A functional dependency $\alpha \rightarrow \beta$ is called a partial dependency if there is a proper subset γ of α such that $\gamma \rightarrow \beta$. We say β is partially dependent on α. A relation schema R is in 2NF if each attribute A in R meets one of the following criteria:

(a) It appears in a candidate key; or

(b) It is not partially dependent on a candidate key.

It can be shown that every 3NF is in 2NF. Unlike the cases of BCNF and 3NF (which are practically used) and 1NF (which is a very basic requirement), for a long time, 2NF was considered of historical interest, because historically, 3NF was developed from 2NF, and BCNF is a further enhancement of 3NF. However, as we have seen in the last few sections, the modern definition of 3NF does not bother 2NF at all. Nevertheless, recently 2NF has received renewed attention, particularly due to the consideration of *denormlization* process involved in data warehouses. In fact, we may deliberately introduce some redundancy if we denormalize 3NF into 2NF. A more detailed discussion can be found in Chapter 11.

4.7.4 DESIRABLE FEATURES FOR DECOMPOSITION -- "GLOBAL" DESIGN CRITERIA

Normalization as discussed so far is concerned with the quality of each individual relation. It is important to keep in mind that an overall quality of the decomposed relations is equally important, because the "whole" is not a simple additive combination of the individual "parts," and a good relational database design is not just a collection of good relations. In fact, even when each relation may have good quality, anomalies may still occur at the global level. In this section we discuss several important "global" design criteria.

4.7.4.1 Lossless-join decomposition

In order to understand the important concern behind the need for lossless join, let us consider the relation R shown in Table 4.7(a).

Table 4.7(a) A relation

A	B	C
a1	b1	c1
a2	b1	c2
a3	b2	c3

Consider the decomposition as shown in Table 4.7 (b) and (c).

Table 4.7(b) R1

A	B
a1	b1
a2	b1
a3	b2

Table 4.7(c) R2

B	C
b1	c1
b1	c2
b2	c3

Now consider $R' = R1 \bowtie R2$. The result is shown in Table 4.5(d).

Table 4.7(d) Result of join (Note: * indicates an additional tuple not in R)

A	B	C	Remark
a1	b1	c1	
a1	b1	c2	*
a2	b1	c1	*
a2	b1	c2	
a3	b2	c3	

Here is a remark on the meaning of *lossless*: Note that the more constraints (requirements) in the query, the fewer tuples in the relation. Therefore, "additional tuples" in the resulting join means "less constraints" which implies "some information has lost" or "lossy." Consequently, "lossless-join" decomposition means when the decomposed smaller relations joined back, there are no additional tuples.

Note that if r_i ($i = 1, 2, ...n$) is a relation decomposed from R, then we *always* have $R \subseteq r_1 \bowtie r_2 \bowtie .. \bowtie r_n$.

The following requirements for lossless join can be used to check whether the lossless join condition is hold: Lossless join requires *at least one* of the following is true:

$$R_1 \cap R_2 \rightarrow R_1$$
$$R_1 \cap R_2 \rightarrow R_2$$

Here the intersection $\cap$ means intersection of attributes; the above actually says the intersection should be at least a superkey of R1 or R2. Back to the previous example: $R_1 \cap R_2 = AB \cap BC = B$, but none of the following is true: $B \rightarrow A$ or $B \rightarrow C$.

Note that this requirement can be used to test lossless join when a relation is decomposed into *two* relations only. In case we have more than two relations, we have to repeat this algorithm several times. Alternatively, we may use an algorithm for testing the lossless join property as introduced in [Elmasri and Nevathe 1994].

4.7.4.2 Dependency preservation

Recall that functional dependencies may cross relation borders (that is, functional dependencies belong to the whole database). Consider the example $R=(ABC)$ with F: $\{A \rightarrow B, B \rightarrow C\}$. Suppose we decompose R into:

   $R1(AC)$ with $F1$: $\{A \rightarrow C\}$

and

   $R2(AC)$ with $F2$: $\{B \rightarrow C\}$

From F1 and F2 we get $F' = \{A \rightarrow C, B \rightarrow C\}$ and there is no way to derive $A \rightarrow B$. So this example does not preserve dependency.

Both lossless-join and dependency preservation are important in decomposition. However, sometimes we cannot satisfy both. In this case, we usually sacrifice dependency preservation (because lossless-join is more important).

4.7.5 DECOMPOSITION ALGORITHMS

Combining the individual and global design criteria, we introduce the following important decomposition algorithms for relational database design.

Algorithm 1: Lossless-join decomposition into BCNF
The key idea of this algorithm can be stated in the following informal way:

While some functional dependency in relation R violates BCNF requirement
- form a new relation R_i consisting of the LHS and RHS attributes of this functional dependency.
- remove RHS of this functional dependency from R.

The collection of R_is and the final relation containing the remaining attributes Of R form a lossless join decomposition of the original relation R.

Note that the algorithm presented in many DBMS textbooks requires us to compute F+. In fact, what is important is to determine what functional dependency is *not* in F+. Note also if we say a functional dependency is *not* in F+, it actually means it violates BCNF. Note also that *this algorithm is not necessarily dependency preserving*. This algorithm can be carried out using a binary "decomposition tree" format, as illustrated in the example shown in Figure 4.1. In this example, we have relation schema $R = (ABCDEG)$ with $F = \{A \rightarrow BC, E \rightarrow AG\}$. We can find the only candidate key is DE (please verify). Each non-leaf node in this binary tree indicates a decomposition (due to the violation of BCNF). The left branch of the binary tree indicates a new relation constructed according to the requirement of BCNF while the right branch indicates the remaining attributes in the original relation. The result of this process consists of three relations $R1$, $R3$ and $R4$.

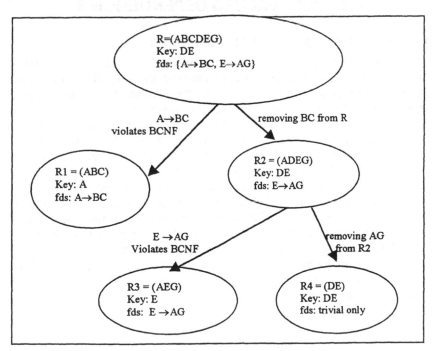

Figure 4.1 A decomposition tree

Algorithm 2: Dependency-preserving, lossless-join decomposition into 3NF
Note that this algorithm starts from functional dependencies in canonical cover to guarantee dependency preservation. An informal presentation of the key idea is given below (not all details):

Algorithm

For each functional dependency in canonical cover
    form a new relation;
If none of these formed relations contain any candidate key of the original
    relation, form a relation consisting of attributes in a candidate key;
The collection of the relations form a dependency-preserving, lossless-join
    decomposition.

As a simple example, consider $R=(ABCD)$ with F: $\{A \rightarrow B, B \rightarrow C\}$. This relation is not in 3NF (Why?). To apply the above algorithm, notice apparently $F_c = F$. We construct two relations R1=(AB) and R2=(BC). However, none of them contains a candidate key. So we form another relation R3=(AD), which contains a candidate key AD. R1, R2 and R3 together is the set of decomposed relations.

4.8 MULTIVALUED DEPENDENCIES

4.8.1 VARIOUS FORMS OF DEPENDENCIES

Functional dependencies are an important form of integrity constraints. However, other forms of dependencies also exist and may play an important role in good relational database design. In this section, we discuss a type of dependency called multivalued dependency. Other dependencies also exist. For example, multivalued dependencies can be further generalized into *join dependency*, which is said to hold over a relation R if R is decomposed into a set of relations *R1, R2, ..., Rn*, which forms a lossless-join decomposition of R. Another example is *inclusion dependency*, which is a statement of the form that some columns of a relation are contained in other columns (usually of another relation). A foreign key constraint is an example of an inclusion dependency, because the referring columns in one relation must be contained in the primary key columns of the referenced relation. Since join dependencies and inclusion dependencies are not very influential in database design, we will not discuss them any more. Interested readers are referred to [Ramakrishnam 1998] for a little more detailed discussion. In the following we will briefly discuss multivalued dependencies.

4.8.2 MULTIVALUED DEPENDENCIES

4.8.2.1 Comparison between FD and MVD

Multivalued dependencies (MVDs) can be considered as a generalization of functional dependencies (FDs). We can introduce MVD by comparing it with FD:

- For functional dependency $\alpha \rightarrow \beta$: α's value uniquely determines β's value; other attributes are not affected in any way.
- For multivalued dependency $\alpha \rightarrow\rightarrow \beta$: α's value does not uniquely determine β's value, but α and β form a constraint for other attributes in the relation (let us call these attributes "the third part"). This constraint can be stated as "the relationship between α and β is independent of the relationship between α and $R - \alpha - \beta$."

FDs are usually referred to as *equality-generating dependencies* while *MVDs* are referred to as *tuple-generating dependencies*, because it requires generation of new tuples if the required property does not hold. The requirement is shown in the formula of the formal definition. In this definition, four tuples are needed; all have same value on α but different on $t_i[\beta]$.

Formal definition of Multivalued dependency (Md) $\alpha \rightarrow\rightarrow \beta$ if and only if we have four tuples which satisfy

$$t_1[\alpha] = t_2[\alpha] = t_3[\alpha] = t_4[\alpha],$$
$$t_3[\beta] = t_1[\beta]$$
$$t_3[R - \alpha - \beta] = t_2[R - \alpha - \beta]$$
$$t_4[\beta] = t_2[\beta]$$
$$t_4[R - \alpha - \beta] = t_1[R - \alpha - \beta].$$

Note that attributes in the relation schema fall in three parts: α, β, and $\gamma = R - \alpha - \beta$ (all of other attributes). Intuitively, these conditions indicate that for the same left-hand side α of an MVD, if we have two different values at the right-hand side β in two tuples, then we should be able to find two other tuples, with their γ values swapped. Note that FDs can be considered as a special case of MVDs; because the right-hand side value is unique, the four required tuples are reduced to one.

We also need the concept of *trivial MVD:* for $\alpha \rightarrow\rightarrow \beta$, either we have $\beta \subseteq \alpha$ or $\alpha \cup \beta$. In other words, the third part is empty; this can be compared with the concept of trivial FD.

4.8.2.2 Important properties

An interesting and important property for MVD is that in the three parts, the second part β and the third part γ are "symmetrical" (this is actually *complementation rule* as to be discussed soon):

If $\alpha \rightarrow\rightarrow \beta$, and if $R \neq \alpha \cup \beta$, then $\alpha \rightarrow\rightarrow \gamma$.

Note that now a set of dependencies may include both FDs and MVDs, and will be denoted by D (instead of F). Similarly, we have D+ (instead of F+). We also have the remarks on primary keys and candidate keys: they are still determined by functional dependencies only. For superkey, the definition stays the same. In other words, MVDs do not contribute to the concept of keys.

As an example, consider the Easter gifts given to children by their mothers, as shown in the relation Gift = (MCRGP) in Table 4.8 (a).

Table 4.8(a)   An example for multivalued dependency

M(Mother)	C(Child)	R(Relationship)	G(Gift)	P(Price)
Jo Ann	David	son	PC	1000
Mary	Kim	daughter	car	10000
Mary	Tom	son	teddy-bear	20

You may think that Mary is unfair with her children, because price values of gifts differ so much. (Jo Ann has only one child, David, so there is no problem.) To be a good mother, Mary should give her son a car and her daughter a teddy bear as well (that is, the previous table should add two rows). This is shown in Table 4.8(b). This example shows why MVDs are called tuple-generating.

Table 4.8(b)   An example for multivalued dependency (cont.)

M(Mother)	C(Child)	R(Relationship)	G(Gift)	P(Price)
Jo Ann	David	son	PC	1000
Mary	Kim	daughter	Car	10000
Mary	Kim	daughter	teddy-bear	20
Mary	Tom	son	teddy-bear	20
Mary	Tom	son	car	10000

The second table satisfies MVD: $M \rightarrow\rightarrow CR$. Note we also have $M \rightarrow\rightarrow GP$.

As a final remark, we point out that Armstrong's axioms can be extended to MVDs, but they are much more complicated, and the detail is not discussed here.

4.8.3 FOURTH NORMAL FORM (4NF)

We should notice that normal form higher than BCNF is needed, because anomalies may still exist even in BCNF (note the relation schema does not have any nontrivial FDs). Fourth normal form (4NF) is such a normal form, which can be defined in terms of FDs and MVDs.

4.8.3.1 Definition of 4NF

A relation schema R is in 4NF with respect to a set D of FDs and MVDs if, for all MVDs in D+ of the form $\alpha \rightarrow\rightarrow \beta$ where $\alpha \subseteq R$ and $\beta \subseteq R$, at least one of the following holds:

(a) $\alpha \rightarrow\rightarrow \beta$ is a trivial MVD;

(b) α is a superkey for schema R.

Note that *if a relation schema is in 4NF then it is also in BCNF*. This is because if a schema R is not in BCNF, then it cannot be in 4NF. Finally, just like the case of BCNF, a database design is in 4NF if all relation schemas are in 4NF.

4.8.3.2 Decomposition into 4NF

The algorithm for lossless-join decomposition to 4NF is similar to BCNF decomposition. In this process we check some $\alpha \rightarrow\rightarrow \beta$ violating 4NF instead of checking some $\alpha \rightarrow \beta$ violating BCNF.

As an example, the Relation(MCRGP) in the above example is not in 4NF (Why?). We can decompose it to two relations MCR (containing information about mother and children) and MGP (containing information about mother and gifts available). (What are the tuples in these two tables?) Each small relation has trivial MVDs only, so is in 4NF. (What is the primary key for MGP?)

4.9 REMARK ON OBJECT-ORIENTED LOGICAL DATA MODELING

Recently object-oriented data modeling approaches have received much attention. The object-oriented data modeling techniques can be considered as out-grown from Non-First Normal Form (sometimes denoted as NF^2). Let us re-consider the example presented in the last section. Instead of decomposing the relation into smaller relations in 4NF, we follow the opposite direction by grouping atomic values into sets. This consideration results in Table 4.9.

The NF^2 representation serves as a model which is semantically clearer than the one in 1NF, because the related information is grouped together. For example, Table 4.10 clearly indicates Mary has two kids, one is Kim, another is Tom, and each kid has a gift Car priced 10000 and a teddy bear priced 20. In other words, each kid can be viewed as a *nested relation* contained in the mother. In fact, we can view "mother" as a *structured* (or *complex*) data type suitable for object-oriented data modeling. Extensions to SQL have been developed to allow complex types, including nested relations, as well as object-oriented features. Some aspects of object-oriented data modeling will be briefly addressed in Chapter 6.

Table 4.9 Example to illustrate NF^2

M(Mother)	C(Child)	R(Relationship)	G(Gift)	P(Price)
Jo Ann	David	son	PC	1000
Mary	Kim	daughter	car	10000
			teddy-bear	20
	Tom	son	teddy-bear	20
			car	10000

4.10 BASICS OF DEDUCTIVE DATABASES

4.10.1 LIMITATION OF RA AND SQL

In the last section we mentioned the need for extending SQL. In fact, there are other limitations which make various extensions desirable. One particularly important feature is lack of recursion in both relational algebra and SQL. In fact, lack of recursion is an important reason why embedded SQL is needed.

Consider retrieval of all ancestors for John in the following ancestor relation (Table 4.10). You cannot do it in RA or SQL. Using formal languages extended from RA or using embedded SQL, you can consider use of a loop (or recursion) to handle this.

Table 4.10 Parent relation

Child	Parent
Tom	Mary
Mary	Tim
Dave	Tim
Tim	Bob

In the rest of this section, we briefly examine the issue of deductive databases. Particularly, we use Datalog to illustrate how relational algebra can be extended.

4.10.2 BASICS OF DATALOG

4.10.2.1 EDB and IDB

A database is a model of some set of integrity constraints, and a query is some formula to be evaluated with respect to this model [Reiter 1984]. From the viewpoint of logic, a DBMS can be seen as a query answering system that views facts (tuples) as axioms of a theorem and queries as the conclusion of a theorem. The inference mechanism provided with logic can be used to deduce the query on the basis of the set of facts and rules. In addition, logic can be used as a uniform language for expressing facts, rules, programs, queries, views, and integrity constraints.

Datalog is the simplest model of *deductive databases*, which are databases with inference power. Datalog is a version (or variation, not really subset) of Prolog (as discussed in Chapter 3) suitable for database systems. A Datalog program consists of two parts: an extensional database and an intensional database, as discussed below.

- *Extensional database* (or *EDB*): This part contains the actual instances in a conventional relational database. It consists of predicates whose relations (instances) are stored in the database; it consists of facts (tuples).

As we have already learned in Chapter 4, the following predicates usually are expressed in a table, but can also be expressed using predicates:

```
parent (john, tom).
```

```
parent (tom, mary).
parent (mary, bob).
parent (ron, john).
parent (ann, john).
```

- *Intensional database* (or *IDB*): This part contains rules involving predicates (namely, relations). They are defined by logical rules; they are actually views.

The following is an example of IDB:

```
ancestor (X, Y) :- parent (X, Y).
ancestor (X, Y) :- parent (X, Z), ancestor (Z, Y).
```

Note that the same predicate may be associated with both EDB and IDB. For example, we can define "grandfather" as:

```
Grandfather(tom,john).  %This is part of EDB
Grandfather(X,Y) :- father(X,Z), father(Z,Y).
                        %This is part of IDB
```

4.10.2.2 Recursion

Note that the definition of intensional database can use *recursion;* for example, predicate "ancestor" in both head and body of the same rule. This is a very important property of using intensional databases.

Before we go on, let us briefly summarize what we have achieved so far. The use of IDB makes recursion be introduced in a database program. Also please note that in our discussion we did not mention negation (namely, we did not consider to negate a predicate) – in fact, at this point we have not included negation in our simple Datalog model. The relationship among RA, RC and the simplest Datalog model can be described as following:

A query can be converted from RA to nonrecursive Datalog;
- A query can be converted from safe, nonrecursive Datalog possibly with negated subgoals to RA;
- A query can be converted from safe DRC to safe nonrecursive Datalog;
- A query can be converted from RA to safe nonrecursive Datalog to safe DRC.

Therefore, we have established the equivalence of the following: RA; safe, nonrecursive datalog programs with negation; safe DRC; safe TRC. In summary, we have the following two formulae:

(Safe) Datalog = RA + recursion - negation

RA = (Safe) Datalog - recursion + negation

These two formulae indicate what is lacking from the basic version of Datalog is negation. In the following, we take a look at this issue.

4.10.2.3 Recursive queries with negation in rule body: Using stratification

Negation can be added into Datalog by introducing new concepts related to *stratification*. A stratified program is a program whose tables can be classified into strata. A stratified program is evaluated stratum by stratum, starting with stratum 0.

In order to explain the basic idea of handling recursive queries with negation in rule body, we informally introduce some terminology. We use the term *strata* to denote layers in a Datalog program. The intuition is to process the Datalog program in a stratum-by-stratum fashion. Furthermore, we can define *stratified rules*: rules are stratified if whenever there is a rule with head predicate *p* and a negated subgoal with predicate *q*, there is no path from p to *q* (namely, *p* does not depend on *q*, directly or indirectly).

A simple example of stratified program is taken from [Ullman 1989]. This program is recursive, because of (2) (although it actually does nothing).

  (1) p(X) :- r(X).
  (2) p(X) :- p(X).
  (3) q(X) :- s(X), not p(X).

In this program, p depends on r, which does not involve negation. Q depends on s and p, but the calculation of p is already done. (q is at a higher stratum than p.) We can use *dependency graph* to depict how the predicates are depending on each other, as shown in Figure 4.2. Note that in a dependency graph, nodes are predicates. Arcs in the dependence graph indicate how predicates depend on each other: There is an arc from predicate *p* to predicate *q* if there is a rule with a subgoal whose predicate is *p* and with a head whose predicate is *q*. Using dependency graph, we can easily check a recursive program: A program is recursive if its dependency graph has one or more cycles. There are three nodes in Figure 4.2, *p*, *q*, and *r*. There is an edge from *r* to *p*, due to rule (1). There is also an edge from *p* to *q*, due to rule (3). Due to rule (2), there is a cycle local to node *p*, which indicates the Datalog program is recursive. The good news is that, however, although *q* depends on *p* (in rule 3, where *p* is negated), *p* does not depend on *q*. If the calculation of *p* involves *q*, we will be in trouble.

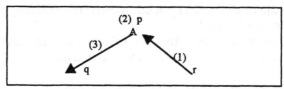

Figure 4.2 A dependency graph

Stratification has an important role in deductive database reasoning. Recall that we have the following relationships:

  (safe) Datalog = RA + recursion - negation
  RA = (safe) Datalog - recursion + negation.

Stratified Datalog with negation subsumes both Datalog and RA, and thus plays an important role in deductive databases. An in-depth discussion of Stratified Datalog can be found in [Ullman 1989].

4.10.3 DEDUCTIVE QUERY EVALUATION

We now briefly discuss how to evaluate (or process) a deductive query (namely, how to get answer(s)). One important concern here is how these methods apply to recursive queries.

4.10.3.1 Bottom-up versus top-down

Top-down (query-driven, similar to Prolog): It starts from query, finds the head of a rule to match, then propagates the variable binding from head to body (from the first subgoal to the last subgoal). The problem of determining precisely the relevant facts is difficult to solve. "Pure" top-down processing for recursive queries has intrinsic problems, and is avoided entirely.

Bottom-up (data-driven): It starts from using facts, but does not consider the query (facts used may not be useful to answer a query at all). Note rules are used in this manner: first, values of the variables are determined to satisfy the body (RHS), then the variable bindings are propagated to the head (LHS). We can use a bottom-up proof procedure for computing consequences of KB until the result does not change. The final C generated in the algorithm is called a *fixed point* because any further application of the rule of derivation will not change C. So the fixed point is actually the solution of the given problem. A fixed point of the Datalog equations (with respect to EDB R_1, ...R_k) is a solution for the relations corresponding to the IDB predicate to the IDB predicates of these equations.

In the following, we introduce two bottom-up query processing methods, using the following example. We assume that "parent(X,Y)" is in EDB.

```
ancestor(X,Y) :- parent(X,Y).
ancestor(X,Y) :- parent(X,Z), ancestor(Z,Y).
```

Query: `ancestor(X, tom).` (Namely, find all of Tom's ancestors.)

- *Naive method:* It can be performed using RA. The problem of this method is that it does redundant, useless work, because it does not take advantage of the actual query: it generates all the facts that can be derived, then selects those related to the query. As an example, we use naïve method for finding Tom's ancestors ("=" denotes assignment):

  ancestor = $\emptyset$;   %initialization

  While ancestor changes do

  ancestor = ancestor $\cup$ parent $|\times|$ ancestor
          %calculating ancestor for all persons
  select ancestors with "Tom" as a descendent

- *Semi-naive method:* It applies rules to *new* tuples produced at the previous step *only*. That is, it focuses on the change. In this sense, it uses an "incremental" method for query processing. As an example, we use semi-naïve method for finding Tom's ancestors ("=" denotes assignment, Δ stands for change, and $\bowtie$ denotes the join operator defined earlier in this chapter):

Δ ancestor = parent;
ancestor = Δancestor;
While Δancestor changes do
    Δancestor =   parent $\bowtie$ Δancestor;
               %calculating changes of ancestors;
               %note that the naïve method does not record
                    the actual change of ancestors.
select ancestors with "Tom" as a descendent

4.10.3.2 Magic sets approach for recursive query processing

The discussion made in this section so far can be summarized as follows. Top-down approach has the advantage of being efficient (because it is query-driven) but is not a realistic method to use, while bottom-up approaches (even semi-naive approach) are not efficient. In fact, in the above example, although the query is only concerned with John's ancestor, this fact is not considered until the last step. To overcome the problems of existing methods, *magic sets approach* employs a rule-rewriting technique so that bottom-up processing is combined with a top-down flavor. The purpose is to discard irrelevant tuples early in the bottom-up query processing. How to tell the query processing system which information is relevant and which is not? The trick is to use the given (known) portion of the query to form a "pseudo-fact" (the "magic" thing!) so that bottom-up processing can take   advantage of top-down processing (while avoid the troubles of using "pure" top-down processing). It is still bottom-up processing but *only searches for paths related to query*. From the perspective of relational algebra, this can be considered as pushing selection to avoid irrelevant inferences.

The magic set rule-writing algorithm given by [Ullman 1989] (Section 13.1 in Volume II) describes detailed steps of rewriting. The result has five groups of rules. The following is revised from an example discussed there:

    r1:   same_gen(X,X) :- person(X).
    r2:   same_gen(X,Y) :-
                           parent(X,Xp), same_gen(Xp, Yp), parent(Y,Yp).

Note that "same_gen" is a recursive predicate, and the program is thus a recursive one. The first rule says a person is always at the same generation of himself (or herself). This is the base case of the recursive. The second rule says X and Y are the same generation if their parents are at the same generation. This is the general case of the recursion.

Note that only the IDB part and the query are shown there; EDB facts (tables) such as   person or   parent are not shown. Here we will not discuss how to rewrite the rules; we will only explain how this new (namely, re-written) program will be processed to answer the query. The query is "same_gen(john, W)", namely, find W (the second argument which is a variable) who is in the same generation with person "john" The magic sets approach requires to construct (from the query) a magic predicate "m-same_gen(john)" as shown in Group V in the algorithm, which indicates that what is to be retrieved should be associated with that particular individual "john" *only*. This magic predicate is treated as a fact for further processing; in this sense, the magic sets approach uses bottom-up. Take a look at the attachment (with the instructor's remark in handwriting). The purpose of this algorithm is to convert the original program so that the re-written program can be processed in the manner as described here. Magic sets approach has been used for maintaining materialized views and query optimization (e.g., [Staudt and Jarke 1996, Harinarayan 1997]).

4.11 KNOWLEDGE REPRESENTATION MEETS DATABASES

In this last section of Chapter 4, we examine the issue of combining requirements of knowledge bases and databases. This discussion takes a logic-based perspective. A continued discussion on combining knowledge bases and databases will be continued in the next chapter (as well as in the remaining part of this book), where more pragmatic concerns will be addressed. The focus of our discussion is on intelligent access to heterogeneous information sources. According to [Baader, Jeusfeld and Nutt 1997, Borgida, Chaudhri and Staudt 1998], researchers seeking logic-based approaches have studied using Datalog (or another language called DL) to achieve integration between computational intelligence and DBMS. Although their approaches are logic-based, the discussion may shed significant insight on the nature of this kind of integration. Both databases and knowledge bases are used to represent the relevant parts of an application domain, and to allow convenient access to the stored information. Research in KR originally concentrated on expressive formalisms with sophisticated reasoning services, usually under the assumption that the size of the knowledge base (KB) is relatively small and resides in main memory. In contrast, DB research was concerned with efficiently storing, retrieving, and sharing large amounts of simple data (usually in secondary memory), but the languages for describing schema information were rather simple, and reasoning about the schema played only a minor role. This difference reminds us the importance of dealing with scaling up problems (which was briefly discussed in Chapter 2). However, the distinction between the requirements and problems in KB and DB are vanishing rapidly. This is because a modern KR system must be able to handle large data values if it is to be employed in realistic applications. This means that techniques developed in the DB area can and should be incorporated. The boundary between KB and DB is diminishing, also because the information stored in DBs is becoming more complex and comes from heterogeneous sources, thus requiring more intelligent construction and retrieval techniques, especially the use of meta-data, which is really knowledge about data. (For a discussion on meta-data, see Chapter 14.) In principle, as long as descriptions of database schemas are expressed as formal concept definitions in a suitable description logic, a computational intelligence tool can reason about them to detect inconsistent descriptions and containment of these schemas. Note that the reasoning is done independently of the specific content of a database. Research work has been carried out to implement KR systems on the top of relational databases or the access to a database through a KR system. Techniques to be introduced in Chapter 5 and Chapter 6 will make important contributions to this integration.

SUMMARY

In this chapter we have extended our discussion of predicates to relations. We discussed relational algebra and relational calculus. Logically, relational databases are just predicates; however, the practical issues considered in DBMS make them deserve special treatment.

We have also discussed relational database design. The basic normal forms (based on functional dependencies and multivalued dependencies) discussed in this chapter can be summarized as follows:

$$4NF \subset BCNF \subset 3NF \subset 2NF \subset 1NF$$

Decomposition algorithms to these normal forms were also introduced. More details on the relational databases, as well as many other basic issues related to database management systems can be found in [Silberschatz, Korth and Sudarshan 1987, Ramakrishnan 1998].

Note that the relational database design theory has a very close relationship with logic-based reasoning. A volume consisting of historically important discussion on deductive databases can be found in [Minker 1987]. The integration between Prolog and DBMS, which was an enthusiastic topic in the 1980's, has been considered as dead. However, this does not indicate that integration itself is a bad idea. The key point here is how to integrate them. Datalog is a useful language for this kind of integration. In this chapter we briefly introduced magic set method for efficient deductive query processing. Other methods also exist. For example, [Lee and Leung 1993] introduced a query-processing method using V graph and SARP techniques. It is based on the analysis of a recursive rule's structure that cuts through the complexity often associated with queries in deductive databases.

Another important development in integrated database design is concerned with combining deductive databases techniques with object-oriented databases, sometimes under the title of deductive object-oriented databases (DOOD). Some basic issues related to deductive and object-oriented bases are discussed in [Gardarin and Valduriez 1989]. A collection of recent papers along with this research direction can be found in [Bry, Ramakrishnan and Ramamohanarao 1997]. A recent survey on deductive database languages (including different Datalog extensions LDL, COL, Hilog and Relationlog) as well object-oriented deductive languages (including O-logic, F-logic, ROL and IQL), can be found in [Liu 1999].

SELF-EXAMINATION QUESTIONS

1. Explain the meaning of safety in relational calculus. Why don't we discuss safety in RA?
2. What is the meaning of the following query in RA? How to re-write it using RC (you don't have to worry about the exact syntax).

$$\sigma_{A1='a'}(r) \times \pi_{A2}(s)$$

3. Verify FDs as a special case of MVDs. Consider R(ABC), with F: {A → B}. Use two tuples (a1, b1, c1) and (a1, b1, c2) and restate in terms of MVD.
4. Consider Table 4.11. Does the following MVD hold in R(ABCDE): C→→BE? If not, add the smallest number of tuples to make the MVD hold.

Table 4.11 Another example of MVD

A	B	C	D	E
a1	b1	c1	d1	e1
a2	b2	c1	d2	e1
a1	b2	c1	d1	e1
a2	b1	c1	d2	e1
a3	b3	c2	d3	e2
a4	b4	c2	d4	c3
a4	b3	c2	d4	e2
a3	b4	c2	d3	e3

REFERENCES

Baader, F., Jeusfeld, M. A. and Nutt, W., Intelligent access to heterogeneous information sources: Report on the 4th workshop on knowledge representation meets databases, *SIGMOD Record,* 26(4), 44-48, 1997.

Borgida, A., Chaudhri, V. K., and Staudt, M., Report on the 5th workshop on knowledge representation meets databases (KRDB'98), *SIGMOD Record,* 27(3), 10-15, 1998.

Bry, F., Ramakrishnan, R. and Ramamohanarao, K. (eds.), *Proceedings of 1997 Deductive and Object-Oriented Databases Conference (DOOD '97),* Springer, Berlin, 1997.

Elmasri R. and Navathe, S. B., *Fundamentals of Database Systems* (2nd ed.), Benjamin Cummings, Redwood City, CA, 1994.

Gardarin G., and Valduriez, P., *Relational Databases and Knowledge Bases,* Addison Wesley, Reading, MA, 1989.

Lee, D.L. and Leung, Y. Y., Fast Query processing in Deductive Databases. *IEEE software,* 10(6), 66-74, 1993.

Liu, M., Deductive database languages: Problems and solutions, *ACM Computing Surveys*, 31(1), 27-62, 1999.

Minker, J. (ed.), *Foundations of Deductive Databases and Logic Programming,* Morgan Kaufmann, Los Altos, CA, 1987.

Ramakrishnan, R., *Database Management Systems,* McGraw-Hill, Boston, 1998.

Reiter, R. Toward a logical reconstruction of relational database theory. In *On Conceptual Modelling* (Brodie, M. L., Mylopoulos, J., and Schmit, J. W., eds.), Springer-Verlag, New York, 191-238, 1984.

Silberschatz, A., Korth, H. and Sudarshan, S.,, *Database System Concepts* (3rd ed.), McGraw-Hill, New York, 1997.

Staudt, M. and Jarke, M., Incremental maintenance of externally materialized views, *Proceedings of Very Large Data Bases* (*VLDB'96*), pp. 75-86, 1996.

Ullman, J. D., *Principles of Database and Knowledge Based Systems,* (Volumes I and II), Computer Science Press, Rockville, MD, 1989.

Chapter 5

RETRIEVAL SYSTEMS

5.1 OVERVIEW

Logic-based representation as discussed in Chapter 3 (as well as an extended discussion provided in Chapter 4) paves the way for presenting several kinds of retrieval systems. In this chapter, three kinds of retrieval systems will be examined: we start with data retrieval in database management systems, and extend our discussion to information retrieval and knowledge retrieval. The emphasis of this chapter is on actual systems which are useful in intelligent decision support. For database retrieval, we discuss basics of database management systems. For information retrieval, we discuss how it differs from database retrieval, some important concepts in information retrieval, as well as the role of the World-Wide Web in building data warehouses, which serve as a low-key solution to get around the problems encountered in distributed database systems. Finally, for knowledge retrieval, we present the concept of expert system as a deductive retrieval systems, and introduce recent development in knowledge management.

An agent-based retrieval system is able to perform interoperation among these different types of retrieval. We should note that retrieval data and knowledge are very different tasks, but they also share some common concerns. A good understanding of their similarities and differences will enhance the chance of integration of information systems. The similarities and differences have significant impact on decision making. For example, a very important problem in both database and knowledge reasoning systems is concerned with the size of the data or knowledge. On the one hand, for database management systems, due to the huge amount of data residing on the secondary memory, performance analysis has traditionally been a focal issue. On the other hand, for computational intelligence, the emphasis of the study has been on the development of algorithms dealing with knowledge residing in main memory. How to scale up these algorithms to satisfy the environment consisting of a huge amount of data poses a big challenge to computational intelligence.

Since in the previous chapter we discussed relational databases, in this chapter we start our discussion on retrieval systems from database management systems.

5.2 DATABASE MANAGEMENT SYSTEMS (DBMS)

5.2.1   BASICS OF DATABASE MANAGEMENT SYSTEMS

A *database-management system* (DBMS) consists of a collection of interrelated data and a set of programs to access those data. The collection of data (the *database*) contains information about one particular enterprise. The primary goal of a DBMS is to provide an environment that is both convenient and efficient to use in retrieving and storing database information. Applications of DBMS include banking systems, airport reservation systems, etc. Functions supported by a DBMS include retrieval, update, as well as others.

There are actors on the scene, including *Database administrators* (who are responsible for authorizing access to the database, coordinating and monitoring its use, and for acquiring software and hardware resources as needed), *Database designers* (who are responsible for identifying the data to be stored in the database and   choosing appropriate structures to represent and store this data), *End users* (including   casual end users, naive users, sophisticated end users (engineers, scientists, business analysts, etc.) and stand-alone users), *system analysts* (who determine the requirements of end users, and develop specifications to meet these requirements) and *application programmers* (who implement specification as programs, involving testing, debugging, documenting and maintenance). There are also actors behind the scene, including DBMS designers and implementers, tool developers and operators and maintenance personnel.

5.2.2 THREE LEVELS OF DATA ABSTRACTION

A major purpose of a database system is to provide users with an abstract view of data. The three levels of data abstraction (three-layer architecture) are depicted in Figure 5.1.

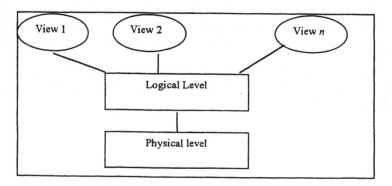

Figure 5.1 Three layer architecture of DBMS

The architecture shown in Figure 5.1 is usually referred to as the 3-layer architecture. The three levels are:

- *View level*: It is the part of the entire database the user is interested in. (Note that the concept of view in this context is more general than the concept in relational databases.)
- *Logical level*: It is referred to *what* data are stored in the database, and *what* relationships exist among those data.
- *Physical level*: It is concerned with *how* the data are actually stored.

From the 3-layer architecture we can distinguish the following two types of data independence, thus benefiting the design of database management systems.

- *Physical data independence*: The ability to modify the physical schema without causing application programs to be rewritten.
- *Logical data independence*: The ability to modify the logical schema without causing application programs to be rewritten.

5.2.3 SCHEMA VERSUS INSTANCES

When relational data model was discussed in Chapter 4, we had already introduced concepts such as schema and instances. In the following, we re-define them in a larger scope.

Database schema refers to the overall design of the database. It is changed infrequently. Database schema may exist at different levels.

- Physical schema. There is only one such schema.
- Logical schema. There is only one such schema.
- Subschemas at the view level. There may be multiple number of subschemas.

Database instances (also called as *database states*) refers to the contents (values) of the database. They are changed more frequently in comparison with the schema. Note a database instance (or database state) refers to all the data stored in the database at a particular moment.

5.2.4 DATA MODELS

A *data model* is a collection of conceptual tools for describing data, data relationships, data semantics, and consistency constraints. Various models exist at different levels.

- *Conceptual model*: This is the highest level. A popular model at this level is the Entity-relationship (ER) model (to be discussed in Chapter 6).
- *Logic model*: Conceptual model can be used for development data models at the logic level. Relational data model as discussed in Chapter 4 is an example of logical level abstraction. Other logical level abstractions also exist, including those usually referred to as legacy systems, such as network data model and hierarchy data model.
- *Physical model*. At the lowest level, physical implementations are developed to realize the logic models.

5.2.5 DATABASE LANGUAGES

In general, two types of languages can be distinguished:

- *Data-definition language* (DDL): Language used to specify database schema.
- *Data-manipulation language* (DML): A language that enables users to access or manipulate data as organized by the appropriate data model. Data manipulation refers to retrieval, insertion, deletion and modification of information. We also have the following terminology:
  - ◆ *Query language:* The portion of a DML that involves information retrieval.

5.2.6 COMPONENTS OF DATABASE MANAGEMENT SYSTEMS

We now discuss the system architecture of DBMSs. A DBMS consists of the following components:

- Users
- DBMS proper:
  - ◆ Query processor
  - ◆ Storage manager
    - ▪ Transaction manager, etc.
- Disk storage (relationship with main memory)

The relationship among these components is shown in Figure 5.2 (following presentations given in [Ullman and Widom 1997, Silberschatz, Korth and Sudarshan 1996]). Related concepts, such as transaction processing and query process will be briefly discussed in Section 5.5.

5.3 COMMERCIAL LANGUAGES FOR DATA MANAGEMENT SYSTEMS

5.3.1 BASIC REMARKS ON COMMERCIAL LANGUAGES

Different from formal languages for relational data model (as discussed in Chapter 4), commercial languages have added "syntactical sugar" (such as ability to deal with string operations). In this section we provide a brief sketch for a well-known commercial language SQL, which stands for Structured query language. It can be considered as a realization of relational algebra, but it also has some flavor of relational calculus. Various versions of SQL have been developed, including SQL-89, SQL-92 (SQL 2), SQL 3 (proposal). Various proposals for extension exist, such as to add temporal aspects. In addition, some variations of SQL have been developed by various venders, such as dynamic SQL. SQL can also be embedded in many other languages, such as C++. In this section, we will only sketch some basic features of SQL.

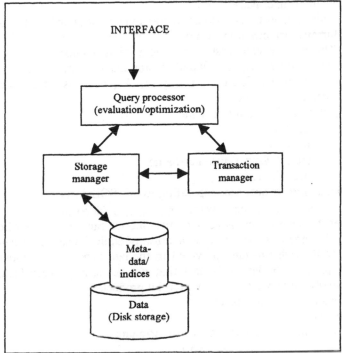

Figure 5.2 DBMS system structure

5.3.2 BASIC STRUCTURE OF SQL QUERY

We can compare SQL clauses with RA operators, as shown below.

SQL Clause	Corresponding RA operator
Select $A_1, A_2, ... A_n$	$\pi_{A1, A2, ..., An}$ (NOT σ!)
From $r_1, r_2, ..., r_m$	$r_1 \times r_2 \times ... \times r_m$
Where(optional) P	σ_P

The entire SQL statement "Select $A_1, A_2, ... A_n$ From $r_1, r_2, ..., r_m$ Where(optional) P" is equivalent to the following RA expression

$$\pi_{A1, A2, ..., An} (\sigma_P (r_1 \times r_2 \times ... \times r_m))$$

Nested SQL queries are allowed. For example, any r_i ($i = 1, ..., m$) in the above SQL query could be an SQL query as well.

5.3.3 EXAMPLES OF SQL QUERIES

Note that although RA provides a good theoretical foundation for SQL, the connection between an RA query and an SQL query may not necessarily be (or not always) a direct translation. Also note that in order to implement a query in SQL, you may need to try more than one way.

Consider a bank relational database with the following relations:
> Own(customer-name, a-no):
> This relation stores customer name and account numbers for saving.
> Borrow(customer-name, l-no):
> This relation stores customer name and loan numbers.

Now let us consider the query "find all customers who have both a loan and an account at the bank." The following query A (which uses the "intersect" operator) should do the work:

(A)   (select distinct customer-name
>   from Own)
>   intersect
>   (select distinct customer-name
>   from borrow)

The relational algebra query corresponding to this SQL query is

$$\pi_{customer-name} (borrower) \cap \pi_{customer-name} (depositor)$$

However, the above query is not the only one we can write. The following are some other answers. This is an indication of equivalence (redundancy) in SQL, due to the rich structures provided in the language. The redundancy is necessary, particularly due to the fact that not necessarily every feature of SQL is actually supported by any commercial product.

(B) select distinct customer-name
> from borrow
> where customer-name in (select customer-name
>   from own)

(C) select distinct customer-name
> from borrow
> where exists (select customer-name
>   from own
>   where own.customer-name = borrow.customer-name)

(D) select distinct customer-name
> from borrow, owns
> where borrow.customer-name = own.customer-name

5.3.4 WRITING SIMPLE SQL QUERIES

Although writing an SQL query is not a translation from RA to SQL, to form an SQL query takes similar consideration as to form a relational algebra query from a given English query. The following is an informal description for some considerations involved in simple SQL queries.

- From interested attributes identify relevant relations:
  - ◆ study relation schema;
  - ◆ given attributes, find relations, find other attributes in same relation;
  - ◆ be aware that same attribute may appear in different relations or may have different names in different relations;

- specify attributes to be retrieved in the **select** clause (the π operator in RA);
- specify all the relation names involved in the **from** clause (to form a **Cartesian product** $\times$;
- specify conditions (e.g. $r.A = s.B$) used for join and select operations (in RA) in the where clause;
- take advantage of "syntactic sugar" of SQL.

5.3.5 WORKING WITH SQL PROGRAMS: GENERAL STEPS

Writing SQL queries is only a portion of the larger task concerning an SQL program. An SQL program consists of DDL and DML, including table creation, insert statements, queries, and others (such as modification). In general, working with SQL programs consists of the following steps. We use a bank database for illustration purposes (the requirement for this database will be described in Chapter 6).

1. Define schema for each relation using SQL DDL. For example, we can create a relation account using SQL DDL:

> create table account
> (account_number char(10) not null,
> branch_name char(15),
> balance integer,
> primary key (account_number));

2. Populate the database by inserting tuples. The following is an example for inserting tuples into the table defined above:

> insert into account values
> ('Aksarben', 'A-5215', 1600);

3. Write SQL queries. After the database has been populated, we can submit SQL queries. We can type in all SQL queries in one file. Alternatively, we can treat each query as a separate file. The general steps involved in writing SQL queries are already discussed in the previous section.

4. Execute the queries. After the database schemas are created and the tables are populated, you can execute queries. It is likely that you need revise your file to correct any syntactic or semantic error.

5.3.6 REMARKS ON INTEGRITY CONSTRAINTS

ICs other than primary keys including the following in SQL, include use of *constraint* (to specify the constraint to be satisfied), *check* (to check the condition specified), as well as *foreign key* (to define the attribute-name used as a foreign key). In addition, domain constraints can be defined, which are similar to user-defined data types in many programming languages. The following is an example of referential integrity in SQL-92:

> create table table-name
> (...
> primary key (...),

  foreign key (...) references relation-name,
  check (...));

5.3.7 AGGREGATE FUNCTIONS

Aggregate functions map a collection (i.e., a set or a multi-set) of values into a single value. Aggregate functions are important because they allow us to obtain important statistics of the data. Aggregation functions play an important role in data analysis for decision support (more discussion can be found in Chapter 11). A brief examination of SQL may help us to understand basic concerns behind aggregation functions. SQL offers five built-in aggregate functions:

- avg(X): average of X (X must be a collection of numbers);
- sum(X): sum of X (X must be a collection of numbers);
- max(X): maximum of X (X can be collections of nonnumeric data types);
- min(X): minimum of X (X can be collections of nonnumeric data types);
- count(X): count the total number (cardinality) of X (X can be collections of nonnumeric data types).

In addition, in order to allow users to apply aggregation functions on a group of set of tuples, SQL offers the "group by" clause. For example, in a banking database, a user may submit a query using "group by" to find the average account at each branch. Furthermore, condition itself may involve aggregation. In this case, the "where" clause in SQL should be extended. This results in a "having" clause in SQL. For the query, "find names and average balance of the branches where the minimum account balance is more than $500," we can write the following SQL query:

  Select branch-name, avg(balance)
  From account
  Group by branch-name
  Having min(balance) > 500

5.3.8 REMARKS ON ENHANCEMENT OF SQL

Finally, we give some advanced features or enhancement of SQL. One feature is concerned with the following scenario: Applications from spreadsheets or graphical front-end tools accept commands from users, and based on the user needs generate appropriate SQL statements to retrieve the necessary data. In these cases we are unable to predict in advance which SQL statements should be executed. SQL provides commands such as *prepare* and *execute* to deal with these problems. These commands are referred to as *dynamic SQL*.

Another feature is an enhanced ability of aggregation. We just discussed the basic structure of aggregation provided by SQL. This structure is not good enough for the need of On-Line Transaction Processing (OLAP). In order to deal with this problem, we consider the *compute clause* supported by *Transact*

SQL from Sybase. It is an important Transact-SQL extension that is used with the row aggregate functions, sum, max, min, avg, and count, to calculate summary values. The results of a query that includes a compute clause are displayed with both detail and summary rows, and look like a report that most DBMSs can produce only with a report generator. compute displays summary values as additional rows in the results, instead of as new columns.

Transact-SQL has been designed to enhance the power of SQL and to minimize the occasions on which users must resort to a programming language to accomplish a desired task. Transact-SQL goes beyond both the ANSI standard and the many commercial versions of SQL. Other features supported by Transact SQL include control-of-flow language, stored Procedures, triggers (a special kind of stored procedure that is used to protect referential integrity-to enforce rules about the relationships among data in different tables), rules and defaults, error handling and set options, as well as others.

5.4 BASICS OF PHYSICAL DATABASE DESIGN

Although this book is not concerned with physical database design, a basic understanding of physical database design is still needed (even for an end user). It is important to keep in mind that searching and sorting methods in a DBMS involves input/output operations with secondary memory.

5.4.1 STORAGE MEDIA

We first give some terminology related to the size of databases:

$$1 \text{ MB (megabyte)} = 10^6 \text{ bytes}$$
$$1 \text{ GB (gigabyte)} = 10^9 \text{ bytes}$$
$$1 \text{ TB (terabyte)} = 10^{12} \text{ bytes}$$
$$1 \text{ PB (petabyte)} = 10^{15} \text{ bytes}$$

It is not uncommon for data warehouses to have size in hundreds of terabytes.

Several types of data storage exist, for a hierarchy of storage devices. At one end of this hierarchy is the fastest storage media called *cache,* and is managed by the operating system. The storage medium used for data that can be operated on is the *main memory.* The primary medium for the long-term on-line storage of data, however, is the magnetic disk. Traditionally, the entire database is typically stored on magnetic disk, although recently *main-memory databases* have drawn more and more attention [Eich 1992]. The advent of main-memory database has apparently enhanced the integration of knowledge-based computational intelligence techniques with database techniques. Note that disk storage is referred to as *direct-access storage,* because it is possible to read data on disk in any order. Having a large number of disks in a system can improve the rate at which data can be read or written, and improve the reliability of data storage by storing redundant information on multiple disks. For this reason, a variety of disk-organization techniques referred to *redundant arrays of independent disks* (*RAID*) have now been widely used. At the other end of the storage-device hierarchy is the tape storage, which is considered as *sequential-access storage*. Tape storage is slow to access, and used primarily for backup and archival data.

5.4.2 FILE STRUCTURES AND INDEXING

A database is mapped into a number of files, which are maintained by the underlying operating system. These files reside permanently on disks (with backups on tables). A file is organized logically as a sequence of records. These records are mapped into disk blocks. Files are provided as a basic construct in operating systems.

A *search key* is the attribute (or attributes) used to look up records in a file. Note that it is different from key concepts (e.g., primary keys) in relational database (which is at the logical level of DBMS).

A query may reference only a small proportion of the records in a file. To reduce the overhead in searching for these records, we can construct indices for the files on which the database is stored. There are many types of indices:

(a) *Index-sequential files*. They are one of the oldest index schemes used in database systems and are designed for applications that require both sequential processing of the file and the random access to individual records. To permit fast retrieval of records in the order of the search key, records should be chained together by pointers. To allow fast random access, an index structure should be used. Indices could be either dense or sparse. In *dense index*, an index record appears for every search-key value in the file; while in *sparse index*, an index record is created for only some of the values.

In a standard index-sequential file, only one index is maintained. If several indices on different search keys are used, the index whose search key specifies the sequential order of the file is referred to as the *primary index* (also called *clustering index*). The search key of a primary index is usually (but not necessarily) the primary key. Each of the other indices is called a *secondary index* (or *non-clustering index*). In other words, a secondary index is an index whose search key specifies an order different from the sequential order of the file (for example, records are ordered by SSN but searched by names). Secondary indices improve the performance of queries that use search keys other than the primary one. However, the price we have to pay is the overhead when the database is modified. Note that regardless of what kind of index is used, the index-sequential file organization suffers from performance degrading as the file grows.

(b) *B+ tree or B tree index*. They are designed to overcome the performance degrading problem. A B+ tree is a balanced tree in which all the leaves (which store the data or contain pointers to the data) are at the same level. The branch factor is usually a relative large number (say, $2^7 = 128$), making only few disk accesses needed. Search operation can be carried out in a straightforward manner. Insert and delete are somewhat complex, because the balanced condition may be violated and need to be restored. B-tree index is a variation of B+ tree where data may be stored in the internal nodes.

(c) *Hash index.* An alternative way of using index is instead of using ordered indices (sorted ordering), we can use a hash function to find the address of a data item directly by computing a function on the search-key value of the desired record. Two kinds of hashing can be distinguished:

- *Static hashing.* It uses hash functions in which the set of bucket addresses is fixed. These hash functions cannot easily accommodate databases that grow significantly larger over time.
- *Dynamic hashing.* It allows the hash function to be modified. Different dynamic hashing techniques have been developed. For example, in *extendable hashing*, buckets used to store the data can be split when the database grows, and can be coalesced when the database shrinks.

5.4.3 TUNING DATABASE SCHEMA

In Chapter 4, we discussed logical database design. The logical design should be followed by the physical database design, where we design the physical schema. It is important to keep in mind that as user requirements evolve, it is usually necessary to tune, or adjust, all aspects of a database design for good performance. There are three kinds of tuning [Ramakrishnan 1998]:

- *tuning indexes:* Based on the observed workload we may refine the initial choice of indexes.
- *tuning the conceptual schema:* This is to make changes to the conceptual schema in order to enhance performance.
- *tuning queries:* This is to rewrite frequently executed queries and transactions in order to run them faster.

5.5 AN OVERVIEW OF QUERY PROCESSING AND TRANSACTION PROCESSING

Although the main interest of computational intelligence for decision support is not directly concerned with what is going on inside of the computer, we still need a basic understanding about two very basic issues, namely, query processing and transaction processing. In the following we give a brief remark on this topic.

5.5.1 QUERY PROCESSING

Query processing refers to the range of activities involved in extracting data from a database. It is concerned with choosing a strategy for processing a query that minimizes the amount of time that it takes to compute the answer. Basic steps in traditional *On-Line Transaction Processing (OLTP)* consist of the following:

(1) Parsing and translation: This is to translate SQL queries into system's internal representation (using extended relational algebra);

(2) *Query optimization*: This refers to the process of selecting the most query-evaluation plan for a query. A *query evaluation plan* is a sequence of primitive operations that can be used to evaluate a query.

(3) *Query evaluation*: In this step, the query is evaluated with the selected plan, and the result of the query is output.

An important concept in query processing is cost model. A *cost model* makes use of statistical information in DBMS catalog to determine the cost of alternative operations optimally, so that the optimizer can select the efficient plan with the least estimated cost. The cost of query evaluation can be measured in terms of a number of different resources, including disk accesses, CPU time to execute a query, and the cost of communication in distributed/parallel database systems.

5.5.2 BASICS OF TRANSACTION PROCESSING

What is a *transaction*? It is a unit of program execution that accesses and possibly updates various data items in a DBMS. A database transaction should hold the ACID properties:

- *Atomicity* (A): All or no operations of the transaction are executed.
- *Consistency*(C): Database should be consistent before and after transaction.
- *Isolation*(I): Each transaction is unaware of other transactions executing concurrently in the system.
- *Durability*(D): Changes made by completed transactions should be made persistent, even if there are system failures.

A transaction could be in different status (usually referred to as *transaction states*), such as active, partially committed (after the final statement has been executed), committed (after successful completion) or aborted. Important issues to be considered in transaction processing include concurrency control and recovery. When several transactions execute concurrently in the same database, the isolation property may not longer be preserved. *Concurrency control* provides a variety of mechanisms to control the interaction among the concurrent transactions. *Recovery* is referred to the part of database system which is responsible for the restoration of the database to a consistent database state (or instance) that existed prior to the occurrence of the failure.

5.5.3 HOW TRANSACTION PROCESSING IS RELATED TO QUERY PROCESSING

It is important to understand how query processing is related to transaction processing. The query manager converts a query into a sequence of requests for stored data (usually involving query optimization). DBMS allows the user to group one or more queries (including possible modification) into a transaction. A transaction usually results from the execution of a user program written in high level language (such as SQL queries). It is convenient to regard a transaction as a series of read operations and write operations of database objects (here the term object is used in its broad sense) and delimited by statements of the form *begin Transaction* and *end transaction*. A system component called *transaction manager* ensures that all these transactions are executed properly so that ACID properties can be supported (see Figure 5.2 in Section 5.2).

5.6 INFORMATION RETRIEVAL (IR)

5.6.1 DIFFERENCES BETWEEN DBMS AND IR SYSTEMS

Extending our discussion on database retrieval, we further examine information retrieval (IR). Unlike database retrieval, information retrieval is concerned with unstructured data (such as documents). A detailed discussion on IR is beyond the scope of this book, and can be found elsewhere [Frakes and Baeza-Yates 1992, Sparck-Jones, Willett, and Larson 1997, Korfhage 1997]. A discussion on the relationship between DBMS retrieval and IR is in [Chen 1994]. IR has drawn much attention recently, particularly due to the popularity of the Internet, and the task of building data warehouses through Internet. In this section, we introduce some most important features of IR, which are useful in building data warehouses for handling decision support queries.

5.6.2 BASICS OF INFORMATION RETRIEVAL

The most basic idea of information retrieval starts with representation of documents. Unlike structured data in databases, documents can be represented as *vectors* in a *vector space*. A document represented as a vector

$$<(d_{t1}, w_1), (d_{t2}, w_2), (d_{t3}, w_3), ... (d_{tm}, w_m)>,$$

where d_{ri} denotes a keyword used to describe the document, and w_i denotes the weight (which could be determined by frequency of use). Similarly, a query is represented as

$$<(q_{t1}, w_1), (q_{t2}, w_2), (q_{t3}, w_3), ... (q_{tm}, w_n)>,$$

where q_{ri} denotes a keyword used to describe the query and w_i denotes the weight (which could be determined by frequency of use). The following are some basic things we should know:

- Each document is a point in an nD space (n-dimensional space);
- Each dimension corresponds to a term (concept);
- Each document is a vector from origin of nD space
- Each query is a vector from origin of nD space;
- Similarity is the cosine of angle between vectors, defined as

$$Similarity(d, q) = \Sigma_i dt_i qt_i / (\Sigma_i dt_i^2 \Sigma_i qt_i^2)^{1/2}$$

We use vector space model to represent documents and queries for Web search. For example, if we consider representation of documents using five keywords, we can use a 5-D space model:

doc-1:   <(internet, 0.1), (database, 0.07), (warehouse, 0.02),
          (data mining, 0.05), (association rule, 0.3)>.
doc-2:   <(internet, 0.09),   (warehouse, 0.1), (data mining, 0.06),
          (association rule, 0.2)>.
doc-3:   <(internet, 0.1), (database, 0.6), (warehouse, 0.3),
          (data mining, 0.1), (association rule, 0.1)>.

Since it is hard to visualize a high dimension space, in the following we use the three dimension (3D) example to illustrate the basic idea of information retrieval. Consider an example as shown in Figure 5.3, where documents and queries are represented in three-dimensional space with terms "data warehouse," "Internet" and "data mining" as three dimensions. Suppose a document is represented as doc(0.4, 0.5,0.2) while the query is represented as query (0, 0.5, 0.5).

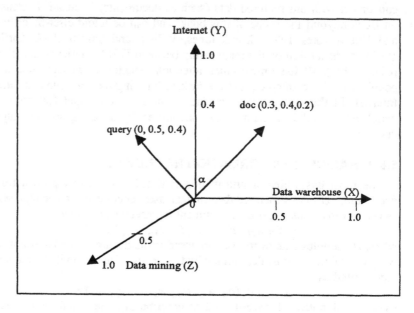

Figure 5.3 Similarity between a query and a document

In Figure 5.3, the similarity between the query and the document can be calculated by plugging in the numbers in the above formula:

$$(0.0 \times 0.4 + 0.5 \times 0.3 + 0.4 \times 0.2)/((0.0^2 + 0.4^2 + 0.5^2)(0.4^2 + 0.3^2 + 0.2^2))^{1/2}$$

There are important issues in information retrieval, such as ranking of documents based on how they are relevant to the query, users' relevance feedback, precision and recall, as well as others. In the following, we provide a brief discussion on *precision* and *recall*:

- Precision =
  |number of relevant documents ∩ number of retrieved documents| / |number of retrieved documents|

- Recall =

  |number of relevant documents $\cap$ number of retrieved documents| / |number of relevant documents|

  For example, suppose for the previous query, documents d1, d3, d6, d8, d12 and d15 are relevant to the query, while documents d1, d3, d4, d6 and d12 are actually retrieved. In this case, documents d1, d3, d6 and d12 are both relevant and retrieved, so we have

$$\text{Precision} = 4/5 = 0.8, \quad \text{Recall} = 4/6 = 0.67.$$

5.6.3 WEB SEARCHING, DATABASE RETRIEVAL, AND IR

The basic idea of information retrieval has been extended to searching the World Wide Web. It is important to note that the same terminology in different contexts may mean different things. For example, in database retrieval, the term *indexing* refers to access methods, i.e., data structures and file organizations for efficient access to data; while in Web searching, just like in IR, it refers to construction of a list of key terms to represent the content of a document. The overall process of Web searching is depicted in Figure 5.1.

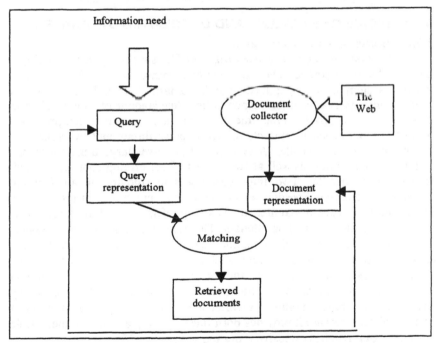

Figure 5.4 **Overall process of Web searching**

We can compare Web searching with information retrieval, which can further be compared with database querying. The result of comparison is shown in

Table 5.1. More detailed discussions on this topic can be found in [Florescu, Levy and Mendelzon 1998, Chaudhuri 1998].

Table 5.1 Comparing web searching with database querying and information retrieval

Database querying	Information retrieval	Web searching
1. Highly structured data	1. Unstructured data (plain text)	1. Semi-structured data
2. Precise query/matching	2. Imprecise querying/matching and feedback	2. Imprecise querying/ matching and feedback
3.Dynamic data allocation	3. Static document allocation	3. Dynamic data allocation

5.7   DATA WAREHOUSING

The Internet provides an excellent chance (and also tremendous challenges) for building data warehouses. In this section, we take a look at this issue. More detailed discussion on data warehousing is provided in Chapter 11.

5.7.1 BASICS OF PARALLEL AND DISTRIBUTED DATABASES

5.7.1.1 Basics of parallel databases

Parallel systems improve processing and I/O speeds by using multiple CPUs and disks in parallel. There are two main measures of performance of a database system: the throughput (the number of tasks that can be completed in a given time interval) and the response time (the amount of time it takes to complete a single task from the time it is submitted). A system that processes a large number of small transactions can improve throughput by processing many transactions in parallel. A system that processes large transactions can improve response time as well as throughput by performing subtasks of each transaction in parallel. Two important issues in studying parallelism are speedup and scale-up. Speedup refers to running a given task in less time by increasing the degree of parallelism. Scale-up refers to handling larger tasks by increasing the degree of parallelism. There are several architectural models for parallel machines used in parallel databases: shared memory (all the processors share a common memory), shared disk (all the processors share a common disk), shared nothing (the processors share neither a common memory nor common disk), and hierarchical (a combination of the preceding architectures). Shared-nothing architecture has been proven the most successful one, because it provides both linear speedup as well as linear scale up, although it requires extensive reorganization of the DBMS code.

The basic idea behind parallel databases is to carry out evaluation steps in parallel whenever possible, in order to improve performance. Individual relational algebra operations (as discussed in Chapter 4) can be parallelized. In addition, we can execute different operations in an query in parallel and execute multiple queries in parallel. In its simplest form, *I/O parallelism* refers to reducing the time required to retrieve relations from disk by partitioning the relations on multiple disks. The most common form of data partitioning in a parallel database environment is horizontal partitioning: the tuples of a relation are divided (or declustered) among many disks, such that each tuple resides on the disk.

- *Interquery parallelism:* In interquery parallelism, different queries or transactions execute in parallel with one another. Transaction throughput can be increased by this form of parallelism. The primary use of interquery parallelism is to scale up a transaction-processing system to support a larger number of transactions per second. However, the response times of individual transactions are no faster than they would be if the transactions were run in isolation.

- *Intraquery parallelism:* Intraquery parallelism refers to the execution of a single query in parallel on multiple processors and disks. Using intraquery parallelism is important for speeding up long-running queries. The execution of a single query can be parallelized in two ways:

  - Intraoperation parallelism: To speed up processing of a query by parallelizing the execution of each individual operation, such as sort, select, project, and join.

  - Interoperational parallelism: To speed up processing of a query by executing in parallel the different operations in a query expression.

5.7.1.2 Distributed database systems

In a distributed database system, the database is stored on several computers. The computers in a distributed system communicate with one another through various communication media, such as high-speed networks or telephone lines. They do not share main memory or disks.

Unlike parallel systems, in which the processors are tightly coupled and constitute a single database system, a distributed database system consists of loosely coupled sites that share no physical components. In addition, the database systems that run on each site may have a substantial degree of mutual independence. In recent years, the need has arisen for accessing and updating data from a variety of preexisting databases, which differ in their hardware and software environments, and in the schemas under which data are stored. A multidatabase system is a software layer that enables such a heterogeneous collection of databases to be treated like a homogeneous distributed database.

A simple and popular distributed DBMS architecture is called client server. A *client-server system* has one or more client processes (which are responsible for user-interface issues) and one or more server processes (which manage data and execute transactions). A client process can send a query to any server process. Howeer, the client-server architecture does not allow a single query to span multiple servers. As a consequence, a client process could be quite complex, and its capabilities would begin to overlap with the server. To deal with these problems, *collaborating server systems* have been developed.

In distributed relational databases, relations are usually fragmented. There are two different schemes for fragmenting a relation: *horizontal fragmentation* splits a relation by assigning each tuple of relation r to one or more fragments; *vertical fragmentation* splits the relation by decomposing the scheme R of relation r so that the original relation can be reconstructed by joining the fragments back (it is often convenient to add a special attribute called tuple-ID for this purpose).

For centralized systems, the primary criterion for measuring the cost of a particular strategy is the number of disk accesses; in a distributed system, we must take into account several other matters, including the cost of data transmission over the network and the potential gain in performance from having several sites process parts of the query in parallel.

Distributed environment also brings more challenges for issues related to transaction processing. For example, in order to ensure atomicity, all the sites in which a transaction T is executed must agree on the final outcome of the execution. T must either commit at all sites, or it must abort at all sites. Therefore, the transaction coordinator of T must execute a commit protocol. The simplest and most widely used is the two phase commit protocol (2PC). Roughly speaking, the first phase is to send prepare message while the second phase is based on the received massages to determine commit or abort.

5.7.2 DATA WAREHOUSING AND DECISION SUPPORT

The complexity involved in distributed database systems has stimulated organizations to find alternative ways to achieve decision support. Data warehousing is an emerging approach for effective decision support. A *data warehouse* is a "subject-oriented, integrated, time-varying, non-volatile collection of data that is used primarily in organizational decision making." [Inmon 1996]. Though considered by some business people that data warehousing is a low-key answer for the "failed" distributed database systems, data warehousing does take advantage of various techniques related to distributed and parallel computing. A discussion on distributed and parallel computing issues in data warehousing can be found in [Garcia-Molina, Labio, Wiener and Zhuge 1999].

Data warehousing provides an effective approach to deal with complex decision support queries over data from multiple sites. The key to this approach is to create a copy (or derivation) of all the data at some one location, and to use the copy rather than going to the individual sources. Note that the original data may be on different software platforms or belong to different organizations.

Data warehouses contain consolidated data from many sources (different business units), spanning long time periods, and augmented with summary information. Warehouses are much larger than other kinds of databases, sizes are much larger, typical workloads involve *ad hoc*, fairly complex queries, and fast response times are important. Data warehousing encompasses frameworks, architectures, algorithms, tools and techniques for bringing together selected data from multiple databases or other information sources into a single repository suitable for direct querying or analysis. Data warehousing is especially important in industry today because of a need for enterprises to gather all of their information into a single place for in-depth analysis, and the desire to decouple such analysis from their OLTP systems. Since decision support often is the goal of data warehousing, clearly warehouses may be tuned for decision support, and perhaps vice versa.

In its simplest form, data warehousing can be considered as an example of asynchronous replication, in which copies are updated relatively infrequently (see [Ramakrishnan 1998] for more discussion). However, a more advanced implementation of data warehousing would store summary data or other kind of information derived from the source data. In other words, a data warehouse stores materialized views (plus some local relations if needed).

It is common in a data warehousing environment for source changes to be deferred and applied to the warehouse views in large batches for efficiency. Source changes received during the day are applied to the views in a nightly batch window (the warehouse is not available to the users during this period). Most current commercial warehousing systems (e.g. Prism, Redbrick) focus on storing the data for efficient access, and on providing extensive querying facilities at the warehouse. Maintenance of warehousing data (in a large degree, maintenance of materialized views) is thus an important problem. A more detailed discussion on data warehousing will be in Chapter 11.

The widespread adoption of Internet technology will profoundly affect *On-Line Analytical Processing (OLAP)*, which refers to applications dominated by stylized queries that typically involve group-by and aggregation operators for analysis purpose. Such queries are extremely important to organizations to analyze important trends so that better decisions can be made in the future. In addition, most vendors of OLAP engines have focused on Internet-enabling their offerings. The true promise of the Internet is in making OLAP a mainstream technology, that is, moving OLAP from the domain of analysts to consumers. E-commerce has emerged as one of the largest applications of the Internet in decision support. The basic concepts of data warehousing and aggregation have naturally made their way onto the web. In fact, some of the most popular Web sits on the Internet are basically databases. For example, search engines such as Alta Vista and Lycos attempt to warehouse the entire web. Aggregation as a means to navigate and comprehend the vast amounts of data on the Internet has to also be recognized. Directory services such as Yahoo and Excite attempt to aggregate the entire web into a category hierarchy and give users the ability to navigate this hierarchy. The infrastructure for decision support is also in the process of improvement [Harinarayan 1997]. A more detailed discussion on data warehousing and related issues will be given in Chapter 11.

5.7.3 MIDDLEWARE

Middleware is a loosely defined term referring to the products to help customers deal with disparate, heterogeneous environments more effectively. In the DBMS arena, middleware products provide a consistent interface to different local and remote data sources. Typically, data sources are supported through one or more specific *drivers* that (among other things) pass requests to a given data source and enable the results to be returned to the application.

From a customer's viewpoint, typical elements of data access middleware offerings include the following:

- an *application programming interface (API)* consisting of a series of available unction calls in C and a series of data access statements in dynamic SQL,
- a component called *middleware engine* for routing requests to various drivers and performing other functions (structures of middleware engine differ, depending on whether a global catalog or directory exists), and
- *drivers* to translate requests issued through the middleware API to a format intelligible to the various back-end data sources.

Gateways may be considered an early attempt at middleware; they provide specific point-to-point connectivity rather than broad-based connectivity.

The logical architecture of a data warehouse, including the roles of the middleware and *data marts* are depicted in Figure 5.5. Each data mart contains a portion of the data stored in the data warehouse (to be further discussed in Chapter 11). Also note source data are assisted by wrappers that facilitate conversion of data for integration.

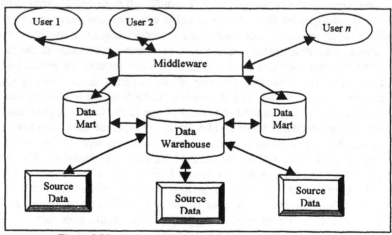

Figure 5.5 Logical architecture of a data warehouse

5.8   RULE-BASED EXPERT SYSTEMS

5.8.1 FROM DATA AND INFORMATION RETRIEVAL TO KNOWLEDGE RETRIEVAL

Although data and information retrieval are important in decision making processes, they lack the power of reasoning. Now that we have covered data and information retrieval systems, we are ready to discuss knowledge retrieval systems that support reasoning.

Typically, management of data refers to retrieval and updating of data, while management of knowledge also requires inference of data. One practical way to distinguish knowledge from data is to view a *database* as consisting of assertions involving constants (e.g., "Professor Tom is 35 years old") , while a *knowledge base* consists of more general statements involving variables (e.g., "Many college professors are middle-aged males") [Wiederhold 1984]. However, a deeper understanding from a knowledge-level perspective (see Chapter 2) would interpret databases as knowledge bases of a certain limited form [Brachman and Levesque 1986]. Therefore, a set of data structures used by a program is both a knowledge base and a database: to ask about implementation mechanisms is to view it as a database, while to delve more deeply into expressiveness (including what is implied) is to adopt a knowledge base perspective. [Freundlich 1990] noticed that the domain of database technology has not required expressive capabilities as sophisticated as those of knowledge-based technology. It has also been noted that practices in knowledge bases required less sophisticated implementation mechanisms, and so have been less concerned with data-level issues. As computers tackle new tasks in new domains, support is needed for large-scale, complex, data-intensive applications in user-oriented environments. Handling these tasks requires a new way of thinking about databases; a shift from the view of data as values (i.e., sets of uniformly formed data types) to a view of data as chunks of knowledge. Another difficulty is that the interests of knowledge base practitioners and database practitioners differ, but this situation is changing very soon. Now, given the physical implementation of a database, what can we do to extend it to the power of processing knowledge?

The relationship between data and information retrieval and knowledge retrieval can also be explained from the nature of computational intelligence. Computational intelligence is concerned with learning, memory organization and access, functional constraints with knowledge analysis, as well as scale-up. The integration of learning with every phase of cognitive processing is extremely important. Inseparable from the importance of learning is the importance of memory organization and access, and learning should not be simply aggregating more of the individually acquired atomic units [Schank 1993]. Knowledge retrieval is such an integrated process concerning memory access (which is comparable with database access) and organization.

5.8.2 DEDUCTIVE RETRIEVAL SYSTEMS

A *deductive retrieval system* refers to any system that stores knowledge in the form of rules and implements procedures for drawing conclusions from that knowledge. Deductive retrieval systems are similar in some respects to theorem proving systems, but are generally tailored for a particular type of problem solving. Most expert systems can be characterized as deductive retrieval systems. One thing that both deductive retrieval systems and theorem provers have in common is that they represent knowledge symbolically and declaratively. A typical deductive retrieval system consists of a collection of facts and rules, and a collection of procedures that operate on the storage, answering queries, noticing when certain conclusions are warranted, expanding the facts and rules as new data are added, and cleaning up when data are withdrawn. The database in most deductive retrieval systems is more than a passive repository for facts and rules. Often the information stored in a knowledge base is supplemented as well as organized (e.g., using a discrimination tree) [Dean, Allen, and Aloimonos 1995].

5.8.3 RELATIONSHIP WITH KEY INTERESTS IN COMPUTATIONAL INTELLIGENCE

In order to understand the importance of expert systems from the key interests of computational intelligence, let us briefly review what we presented in Chapter 2. We started with the notion of problem solving as search and discussed the importance of representing knowledge for search. We also notice although search is useful, it may be a time-consuming process. Therefore, there is the need for limiting search (to improve performance). In order to achieve this, we have several choices. One way is to find better (namely, more efficient) search methods; for example, we may employ heuristics to search only promising states. Another way to limit search is to resort to knowledge, because knowledge is power. The more knowledge, the less search is needed. The philosophy used here is to emphasize the need to encode a huge amount of domain specific knowledge while using some relatively simple (and fixed) inference mechanism. Comparing with general problems solvers in early history of computational intelligence, expert systems represent a sharp philosophical change in achieving intelligent behavior.

5.8.4 BASICS OF EXPERT SYSTEMS

An *expert system* is an interactive system which is able to demonstrate expertise (expert level of knowledge) in a specific knowledge domain (such as diagnosis, trouble shooting) and solve problems in this specific domain for consultation. The term expert system is closely related to the concept of *knowledge-based system*, and these two terms are usually used interchangeably. However, we should point out unlike an expert system, a knowledge-based system does not require expert-level knowledge.

It is important to understand when an expert system solution is appropriate. This is because just like anything else, the expert system approach has pros and cons. Successful application areas are abundant, but lessons learned are also important.

5.8.5 PRODUCTION SYSTEM MODEL

A popular approach to build expert systems is by using the production system model. In this section we briefly introduce this model.

5.8.5.1 Important components

Production systems provide an important model for building expert systems. (A variation of this model has been called the blackboard structure model, with emphasis on distributed knowledge sources.) The following are important components in the production system model.

- *Production rules (long term memory);*
- *Working memory (short term memory);*
- *Recognize-act cycle.*

Let us take a brief look at the first two components. A production rule has the following format:

if antecedent (premise/condition) then consequence (conclusion/action)

Here are some examples:

- If it does not rain, then Tom will go.
- If the engine does not turn over, and the lights do not come on then the problem is battery or cables.

The set of production rules form the long term memory (namely, the knowledge base). The case-specific data (namely, data or facts directly used in the current session) are stored in the working memory. Contents in working memory are either conditions or actions of those rules which were fired in current session. After the session ends, the content stored there are all gone. Working memory thus works like a buffer, and can be used to make reasoning process efficient.

5.8.5.2 The recognize-act cycle

The recognize-act cycle is the heart of the production systems model. It consists of three elements: match, select, and act. The cycle is repeated until the problem has been solved or there are no rules in the conflict set.

Note the recognize-act cycle does not specify the direction of search. In general, a query can be answered by using *goal driven (backward reasoning)* or *data driven (forward reasoning)*. (The term backward chaining means that we are trying to prove a hypothesis by looking for evidence to support it.)

We use the following example to illustrate the difference between goal driven versus data driven. Given facts a, h and e, along with the following rules:

(1) if a then b,
(2) if a and c then d,
(3) if h and e then d,
(4) if d and m then g.

Suppose we want to search for goal g. The different behavior of goal driven and data driven is depicted in Figure 5.6, where two search trees are constructed along with different directions. Note that in case of data driven, if we start with rule (1), since from b we can go nowhere, alternative rules must be used. In case of goal driven, we reach a dead end at c, because it is not a given fact. As for the design choice itself, it is an important design decision to determine whether goal driven or data driven should be used. For example, if there are a lot of facts to choose while there is only one clearly defined goal, then the goal-driven approach makes sense.

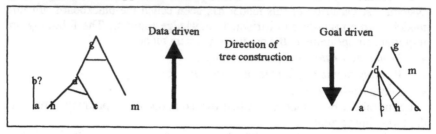

Figure 5.6 Direction of search

In the following, we will consider the recognize-act cycle in the case of data driven approach.

- *Match (Recognize):* During the match portion of the cycle, the conditions in the left-hand side of the rules are matched against the contents of working memory to determine which rules have their LHS conditions satisfied with consistent bindings to working memory terms. Rules which are found to be applicable are put in a *conflict set*.
- *Select:* From the conflict set, one of the rules is selected to execute. The selection strategy may depend on recency of usage, specificity of the rule, or some other criteria. This is usually referred to as *conflict resolution*: several candidates of rules to *fire* (which means to activate or apply).
- *Act (Execute):* The rule selected from the conflict set is executed by carrying out the action or conclusion part of the rule, the RHS of the rule.

The production system model can be summarized in Figure 5.7.

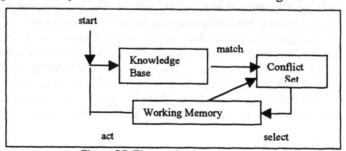

Figure 5.7 The production system model

In order to improve the efficiency of the match process, an algorithm called *RETE algorithm* has been developed (along with an expert system development language called OPS5). The main time-saving features of RETE are:

- In most expert systems, the contents of working memory (see below) change very little from cycle to cycle. There is a persistence in the data known as temporal redundancy. This makes exhaustive matching on every cycle unnecessary. Instead, by saving match information, it is only necessary to compare working memory changes on each cycle.

- Many rules in a knowledge base will have the same conditions occurring in their LFS. Repeated testing of the same conditions in those rules could be avoided by grouping rules which share the same conditions and linking them to their common terms.

For a more detailed discussion on RETE algorithms, see [Giarratano and Riley 1998].

5.8.5.3 The need for a separate knowledge base

In order to employ production systems model to build expert systems, we should first understand what is the architectural implication of this model. A storage of explicitly represented problem-solving knowledge (namely, a knowledge base) is maintained to separate its content from the control knowledge. This separation of domain knowledge from control knowledge is one of the most important principles offered by the production systems model. In order to understand the meaning of separating knowledge from control, let us compare the following two versions of Prolog code as shown below. Our task is to print the names of state capitals. We have two choices. As shown in Version 1, we have a hard-code version; for each state, we write a statement to print its capital. In Version 2, however, we separate the print statement from the domain knowledge of state capitals. Version 2 is superior to Version 1 because of modularity and flexibility.

Version 1 (Hard-code version):

```
print_capital(texas) :- write(austin).
print_capital(kansas) :- write(topeka).
print_capital(nebraska) :- write(lincoln).
print_capital(louisiana) :- write(baton-rouge).
print_capital(_) :- write('Capital is not known').
```

Version 2 (Separate print control knowledge from domain knowledge):

```
%Print control knowledge
print_capital(Capital) :-
                  capitalcity(State, Capital), write(Capital).
print_capital(_) :- write('Capital is not known').
%Knowledge base of state capitals
capitalcity(texas, austin).
capitalcity(kansas, topeka).
capitalcity(nebraska, lincoln).
capitalcity(louisiana, baton-rouge).
```

The advantage of separating inference control is that it keeps inference mechanism simple and makes the knowledge base easy to maintain. This separation has been used as an important principle for designing rule-based expert systems. An expert system is a knowledge-based system which demonstrates expert-level of knowledge. The power of these systems mainly comes from the huge amount of knowledge, rather than the inference mechanism.

5.8.6 KNOWLEDGE ENGINEERING

The process of building an expert system is referred to as *knowledge engineering*. It would be beneficial to compare knowledge engineering versus software engineering:

*   Type of knowledge being represented is different: Software engineering involves representing well-known and well-defined algorithmic procedures that are widely known, while knowledge engineering involves representing the extensive imprecise, and ill-defined heuristic knowledge that is stored in the minds of a few experts.
*   The nature and quantity of the knowledge is different: Typically, the nature and quantity of the problem-solving knowledge required within a knowledge-based system is not well-known even by the experts themselves.

Knowledge engineering is a design process, and knowledge acquisition has been considered as the "bottleneck" of knowledge engineering.

It is important to distinguish different kinds of people involved in expert systems.

*   *knowledge engineer*: A person who develops the expert system. It is often useful for the knowledge engineer to be a novice in the problem domain because they should be able to spot domain experts' conceptual jumps and ask for clarification;
*   *domain experts,* who have cooperated knowledge engineers for system development; and
*   *users*, who are usually domain experts as well.

An important task in knowledge engineering is evaluation. Evaluation means to carry out a technical judgment of the ontologies, their software environment, and documentation with respect to a frame of reference (the requirements specification document) during each phase and between phases of their life cycle. Evaluation subsumes the terms verification and validation. A colloquial definition of the terms from software engineering is:

*   Verification: This is to answer the question: "Am I building the product right?" The purpose is to make sure that the new rule is in the right form.
*   Validation: This is to answer the question: "Am I building the right product?" The purpose is to determine that a chain of correct inferences leads to the correct answer in expert systems. Verification refers to the technical process that guarantees the correctness of an ontology, its associated software environments, and documentation with respect to a frame of reference during each phase and between phases of its life cycle. Validation guarantees that the ontologies, the software environment, and documentation correspond to the system that they are supposed to represent.

5.8.7 BUILDING RULE-BASED EXPERT SYSTEMS

5.8.7.1 Expert system architecture

The components of a typical expert system (built on production system model) is shown in Figure 5.8.

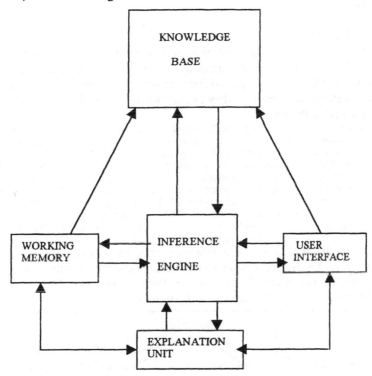

Figure 5.8 Architecture of an expert system

5.8.7.2 Some important features of rule-based systems

A rule-based expert system contains components that usually can be found in the production systems model, and more. It usually includes the following components:

- *Inference engine:* An inference engine separate from the domain knowledge is the most important factor for a successful system. The inference engine usually works in a simple and fixed manner; for example, it could be designed as either data driven (i.e. forward reasoning) or goal driven (i.e. backward reasoning).
- *Knowledge-base* ("long term memory"): This is where the domain knowledge is stored. The most common form of knowledge bases are rule-based systems consisting of rules (may be heuristic rules) and facts

(rules may be indexed and the rule base may be partitioned into several parts).

- *Working memory* ("short term memory"): This is the place to store case-specific data (initialized as empty when a session starts).
- *Explanation unit:* In addition to provide a consultation to a user, an expert system can explain its own behavior. This will enhance the confidence of the user.

5.8.7.3 A simple example

We use the following simple example to illustrate how a rule-based expert system works. Consider a troubleshooting system. We want to diagnose the problem of a TV set using goal-driven reasoning. Suppose we have the following rules (for convenience, they are written in Prolog, but do not have to be implemented in Prolog):

```
diagnose(a) :- symptom-1, symptom-2.              %Rule 1
symptom-1 :- symptom-3, symptom-4.                %Rule 2
diagnose(b) :- symptom-5, symptom-6.              %Rule 3
sumptom-6 :- symptom-7, symptom-8.                %Rule 4
symptom-2 :- write('symptom 2?'), read(yes), nl.  %Rule 5
symptom-3 :- write('symptom 3?'), read(yes), nl.  %Rule 6
symptom-4 :- write('symptom 4?'), read(yes), nl.  %Rule 7
symptom-5 :- write('symptom 5?'), read(yes), nl.  %Rule 8
symptom-7 :- write('symptom 7?'), read(yes), nl.  %Rule 9
symptom-8 :- write('symptom 8?'), read(yes), nl.  %Rule 10
```

In order to understand how the system works, let us take a look at two sample sessions. Let us also assume to use smallest-numbered rule as a simple way for conflict resolution. The *static structure of the rules* (namely, how these rules are related to each other) is shown in Figure 5.9.

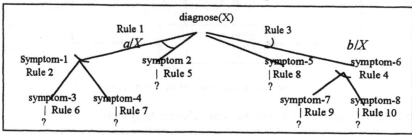

Figure 5.9 Static structure of the rules

In order to show the *dynamic construction* of the search tree (in the sense discussed in Chapter 2), let us consider the following sample scenario.

```
Symptom 3?
no
symptom 5?
yes
symptom 7?
yes
symptom 8?
yes
X = b
```

An ideal inference engine should construct the dynamic search tree in the manner shown in Figure 5.10. Comparing with Figure 5.8, we note only the portion in the static structure which is related to the current session (which depends on the user's answers) is shown in the figure (others are pruned).

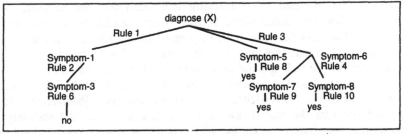

Figure 5.10 A dynamic search tree

5.8.7.4 Expert system shells

An expert system shell is a tool that can be used for expert system development. In a sense, it can be considered as an expert system with an "empty" knowledge base (namely, one knowledge base can be replaced by another knowledge base). Prolog can serve as an expert system shell, because its built-in search mechanism can serve as a backward reasoning inference engine. More flexible ways of reasoning, however, can be achieved by building an inference engine on the top of Prolog. Many other commercial expert systems shells have also been developed to meet various user needs.

5.8.7.5 Explanation facility

The reason to have explanation facility is to improve user confidence. Traditionally there are two kinds of problems:

- *Why*: The user asks the computer "why do you want to know this?" and the computer returns a rule to be fired. In this case, the system looks at the upper level of the tree (i.e., one level above the node accessed).
- *How*: The user asks "how did you get here?" and the computer returns rule(s) fired. In this case, the system looks at the subtrees rooted at the accessed node.

For example, in the previous session, suppose the user wants to know why she is asked about symptom 3. The system provides an explanation by looking at one level above the node representing symptom 3. After the explanation, the same question is repeated so the user is given a second chance to enter yes or no:

```
symptom 3?
Why
Because I am trying to fire rule 2 which requires symptom
3 and symptom 4
symptom 3?
no
symptom 5?
...
```

5.8.8 SOME OTHER ASPECTS

5.8.8.1 Weak methods, Strong methods and Role-limiting methods

From expert system shells we can provide the following comments. During the 1960s, a significant piece of the computational intelligence community's attention was devoted to identifying and analyzing the so-called *weak methods*. They are called weak because their usefulness is only weakly constrained by task features; each is potentially applicable to a broad set of task types. A weak method does not put any limits on the nature nor complexity of the task-specific control knowledge it can use. A *role-limiting method* can be viewed as a specialization of a weak method that predefines the task-related control knowledge the method can use. [McDermott 1988] pointed out that the underlying idea here is that if we take seriously the knowledge base/inference engine distinction that expert system developers have made so much of, it should be possible to devise a set of role-limiting methods, where each method defines the roles that the task-specific knowledge requires it must play and the forms in which that knowledge can be presented. A role-limiting method typically consists of a simple loop over a sequence of 5 or 10 steps. These role-limiting methods serve as knowledge-acquisition tools.   One method is called cover-and-differentiate, a method suitable for certain types of diagnostic tasks, as demonstrated in a tool called MOLE. A MOLE-built program searches a space of possible explanations. MOLE has the following control knowledge:

1. Determine the events that potentially explain the symptoms.
2. If there is more than one candidate explanation for any event, then identify information that will differentiate the candidates by performing the following: ruling out one or more of the explanatory connections, ruling out one or more of the candidate explanatory events, providing sufficient support for one of the candidate explanatory events, and providing a reason for preferring some of the explanatory connections over others.
3. Get this information (in any order) and apply it (in any order).
4. If Step 3 uncovers new symptoms, go to step one.

Chandrasekaran proposed a theoretical framework for looking at knowledge-based problem solving in terms of generic tasks [Chandrasekaran 1986]. Abstractly, the generic tasks can be characterized by providing information about a task specification in the form of generic types of input and output, domain knowledge and a family of control regimes. Six generic tasks have been found; they are considered as very useful as building blocks for the construction (and understanding) of knowledge-based systems. Furthermore, role-limiting methods have been studied [McDermott 1988]. In a sense, role-limiting methods provide a concrete way to realize generic tasks in knowledge-based reasoning.

5.8.8.2 Remarks on other features of expert systems

We have discussed the most fundamental features of rule-based expert systems. There are many other important features. One such important feature is about *reasoning under uncertainty*. In fact, frequently rules represent heuristic knowledge, they are not necessarily always true or only true to some degree. In fact, reasoning under uncertainty is an important issue, and we will take a look at this issue in a broader sense (i.e., not restricted to expert system context) in Chapter 12 and Chapter 13.

Another remark is that expert systems can be built with models other than the production system model (for example, using neural networks). However, many general principles involved in building expert systems remain same.

5.8.9 CLIPS: A BRIEF OVERVIEW

CLIPS (an acronym for C Language Integrated Production System, [Giarratano and Riley 1998]) is a multi-paradigm programming language that provides support for rule-based, object-oriented, and procedural programming. CLIPS is a forward-chaining, rule-based production-system language, based on the RETE algorithm for pattern-matching. A command-line interpreter is the default interface for CLIPS. CLIPS programs are expressed by means of commands, functions and constructs. In CLIPS, a fact is presented as an ordered list of fields; the system also supports template (or non-ordered facts). Rules allow the user to specify a set of conditions to CLIPS, such that when the conditions in the left-hand side (LHS) are satisfied, a set of actions in the right-hand side (RHS) are executed. Note that here we will not focus on the syntactic issues. We want to emphasize some important things that may or may not be explicitly stated in literature.

It would be beneficial to compare CLIPS with Prolog. The problem is *how* to compare. The following is a list of questions that could be used for comparison:

- Is it based on production-system model?
- Does it use functions or predicates?
- Does it use recursion or iteration?
- What is the direction of search for problem solving?
- What should be on LHS and RHS of a rule?
- Could you make a simple rule in CLIPS? How would you write the same rule in Prolog?
- How is matching performed?
- Is it a typed language?
- Does it use global variables?
- Can you think about other criteria for comparison?

The reader is encouraged to check the CLIPS manual and answer these questions by herself. Nevertheless, we can briefly answer some of the questions below. Unlike Prolog which is a logical language, CLIPS has a more direct connection with the production systems model. Unlike Prolog which uses unification, CLIPS puts emphasis on the efficiency of matching by manipulating the working memory. In particular, CLIPS employs a data structure called agenda, to keep on tracking current activities.

CLIPS also incorporates some considerations involving computational intelligence for decision supports as discussed in early chapters. For example, the way used in removing a rule and the use of logical conditional elements resemble the considerations behind integrity constraints as discussed in DBMS.

Basic constructs in CLIPS include *deftemplate, defrule, defmodule,* as well as others. CLIPS has been undergoing various kinds of extensions. For example, the object-oriented programming capabilities in CLIPS, collectively referred to as the *CLIPS Object-Oriented Language (COOL),* are a hybrid combination of features found in other object-oriented languages along with some new ideas. extended to add object-oriented features. Another important extension is FuzzyCLIPS, which will be discussed in Chapter 12.

5.9   KNOWLEDGE MANAGEMENT AND ONTOLOGIES

In this chapter, started from data retrieval systems, we extended our discussion to information retrieval systems, and further discussed knowledge retrieval systems. Finally, in this section, we take a look at the issue of manipulating *multiple* knowledge bases for knowledge management [O'Leary 1998a, 1998b].

5.9.1   WHAT IS KNOWLEDGE MANAGEMENT?

Knowledge management (KM) is the formal management of knowledge for facilitating creation, access, and reuse of knowledge stored in various knowledge bases, typically using advanced technology. Typical KM tools include the World Wide Web, Lotus notes, the Internet, and intranets.

Knowledge management shares some common concerns with computational intelligence, but with somewhat different focus. For example, knowledge bases employed by knowledge management systems are used for both machine *and human* consumption, rather than for machine alone. KM thus can be viewed as a further development of computational intelligence, and computational intelligence techniques, such as intelligent agents, knowledge bases, knowledge discovery, and ontology (see below) play an important role in KM systems.

In order to stimulate group decision making in organizations, knowledge management systems often allow discussion groups that focus on a single set of issues or a specific activity, such as particular software or a single consulting engagement. KM is a process of *converting* knowledge from the sources accessible to an organization and *connecting* people with that knowledge.

An underlying philosophy of knowledge management is that it assumes an organization gathers all its important knowledge in a single place, and employees use it to make good decisions that will benefit the organization.

Therefore, there is an interesting similarity between the mission of KM and data warehousing (as discussed in Section 5.7 of this chapter), although the emphasis here is more on the reasoning (rather than on the analysis of aggregate data). To reach this end, there is a full range of KM *converting* capabilities involving individuals and groups, data and text, as well as a full range of KM *connecting* capabilities involving people and knowledge. The capabilities include converting individual to group-available knowledge, as well as converting data or text to knowledge. The *connecting capabilities* involve two factors: people and knowledge from both directions.

5.9.2 INFORMATION TECHNOLOGY FOR KNOWLEDGE MANAGEMENT

Knowledge workers now believe it is knowledge that makes organizations work. Knowledge management systems contain numerous knowledge bases, made up of numeric and qualitative data (such as searchable Web pages). Knowledge bases typically have several kinds of knowledge, including *engagement knowledge bases* (which summarize information about different jobs that are captured in working papers, either actual or virtual), *Proposal knowledge bases, news knowledge, best-practices knowledge bases,* as well as *expert knowledge bases* that identify who in the firm is expert in a particular set of activities.

However, knowledge management is not only concerned with utilizing existing knowledge bases. Among other things, it is also concerned with *creation* of new knowledge. Where is this new knowledge from? The knowledge movement in organizational thinking is about refining rules of thumb used by investors into techniques and methodologies for the knowledge auditing of organizations. This new view of organizations should help investors to make their decisions in a sound and systematic manner. In addition, it also aids knowledge workers to identify the real weaknesses and strengths of the organizations they run, and to set up the priorities in order to make them grow [Borghoff and Pareschi 1997]. Organizational knowledge is something inherently fluid and elusive. Knowledge management is complicated due to the need for incorporating two very different kinds of organizational knowledge: *explicit knowledge,* which is the formal knowledge that can be packaged as information and can be found in the documents of an organization; and *tacit knowledge,* which is the personal knowledge embedded in individual experience and shared and exchanged through direct, eye-to-eye contact.

Knowledge management can be enhanced by using information technology, and related aspects include:

- *Process knowledge.* It is explicit, formalized knowledge about executing sequences of work activities. An important issue here is how to enrich process knowledge.
- *Corporate (or organizational) memories.* They record the accumulated knowledge about the services and the products of an organization, with

the purpose of supporting the continuous enhancement of knowledge-intensive work practices and of alleviating the risk of "corporate amnesia" due to experts taking away their knowledge when they leave.

- *Information filtering.* It is a crucial type of information technology due to the huge amount of information available, particularly through the World Wide Web.

5.9.3 DATA AND KNOWLEDGE MANAGEMENT ONTOLOGIES

Since the knowledge available in a knowledge management system comes from various sources and takes various formats, it is a big challenge to use and reuse such acquired knowledge in an integrated manner. Similarly, in distributed database management systems, multi-database systems or data warehouses, ontologies also play an important role. To deal with this challenge, we have to consider issues related to *ontology*, which is explicit, knowledge-based specifications of conceptualizations. These specifications typically describe a taxonomy of the tasks that define the knowledge. Within the context of knowledge management systems, ontology is the specifications of discourse in the form a *shared vocabulary*. Ontology thus plays an important role of integrated use of knowledge in an organization.

There are significant advantages of using ontology in knowledge management. First of all, ontology defines the scope of group discussions needed by knowledge management systems and serves as the common language for collaboration. As a consequence, ontology also facilitates reusability of artifacts achieved in knowledge management systems. In addition, ontology provides more focused search capabilities needed in organizations, filters substantial amounts of information, and directs the information of interest to the appropriate source. In order to select an appropriate ontology, a number of factors should be considered. More discussion on knowledge management can be found in [O'Leary 1998a, 1998b, Borghoff and Pareschi 1997].

A collection of papers on ontologies can be found in [Swartout and Tate 1999] and a collection of papers on ontologies in distributed databases can be found in [Bougurettaya 1999]. The American Heritage Dictionary defines "ontology" as "the branch of metaphysics that deals with the nature of being." (Metaphysics refers to the branch of philosophy that systematically investigages first causes and the nature of ultimate reality.) The term has recently been adopted by the computational intelligence community to refer to a set of concepts or terms that can be used to describe some area of knowledge or build a representation of it. An ontology can be either very high level (consisting of concepts that organize the upper parts of a knowledge base) or domain specific. An ontology provides the basic structure or armature around which a knowledge base can be built. The distinction between an ontology and a knowledge base lies in that an ontology provides a set of concepts and terms for describing some domain, while a knowledge base uses those terms to represent what is true in that domain. Interest in ontologies is largely due to reusing or sharing knowledge across systems [Swartout and Tate 1999]. One key impediment to sharing knowledge is that different systems use different concepts and terms for describing domains. Ontologies will fundamenally change the way in which systems are constructed. Of particular interest is the issue of the use of databases over the Web. Because of the sheer size of the Web, the data volume is steadily becoming larger, and the information space is increasingly dynamic. In light of these developments, one emerging area that holds promise to define a common representation and understanding is the use of ontologies in databases, which have drawn from computational intelligence, linguistics and philosophy [Bouguettaya 1999].

SUMMARY

In this rather long chapter we discussed various kinds of retrieval systems: database retrieval, information retrieval and knowledge retrieval. A good understanding on the similarities and differences of these systems is crucial for the integrated use of these systems for decision support. Materials presented in this chapter, along with those presented in the next chapter, will form the core of database and knowledge-based systems. A collection of recent research papers [Yang 1999] examine recent development in intelligent information retrieval, including searching, filtering and navigating on the Web; multimedia information retrieval; and the incorporation of machine learning techniques into intelligent retrieval (see Chapter 10 for a discussion on machine learning). Some advanced issues related to intelligent retrieval, including reasoning through extended retrieval, as well as integrated retrieval involving creativity, will be further discussed in Chapters 7 to 9.

SELF-EXAMINATION QUESTIONS

1. Make your examples to illustrate how to integrate information retrieval and database retrieval, and discuss some advantages as well as some issues that must be considered.
2. Suppose you heard from the news report that Miami is declared as the capital of the United States.
    (a) Indicate all the possible implications you can make from this news.
    (b) Suppose you want to write a Prolog program to produce these implications. Discuss what kind of facts and assumptions should be stored in the knowledge base.
    (c) Instead of writing a Prolog program, suppose you are asked to accomplish the same task indicated in (b) by developing a knowledge-based system. The knowledge-based system will not store any facts; rather, it is to be integrated with a database

management system to retrieve all the data needed (such as geographical information) for reasoning. Discuss some important issues that must be considered in developing such a system.

3. Consider the issue of handling duplicates in RA and SQL. (A tuple is a duplicate of another one if they are identical.) Answer the following questions in regard to operators used in RA and SQL:
    (a) Which operators retain duplicates?
    (b) Which operators automatically eliminate duplicates?
    (c) When and why should duplicates be retained?
    (d) Are duplicates explicitly removed or retained?

4. Consider the simple expert system example discussed in Section 5.8.7.3. Design a system-user conversation under which the right subtree at the node diagnose(X) will not be searched at all. Is it possible to prune the left subtree at the same node?

REFERENCES

Borghoff, U. M. and Pareschi, R., Information technology for knowledge management. *Journal of Universal Computer Science*, 3(8), 835-842, 1997.

Bouguettaya, A. (guest ed.), Ontologies and databases (special issue), *Distributed and Parallel Databases*, 7(1), 5-98, 1999.

Brachman, R. J. and Levesque, H. J., What makes a knowledge base knowledgeable? A view of databases from the knowledge level, in Kerschberg, L. (ed.), *Expert Database Systems*, 69-78, 1986.

Chandrasekaran, B., Generic tasks in knowledge-based reasoning: High-level building blocks for expert system design, *IEEE Expert*, 1(3), 23-29, June 1986.

Chaudhuri, S. (ed.), Special issue on databases and the World Wide Web, *Data Engineering Bulletin*, pp. 3-52, 21(2), 1998.

Chen, Z., Enhancing database management to knowledge base management: the role of information retrieval technology, *Information Processing and Management*, 30(3) 419-435, 1994.

Dean, T., Allen, J. and Aloimonos, Y., *Artificial Intelligence: Theory and Practice*, Benjamin/Cummings, Redwood City, CA, 1995.

Eich, M. (ed.), Special section on mian memory databases, *IEEE Transactions on Knowledge and Data Engineering*, 4(6), 507-571, 1992.

Floreskcu, D., Levy, A. and Mendelzon, A., Database techniques for the World Wide Web: A survey, *SIGMOD Record*, 27(3), 59-74, Sept. 1998.

Frakes, W. B. and Baeza-Yates, R. (eds.), *Information Retrieval: Data Structures and Algorithms*, Prentice-Hall, Englewood Cliffs, NJ, 1992.

Freundlich, Y., Knowledge Bases and Databases: Converging Technologies, Diverging Interests, *IEEE Computer*, 23(11), 51-58, 1990.

Garcia-Molina, H.L., Labio, W. J., Wiener, J. L. and Zhuge, Y., Distributed and parallel computing issues in data warehousing, *Proceedings of ACM Principles of Distributed Computing Conference,* 1999.

Giarratano, J. and Riley, G., *Expert Systems: Principles and Programming* (3rd ed.), PWS Publishing Co., Boston, 1998.

Harinarayan, V., Issues in interactive aggregation, *Data Eng. Bulletin,* 20(1), 12-18, 1997.

Inmon,W. H., *Building the Data Warehouse.* John Wiley, New York, 1996.

Kimball, R., *The Data Warehouse Toolkit,* Wiley, New York, 1996.

Korfhage, R., *Information Storage and Retrieval,* John Wiley, New York, 1997.

McDermott, J., Preliminary steps toward a taxonomy of problem-solving methods, Chap. 8 in Marcus, S. (ed.), *Automating Knowledge Acqusition for Knowledge Based Systems,* pp. 120-146, Kluwer, Boston, 1988.

O'Leary, D. E., Knowledge-management systems: Converting and connecting, *IEEE Intelligent Systems,* 30-33, May/June, 1998a.

O'Leary, D. E. Using AI in knowledge management: Knowledge bases and ontologies, *IEEE Intelligent Systems,* pp. 34-39, May/June, 1998b.

Ramakrishnan, R., *Database Management Systems,* WCB McGraw-Hill, Boston, 1998.

Schank, R. C., Issues for psychology, AI, and education: a review of Newell's Unified Theories of Cognition, *Artificial intelligence,* 59(1/2), 375-388, 1993.

Silberschatz, A., Korth, H. F. and Sudarshan, S., *Database System Concepts* (3rd ed.), McGraw-Hill, New York, 1996.

Sparck-Jones, K., Willett, P. and Larson, R. (eds.), *Readings in Information Retrieval,* Morgan Kaufman, San Mateo, CA, 1997.

Swartout, W. and Tate, R. (guest eds.), Ontologies, *IEEE Intelligent Systems & Their Applications,* special issue papers appearing in 14(1), 18-54, 14(2), 63-80, 14(3), 73-79, 14(4), 79-85, 1999.

Ullman, D. D. and Widom, J., *A First Course in Database Systems,* Prentice Hall, Upper Saddle River, NJ, 1997.

Wiederhold, G., Knowledge and database management, *IEEE Computer,* 17(1), 63-73, 1984.

Yang, Y. (guest ed.), Intelligent Information Retrieval, *IEEE Intelligent Systems & Their Applications,* 14(4), 30-69, 1999.

Chapter 6

CONCEPTUAL DATA AND KNOWLEDGE MODELING

6.1 OVERVIEW

In Chapter 5 we discussed data and information retrieval systems, as well as knowledge retrieval systems. The discussion given there was based on the assumption that data and information were already properly stored. Now we discuss the important issue of how to put data and knowledge into a system. This process starts with the task of conceptual modeling. The term *conceptual modeling* refers to the process of capturing semantics reflected in the design requirements. Conceptual modeling is the starting point of building agent-based systems. There are different aspects for different kinds of conceptual modeling. In the first part of this chapter (Sections 6.2 and 6.3) we discuss conceptual data modeling, with an emphasis on Entity-Relationship (ER) modeling and its relationship with object-oriented (OO) approaches. The remaining part of this chapter is devoted to conceptual knowledge modeling, as well as a discussion on knowledge representation and reasoning (KRR) from this perspective. Two specific structured knowledge representation schemes are discussed, namely, frames and conceptual graphs (along with its relationship with logic). Finally, we extend our discussion on modeling to a wider scope. Since users are always an important factor in the integrated problem solving process involving all parties (including intelligent agents and human beings), we close this chapter with a brief discussion on the issue of user modeling.

6.2 ENTITY-RELATIONSHIP DATA MODELING

6.2.1 WHAT IS THE ENTITY-RELATIONSHIP (ER) APPROACH?

The entity-relationship (ER) [Chen 1976] approach provides an effective way for conceptual modeling of data. (Actually, ER approach goes beyond database modeling, such as in software engineering, but we will not discuss this issue here.) The underlying idea is simple: Data can be described in terms of "things" and their connections. Consequently, there are two kinds of basic constructs in an ER model: *entity sets* consists of entities, as well as *relationship sets* connecting the entity sets. Both entity sets and relationship sets can be described by *attributes*. ER modeling typically makes use of *ER diagrams*. An ER diagram (ERD) is the graphical expression of the overall

141

logical structure of a database. In an ERD, each entity set is represented by a rectangle, each relationship set is represented by a diamond and is connected to associated entity sets by lines, and each attribute is represented by an oval.

6.2.2 A SIMPLE EXAMPLE

Consider a university database of student information, the courses offered, and the courses taken by individual students. Information recorded for students includes S-ID, name, major, etc. Information recorded for courses include call numbers, department offering this course, and the section of this course. For the time being, we will assume a course can have many students enrolled, but each student can only register for one course. The information for the date a course is taken is also recorded. Based on this design requirement, an ERD like Figure 6.1(a) can be developed to capture this mini-world. Note that an arrow has been used to denote the restriction that each student can only take one course.

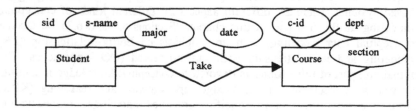

Figure 6.1 (a) An ER diagram

A shorthand form may be more convenient for drawing the ERD. In this shorthand form, rectangles, diamonds and ovals are replaced by squared brackets, acute brackets and parentheses, respectively. (Each weak entity set will be represented using double squared brackets, like [[child]].) We will refer this form of ERD as its *linear representation*. This form is particularly suitable for small, non-sophisticated ERDs. In the remaining part of this book we will stay with this form.

```
(s-id) (s-name) (major)        (date)       (c-id, dept, section)
         [student]   ———   <take>   →      [course]
```

Figure 6.1 (b) An ER diagram (in linear notation)

Although the ER approach seems to be simple, there are a lot of design issues to be considered. For example, we should decide which "things" should be treated as entity sets. Other issues should be considered including which attributes should go to the "student" entity set, which should go to the relationship set "takes," etc.

6.2.3 MAJOR CONSTRUCTS

We now discuss the major constructs involved in ER modeling in more detail. An *entity set* (i.e., a *strong entity set*) is a set of entities of the same type that share the same properties (or attributes). An entity is a thing or object in the real world that is distinguishable from all other things. Entity sets do not need to be disjoint. An entity is represented by a set of attributes.

A *relationship set* is a set of relationships of the same type. A relationship is an association among several entities. The degree of a relationship set is determined by the number of entity sets associated. Typically we have binary relationship sets, but we may also have n-ary relationship sets. A relationship set may have its own attributes (just like an entity set). An important aspect of a relationship set is the *mapping constraint* (namely, *cardinalities*):

- one to one (1:1) $\leftarrow\rightarrow$. For example, a student can only take one course and each course can only have one student. (Of course, this restriction is not realistic.)
- one to many (1:N) $\leftarrow$ For example, a student can take many courses, while each course can have only one student. (Again, not realistic in our current example.)
- many to one (N:1) $\rightarrow$. For example, many students can take one course, and each course can have many students.
- many to many (M:N) —. For example, each student can take one or more courses and each course may have more than one student. This is a reasonable assumption in our example.

The function that an entity plays in a relationship is called that entity's *role*. For example, a graduate student can play the role of either a student as well as an instructor.

Both entity sets and relationship sets are described by *attributes*. There are different kinds of attributes, such as simple versus composite attributes, single-valued versus multivalued attributes, null attributes and derived attributes (such as age being derived by date of birth and today's date). The collection of attributes is referred to as the *schema* (as we already discussed earlier in this chapter).

6.2.4 SOME IMPORTANT CONCEPTS

In relational databases, we have already learned concepts related to keys, such as candidate key or primary key. These concepts can be extended to entity-relationship models.

- *Keys for entity sets:* There are several different types of *keys* for entity sets (collection of attributes). They are different to search keys at file structures level, and are also different to each other.
  - *Superkey:* It uniquely identifies an entity in the entity set.
  - *Candidate key:* It is the minimal super key (attributes used as candidate key are usually underlined).
  - *Primary key:* It is the designated candidate key.

♦   *Foreign key*: It is a set of attributes that form the primary key of another relation.
- *Keys for relationship sets:* Primary keys for relationship sets are formed from primary keys of associated entity sets.
- *Existence dependency*: If the existence of entity x depends on the existence of entity y, then:
  - ♦   x is existence dependent on y;
  - ♦   Entity y is a dominant entity,
  - ♦   Entity x is a subordinate entity.
- *Total versus partial participation* of entity set E in relationship set R:
  - ♦   Total participation: every entity in E participates in at least one relationship in R (closely related to existence dependency).
  - ♦   Partial participation: only some entities in E participates in relationships in R.
- *Weak entity sets*: An entity set which does not have sufficient attributes to form a primary key. For example, the employees' dependents in a company database are reasonably treated as weak entities, because the dependents' information is included only because their existence would affect the benefit of the employees. The *discriminator* of a weak entity set is a set of attributes that distinguish among all the entities in the weak entity set. *The primary key of a weak entity set* is formed by the primary key of the strong entity set on which the weak entity set is existence dependent, plus the weak entity set's discriminator. A portion of an ERD involving a weak entity set "dependent" is depicted in Figure 6.2, where "dependent" is a weak entity set. The discriminator of this weak entity set is "d-first-name," and the primary key of the set "dependent" is the combination of e-id and d-first-name.

```
(e-id, e-first-name, e-last-name)          (p-id, dept-name)
      [employee] --- <participate> --- [project]
            ||                   (start-time)
         <<has>>
            ||
      [[dependent]]
      (d-first-name)
```

Figure 6.2 An ERD with a weak entity set

6.2.5 DESIGN ISSUES IN ER MODELING

The following is the general process of developing an ERD:
- Obtain data requirements;
- Entity sets designation;
- Relationship sets designation (refinement of entity sets designation)

Designing an ER diagram could be tricky. The following are some issues that need to be considered.
- Use an attribute or an entity set to represent an object?

- Use an entity set or a relationship set to represent a real world concept? (Note: The notions of an entity set and a relationship set are not precise.)
- Use binary relationship set or n-ary relationship set?
- Use a strong or weak entity set?
- Use extended ER features?

Readers are referred to [Elmasri and Navathe 1994] for a more detailed discussion on ER modeling, including a description of the Enhanced-ER model.

6.2.6 MAPPING ER DIAGRAMS INTO RELATIONS

ERDs can be converted to a form closely related to predicate logic, which is a relation. The general steps needed for converting an ERD to tabular format are stated below (an example can be found in Section 6.2.8). After the ERD is converted to the table format, relational database techniques (as described in previous chapters) can then be used.

- For strong entity set E:
  We represent E by a table with distinct columns; each column corresponds to one of the attributes of E. Each row corresponds to an entity of the entity set.
- For weak entity set A owned by strong entity set B:
  We represent it by a table with distinct columns; each column corresponds to one of the attributes of A or attributes of the primary key of B.
- For relationship set R (R does not link a weak entity set to its owner strong entity set):
  We represent it by a table with distinct columns; each column corresponds to one of the attributes in primary keys of associated entity sets or R's own descriptive attributes.
- For many-to-one relationship:
  For a N:1 relationship set R from entity set A to entity set B, if there is an existence dependency of A on B, combine the tables A and R.
- For multivalued attribute M:
  We create a table T with a column C that corresponds to M and columns corresponding to the primary key of the entity set or relationship set of which M is an attribute.

6.2.7 KEYS IN CONVERTED TABLES

Important to relational database design is the concept of key. We have already discussed various issues related to keys in Chapter 4. When the ER approach is used, primary keys and foreign keys in the converted tables can be determined from the primary keys in the corresponding constructs (entity sets or relationship sets) in the ERD. Examples for the following definitions can be found in Section 6.2.8.

Primary keys:

- Entity relation: The primary key of the entity set in ERD becomes the primary key of the entity relation.
- Relationship relation: The union of the primary keys of the related entity sets becomes a superkey of the relation. (Note here union refers to put together all the attributes in both primary keys.)

Foreign key: An attribute in a relation is a primary key of another relation.

6.2.8 AN EXAMPLE: A BANKING ENTERPRISE

6.2.8.1 Data requirements

We use an example to illustrate ER modeling and its conversion to table format. The example used here is a banking enterprise, which is similar to the one discussed in some other books (such as the one in [Silberschatz, Korth and Sudarshan 1997]). The most important feature of our treatment lies in the common treatment of knowledge and data. Since a relationship resembles a predicate, it would be beneficial to use a verb or a noun or an adjective as the name of a relationship. Also we will use the linear format to represent an ERD.

The data requirements for a banking enterprise are described below. The bank is organized into branches. Each branch is located in a particular city, and identified by a unique name. The assets of each branch are recorded. The bank offers accounts to customers. For each customer, his or her name, city and street information is recorded. Accounts can be held by more than one customer, and a customer can have more than one account. Each account is assigned a unique account number. The balance of each account is maintained. The bank also provides loans to customers. For each loan, a unique loan number is assigned and the amount of loan is maintained.

6.2.8.2 ER Diagram for banking enterprise

The ER diagram can be constructed as shown in Figure 6.3, with primary keys in entity sets underlined.

```
(a-no, bal)                          (b-name, b-city, assets)
        [account]  —<deposit> → [branch]
            |                        ↑
          <own>                  <approve>
        [customer]  —  <borrow>  —  [loan]
   (c-name, c-addr, c-city)      (l-no, amount)
```

Figure 6.3 The banking ER diagram

6.2.8.3 Converting to tables

Applying the conversion method described in the previous section, we obtain the following tables (each represents a relational schema). Note that while each entity set is converted to a table, only those relationship sets which do not involve a 1 to *n* mapping are converted into tables (otherwise they are "absorbed" into one of the associated entity tables). Primary keys are underscored.

>Account relation: <u>a-no</u>, balance, b-name
>Branch relation: <u>b-name</u>, b-city, assets
>Borrow relation: <u>c-name</u>, <u>l-no</u>
>Customer relation: <u>c-name</u>, c-addr, c-city
>Loan relation: <u>l-no</u>, amount, b-name
>Owns relation: <u>c-name</u>, <u>a-no</u>

Note that relationships "approve" and "deposit" are not converted to tables. Also note that b-name in both Account relation and Loan relation is a foreign key, because it is a primary key in Branch relation.

6.2.9 EXTENDED ER FEATURES AND RELATIONSHIP WITH OBJECT-ORIENTED MODELING

There are some well-known problems of ER modeling which have been used to lead to more advanced modeling techniques, including extended ER models and object-oriented models:

- *Specialization*: For example, in a university database, both instructors and students are specialization of "persons." Semantically, these two entity sets should have a closer relationship than relationship with other entity sets. The original ER modeling technique does not reflect this.
- *Generalization*: For instance, in the above example, "persons" is the entity set generalized from instructors and students. Common attributes such as Social Security Number, first name and last name, can be stored in the persons entity set. However, the original ER modeling technique does not support this.
- *Aggregation*. Another limitation of the ER model is that it is not possible to express relationships among relationships. For example, in a banking database, a customer may be both a depositor and a borrower, but according to the standard ER modeling technique, we have to treat "deposit" and "loan" as two separate activities.

Efforts have been made to enrich the ER model. However, most extensions are much less well known than the original ER modeling approach. In addition, these extensions have been overshadowed by object-oriented data modeling approaches (which have become increasingly popular). Loosely speaking, an object corresponds to an entity in the ER model. The object-oriented paradigm is based on encapsulating data and code related to an object into a single unit. Conceptually, an object communicates with the rest of the system by sending *messages* to invoke various *methods*. Because of this feature, object-oriented data modeling has a behavior part (in addition to the conventional structure part), with inheritance a strength of this kind of modeling. We will take a look at the issue of inheritance in Section 6.6 when we discuss frame systems.

One criticism of the ER approach is its lack of the behavior part (which is supported by object-oriented modeling approaches). Nevertheless, the simplicity of ER modeling makes it continuously a favorable tool in many applications.

6.3 REMARK ON LEGACY DATA MODELS

Historically, Entity-Relationship model was introduced to unify three existing logical models: relational, network, and hierarchical. We have studied relational data model in Chapter 3. In this section, a brief sketch of the other two models is provided.

Roughly speaking, the *network data model* is the ER model with all relationships restricted to be binary, many-one relationships. Entity sets are represented directly by logical record types with attributes as their fields. Binary, many-one relationships are kept; arbitrary relationships should be converted by creating new logical record types. We can use a simple directed graph model for data. Retrieving data requires users to write queries to express *how the links are navigated.*

The *hierarchical data model* can be considered as a special case of the network model. A hierarchy is a network that is a collection of trees in which all links point in the direction from child to parent.

The two query languages for network model and hierarchical model are sometimes considered as "object-oriented" because these languages support object identity, and thus present significant problems and significant advantages when compared with relational languages [Ullman 1989]. Queries in object-oriented data model may follow similar considerations as the network model, such as specifying navigation path.

Since object-oriented data model may be considered as the "current" data model, relational database systems sometimes are also considered as "legacy" systems. But in this book, we will not take this perspective. In fact, building data warehouses largely depends on relational data modeling techniques.

There are some reasons for studying legacy data models, including the following:

- *Data re-engineering:* In some cases, we have to re-implement legacy systems. In order to understand the data modeled in these systems, we have to learn legacy systems.
- *Building data warehouses:* It has been increasingly popular to build data warehouses for decision support queries. The source data used for building a data warehouse may be acquired from legacy databases. A good understanding of legacy systems is thus critical for the success of building data warehouses.
- *Object-oriented implementation:* In addition, as already implied in the brief discussion provided earlier in this chapter, legacy systems may shed light on learning object-oriented data modeling techniques.

6.4 KNOWLEDGE MODELING FOR KNOWLEDGE REPRESENTATION

Just like data modeling is concerned with how to conceptually view the data, knowledge modeling is concerned with how to conceptually view the knowledge to be represented. Of course, there is no "clear up" between data modeling and knowledge modeling. For example, while relational model captures the logical representation of data, an ER diagram, which roughly represents the schema of the corresponding relational model, can also be viewed as a primitive version of knowledge modeling. In fact, as we can see from the remaining part of this chapter, the underlying philosophy used in ER approach, namely, modeling the world using nodes and their connections, has been adopted and enhanced in modeling structural aspects of human knowledge.

Knowledge modeling serves as an intermediate step for knowledge representation and reasoning, because it is preferable to have the contents of the knowledge captured before the exact format of representation is determined. In this sense, knowledge modeling versus knowledge representation resembles abstract data types versus data structures, or conceptualization versus implementation. For example, we can use graphs or flow charts to acquire the knowledge needed for problem solving without considering how the acquired knowledge will be represented. At this stage, we are doing knowledge modeling. We can then further consider how to implement the acquired knowledge using production rules or other representation schemes (whichever is appropriate). Therefore, using knowledge modeling approach for building knowledge-based systems may be carried out through two steps: (a) capture the contents of knowledge (which can be assisted by knowledge modeling tools) and (b) select the appropriate knowledge representation scheme and convert the captured knowledge into that scheme. An example of using knowledge modeling to build a TV-troubleshooting expert system is described in [Lockwood and Chen 1994].

Knowledge modeling is important, because knowledge acquisition (which is crucial in knowledge engineering, as discussed in Chapter 5) is a modeling process, not merely an exercise in "expertise transfer" or "knowledge extraction." Various tools have been developed for knowledge modeling [Ford and Bradshaw 1993]. However, knowledge is at a higher conceptual level than data; unlike data modeling, so far there is no general consensus on how knowledge modeling should be. Since considerations behind structured knowledge representation schemes largely reflect concerns related to knowledge modeling, instead of focusing on knowledge modeling itself, a discussion on structured knowledge will follow.

6.5 STRUCTURED KNOWLEDGE REPRESENTATION

6.5.1 SOME IMPORTANT ISSUES INVOLVED IN KNOWLEDGE REPRESENTATION AND REASONING

Knowledge representation and reasoning is not a simple task. Many factors contribute to this complexity. Here we just give several examples to illustrate this point.

One factor is *granularity:* We have already learned several knowledge representation schemes. For both FOPL and production rules, they represent knowledge in small pieces, and thus support modularity and are easy to revise. However, they also suffer some problems such as the lack of "global" perspective and a leaning to cause inconsistency. In many applications, knowledge should be represented in a more structured manner. For example, pieces of information related to the same customer are preferably grouped together. *Structured knowledge representation schemes* (such as associative networks, frames and conceptual graphs) have been developed for this purpose. Note that the term "structured knowledge" used here is also called aggregated knowledge, but we will reserve the word "aggregation" to summary data (such as sum, average, etc.) as used in database management systems (discussed in Chapter 5 and to be further discussed in Chapter 11). Note also predicate expressions and productions rules themselves may also be called as "structured knowledge," mainly from researchers in neural network community, because they are more structured than subsymbolic representation, and can be obtained from machine learning algorithms applied on neural networks. However, in this book, we will only use the term "structured knowledge" in the sense described above.

Another issue is *nonmonotonic reasoning.* We briefly discussed this issue in the context of logic. However, there are other important aspects we have not addressed. A specific problem in nonmonotonic reasoning is *the frame problem,* which is concerned with how to represent change. In order to understand the importance of this problem in knowledge representation and reasoning, let us consider the following two scenarios. Suppose we have three apples on the table, and three birds in a tree. Now I have just taken one apple from the table and eaten it. I also have also used a gun to shoot a bird. Now consider the following retrieval problems (both require aggregating answers): How many apples remain on the table? Apparently it is two. How many birds on the tree? None -- because the other two birds are gone! Frame relations are rules to tell which predicates describing a state are not changed by rule applications and are thus carried over intact to help describe the new state of the world. Truth maintenance systems have been developed to deal with nonmonotonic reasoning in knowledge-based systems. Their task is to check the validity of knowledge stored in the knowledge base.

There are several general issues of knowledge representation and structured knowledge representation schemes. Knowledge representation schemes serve the role of "languages" at the symbol level. Desired features of

KR languages include the ability to do the following [Luger and Stubblefield 1998]:

a. Handle qualitative knowledge;
b. Allow new knowledge to be inferred from a set of facts and rules;
c. Allow representation of general principles as well as specific situations;
d. Capture complex semantic meaning; and
e. Allow for meta-level reasoning (see Chapter 14 for a brief discussion).

6.5.2 BASICS OF STRUCTURED KNOWLEDGE REPRESENTATION SCHEMES

To represent structured knowledge, we can represent knowledge as a graph, with *nodes* corresponding to facts or concepts, and *arcs* corresponding to relations or associates between concepts. Both nodes and links are usually labeled. Using network representations, we view knowledge as *organized* using explicit links or associations between objects in KB. There have been many proposals, focusing on either structures or actions, but for a long time, there has been a lack of "standard" network representation. However, recently, conceptual graphs have emerged as a potential candidate for this standardization.

In the remaining part of this chapter, we discuss frame systems and conceptual graphs. Both of these approaches can be considered as extensions of data modeling using an ER approach. Roughly speaking, frame systems put emphasis on extending the entity types (taking considerations as discussed in Section 6.2.9) to meet the requirements in object-oriented modeling, while conceptual graphs tend to represent the complexity of the world by extending the relationship types.

6.6 FRAME SYSTEMS

6.6.1 BASICS OF FRAMES

A frame is based on the metaphor of a single frame in a film. A frame system may be viewed as an alternative to network representations. We discuss frame systems through two levels: first individual frames, and then frame systems.

Frame contents (slots) include: an identifier; relationship with other frames; descriptors of requirements for frame match; procedural information; default information; new instance information (unspecified at beginning) and others. Examples of frames will be shown in the next section when the issue of inheritance is discussed.

Frame systems extend semantic networks in a number of important ways. They provide a much clearer picture than semantic networks themselves. Frames add to the power of semantic nets by allowing complex objects to be represented as a single frame, rather than as a large network structure.

6.6.2 CLASSES, SUBCLASSES AND INSTANCES

Parallel to the development of frame languages has been the development of object-oriented programming languages (OOPL). Due to the popularity of object-oriented concepts, in this section we present some key concepts in frame systems by connecting them with object-orientation. Frame systems and OOPLs are quite similar, differing primarily in emphasis. An object-oriented programming language is viewed as a practical programming language able to compete with standard programming languages, whereas a frame system representation tends to be either a research tool or a language to be used in the construction of intelligent information systems and to facilitate reasoning in these systems.

Since object-oriented paradigm has gained much popularity, here we will only summarize In order to fully support the needs of object-oriented paradigm, a programming language should support capabilities of encapsulation, polymorphism and inheritance. Object-oriented *encapsulation* is unique in that it combines both data items and the methods or procedures used for their manipulation into a single structure, called a *class*. A class is a set of object instances with shared features. Methods or procedures characterize the behavior of a class. A method is *polymorphic* if it has many different behaviors, depending on the types of its arguments. Associated with the concept of the class is *inheritance,* which is a mechanism for supporting class abstraction in a programming language, as well as in a knowledge representation scheme. A class can inherit properties from its *superclass(es);* these properties, along with the properties owned by this class itself, can be inherited by its *subclasses.*

Frames have many similarities with classes, but also some differences. For example, both classes and instances can be represented by frames and the difference is not reflected in the definition of frames. In the following, we will examine issues related in inheritance in frame systems.

6.6.3 INHERITANCE, MULTI-LEVEL AND MULTIPLE INHERITANCE

6.6.3.1 Inheritance in frame systems

Inheritance allows a frame to inherit properties from its parent. Frames can be connected through class-subclass relationships to form a *frame system.* As indicated earlier, the notion of frame does not distinguish its use of a frame as a class or an instance. In this context, we will assume that inheritance will occur between classes, although we do allow that instances inherit properties from the class they belong to. One important thing we should know about inheritance is that it is not mandatory; in fact, a subclass (or an instance) can override some of the properties of the class it belongs to. This is advantageous in many real-world situations, where we may not be able to assign all the initial values of properties for a new subclass or instance. We may set up default values for these properties, because these values may be overridden later. Note that the overriding feature involved in inheritance gives frame systems the power of nonmonotonic reasoning (see Chapter 3). The Prolog code for implementing a frame system will be provided in Chapter 8.

6.6.3.2 Multiple inheritance

The definition of inheritance allows a property of a class to be inherited by its subclasses, then the subclasses of the subclasses, and so on. In general, we have *multiple-level of inheritance*. On the other hand, subclass may not necessarily inherit all the properties from the same parent class; in other words, a subclass may have several classes as its parents. In this case, we have a *multiple-inheritance*. It is important to keep in mind that multiple inheritance is not multiple-level of inheritance.

A sample frame system is depicted in Figure 6.4 on the next page. To distinguish an object instance from a class, we will use a double-bordered box indicate an instance. In this figure, the pick-up class inherits the property "number of wheels" with values 2 to 10 from class "vehicle" through multi-level inheritance. Note also the pick-up has two parents "car" and "truck," so there is a multiple-inheritance as well. Note that in case there is more than one parent, inconsistency may occur. For example, the values for the property "passenger" are different from car and truck, so there is a need to assign the value of the property "passenger" for pick-ups.

6.7 CONCEPTUAL GRAPHS

6.7.1 WHAT IS A CONCEPTUAL GRAPH?

In this section, we discuss conceptual graphs (CGs) in the context of conceptual modeling. It is important to note, however, that some other factors had impact on CG, such as Logic, Natural Language Processing (NLP), to name a few.

A CG is a finite, connected, bipartite graph. The nodes of the graph are either concepts or conceptual relations; each node is connected to the other kind of node. The following are some basic definitions:

- *Concept* node: It is represented as a box. A concept can be either a concrete or abstract entity. A concept node connects to conceptual relations. A concept node may represent an individual or a type.
- *Conceptual relation*: It is represented as ellipses connecting concepts and plays the role of a labeled arc. Although usually it connects two concept nodes (and is thus binary), it could be an n-ary relation.

Note that CGs do not use labeled arcs; instead the conceptual relation nodes represent relations between concepts.

There is an interesting connection between conceptual graphs (CGs) and ERDs. Historically, CGs have outgrown from ERD and extended its power of data modeling to knowledge representation. Consequently, we may view an ERD as a restricted form of CG and the linear form developed for CGs can thus be borrowed. We may note that concepts in CG resemble concepts in

ERDs while conceptual relations resemble relationship sets. However, the similarity stops here, because the CGs do not have the stored data associated with concepts and conceptual relation nodes. Therefore, the similarity between CGs and ERDs does not go beyond the data schema level.

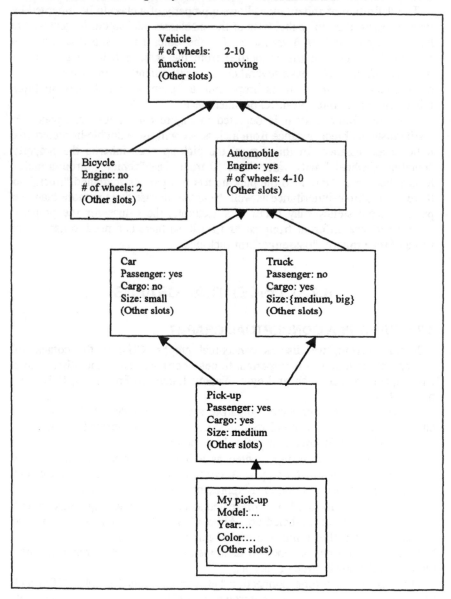

Figure 6.4 A frame system

6.7.2 USING LINEAR FORM TO REPRESENT CONCEPTUAL GRAPHS

Let us consider the following example: "Tom donated a computer to Aksarben College." The conceptual graph is shown in Figure 6.5(a).

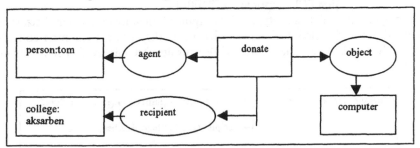

Figure 6.5(a) A conceptual graph

Similar to the case in an ER diagram, the linear form of conceptual graph is easier to present as text. A concept node is represented by a pair of squared brackets while a conceptual relation is represented by a pair of parentheses. The linear form equivalent to the above conceptual graph is depicted in Figure 6.5(b).

```
          [person:tom] ← (agent) ← [donate] → (object) → [computer]
                                          |
     [college:aksarben] ← (recipient) ← |
```

Figure 6.5 (b) A conceptual graph in linear form

How to construct a conceptual graph? Although there are no simple rules, in many cases conceptual graphs can be constructed by organizing concepts and conceptual relations around some "key" activities (which are usually verbs). For instance, in the above example, the conceptual graph is constructed around the verb "donate" (which is a conceptual node), and other conceptual nodes, such as person, computer and college, reflect different aspects of the activity "donate."

6.7.3 OPERATIONS

The following operations defined on CGs can be viewed as rules, but they are not inference rules:

- *Simplify*: It allows deletion of duplicated relations.
- *Copy*: This is the operation for duplicating a CG.
- *Restriction:* It allows concept nodes in a graph to be replaced by a node representing their specialization. A type label is replaced by an individual or subtype; note the similarity with object-oriented considerations.

- *Join*: It combines two CGs sharing some concept node into one CG. This operation may be done through restriction. This operation can be compared to natural join in relational algebra (Chapter 3).

Now consider a conceptual graph in linear format:

[ibmPC] → (price) → [$2000]

Suppose ibmPC is a subtype of "computer;" then this graph can be joined with the one depicted in Figure 6.5(b), since they share a common concept node "ibmPC." The linear form of the result after join is shown in Figure 6.5(c).

[person:tom] ← (agent) ← [donate] → (object) → [ibmPC] → (price) →[$2000]

⊢→ (recipient) → [college:aksarben]

Figure 6.5 (c) A conceptual graph after join

The combined results indicates that Tom donated to Aksarben College an IBM PC which is worth $2000.

6.7.4 LOGIC-RELATED ASPECTS

6.7.4.1 Propositional node

Conceptual graphs employ propositional nodes to handle issues in logic. A propositional node is a kind of high level node -- that is, a node itself may be a graph. For example, consider the statement "John believes that Tom donated a computer to Aksarben College." Here "believes" is a relation that takes a proposition as an argument. To deal with such needs, conceptual graphs include a concept type called proposition that takes a set of conceptual graphs as its referent and allows us to define relations involving propositions. A propositional concept is indicated as a box that contains another conceptual graph. These proposition concepts may be used with appropriate relations to represent knowledge about propositions. The statement "John believes that Tom donated a computer to Aksarben College" can thus be represented in the form shown in Figure 6.6.

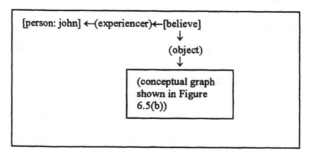

Figure 6.6 A conceptual graph with propositional node

- *Negation.* Propositional nodes allow us to express negation. For example, if we want to indicate "IBM PC is not priced at $2000," Figure 6.7 illustrates how this can be done.

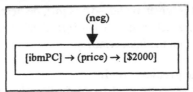

Figure 6.7 Propositional node with negation

- *Quantifier.* When we discussed basics of Prolog in Chapter 3, we pointed out although Prolog does not use quantifiers explicitly, variables appearing in both head and body are universally quantified while variables appearing in body alone are existentially quantified. Conceptual graphs do not explicitly use quantifiers either. In fact, it has been established that variables in conceptual graphs are existentially quantified. So what should we do if we want to use universal quantifiers? Since negation can be handled by using propositional nodes, by utilizing deMorgan's law as discussed in Chapter 3, we should be able to express variables which are universally quantified.
- *Modal logic.* Furthermore, conceptual graphs with propositional nodes may be used to express the modal concepts of knowledge and belief. For a brief discussion on modal logic, see [Turner, 1984].

6.7.4.2 Inference rules

It is important to point out that the operations discussed above are *not* inference rules. For example, the join operation simply combine relevant information together; the result is simply a combination of facts rather than inference. However, inference rules do exist, as shown below. We also use examples to show how inference can be carried out (we assume *u* and *v* are two conceptual graphs). Our presentation follows [Patterson 1990]. For more detailed discussion on conceptual graph inference rules, please see [Sowa 1984].

- *Erasure.* Any conceptual graph enclosed by an even number of negations may be erased. Suppose w is a conceptual graph; it can be erased from the consequent of an implication ¬[u ¬ [v]] to derive . ¬[u w ¬ [v]]
- *Insertion.* Any conceptual graph may be inserted into another graph context which is enclosed by an odd number of negations. Suppose w is a conceptual graph, it can be inserted into the consequent of an implication ¬[u ¬[v w]] to derive ¬[u ¬ [v]].
- *Iteration.* A copy of any conceptual graph C may be inserted into a graph context in which C occurs or in which C is dominated by another concept.
- *De-iteration.* Any conceptual graph which could be the result of iteration may be erased from a conceptual graph context.

- *Double negation.* A double negation may be erased or drawn before any conceptual graph or set of graphs.

An interesting aspect is that de-iteration and double negation are equivalent to modus pones. That is, given p and $\neg[p \neg [q]]$, de-iternation permits erasure of p inside the first bracket to get $\neg [\neg [q]]$. Double negation then permits erasure of $\neg [\neg]$ to obtain the final result q.

6.7.4.3 Converting to predicate logic

Conceptual graphs are equivalent to predicate calculus in their expressive power. There is a straightforward mapping from conceptual graphs into predicate calculus notation. The following is an algorithm for converting a conceptual graph g into a predicate calculus expression. (Our presentation follows [Luger and Stubblefield 1998].)

1. Assign a unique *variable* to each of the *n generic* concepts in g.
2. Assign a unique *constant* to each *individual* concept in g.
3. Represent each concept node by a unary predicate with the same name as the type of that node and with the variable or constant assigned in step 1 or 2 as its argument.
4. Represent each n-ary conceptual relation in g as an n-ary predicate whose name is the same as the relation. Let each argument of the predicate be the variable or constant assigned to the corresponding concept node linked to that relation (the order may follow the direction of the arrows).
5. Take the conjunction of all atomic sentences formed in steps 3 and 4. Attach an existential quantifier to each variable.

For example, the sample conceptual graph can be converted to logic as follows.

1. Generic concepts are "donate" and "computer." We assign X and Y to these two concepts, respectively.
2. Individual concepts are "person" and "college." We assign the two constants "tom" and "aksarben" to these two concepts, respectively.
3. Represent concept nodes as follows:
   donate(X)
   computer(Y)
   person(tom)
   college(aksarben)
4. Represent conceptual relation as following:
   agent(X, tom)
   object(X, Y)
   recipient(X, aksarben)
5. Take the conjunction and attach the quantifier, we obtain the following result:

$$\exists X \ \exists Y \ (\text{donate}(X) \ \wedge \ \text{computer}(Y) \ \wedge \ \text{person(tom)} \ \wedge$$
$$\text{college(aksarben)} \ \wedge \ \text{agent}(X, \ \text{tom}) \ \wedge \ \text{object}(X, Y) \ \wedge$$
$$\text{recipient}(X, \text{aksarben}))$$

6.7.5 REMARKS ON SYNERGY OF FRAME SYSTEMS, CONCEPTUAL GRAPHS AND OBJECT ORIENTATION

We summarize our discussion on conceptual graphs (and frame systems) by providing the following remarks on object orientation. Historically, the development of frame systems closely parallel object-oriented programming. (Note that the term frame used here is not necessarily closely related to the term frame as in the frame problem.) Roughly speaking, frame systems are more appropriate in representing structures while conceptual graphs are more appropriate in representing actions (as well as in natural language representation). The knowledge represented by frame systems may also be represented by a conceptual graph (and vice versa), but the frame system representation may be more appropriate.

In the previous section we have already discussed the close relationship between frame systems and object-oriented approaches. We have just mentioned the relationship between frame systems and conceptual queries. We now point out considerable similarity is also encountered between the object-oriented formalism and the conceptual graph formalism. There seems to be a one-to-one relationship between the notion of class in object orientation and the notion of type in conceptual graphs.

6.8 USER MODELING AND FLEXIBLE INFERENCE CONTROL

So far in this chapter we have examined various issues related to data modeling and knowledge modeling. Intelligent agents and knowledge workers share the same problem-solving environment that is modeled by using the discussed techniques. It is important to note, however, that knowledge workers and other human users are also an integrated part of this environment. This consideration leads us to take a brief look at *user modeling* from the perspective of computer-user symbiosis -- a desirable environment for decision support. In the following, we briefly discuss flexible inference control from the perspective of user modeling, and introduce some important terminology.

There is a need for more flexible styles of inference and control over the strategies used for guiding the order of inferences in knowledge-based systems. One choice is to attach a scheduler in inference engine that enables explicit decisions to be made about which actions are to be taken (for example, which rules to apply, whether to use forward or backward chaining, and so on). The main consideration is to provide flexible inference control to reduce the work of search in knowledge bases. We briefly examine two application areas.

There are some common considerations behind real-time expert systems. In order to provide timely response, most approaches have imposed a restricted manner of searching, namely, to restrict the portion of knowledge base to be searched. The difference is only in how to get this done. In the *designated inference engine approach,* each inference engine only processes a particular kind of data, so that only part of the knowledge base will be searched by a particular inference engine. Some other approaches rely on *meta-level reasoning* and change of focus in searching. The term "meta-level inference" means "inference performed at one level is concerned about another level." To assure flexibility, some degree of domain-dependent control has also been introduced. A discussion on meta-level inference control can be found in [Chen 1993a], and a related issue on participatory design can be found in [Chen 1993b].

We now give a brief remark on user environments, user modeling, system adaptability and perturbation models. The four items mentioned here are all concerned with the role of users in flexible inference control, but each has its unique focus. For example, the flexible inference control may be needed in different circumstances or environments in which users use the system (which is referred to as *user environments).* Flexible inference control is also justified from the perspective of different user groups of user models. This discussion leads to the issue of system adaptability.

Another interesting concept is the *perturbation model.* According to the theory of perturbation models, each user is assumed to have a mental model similar to the domain model (the "true" model of the system), differing only in certain perturbations to the domain model. To support such kind of system adaptability, flexible inference control is needed. A more radical approach of flexible inference control requires the user's participation of reasoning. A brief discussion on this issue can be found in Chapter 14.

SUMMARY

In this chapter we have covered a wide-range of issues related to data and knowledge modeling. The materials presented in Chapters 4, 5 and 6 are closely related to each other. When we build and access an information system, we take the following order: conceptual modeling for data/knowledge representation, design of the system, implementation and retrieval. In this chapter we discussed issues related to conceptual modeling. In addition, we pointed out the importance of user modeling in the computer-human symbiosis.

SELF-EXAMINATION QUESTIONS

1. A travel agency wants to keep tracking its customers (including those who just have inquires only). For people who are travelling together, a group number is assigned. (A person who travels alone will be considered as a group.) For each traveler in the group, his or her name, address and occupation are recorded. For each travel, the tour identifier, the place of departure, the destination, and the departure date are recorded. Draw an ER diagram for the travel agency database.
2. Suppose we want to represent the knowledge of travel agency (as described in Problem 1) using the conceptual graph approach. Compare the resulting representation with the ERD obtained in Problem 1.
3. In Problem 2, instead of using a conceptual graph, suppose a frame system is used. Do you think this is a better choice? Give your comments.
4. Draw a conceptual graph indicating "All basketball players are tall."

REFERENCES

Chen, P., The Entity Relationship Model -- Toward a unified view of data, *ACM Transactions on Database systems*, 1(1), 9-36, 1976.

Chen, Z., User modeling for flexible inference control and its relevance to decision making in economics and management, *Computational Economics*, 6, 163-175, 1993a.

Chen, Z., From participatory design to participatory problem solving, *AI & Society*, 7(3), 238-247, 1993b.

Elmasri, R. and Navathe, S. B., Fundamentals of Database Systems (2nd ed.) Redwood City, CA: Benjamin/Cummings, 1994.

Ford, K. M. and Bradshaw, J. M., Introduction: Knowledge acquisition as modeling, *International Journal of Intelligent Systems*, 8(1), 1-7, 1993.

Lockwood, S. and Chen, Z., Modeling experts' decision making using knowledge charts, *Information and Decision Technologies*, 19, 311-319, 1994.

Luger, G. F. and Stubblefield, W. A., *Artificial Intelligence: Structures and Strategies for Complex Problem Solving* (3rd ed.), Addison-Wesley Longman, Harlow, England, 1998.

Patterson, D. W., *Introduction to Artificial Intelligence & Expert Systems,* Prentice Hall, Englewood Cliffs, NJ, 1990.

Silberschatz, A., Korth, H. F. and Sudarshan, S., *Database System Concepts* (3rd ed.), McGraw Hill, New York, 1998.

Sowa, J. F, *Conceptual structures: information processing in mind and Machine,* Addison-Wesley, Reading, MA, 1984.

Turner, R., *Logics for artificial intelligence,* Chichester: E. Horwood, 1984.

Ullman, J., *Principles of database and knowledge-base systems* (Vols I and II), Computer Science Press, Rockville, MD, 1989.

Chapter 7

REASONING AS EXTENDED RETRIEVAL

7.1 OVERVIEW

In the last two chapters we discussed different kinds of retrieval systems. As already indicated earlier, the purpose of discussing them in parallel is aimed at integrated use of these systems for decision support. We have also noted that retrieval in knowledge-based systems is different from data retrieval, because the former is actually a reasoning process. In this chapter we continue to examine the relationship between retrieval and reasoning, but from a different perspective. Our emphasis is on the *boundary* between these two. The *interplay* between knowledge reasoning and data retrieval can be achieved by *viewing retrieval as an extreme of reasoning and vice versa*. We start with a brief review on several cases of this blurred boundary. Analogical reasoning is used as an example to illustrate the connection between retrieval and reasoning. Much of the rest of this chapter is devoted to a computer model (called the COGMIR model) which illustrates the concept of reasoning as extended retrieval.

7.2 BEYOND EXACT RETRIEVAL

7.2.1 SOME FORMS OF NON-EXACT RETRIEVAL

The various kinds of retrieval systems discussed in the last two chapters can be characterized as *exact retrieval*, because the answers produced in these systems are either previously stored (in the cases of database and information retrieval) or derived on demand based on what was stored (in the case of knowledge retrieval). However, there are many situations where retrieval should be handled in a more flexible manner. If there is no exact match to a user's query, an approximate answer may be better than no answer at all. In addition, as we will see soon, non-exact, or approximate answers may have some other interesting aspects which exact retrieval may not possesses. The tricky thing here is that the word "approximate" may have different meanings. In the remaining part of this section, we provide several examples to illustrate what the non-exact retrieval means and what the advantages are.

We start with fuzzy queries in databases. Fuzzy set theory will be discussed in later chapters, and here we just want to raise questions instead of solving them. Roughly speaking, fuzzy set theory has been developed to deal with vagueness. A fuzzy query interface to a relational database allows giving fuzzy terms as values for the attributes, which are not stored in the relational database. An example of such a query is to retrieve company names which have made large profit in the first quarter of 1999. In this query, "large profit" is a fuzzy concept, because profits are usually stored in numerical numbers. Another approach in fuzzy information retrieval is to build fuzzy databases. There are several different approaches toward creating fuzzy databases, such as:

(a) The fuzzy database as an extension to a relational database.
(b) Possibility-distribution relational databases.
(c) Modular fuzzy databases, which consists of three parts: (1) the value database which is same as (b); (2) the explanation database, which contains the definition of the fuzzy terms, and is subject to update depending on the particular applications; and (3) conversion rules for processing modifiers and qualifiers.

There are many other forms of non-exact retrieval, and some of them involve the use of analogical reasoning. Analogical reasoning is pervasive in human reasoning. Briefly, analogical reasoning assumes that if two situations are known to be similar in some respects, it is likely that they will be similar in others. So if two brands of CD boom boxes have the same quality and are made in places with cheap labor, you may expect they should have similar price. Analogical reasoning has been studied extensively by computer scientists for many years. For example, the Copycat project (by Douglas Hofstadter and his research group [Hofstadter 1995]) is a computer program intended to be able to discover insightful analogies in a psychologically realistic manner. This research is a continuation of Hofstadter's original research goals set up during the late 1970's, namely, to uncover the secrets of creativity, and to uncover the secrets of consciousness, by modeling both phenomena on a computer.

Analogical reasoning can play an interesting role in non-exact retrieval, and here is a simple example. Suppose a relational database has information for average housing prices for a number of selected cities in the United States. Now a user wants to know the average housing price in Omaha but it is not available. A retrieval system with analogical reasoning ability may suggest the user try, say, Lincoln or Wichita. Here is why: Lincoln is close to Omaha and is in the same state of Nebraska, so their property values should be similar. And why Wichita? Because just like Omaha, it is also located in the heartland of the country, and it has the similar size of Omaha. Analogical reasoning is also useful in *text mining*, where analogy is used for guiding meta-data search [Soto 1998]. As a real-world example, according to CBS Morning Business Report (Jan. 18, 1999), Robert Morrow has 37 patterns for solving vibration problems in engineering. He has utilized his expertise to predict vibration in markets with great success.

Due to the importance of analogical reasoning for approximate retrieval, in the next subsection we provide a brief discussion on analogical reasoning.

7.2.2 BASICS OF ANALOGICAL REASONING

According to the popular computational model of analogy [Gentner 1983], the two analogs involved in analogical reasoning are referred to as the source and the target. The *source* of an analogy is a problem solution, example, or theory that is relatively well understood. The *target* is only partly known. Analogy constructs a mapping between corresponding elements of the target and the source. Analogical inferences extend this mapping to unknown or missing elements of the target. Note that the source and the target are usually in different knowledge domains. For example, consider the "electricity is like water" analogy. Here "water" is the source, which is in the domain, say, of hydrodynamics; and "electricity" is the target, which is in the domain, say, of electrodynamics. Since electricity was a new concept in the 19th century, the knowledge of water and hydrodynamics had greatly helped human beings to understand this new concept. For example, if we know that this analogy maps switches onto valves, amperage onto quantity of flow, and voltage onto water pressure, we may reasonably infer that there should be some thing similar to the capacity (i.e., the cross-sectional area) of a water pipe; this could lead to an understanding of electrical resistance [Luger and Stubblefield 1998].

We will get back to the issue of relationship between retrieval and reasoning, and discuss the role of analogical reasoning in this exploration. But before we leave, we give a brief remark on two related reasoning or learning approaches.

1) *Case-based reasoning.* In order to solve problems or answer questions using analogical reasoning, one important issue is how to effectively and efficiently retrieve source analogs. *Case-based reasoning* (CBR) is closely related to analogical reasoning (and can be used in combination with analogical reasoning) because it employs an explicit knowledge of problem solutions (referred to as cases) to address new problem-solving situations. Therefore, CBR provides an effective way to retrieve solutions of previously solved problems, and to adapt this solution to the current problem by mapping the old solution to a new one. For more detail of CBR, please see [Kolodner 1993].

2) *Explanation-based learning.* Analogical reasoning can be considered as a species of single instance induction. In contrast, *explanation-based learning* (EBL) also performs learning based on a training example, but uses deductive method. EBL uses an explicitly represented domain theory to construct an explanation of a training example, usually a proof that the example logically follows from the theory. By generalizing from the explanation of the instance, rather than from the instance itself, EBL organizes training data into a systematic and coherent structure.

7.3 REASONING AS QUERY-INVOKED MEMORY RE-ORGANIZATION

7.3.1 REASONING AS EXTENDED RETRIEVAL

In this section we describe a computer model based on the notion of reasoning as extended retrieval. The underlying philosophy of this exploration is based on the following observation given by [Frisch and Allen 1982]. Knowledge retrieval must respect the semantics of the representation language and is therefore inference. A query is a request for the retriever to attempt to infer a specified sentence of the representation language. The knowledge base module should perform only those inferences for which it has adequate control knowledge to perform efficiently. Knowledge retrieval is thus a limited form of inference operating on the stored facts. We should note that although viewing retrieval as limited inference is important, it is mainly a performance issue regarding computer implementation. The *inverse* side of this statement is equally important, which is concerned with the notion of viewing inference as an extension of retrieval. In fact, it reveals that when retrieval goes beyond a certain threshold, it may *become* reasoning. In the following, we examine this model and provide examples on how it works. We also examine the role of memory organization in the integrated task of retrieval and reasoning.

7.3.2 STRUCTURE MAPPING FOR SUGGESTION-GENERATION

Research work has been conducted to support analogical problem solving or achieve creativity support systems through computerized metaphor generation. In the following, we describe a model as well as an experimental system (both will be referred as COGMIR, which stands for a Cognitive Model for Information Retrieval) [Chen 1996].

This model deals with storage and retrieval of short scientific documents written in restricted English defined by simple grammar. The model consists of the following components. There is a document space (or document base) D, which is the conceptual place to store the documents. There is also a knowledge space (or knowledge base) K (consisting of nodes connected by links) which is the actual place to store the knowledge converted from the documents. Each acquired document is assigned a unique sequential identifier, is converted to its internal form (called document stem) and then stored in a global knowledge base. Each document stem occupies a certain area in the knowledge base; each area is confined by its own boundary. A system component called document description list (or keyword list) L identifies the boundaries of the document stems. The system also consists of a conceptual memory, which is a hierarchically structured thesaurus used for indexing of documents. Finally, the system consists of a set of mapping functions M between various system components. In summary, the COGMIR model consists of the following basic components:

D - Document base (also called document space)
K - Knowledge base (also called knowledge space)
C - Conceptual memory (extension of indexing by combining a hierarchical thesaurus)
L - Document description list
Q - Queries

This computational model provides dual modes for dealing with queries. If information is available to answer the user's request (in terms of keywords), a document (or a *fact* consisting of portions of several documents) is reconstructed from its internal form in the knowledge base (called document stem), and presented in the text format to the user. This is *the regular mode*. In case the requested information is not available, the user may use *the analogy mode* to ask the system to *generate* a document using analogical reasoning. This generated document may serve as a *suggestion* or *an advice* to the user. One option to consider here is to map the keywords in the query list submitted by the user to another list. Since both the document description list and the query description list consist of objects, if a suggestion is to be generated using analogy reasoning, it has to be done by mapping of objects only. A pseudo-fact is a document-like unit containing a portion which is generated through structure mapping. This model thus provides a detailed solution for analog retrieval for generating suggestions. For example, the system may have no knowledge about how to detect an enemy plane. But if it has knowledge (in one document or several documents) about bats' behavior, it is able to use this analogy to construct a pseudo fact for the user, and suggest producing a "sound-like" thing for people to detect an enemy plane.

The components of the system, as well as an overview on the general pseudo-fact generation process in our computational model (as well as in the experimental system) are depicted in Figure 7.1.

7.3.3 DOCUMENT STORAGE AND RETRIEVAL THROUGH RELATIONAL DATABASE OPERATIONS

Although COGMIR was designed as a system for intelligent information retrieval, it was implemented as an unstructured database residing in the main memory. Therefore, its implementation demonstrates aspects from both database systems and conventional information retrieval systems. Some features of this implementation are highlighted below.

7.3.3.1 Conversion of documents into unstructured databases

The model was implemented using Prolog with some restrictions, such as documents must be written following a small set of grammatical rules. The motivation of imposing these restrictions is to avoid technical difficulties while still demonstrating the usefulness of our model. The parser converts these documents into items to be stored in the knowledge base.

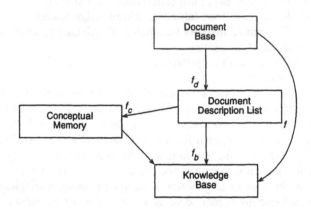

Figure 7.1 The COGMIR model for storage and retrieval

There are two basic constructs in the knowledge base: objects and relationships. Relationships indicate how the objects are associated, and objects indicate what relationships are associated with them. All the data structures are represented in terms of Prolog lists. Lists can be nested, and the contents of a list are put in squared brackets. The conversion (i.e. parsing) from document to document stems (consisting of objects and relationships) is done through the system function f (which works like a parser). In the following, we will only discuss the representation issue.

Representation objects. An object can be attached to an attribute list as well as other associate lists. Each object is represented by a tuple written in list form. Each object tuple has the following format:

$$[L, [N], [A], [R_L]],$$

where L is the unique location of the object in the knowledge base, N is the name of the object, A is an attribute list, and R_L represents the location of related relationships in the knowledge base (notice that an object may be associated with several relationships).

Representing relationships. We will consider binary relationships only. (If a relationship is not binary, it will be first converted to several binary relationships by the parser. However, in this book, we will not address this issue.) A relationship name is a verb or verb phase. Each relationship takes the form of a tuple with the following format:

$$[L, [N], [A], [A_r, A_e]],$$

where L is the unique location of the relationship in the knowledge base, N is the name of the relationship, A is an attribute list, A_r is the location of the first object associated with the relationship, and A_e is the location of the second object associated with the relationship.

For instance, the sentence (in restricted English) "the scientist discovers capillaries" can be presented by two sublists in the object list and one tuple in the relationship list. In the object list, we have

[115, [scientist], [], [116]],
[117, [capillaries], [], [116, 118, 120]]]

The meaning of the first item is: an object, 'scientist,' is stored at memory location 115, does not have its own attributes, and is associated with a relationship stored at memory location 116. The second item represents an object, 'capillaries,' which is stored at location 117, does not have its own attributes, and is associated with relationships stored at location 118 and 120.

In the relationship list, we have

[116, [discovers], [ ], [115,117]]

This item represents a relationship, 'discover,' and is stored at memory location 116. This relationship represents an action taken by the object stored at location 115, with an object stored as location 117 as the receiver of this action.

These lists can be viewed as relational databases with fixed fields of attributes. Therefore, the underlying structure of the knowledge base resembles relational databases. All the objects list can be considered a tuple in a relation. All the object tuples form a relation *object*, which has fixed fields. L, N, A, R. One difference that must be noted here is that the sublists are ordered according to the location numbers assigned to objects or relationship; while for relational databases, tuples are not ordered. But this kind of order just imposes some additional restrictions on the relations, and the standard relational operations such as select or union can be adopted with only minor revisions (as explained in the next subsection). Each sublist in the relationship list can also be considered a tuple in a relational database. All the relationship tuples form another relation, *relationship*, which has fixed fields, L, N, A, A_r, A_e. Notice that unlike the relations discussed in Chapter 4, these relations are *schema-free*, because they represent unstructured data [Motro 1986]. In these relations, the meaning of the *key* of a relation should be explained as the location of an object or a relationship in knowledge base.

Representation document stems. A *document stem* consists of object tuples along with some relationships between these objects. In other words, a document stem is the collection of related object tuples and relationship tuples. A document stem has the following format:

[O, R],

where O is its object list and R is its relationship list.

Therefore, a document stem is implemented as a relation. Similarly, other system components, such as the concept memory, form a relation, as does the document description list. But in our approach, instead of a tabular form, a list form is used, due to the considerations from Prolog language. By mapping the input documents into a frame-like list representation, which is much more regular than that in the original documents, the power of manipulating a regular, homogeneous structure, such as that demonstrated in a relational database, is adopted.

A document stem with O and R as its object list and relationship list, respectively, can then be expressed as $(\delta^{(O)}, \delta^{(R)})$, or $\delta^{(O,R)}$ for short (the superscripts are used to denote its associated object list and relationship list). We will also use the notation $r^{(O)}$, $r^{(R)}$, $r^{(O,R)}$ to denote the relations that implement $\delta^{(O)}$, $\delta^{(R)}$, or $\delta^{(O,R)}$, respectively.

As a comprehensive example, consider the documents (written in restricted English) in Figure 7.2(a). The correspondent object list and relationship list of their document stems are shown in Figure 7.2(b); each can be viewed as a relation, and each row in a list can be viewed as a tuple in that relation.

1.. the arteries carry blood from the heart, the veins carry blood to the heart.
2. a bat emits sound, the sound is inaudible. an obstacle reflects the sound, the obstacle is invisible. the bat detects the obstacle.
3. a scientist discovers the capillaries. the capillaries connect the arteries. the capillaries connect the veins.

(a) Several documents

Object list:	Relationship list:
[101, [arteries], [], [102],	
[103, [blood], [], [102]],	[[102, [carry], [], [101, 103]],
[105, [heart], [], [104]],	[104, [to], [], [103, 105]],
[106,[veins], [], [107]],	[107, [carry], [], [106, 103]],
[109, [bat], [], [110,114]],	[108, [from] , [], [103, 105]],
[111, [sound], [inaudible], [110,112]],	[110, [emits], [], [109, 111]],
[113,[obstacle], [invisible], [112,114]],	[112, [reflects], [], [113, 111]],
[115, [scientist], [], [116]],	[114, [detects], [], [109, 113]],
[117, [capillaries], [], [118,120]],	[116, [discovers], [], [115, 117]],
[119, [arteries], [], [118]],	[118, [connect], [], [117, 119]],
[121, [veins], [], [120]]].	[120, [connect], [], [117, 121]]].

(b)

Figure 7.2 (a) Original documents (b) Corresponding document stems in knowledge base

7.3.3.2 Document algebra: an algebra on document stems and relations

Document storage and retrieval in such a system is done through the various components of the system. In the following, we define *document algebra* to handle documents that are operated as relations. Essentially, document algebra is an extension of relational algebra discussed in Chapter 4. But first, we should notice that there is a need to distinguish operations at two levels: the higher level of document stems, and the lower level of relations.

Operations on document stems. We start with the following remark. Since the relations used in the COGMIR model are schema-free, some operations originally defined on conventional relations become meaningless. Unlike conventional relational databases, we have only two relations to handle: the object relation and the relationship relation. Therefore, the join operation as defined in conventional relational database now does not make sense. In addition, since both the object relation and the relationship relation have fixed attributes, project operation as defined on conventional relational database will not be of interest. Based on these considerations, we will not include join and project as operations in our implementation. On the other hand, the concept of document stem is new, and no previous definitions have been given on the document stems. Therefore, we will borrow the names project and join, to redefine these two operations on the document stems (rather than relations).

Project. A document (or its correspondent document stem) relevant to a query does not necessarily imply the entire document is relevant to that query. The operation $\pi_q(\delta)$, that is, project operation over a query q for a document stem δ, is to exclude, from that document stem, those object tuples and relationship tuples that are not relevant to q.

Join. The join operation connects two document stems if they share an object with the same name. The join of two document stems δ_i and δ_j (here i, j are two document identifiers and $i < j$) is denoted as $\delta_i \bowtie \delta_j$. This operation is very important in our model, since separately acquired information stored in different document stems can be connected. A note to be made here is the role of the document identifier in the join operation of document stems; they are used as *time stamps* of the corresponding documents, because they are assigned according to the order in which they are acquired by the system. Although better methods may be desirable, in the current implementation, we have assumed documents acquired earlier record things which happened earlier. In the current implementation, $\delta_i \bowtie \delta_j$ is not defined if $i > j$.

Operations on relations. Operations defined on document stems are *conceptual* operations; the purpose of defining these operations is to provide a convenient way to envision the system behavior. These operations are actually performed through operations defined on relational databases, because the object list and relational list resemble relations. We will use the following operations on schema-free relations.

Select. The select operation $\rho_q (R)$ selects tuples (rows) relevant to query q from the schema-free relation R. This operation is much like the standard select operation; the only exception is to keep the selected tuples in their original order. For instance, we can select one or more rows (i.e., tuples) from any of the two lists in Figure 7.2(b).

Union. The union of two schema-free relations R_1 and R_2 is denoted as $R_1 \cup R_2$. This operation is much like the standard union operation on relations, except for the requirement of keeping the original order to tuples in two relations. Therefore, in general, $R_1 \cup R_2$ cannot be replaced by $R_2 \cup R_1$. For instance, we can perform the union operation on two or more rows (tuples) selected from the above operation.

The major step of performing retrieval from several documents can be expressed as below. As already stated, we will use the notation $\delta^{(O, R)}$ to denote a document stem with object list O and relationship list R. In the following, we will also use the notation $\delta_q^{(O, R)}$ to denote a document stem with object list O and relationship list R in answering query q. if q_s and q_t are two subqueries of the original query q, $q_s \cup q_t = q$ (where $\cup$ denotes set union), if we define the answer for the union of two queries as the union of the answers of these two queries, namely,

$$\delta_{(qs \cup qt)}^{(O)} = \delta_{qs}^{(O)} \bowtie \delta_{qt}^{(O)}$$

then we have

$$\delta_q^{(O)} = \delta_{(qs \cup qt)}^{(O)} = \delta_{qs}^{(O)} \bowtie \delta_{qt}^{(O)}$$
$$= \pi_{qs} (\delta^{(O)}) \bowtie \pi_{qt} (\delta^{(O)})$$

(due to the definition of projection on document stems and the meaning of query), and

$$= \sigma_{qs} (r^{(O)}) \cup \sigma_{qt} (r^{(O)})$$

(due to the definitions of selection and union on unstructured relations). Similarly, we have

$$\delta_q^{(R)} = \delta_{qs}^{(R)} \bowtie \delta_{qt}^{(R)}$$
$$= \pi_{qs} (\delta^{(R)}) \bowtie \pi_{qt} (\delta^{(R)})$$
$$= \sigma_{qs} (r^{(R)}) \cup \sigma_{qt} (r^{(R)}).$$

The above two formulas can be combined to

$$\delta_q^{(O,R)} = \delta_{qs}^{(O,R)} \bowtie \delta_{qt}^{(O,R)}.$$

Note that *the join* ($\bowtie$) *of document stems* δ_{qs} and δ_{qt} is realized through *the union of tuples* in schema-free relational databases. The union operation will be performed only when $\delta_{qs} (O)$ and $\delta_{qt} (O)$ share some common object name. In our implementation, an auxiliary list of object names is constructed for each involved document stem ($\delta_{qs} (O)$ and $\delta_{qt} (O)$); the intersection of these two lists is then checked to determine whether any object name is shared.

In summary, when dealing with a retrieval, first, relevant document stems are identified through **L** and **C**. The remaining steps are carried out by using the following four formulae:

$$\delta_{qs}^{(O)} = \sigma_{qs}(r^{(O)}), \tag{1}$$

$$\delta_{qs}^{(R)} = \sigma_{qs}(r^{(R)}), \tag{2}$$

$$\delta_{q(s \cup t)}^{(O)} = \delta_{qs}^{(O)} \bowtie \delta_{qt}^{(O)} = \sigma_{qs}(r^{(O)}) \cup \sigma_{qt}(r^{(O)}), \tag{3}$$

$$\delta_{q(s \cup t)}^{(R)} = \delta_{qs}^{(R)} \bowtie \delta_{qt}^{(R)} = \sigma_{qs}(r^{(R)}) \cup \sigma_{qt}(r^{(R)}). \tag{4}$$

The meaning of these formulae can be shown in the following example. Consider the knowledge base depicted in Figure 7.2(b), and suppose the objects specified in a query are a set q = {capillaries, heart}. Figure 7.3(a) is basically a duplication of Figure 7.2(b), with rows (tuples) from different documents separated by blank lines. (Identifying tuples from different documents is handled by the document description list, but the details will not be addressed in this article.) Document description list **L** and conceptual memory **C** determine that only document stem δ_1 and δ_3 are relevant to the query q. Figure 7.3(b) depicts relevant document stems (which include only those tuples that are relevant to the current query q). The result of performing a select operation on relations is shown in Figure 7.3(c), where tuples are in the relevant documents but those not directly related to the current query (namely, tuples that correspond to "a scientist discovers the capillaries") are excluded. This is done by applying formulae (1) and (2). Starting from Figure 7.3(c), we now apply formulae (3) and (4), where q_s = {heart} while q_t = {capillaries}. The object names involved in two document stems are {arteries, blood, heart, veins} and {capillaries, arteries, veins}, respectively. Since these two document stems share object names {arteries, veins}, the union of tuples can be performed, resulting in Figure 7.3(d). From this resulting document stem, a *fact* in restricted English can be reconstructed. (Here the term *fact* is used in the same sense as the term "fact retrieval" has appeared in IR literature, which refers to a part of the contents.)

Notice that the two occurrences (with two different memory location numbers, 106 and 121) of object 'vein' as it appears in two documents are treated as one thing, and so are the two occurrences of the entity 'arteries' (with two location numbers, 101 and 119). *Sharing object names is a necessary condition for performing the join operation.* As a result, the following fact can be constructed to answer the query {heart, capillaries}:

arteries carry blood to heart. vein carries blood to heart.

capillaries connect arteries. capillaries connect veins.

Note that, although this short paragraph looks like a document, it is not. Instead, it is generated from the document stems that contain contents relevant to the query.

Object list:	Relationship list:
[101, [arteries], [], [102],	
[103, [blood], [], [102]],	[[102, [carry], [], [101, 103]],
[105, [heart], [], [104]],	[104, [to], [], [103, 105]],
[106,[veins], [], [107]],	[107, [carry], [], [106, 103]],
[109, [bat], [], [110,114]],	[108, [from] , [], [103, 105]],
[111, [sound], [inaudible], [110,112]],	[110, [emits], [], [109, 111]],
[113,[obstacle], [invisible], [112,114]],	[112, [reflects], [], [113, 111]],
[115, [scientist], [], [116]],	[114, [detects], [], [109, 113]],
[117, [capillaries], [], [118,120]],	[116, [discovers], [], [115, 117]],
[119, [arteries], [], [118]],	[118, [connect], [], [117, 119]],
[121, [veins], [], [120]]].	[120, [connect], [], [117, 121]]].

Figure 7.3 (a) Document stems (knowledge base containing δ_1, δ_2, δ_3)

Object list:	Relationship list:
[101, [arteries], [], [102],	
[103, [blood], [], [102]],	[[102, [carry], [], [101, 103]],
[105, [heart], [], 104]],	[104, [to], [], [103, 105]],
[106,[veins], [], [107]],	[107, [carry], [], [106, 103]],
[115, [scientist], [], [116]],	[108, [from] , [], [103, 105]],
[117, [capillaries], [], [118,120]],	[116, [discovers], [], [115, 117]],
[119, [arteries], [], [118]],	[118, [connect], [], [117, 119]],
[121, [veins], [], [120]]].	[120, [connect], [], [117, 121]]].

Figure 7.3 (b) Document stems relevant to the query (δ_1, δ_3)

Object list:	Relationship list:
[101, [arteries], [], [102],	
	[[102, [carry], [], [101, 103]],
[103, [blood], [], [102]],	
	[104, [to], [], [103, 105]],
[105, [heart], [], [104]],	
	[107, [carry], [], [106, 103]],
[106,[veins], [], [107]],	
	[108, [from] , [], [103, 105]],
[117, [capillaries], [], [118,120]],	
	[118, [connect], [], [117, 119]],
[119, [arteries], [], [118]],	
	[120, [connect], [], [117, 121]]].
[121, [veins], [], [120]]].	

Figure 7.3 (c) Document stems after projection through select operation on relations [using formulae (1) and (2)].

Object list:	Relationship list:
[101, [arteries], [], [102],	
	[[102, [carry], [], [101, 103]],
[103, [blood], [], [102]],	
	[104, [to], [], [103, 105]],
[105, [heart], [], [104]],	
	[107, [carry], [], [106, 103]],
[106,[veins], [], [107]],	
	[108, [from] , [], [103, 105]],
[117, [capillaries], [], [118,120]],	
	[118, [connect], [], [117, 119]],
[119, [arteries], [], [118]],	
	[120, [connect], [], [117, 121]]].
[121, [veins], [], [120]]].	

Figure 7.3 (d) Join of document stems through union operation on relations [using formulae (3) and (4)]

From the above simple example, we have seen that the operations are not trivial. In order to see why these nontrivial operations are needed, let us summarize some features of the overall system by associating system components (other than the knowledge base) to the retrieval process. First , let us recall that conceptual memory identifies relevant document stem. The boundary consists of only part of object names; starting from the boundary, the interior of the document stem can be examined by processing a portion of the object list and relationship list.

Implementing knowledge base as an unstructured database with necessary operations defined on it has some significant merit over the use of a plain "sentence base" consisting of all sentences acquired from documents. This is partly because, in our model, the conceptual memory will identify document stems that are relevant to the current query; only a portion of the knowledge base (instead of the entire "sentence base") will be searched. This will represent a significant saving when the number of document stems becomes large. Storage using object tuples and relationship tuples actually implements a net-like structure.

This net-like structure clearly indicates which relationships are related to an object. Determining the connection between different document stems through objects is thus much easier than directly checking the sentences one by one, particularly when the number of sentences that need be checked becomes large. In addition, due to the net-like structure (implemented as tuples), our system is able to generate new documents through structure mapping (using information concurrently available in the knowledge base), thus realizing a kind of analogical reasoning. Document generation through structure mapping might be a more difficult problem if a "sentence base" (rather than the knowledge base consisting of object and relationship tuples) is maintained.

There are also some limitations of this implementation, such as documents being acquired in the order of the events (as described by these documents) that occur; documents with larger identifiers are acquired later, thus containing more updated information; the event which occurred or information contained in a document with a larger identifier may update those in a document with a smaller identifier, but may not be consistent (namely, contradictory) with them.

These assumptions have caused some limitations on our experimental system. Some limitations related to the management of the unstructured databases used in the experimental system are listed below.

1. *Order requirement of join.* As stated earlier, two document stems δ_i and δ_j can only be joined to form a resulting document stem $\delta_i \bowtie \delta_j$ if they share at least one object name and $i < j$. In this case, $\delta_j \bowtie \delta_i$ is not defined, and consequently, the relationship $\delta_i \bowtie \delta_j = \delta_j \bowtie \delta_i$ is not true. The rationale of this requirement is due to assumption (i); consequently, in the result after join, knowledge contained from the document acquired later always appears later, even though it may be concerned with some earlier event.

2. *Simplified treatment for partially redundant documents.* Due to the above assumptions (i), (ii), and (iii), if two document stems contain redundant information, the information contained in the document with the larger identifier will always be used.

3. *The need for dealing with inconsistency.* Current implementation simply assumes that inconsistency does not exist. Therefore, even if a document contains information which is contradictory to an existing one, the implemented system cannot detect it.

All these limitations can be removed or reduced to a lesser degree, although the tasks may not be trivial. For instance, in order to remove limitation 3, we may add an independent component which employs an advanced computational technique (such as the approach described in [Baral, Kraus and

Minker 1991]) so that only consistent information will be included in the final result.

7.3.4 GENERATING SUGGESTIONS

7.3.4.1 Basic idea and an example

The overview given in the last section indicates that our computational model provides dual modes to deal with user queries. On the one hand, if information requested by the user is available, a document is reconstructed from its internal form (called the *document stem*) in the knowledge base and presented in the text format to the user. This is the *regular* mode which is already briefly described in the previous section. On the other hand, in case the requested information is not available, the user may use the *analogy* mode to ask the system to *generate* a document using analogical reasoning. This generated document may serve as a *suggestion* or *advice* to the user. One option to be considered here is to map the keywords in the query list submitted by the user to another list. For example, if the user wants to know how people deal with planes dispatched by enemies, he may submit a query "people, enemy, plane." Suppose no relevant document is found. Since both the document description list and the query description list consist of objects, if a suggestion is to be generated using analogy reasoning, it has to be done by mapping of objects only. However, as we have briefly summarized in an earlier section, at the heart of the structure mapping theory is the mapping of *relationships* among these objects. Such structure information is not implied in the query consisting of keywords "people, enemy, plane"; it must be explicitly stated. In other words, in order to perform structure mapping, it is not enough for the user to simply enter a few keywords. A reasonable way to deal with this situation is to ask the user to provide some help. Although the user does not have the answer (otherwise he will not consult the system), he can still provide some information concerning the relationship between the objects to be retrieved. For example, he can tell the system what he knows, namely, the enemies have dispatched a plane and the plane is not visible; he should also tell the system what he wants to know, that is, how to detect the planes. The system can acquire such structural information by asking the user to enter this query in a form similar to a document, but with some missing information to be filled. By doing so, the user describes the structure of the target analog; the system can then find one or more source analogs (i.e., document stems) from which structure mapping can be performed to generate a new structure so that the missing information in the target analog can be filled. The target analog, since it takes the form of a regular document, will be referred to as an *incomplete* document. Just like a regular document, an incomplete document is written in restricted English, but it differs from a regular one in that it contains unknown information to be answered. An incomplete document always has a sentence appearing at the end, started with a word "how" and ended with a question mark ("?"). In our example, the incomplete document takes the following form:

the enemy dispatches a plane.
the plane is invisible.
How do people detect the plane?

The last sentence of an incomplete document indicates an *unknown part*, while the other sentences form the *known part* of the incomplete document (the known part is similar to a regular document). An incomplete document and its correspondent incomplete document stem will be denoted as d^- and δ^-, respectively.

Now let us consider the entire process of suggestion generation. Suppose the user wanted to retrieve a document for detecting an enemy's plane. He used the regular retrieval mode by providing several keywords but no relevant document could be retrieved. Then he had to switch to the mode of analogical reasoning. In order to let the system find a structurally similar document, the user provided an incomplete document as shown above. To answer this query, the system formed a query description list from this incomplete document. In the simplest case, the query description list could be obtained by taking the first object (noun) of each sentence; in this example, it consists of "enemy, plane, people." What the system would perform is not to retrieve a document (or a fact) consisting of the words in the query description list, but rather, a document (or a fact) which consists of words *similar* to the query description list and contains a portion which has the *same structure* with the known part of the incomplete document. The retrieved document (or fact) also contains a portion that does not have a counterpart in the incomplete document. The incomplete document can then be *filled* by mapping this portion into the domain which the incomplete document belongs to. A new document in the target domain is thus generated, which provides a suggestion to the user. If the user is satisfied with it, it can be further stored as a regular document.

Back to our example, assuming that the document concerning the bat is a document acquired by the system earlier, which has the *structure similarity* with the incomplete document, and can thus be used as a source (base) analog. This document will be retrieved. For convenience of our discussion, the document is repeated below.

a bat emits a sound.
the sound is inaudible.
an obstacle reflects the sound to the bat.
the obstacle is invisible.
the bat detects the obstacle.

The incomplete document itself, on the other hand, becomes part of the target analog. With the help of the conceptual memory, the system determines the similarity between the incomplete document and this existing document. Using a structure mapping algorithm (detail will be provided later), the system will generate the following document as a *suggestion* to fill the incomplete document originally provided by the user:

the enemy dispatches a plane.
the plane is invisible.

people emits [sound-like].
the [sound-like] is inaudible.
the plane reflects [sound-like] to the people.
people detects plane.

The third, fourth and fifth sentences (italicized) in the above document are generated by the computer. Here a word in the pair of squared brackets [ ] indicates a new object generated through structure mapping. For example, the object [sound-like] is an object generated from the object "sound"; it means "something similar to the sound."

As illustrated by this example, document generation using analogical reasoning is the process of *filling* an incomplete document stem $\overline{d}$ (i.e., the internal structure of the incomplete document provided by the user). This can be denoted as

$$\delta = \delta_0 \bowtie \psi,$$

where δ is the completed document by filling $\overline{\delta}$, δ_0 is the known part of $\overline{\delta}$ and ψ is the generated part through structure mapping, and $\bowtie$ is the join operation of δ_0 and ψ. Since document stems are nodes and links in the knowledge bas, both δ_0 and ψ can be treated as document stems.

In the previous incomplete document, we have $= \delta^0$:

the enemy dispatches a plane.
the plane is invisible.

and the generated part is ψ:

people emits [sound-like].
the [sound-like] is inaudible.
the plane reflects [sound-like] to the people.

In general, the known part δ_0 consists of more sentences, thus having a more complicated structure. This example is made simple so that the structure of the document can easily be visualized (as indicated in figures later in this chapter).

Since the last few sentences are generated rather than retrieved, they are not necessarily *true* knowledge; in other words, they just form a *suggestion* to the user. In this example, these generated sentences suggest that in order to detect the enemy plane (as submitted in a user request), people may use some thing which is similar to the inaudible sound (as used by a bat) so that the invisible plane will reflect the sound to the people. This is of course a highly simplified reproduction of invention of radar (which is a device to produce inaudible sound for detecting distant objects).

7.3.4.2 Steps for analogical problem solving

We now describe the steps for performing document structure mapping in our computational model in terms of a general framework as summarized in [Burnstein 1988]. The framework provides a process theory of analogical reasoning consisting of six stages:

1. Base domain memory retrieval;

2. Comparison of base and target models;
3. Mapping a partial model from the base to the target;
4. Justification and integration of the mapped model;
5. Debugging the target model;
6. Generalization of shared structure.

COGMIR implemented the first three steps. Among these three stages, the first stage is also the most critical one. The last few steps were not considered because the model treats a newly generated document (namely, the filled incomplete document) in the target domain as a *suggestion* or possible solution produced from the system's currently available knowledge, leaving the responsibility of determining the quality of the suggestion to the user. If the suggestion is acceptable, upon the user's request, the system will store it as a regularly required document.

According to the structure mapping theory, objects and relationships in the source (or base) domain are mapped into the target domain. In our computational model, we consider the structure mapping from a source analog (consisting of one or more stored documents) to a target analog (which is a *pseudo-fact*). A pseudo-fact (where the term "fact" is used in the sense defined earlier) is a document-like unit containing a portion which is generated through structure mapping.

In the implementation, parsing an incomplete document is similar to parsing a regular document. The internal form of the incomplete document (the document stem) is stored in a *temporary area* separated from the knowledge base. Each object or relationship is assigned a negative integer as its sequential location number (instead of a positive one, as used in the knowledge base), so that the incomplete document and the generated structure will not be mixed with the actual knowledge base. However, a procedure exists so that upon the user's request, the pseudo-fact can be converted as a regular document and is then stored in the knowledge base.

An overview on the general pseudo-fact generation process in this computational model (as well as in the experimental system) is depicted in Figure 7.4.

7.3.4.3 Structure mapping for generating suggestions

We now provide some detail on structure mapping for generating suggestions. Since the basic idea of document mapping can be clearly illustrated in the case of source analog consisting of only one document, the discussion will be mainly around the case of using single document. The entire process of suggestion generation is to be performed as two steps: construct a document stem Δ as the source analog, followed by a mapping and structure generation process $\phi\Delta$.

As indicated in the previous section, parsing an incomplete document is similar to parsing a regular document. A little more detail is given below. A description list for this incomplete document (which will be referred to as a *query description list*), is constructed in the same way as for a document description list. In order not to let the basic idea become mixed with technical difficulties involving natural language processing, the following simplified treatment has been taken. If a sentence is a regular sentence, this list is constructed from the first noun of each sentence. On the other hand, if a sentence is a question, we first change the sentence from the original form into one consisting of an object with unknown name "?" and a relationship with unknown name "?". The document stem converted from the incomplete document is stored in the temporary area separated from the knowledge base. There will be a sequential location number, but it will be indicated by a negative sign (instead of a positive one, as used in the knowledge base).

We now consider the general process of using analogical reasoning to generate suggestions. The basic idea of structure generation in the system can be explained in the case where the structure to be mapped is from a single document. In this case, the pseudo fact is generated by mapping a document to the incomplete document.

The heuristic used in generating new structure is that since the structure as described in two documents is similar in part, it is reasonable to expect that the rest of their structures should also be similar. The entire process of generating document (which serves as a suggestion) is performed in two phases: find a source analog (which is fact constructed from stored document stems), and then map this source analog to generate a new document. Unlike the retrieval in the regular mode, in the analogy mode what to be retrieved is not precisely specified in the original query; rather, the task is to retrieve a document which is structurally similar to the query.

We use the term *object similarity* to refer to the similarity between an object in the incomplete document and an object in the source analog. Object similarity is determined by using conceptual memory and attribute similarity. We use the symbol $a \sim b$ to denote object similarity between two objects a and b. We also use the term *document similarity* between two documents. Object similarity is used in document similarity, but the similarity between relationships in these two documents is of fundamental importance in determining document similarity. This is compatible with Gentner's principle of systematicity of structure mapping theory [Gentner 1983], as briefly mentioned in Section 1.2. Relationships in the two document stems (referred to as *relationship pairs*) are considered similar if they have exactly the same name or carry the same semantic information using auxiliary rules (a topic which will not be addressed here). We use the symbol $d_1 \cong d_2$ (or $\delta_1 \cong \delta_2$) to denote similarity between two documents d_1 and d_2 (or their corresponding document stems δ_1 and δ_2).

Both object similarity and document similarity can be numerically determined and are controlled by a predefined threshold. Since the purpose of this paper is to explain the basic idea of structure mapping, details are omitted here. Some key ideas of a top-level algorithm for document structure mapping are summarized below.

1. Convert the incomplete document (whose document stem is δ_0) into internal form (in a temporary area). Identify the objects on the query description list. Suppose the query description list is $Q = (q_1, q_2, \ldots, q_n)$.

2.   Retrieve (with the assistance of the conceptual memory) a document or a fact which satisfies the following requirements:

- The document to be retrieved satisfies the query description list $Q' = (q'_{r1}, q'_{r2} \ldots q'_{rm})$ $(m \leq n)$, $q_1 \sim q'_{r1}$, $q_2 \sim q'_{r2}, \ldots, q_m \sim q'_{rm}$. This is to construct a list Q' consisting of words similar to Q and use Q' instead of Q itself to retrieve relevant documents.
- The document stem of the retrieved document δ' satisfies $\delta' \cong \delta_0$. This is to retrieve a document which is structurally similar to the incomplete document.
- Construct structure mapping function Φ based on similarity between δ_0 and δ': $\Phi: \delta' \rightarrow \delta_0$,

so that $\delta_0 \subset \Phi(\delta')$. (Here the notation $\subset$ indicates that δ_0 is contained in $\Phi(\delta')$.) As stated earlier, δ' can be considered as consisting of two parts δ'_0 and ψ'. (each can be considered as a document stem): $\delta' = \delta' \bowtie \psi'$. where δ'_0 satisfies $\delta_0 = \Phi(\delta'_0)$. Here $\bowtie$ denotes the join operation of two document stems (the operation on document stems was defined in [Chen 1994]).

- Perform structure mapping to generate new structure to fill the incomplete document: $\psi_* = \Phi(\psi_*)$.

In the steps described above, it is important to determine the object similarity and document similarity. The object similarity sim is determined by applying the following rules:

1.   If two objects have the same name, then they are treated as the instances of the same object; assign $sim = 1$.
2.   If two objects have the same parent in the hierarchical conceptual memory, assign $sim = W$ $(0 \leq W \leq 1)$. If in the hierarchical conceptual memory, one object is the parent of the other object, assign $sim = W'$ $(0 \leq W' \leq 1)$. Both W and W' are some constants indicating certain degrees of similarity; for example, they can be assigned as 0.6 and 0.5, respectively.
3.   Compute similarity based on the ratio of attributes shared by both objects. For example, if the object "ship" has attributes "people-mover," "big" and "in-water," and the object "car" has attributes "people-mover," "big" and "in-land," then two out of three attributes are shared by both objects. Therefore, sim (ship, car) is 2/3 or 0.67. Similar rules have also been developed to deal with two objects which have a different number of attributes.
4.   If none of the above rules are applicable, then assign $sim = U$ (for unknown). The purpose of assigning U for some pairs is to give a chance to the pairs whose similarity cannot be decided immediately.

In addition, relationships in these two document stems (also called relationship pairs) are considered similar if they have exactly the same name,

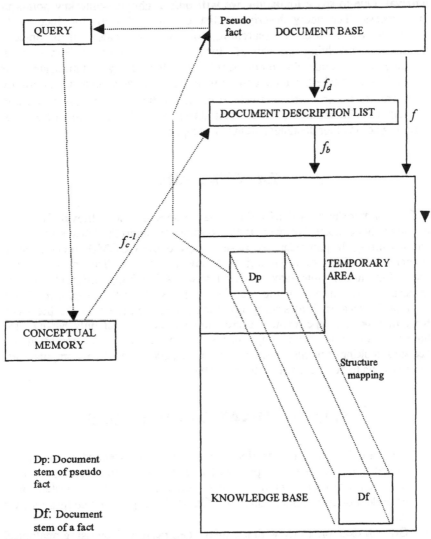

(Note: Solid lines indicate operations related to storage: dashed lines indicate operations related to query) (f, f_b, f_d, f_c^{-1} denote mappings)

Figure 7.4 Overview of pseudo-fact generation process

or if they can be treated as similar by using additional heuristic rules (such as relationships "like" and "love"). Based on the notions of object similarity and relationship similarity, the similarity between two parts of document stems can be determined. In general, the overall similarities between two document stems are the minimum similarity among all the involved object pairs and relationship pairs as stated above.

The search process in the conceptual memory is revised from regular retrieval. Due to space limitation, we will only highlight some key points in this process. The query description list constructed from the incomplete document will be used for searching; for each candidate pair of objects, relationships involving this pair of objects will be compared. Furthermore, compute the overall document similarity after every relationship pair comparison is checked, and the comparison is aborted as soon as the similarity is determined under a certain threshold η. Repeat the same process by starting to compare different objects on the boundaries of the two document stems, or choosing some other document stems to compare.

7.4 SUMMARY

This chapter started with a brief discussion on non-exact retrieval. The main theme of this chapter, however, is to examine the interplay between retrieval and reasoning. In particular, we have reviewed the COGMIR model, which supports the notion of reasoning as extended retrieval. This perspective is useful for building integrated retrieval systems involving different kinds of retrieval. However, we should also be cautious about this approach. Some important issues, such as scaling up, were never mentioned in the literature. Nevertheless, the experiment deserves some attention, not only because the holistic perspective concerning retrieval and reasoning is important for decision making, but also because of the aspects related to computational creativity, as to be discussed in the next chapter.

SELF-EXAMINATION QUESTIONS

1. What are the pros and cons of viewing retrieval as extended reasoning?
2. In order to carry out an experiment to remove a human tumor, a doctor designed a machine which is able to remove seeds from a watermelon. Provide a brief discussion on how COGMIR can generate suggestions for this.
3. Give an example to show that a query can be solved by using analogical reasoning but cannot be answered by COGMIR as described in this chapter.
4. What are the major differences between reasoning as extended retrieval as discussed in this chapter with knowledge retrieval discussed in Chapter 5?

REFERENCES

Baral, C., Kraus, S. and Minker, J., Combining mulitiple knowledge bases, *IEEE Transactions on Knowledge and Data Engineering,* 3(2), 208-220, 1991.

Burnstein, M. H., Combining analogies in mental models, in Helman, D. H. (ed.), *Analogical Reasoning,* Kluwer, Dordrecht, 1988.

Chen, Z., Reasoning as extended retrieval: document generation through structure mapping, *Communication and Cognition - Artificial Intelligence (CC-AI),* 10(4), 343-356, 1993.

Chen, Z., Enhancing database management to knowledge base management: the role of information retrieval technology, *Information Processing and Management,* 30(3), 419-435, 1994.

Chen, Z., Generating suggestions through document structure mapping, *Decision Support Systems,* 16(4), 297-314, 1996.

Frisch, A. M. and Allen, J. F., Knowledge retrieval as limited inference, *Proceedings of the 6th Conference on Automated Deduction* (Lecture Notes in Computer Science), Loveland, D. (ed.), 274-291, 1982.

Gentner, D., Structure mapping: A theoretical framework for analogy, *Cognitive Science,* 7, 155-170, 1983.

Hofstadter, D. (and the Fluid Analogies Research Group), *Fluid Concepts and Creative Analogies: Computer Models of the Fundamental Mechanisms of Thought,* Basic Books, New York, 1995.

Kolodner, J. L., *Case-Based Reasoning,* Morgan Kaufman, San Mateo, CA, 1993.

Luger, G. and Stubblefield, W., *Artificial Intelligence: Structures and Strategies for Complex Problem Solving* (3rd ed.), Addison Wesley Longman, Harlow, England, 1998.

Motro, A., Assuring retrievability from unstructured databases by contexts, *Proceedings of International Conference on Data Engineering (ICDE 86),* 426-433, 1986.

Soto, P., Text mining: Beyond search technology, *IBM Systems Journal,* 3(3), 14-19, 1998.

Chapter 8

COMPUTATIONAL CREATIVITY AND COMPUTER ASSISTED HUMAN INTELLIGENCE

8.1 OVERVIEW

The COGMIR model as examined in Chapter 7 is an example of how computational creativity can be achieved. In fact, creativity is an important aspect of intelligence, and intelligent agents should be able to support creativity in decision making. In this chapter we will take a look at this issue and its importance with decision support. Our discussion will be focused on the following two tasks: *computational creativity* (that is, how to make computers demonstrate some kind of creativity), and *computer assisted human intelligence* (that is, how to make computers assist human creativity). These are two related issues, but with different emphases. For example, the former task is closely related to the study of computational intelligence, while the latter one is more closely related to human-computer interaction (HCI).

8.2 COMPUTATIONAL ASPECTS OF CREATIVITY

8.2.1 REMARKS ON CREATIVITY

Most researchers have agreed that creativity is generally defined as the production of something (e.g., a scientific theory, work of art, poem, novel, etc.) which is both novel and valuable according to consensual judgment. Rothenberg studied creativity, connecting it with dream, and designated the process of actively formulating simultaneous antitheses *janusian thinking*, which consists of actively conceiving two or more opposite or antithetical ideas, images, or concepts simultaneously. A related concept is *homospatial thinking*, a sort of spatial abstraction which consists of actively conceiving two or more discrete entities occupying the same space, a conception leading to the articulation of new identities [Rothenberg 1979].

There are different viewpoints within the computational intelligence research community about the nature of intelligence. One influential viewpoint from Boden is to view creativity as representation redescription. Problem solving is a search over a given search space defined by a set of constraints, operators, and representations. Creative problem solving involves finding important solutions that other searchers miss. The extra search power comes from an ability to transform the search space. That is, creative search involves changing or extending the constraints, operators, or representation, using an additional set of operators whose job is to modify the first set. Therefore, ordinary thought is a search over an ordinary search space, while creative thought is a meta-search using a separate set of operators.

Creativity often has an emotional surprise or "aha!" aspect (which implies something that violates our expectations has happened). Boden likens intelligence to a generative system. Creativity results from changing one's conceptual system to produce new thoughts which were impossible under the old conceptual system. Creative thought is distinguished from ordinary problem solving by conceptual restructuring [Boden 1990].

8.2.2 THEORETICAL FOUNDATION FOR STIMULATING HUMAN THINKING

A central task of management is decision making, and a crucial aspect of decision making is having good alternatives from which to choose. Based on a conceptual framework considering creative processes, environments, outputs, and individuals, generating alternatives is viewed as a process of "making connections" -- internal connections among problem elements and external connections between a problem and its environment. Making connections refers to the creation of new ideas through association between existing ideas. Such connections (associations) can come in many forms. A central distinction is between internal connections and external ones. Internal connections are those between elements of the focal problem itself. External connections are those between the focal problem and external factors. Internal connections may focus either on the form of the problem or on the purpose; external connections may be local or distinct. Connections can also be established by incorporating machine learning algorithms (such as genetic algorithms, to be discussed in Chapter 10).

New ideas may be generated by introducing new elements into a problem context, by altering the relationships between the elements of a problem, or a combination, namely, by introducing new elements as well as by altering the relationships between elements.

Two principal preferred creativity styles have been identified, namely, adaptation and innovation. Corresponding to these two styles are two kinds of creative products, *paradigm-preserving* (*PP*) and *paradigm-modifying* (*PM*). In addition, some heuristics related to creativity style have been observed, for example, the following heuristics on stimulus relatedness:

- The more related the stimulus, the more likely is the generation of PP ideas. The less related the stimulus, the more likely is the generation of PM ideas.
- Free association is likely to generally result in PP ideas, while forced relationships are likely to result in PM ideas.

- Simultaneity could result in the generation of PP ideas. Conversely, turn-taking could potentially encourage the generation of PM ideas, relative to simultaneous idea generation.

A kind of reasoning process closely related to PM is analogical reasoning. Suggestions generated in more advanced programs such as COGMIR (see Chapter 7) have a better quality than those ideas generated in conventional idea processors, because the system includes a kind of evaluation process so that only the most promising ideas will be further explored.

In order to study computational intelligence in a systematic manner, computational models for creativity have been developed. The following are two examples. For more detailed summary of computational models for creativity, see [Chen 1999a].

Achieve computational creativity through transformation. The engineering aspect of computational intelligence has encouraged many researchers to develop exploratory programs to achieve computational creativity. According to an approach for computational creativity, problem solving is seen as the search of an explicit knowledge space for known solutions and creativity as the search of a vast, implicit knowledge space for new solutions. Creativity is distinguished from problem solving not by a single distinguished mechanism (i.e., representational re-description) but by the types of solutions it discovers: solutions incorporating knowledge not found by ordinary problem solving. New problem solutions can be created by transforming a problem into a new problem, solving the new problem, and then adapting the solution back to the original problem. This model also provides an explicit mechanism by which a problem solver can perform the kinds of knowledge re-descriptions needed to be creative.

Case-based reasoning framework. In a framework revised from case-based reasoning, creative thought, like all thought, is treated as involving processes of problem interpretation and problem reformulation, case and model retrieval, elaboration and adaptation, and evaluation. Creativity arises from the confluence and complex interaction of inferences using multiple kinds of knowledge in the context of task or problem and in the context of a specific situation.

8.2.3 CREATIVITY IN DECISION SUPPORT SYSTEMS

In the interdisciplinary area of decision support systems, [Holsapple and Whinston 1996] predicted that knowledge-based systems in future knowledge-based organizations should be "computer co-workers" with the ability to "recognize needs, stimulate insights and offer advice." Analogy and metaphor can provide an important role in offering advice. Research work has been conducted to support analogical problem solving or achieve creativity support systems through computerized metaphor generation. For example, in [Young 1987, 1988], three levels have been defined for supporting metaphoric thinking:

- the *secretarial level* (the computer is used essentially as a dynamic electronic blackboard),
- the *framework-paradigm level*: the computer can provide frameworks to organize the user's thoughts and to provide examples to serve as both thought stimuli and guides to the user), and
- the *generative level* (the computer can automatically synthesize and display new ideas).

The three support levels are hierarchical and cumulative; thus the generative level includes the prior two levels.

8.3   IDEA PROCESSORS

8.3.1 BASICS OF IDEA PROCESSORS

A typical example of computer-assisted human creativity can be examined through *idea processors*. Two types of programs can be developed to elicit or facilitate human creativity: the creativity acquisition programs (somewhat similar to knowledge acquisition in knowledge-based systems) and the creativity facilitation programs. Idea processors belong to the latter category. They are tools at the generative level (see definitions given at the end of section 8.2.3). Idea processors represent computerized endeavors to generate and organize ideas, thus enhancing (or amplifying) human creativity. The term idea means an understanding, insight or some primitive form of solution to a problem. In a looser sense, the term idea processor also covers various creativity support systems. Idea processors are used to support work in early, emergent and usually creative stages of human intellectual activities such as research planning, conceptual design, software requirement analysis, knowledge acquisition, decision making, counseling, motivation, as well as others.

The purpose of idea processors is to assist human intelligence, namely, to provide computer support for ordinary people. We are interested in human creative potential -- not just with analyzing it, but with asking how people can become more creative. An individual's natural creative potential is biologically determined and established early in life, and is not expected to vary significantly over time. However, through training, an individual's creative performance can be amplified or inhibited. Creativity training represents the individual's past knowledge and developmental history concerning his or her creative behavior. Idea processors have been developed for this purpose; they influence an individual's performance by providing the necessary suggestions and cures to produce a creative response.

Idea processors can be examined from the computerized problem solving perspective. Since their main tasks are idea generation and organization, idea processors fall in the scope of knowledge-support systems, and can be viewed as a partner for human beings in problem solving. However, unlike some other partner machines, idea processors usually are not participants of the whole problem solving process; instead, they are only used for idea generation and organizations in some specific stages of problem solving.

Creative thinking is usually considered as relating things or ideas which were previously unrelated. For many idea processors, the most important technique is to generate ideas through electronic brainstorming. Brainstorming, first proposed by Alex Osborne in 1930s from management science, is a method of getting a large number of ideas from a group of people in a short time [Osborne 1963]. [Koestler 1974] used the term "bisociative thinking" to show the linking of two unrelated planes or matrices in the creative act. Two or more quite unrelated concepts can be combined to give a totally new concept. Idea processors use electronic means to achieve effects similar to conventional brainstorming for idea generation, but they do not necessarily rely on the group effort.

Several guidelines for brainstorming are available, such as suspend judgment, free-wheel, quantity, and cross-fertilize. Brainstorming can be conducted through several stages include (i) state the problem and discuss, (ii) restate the problem in the form of "How to...", (iii) select a basic restatement and write it down, "In how many ways can we...", (iv) warm-up session, (v) brainstorm, and (vi) identify wildest idea. Some evaluation method should be used to identify the few good ideas for implementation [Rawlinson 1981]. An implicit assumption used here is the quantitative measure: if a large quantity of ideas was generated, then the idea pool very likely would contain high-quality ideas. An important note: despite the controversial (sometimes poor) laboratory performance of techniques such as brainstorming (based largely on quantitative measures), the business world continues to rely on them. Brainstorming has also been used for engineering design process to offer strategic support, because it separates the production of ideas or plans from any criticism of them. Related to brainstorming is brainwriting, which is characterized by silent, hand-written communication. Brainwriting can be categorized as either interactive or nominal (which is non face-to-face idea generation). Electronic brainstorming is actually electronic brainwriting.

Two related issues that must be addressed in brainstorming are convergence and divergence of ideas. In the context of creative thinking, *convergence* refers to analytical thinking where the process converges to a single answer, while *divergence* refers to creative thinking where the process diverges to a large number of ideas and ranges far and wide over the problem. Creative thought has both divergent and convergent aspects, as to be further explained in the next section. The process of brainstorming is divergent, with participants ranging far and wide in their endeavor to find possible solutions. Evaluation is convergent, seeking to convert the many ideas into the few solutions.

Electronic brainstorming tools are frequently used as components of group decision systems to brainstorm ideas. These thoughts are then organized into categories using the categorizer or idea organization tools. A ranking/ordering/voting process is carried out to prioritize the final categories and achieve consensus. An alternative sequence may consist of stages of diverge (brainstorm or collect ideas), converge (consolidate, or make some sense of the ideas), evaluate (typically vote in some fashion), debate or lobby (to gain a better understanding), and finally organize the results (to develop presentable output).

Traditionally, idea generation has been seen as a group task. Techniques have been designed to facilitate the sharing of ideas and the refinement of ideas generated by other individuals, although techniques which helped the individual problem solver come up with more or better alternatives have also been studied.

8.3.2 COMMON COMPONENTS IN IDEA PROCESSORS

A survey of idea processors can be found in [Schorr 1995]. Although the structure of idea processors highly vary, some common components can be found. A typical idea processor usually consists of the following:

- a user interface;
- an idea generator;
- an idea organizer;
- an idea base;
- an idea presentor;
- a computer network; and
- supporting components (such as an editor, a visualization tool, etc.) .

Figure 8.1 depicts the components (except the computer network) in a typical idea processor. In this figure, boxes denote components directly related to functionality of idea processors, while ovals indicate components related to user interface. Arrows are used to indicate major connections between components. Supporting components can be used in various ways, and are thus not connected to other components by arrows.

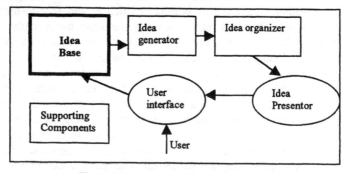

Figure 8.1 Components in an idea processor

8.3.3 HOW IDEA PROCESSORS WORK

Many idea processors rely on brainstorming techniques. Directly related to this is the rearrangement heuristic: ideas and thoughts are solicited from the user(s), followed by a possible randomization, and then rearranged into topics later. The Gestalt psychologists suggest that creative thinking proceeds neither by piecemeal logical operations nor by disconnected associations, but by more determinate restructuring of the whole situation. Creativity lies in the ability to redirect a line of thought taken in solving a problem. We can gain useful insights into problems by making use of computer programs that help us to de-structure our thinking and then to restructure it in a different way.

Categorically, creative thought can be viewed as responses from two types of mental processes: generative and exploratory [Finke, Ward and Smith 1992]. Within the *generative mode*, divergent ways of thinking, including remote association and pattern switching, produce novel, unique concepts. In the *exploratory mode*, convergent thought such as elaboration or successive refinement reformulates a unique concept into a meaningful and valuable response. The nature of the decision task defines which mode is likely to dominate response formation [Finke, Ward and Smith 1992].

Although commercial products are abundant, some idea processors may have an exploratory focus. They are developed either for practical applications or serving as research prototypes. Rather than ask open-ended questions or offer lists of generic ideas, they provide a means for users to embellish, emphasize, and polish ideas. For example, the user may be given a chance to type concepts into the so-called idea-boxes, which could then be linked laterally or hierarchically. Visually clustering the idea symbols on screen allows the user to see emerging relationships, thought patterns, and terms.

8.3.4 THE NATURE OF IDEA PROCESSORS

Idea processors are developed to assist human thinking, including idea generation and organization. This task is a very special kind of symbolic problem solving, and is of an open-ended nature. In order to assist, enhance, and amplify human intelligence, studies in psychology (some are from folk-psychology), management science, as well as computational intelligence, have served as useful sources and have made important contributions.

Creative problem solving has been commonly viewed as a multistage process. The following stages are involved: preparation, incubation (a part conscious, part unconscious deliberation and idea finding phase), illumination (the moment of recognition when an idea has been found), and verification.

Ideally, one might like to see a programmed or programmable idea generation procedure, although such a procedure may seem antithetical to the very concept of creativity. Nevertheless, there are a number of heuristics to facilitate problem structuring and idea generation. For example, several heuristics focus on "asking the right questions," while other heuristics involve linking the present problem with a remote context.

Techniques for brainstorming can be viewed as various kinds of heuristics to stimulate human thinking. Some idea processors intend to help users to take a fresh look at problems by guiding what may be a user's otherwise undisciplined intuition through a series of problem-solving exercises. Some of these programs deliberately force people to think in nonlinear, non-logical, playful ways. The idea behind them is to divert one's thinking from the channels that day-to-day work has forced it into, sparking new ideas and new ways of thinking. Others focus one's attention on the psychological aspects of overwork, such as motivation, stress, and depression. Guided problem-solving supplies frameworks into which a person plug his ideas. The main advantage of computerized, guided problem-solving is that the programs will prompt a user for his ideas in a thorough manner.

As discussed in Chapter 2, problem solving in computational intelligence is conducted as state space search. It has been noted that for a given set of variables and processes operating within a bounded context or focus, any computational model will construct a bounded state space. Creative design can be represented in such a state space by a change in the state space. Recent development in computational intelligence has also emphasized knowledge-based approaches. Frequently, new ideas are sparked by reviewing old ones. In order to achieve the goal of assisting human thinking, idea processors usually perform extensive search in "memories," including large databases, knowledge bases, or text bases. New ideas may be produced by summarizing or reorganizing unorganized chunks in such memories.

In a large degree, computational intelligence is about knowledge representation and reasoning. In contrast, idea processors usually set emphasis on the broader sense of thinking instead of reasoning. As defined in dictionaries, the most basic meaning of thinking is "to have as a thought; formulate in the mind." Although both computational intelligence and idea processors are concerned with using computers to achieve creativity, the role of idea processors in creative thinking is quite limited: they can only generate ideas that are the starting point of a lot of work which needs be done by human beings.

Due to these different aspects and different emphasis, idea processors may employ methods quite different from computational intelligence. For example, instead of developing efficient searching algorithms for reasoning, idea processors may rely on much less sophisticated methods (e.g., random combination or permutation) to generate ideas, although computational algorithms (such as genetic algorithms) may also be used. Academia research work in computational intelligence is not around the study of divergence.

Nevertheless, some overlap exists between the study of computational intelligence and the practice of idea processors. It is noted that in the computational intelligence research community, efforts at modeling discovery processes have sometimes been aimed at developing a theory of human discovery, sometimes at constructing systems that can, in collaboration with scientists autonomously, engage in discovery work. Some interactive software and database search strategies have been developed to facilitate the discovery of previously unknown cross-specialty information of scientific interest. The software can help to find complementary literatures and reveal new useful information that cannot be inferred from either set alone.

8.4 RETROSPECTIVE ANALYSIS FOR SCIENTIFIC DISCOVERY AND TECHNICAL INVENTION

8.4.1 RETROSPECTIVE ANALYSIS OF TECHNICAL INVENTION

An aspect of idea processors is that they are more directly related to everyday thinking rather than scientific thinking. However, there are strong similarities between everyday thinking and scientific thinking, an issue to be discussed here.

Although scientific discovery and technical invention have different aspects or emphases: the task for *discovery* is to reveal or uncover some existing features or relationships; while the task for *invention* is to generate new solutions (or possibly generating new problems as well), they share some common concerns. There are some famous landmark programs in computational intelligence history [Langley, Simon, Bradshaw and Zytkow 1987].

In computational intelligence, computational creativity has been studied along with both the directions of discovery and invention. In a discovery system, given an appropriate set of data or a database, a clever computer program can "re-discover" important scientific laws [Langley, Simon, Bradshaw and Zytkow 1987; Piatetsky-Shapiro and Frawley 1991]. In contrast, generative systems exemplify the study along the direction of invention [Boden 1990].

Computerized discovery and invention systems have much more sophisticated structure than idea processors. Although some techniques may be eventually incorporated into some idea processors, most will not. The real reason to study computational aspects in invention and discovery largely lies in *the analysis* of the thinking process behind invention and discovery. For this purpose, retrospective approaches are frequently used to trace the mental processes involved in invention and discovery. Such analysis may produce useful hindsight serving as heuristics. These heuristics can then be used in generating new ideas for idea generation, or *meta-idea generation*.

Creative studies are a way of cultural self-inquiry: Explaining creativity would mean for a culture to be able to transcend itself and look at itself from the outside [Dartnal 1994]. This can be carried out at a high, philosophical level; but more directly related to our interest, detailed studies in various concrete knowledge domains are important. Two fundamental questions that need to be answered in technical invention are whether we can describe invention in a general way, and whether we can extract principles (heuristics) of invention from particular cases that have some generality across inventions [Weber and Perkins 1992]. To illustrate, consider heuristics which are concerned with *join*, an activity which combines several things together if they share some common part. For example, a claw hammer is the join of a striker head and a claw that share a common handle. Observations like "what the striker part of the hammer will do, the claw will undo, and vice versa" may suggest the inverse join heuristic: "Combine only those tools or ideas that are inverses of one another." [Weber and Perkins 1992]. Heuristics obtained through retrospective analysis, such as the join heuristic and the invention cycle mentioned above, can be incorporated into knowledge bases of idea processors. Within computer science, [Dasgupta 1994] provided an explanation on Maurice Wilkes' invention of microprogramming; Here are some of Dasgupta's hypotheses used in his study:

- invention as a goal-directed endeavor, and goals as working hypotheses in inventive design;
- the gradualistic nature of an insight;
- bisociation or the combining of ideas;
- creative processes are reasoning processes;
- the creative agent is not only knowledge-rich, it also has the capability to freely and associatively wander about the knowledge space and retrieve whatever tokens seem related to the goal at hand;
- the process of inventing artifactual forms (or creating original designs) in the artificial sciences is cognitively indistinguishable at the knowledge level from the process of inventing theories or discovering laws in the natural sciences.

As a more general study, [Simonton 1984] noticed that the greatest thinkers in the Western philosophical tradition have tended to be unrepresentative of their times. The most eminent thinkers are oddly backward-looking in their ideas. They are more representative of the previous generation's ideological consensus than of those of present or succeeding generations. Notice that these backward-looking people have made a profound impact on the generations beyond them. Therefore, the above citation seems to suggest that genius people nurtured themselves using what they have learned *from the past* to guide their activities *for the future*.

The field of creativity needs to make room for commonplace inventions. When examined on a conceptual basis, these simple implements reveal a rich set of concepts and principles that provide a first approximation to a framework of invention and synthetic thinking. Invention draws on a variety of thinking modes: analysis, evaluation, decision making, problem finding and problem solving. What makes invention different from many other modes of thinking is its emphasis on synthetic thinking, that is, the ability to build complexity out of simpler ideas or components. What is needed is an explicit framework and representation for understanding and talking about invention and synthetic thinking. To summarize the common patterns behind invention, Robert Weber proposed the "Evaluation $\rightarrow$ Fix$\rightarrow$ Produce" cycle [Weber 1996].

The heuristic rules of such acquired knowledge can be used along with domain knowledge to improve the power of inference. Interesting results can be obtained by developing some useful operators from the heuristics, and by combined use of these operators. For example, we may consider the *inverse* of an activity, and combine it with join. This illustrates the motivation of an *invention algebra*, as briefly discussed in [Chen 1997a].

8.4.2 RETROSPECTIVE ANALYSIS FOR KNOWLEDGE-BASED IDEA GENERATION OF NEW ARTIFACTS

When comparing idea processors with theoretical studies in computational intelligence research, we may notice that although both divergence and convergence techniques are important for idea processors, various divergence techniques around brainstorming have been the soul of idea processors. Idea processors deal with idea generation and organization only (rather than solving the entire problems), they are typically application-driven, with little care of their theoretical foundation. The methods used by idea processors are usually vivid and colorful, although they are simple and shallow. In contrast, divergence has not been in the center of computational intelligence studies. Rather, by developing sophisticated algorithms, computational intelligence researchers have pursued more rigorous approaches to solve entire problems (not just for idea generation), and furthermore, to explore the nature of creativity. Although the ultimate goal of computational intelligence studies is still for application, a more direct goal is to establish a good understanding of intelligence and a sound theoretical foundation of computational creativity.

This comparison suggests an alternative approach for computational creativity support. Our purpose is still to generate new ideas in a creative manner. We still want to keep the vivid and colorful aspects of idea processors to support divergent thinking. However, we hope that *ideas will be generated in a more controlled manner*, which should be supported by well-established techniques in computational intelligence. In other words, the activity of idea generation itself needs a better foundation. Retrospective analysis can serve this purpose for idea generation of new artifacts. In addition, this process can be largely computationalized. In fact, retrospective analysis suggests a knowledge-based approach for idea generation. There are two kinds of knowledge involved, both of which can be captured by retrospective analysis:

      (a) knowledge of existing artifacts;
      (b) knowledge of heuristic rules needed for invention.

Although most existing idea processors also use knowledge-based approaches, the proposed approach is unique due to its natural connection with frame structures. Since frame systems readily lend themselves to object-oriented techniques (as discussed in Chapter 6), we can take advantage of these techniques to achieve our goal of generating ideas in a controlled manner. For example, object-oriented features allow us to generate a new artifact with multiple parents, and bisociation of different thoughts can thus be realized through multiple inheritance. By combining different components and operations in different ancestors for a newly generated artifact, multiple inheritance supports divergent thinking. In addition, since only those combinations which are involved in multiple inheritance will be generated, computational exploration can be avoided, and convergence can be achieved in a more effective manner.

8.4.3 A PROLOG PROGRAM TO EXPLORE IDEA GENERATION

In this section, we provide a sketch of a Prolog program for idea generation (as outlined in the previous section).

8.4.3.1 Frames and inheritance in artifact representation

Technical invention may involve many heuristic rules; here we will only briefly touch one heuristic (the join heuristic) used in technical invention of artifacts [Weber and Perkins 1989]. The join heuristic suggests to use a frame join operation to create general new entities that integrate the properties of the simpler components by combining simpler frames.

We treat each artifact as a conceptual graph (CG, as discussed in Chapter 6) describing its structure, functions and various features. A library of CGs consists of known artifacts. The task of invention requires us to construct new artifacts from these existing artifacts. The task of artifact invention can be viewed as: given the user specification of a new tool to be constructed (the specification can be viewed as an *incomplete* artifact with incomplete information to be filled), determine which existing CGs partially match the specification, and then create a CG as a combination (or partial combination) of these CGs. A new frame representing the CG of a proposed artifact can be constructed, with the retrieved frames as its multiple parents. The new frame is the result of the invention [Chen 1999b].

As an example, let us consider how to describe a knife as an artifact. Structurally, a knife has a blade and is made of metal. Functionally (or operationally), a knife can be used to cut vegetables. We use paired squared brackets to represent a concept node and a paired parentheses along with arrows to represent a conceptual relationship. The conceptual graph in Figure 8.2 represents this artifact.

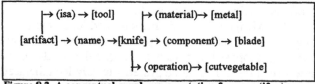

Figure 8.2 A conceptual graph representation for an artifact

This conceptual graph can be represented in Prolog as a frame. The Prolog predicate is basically a straight translation from the conceptual graph with minor revisions (due to implementation-related considerations from Prolog):

```
toolframe(name(artifact,knife), isa(artifact,tool),
         [component(knife,blade),
          material(knife,metal)],
         ops(knife, [cutvegetable]),
```

[]).

As a slightly more complicated example, consider the definition of scissors as an artifact. A pair of scissors is a cutting implement of two blades joined by a swivel pin; it can be opened, closed and can be used to cut paper. We can draw a conceptual graph to represent it and further implement it as a frame in Prolog. The frame definition can be found in the Prolog code appearing in the next section.

The collection of frames forms a library of artifacts, which can be used for recognition purposes. But a more interesting issue is to generate (or create) new artifacts using existing artifacts.

Each artifact is a tool-frame with arguments of Name, Parent, Structure, and Operations. The most important part is operations, which characterize the functionality of the tools, and selecting various operations from different parents, new tools can be generated later (through multiple inheritance). The following are two examples of tool-frame in the knowledge base. The first tool-frame is an artifact called scissors, with components such as two cutting edges and a swivel pin which connects the two edges. Operations available for scissors including cutting paper, open and close. The second tool-frame is a knife, which has a blade as its component, and has the operation of cutting vegetable.

```
toolframe(name(artifact,scissors),isa(artifact, tool),
  [component(scissors,cuttingedge1),
   component(scissors,cuttingedge2),
   component(scissors,swivel-pin),
   connect(swivel-pin,cuttingedge1),
   connect(swivel-pin,cuttingedge2),
   material(scissors,metal)],
   operations(scissors, [cutpaper,open,close])).

toolframe(name(artifact,knife),isa(artifact, tool),
 [component(knife,blade),
   material(knife,metal)],
   operations(knife, [cutvegetable])).
```

Generation of new ideas first requires retrieval of knowledge of existing tool-frames. This can be done using the following code (adopted and revised from [Luger and Stubblefield 1998]):

```
retrieve_multiple(Op, [Parent|_]) :- retrieve(Op, Parent).
retrieve_multiple(Op, [_| Rest]) :- retrieve_multiple(Op,
Rest).

retrieve(Op, Obj) :- toolframe(name(_,Obj), _, _, ops(Obj,
Lst_P)),
                     member(Op, Lst_P).
retrieve(Op, Obj) :- toolframe(name(_,Obj),_,_,_,Lst_d),
                     member(Op, Lst_d).
retrieve(Op, Obj) :-
toolframe(name(_,Obj),isa(_,Parent),_,_),
                     retrieve(Op, Parent).
retrieve(Op, Obj) :-
toolframe(name(_,Obj),isa(_,List),_,_),
                     retrieve_multiple(Op, List).
```

Finally, idea generation for new tool-frames takes place. The following Prolog is used to retrieve operational functions to recognize potential parents so that a new parent tool-frame class can be created through multiple inheritance:

```
newparent([], L, L).
newparent([H|T], OL, L) :- retrieve(H, O),
                           append([O], OL, L1),
                           newparent(T, L1, L).
```

We now illustrate how the Prolog program can be used for new idea generation. The following is a sample execution of the program.

```
?- create(L).
    input a desirable operation for new artifact, end
    to stop:
    cutvegetable.
    input a desirable operation for new artifact, end
    to stop:
    cutpaper.
    input a desirable operation for new artifact, end
    to stop:
    end.
    NEW FRAME GENERATED:
    toolframe(name(newframe,invention_1),
    isa(newframe,[scissors,knife]),[],[]).
    L=[scissors,knife]
```

In this example, the user specifies desirable operations of a new artifact: cut vegetable and cut paper. The program is able to search for existing artifacts which provide these operations, and uses these artifacts as parents to generate a new artifact. The search process is carried out to find parents for multiple inheritance. The resulting frame indicates a new artifact which has two parents (scissors and knife), from which it can inherit properties of both parents to provide all the desired operations. This example can be considered as a highly simplified scenario for the invention of a Swiss army knife. (To focus our discussion, the slots of structure, operations and default values are intentionally left as empty lists.)

As an example of the analysis, here we briefly describe how the size of tool-frame knowledge base would affect convergence and divergence of idea generation. Inventing new artifacts based on existing knowledge in the tool-frame base is limited by the size of the existing knowledge base. Using a small knowledge base, the program can only generate simple new artifacts limited by the set of existing operations defined in all tool-frames. A large library of knowledge increases the chance of divergent ideas. However, as the knowledge base expands, the possibility of conflicting ideas or artifacts rises. It takes a longer time to process the increased knowledge base to create new ideas. A related factor is user's satisfaction. A larger knowledge base offers better opportunity for generating exciting ideas, but the large amount of new ideas may also cause confusion to the user. To achieve a good balance between divergence and convergence, various control mechanisms should be developed and tested.

8.5 COMBINING CREATIVITY WITH EXPERTISE

8.5.1 THE NEED FOR COMBINING CREATIVITY WITH EXPERTISE

Creativity and expertise have been treated as separate issues in computational intelligence. A conjecture is that pursuing creativity or resorting to expertise have quite different philosophical roots. In fact, expert systems can even be viewed as a reactionary activity of creativity in the 19th century. As noted by [Friedel 1992], for most of the 19th century, technical novelty was largely seen as the product of human ingenuity and was closely associated with the "genius" of individuals and of the nation or race. In the 20th century, by contrast, we have come to look for new technology from institutions and individuals who are characterized not by their creativity, imagination, and brilliance but by their ability to marshal expertise.

However, there is a strong indication of combining creativity with expertise. It would be ideal to store useful heuristic knowledge demonstrated in creative activities across many application domains. It may also be beneficial to store heuristic rules to creatively utilize existing domain knowledge (namely, expertise) to enhance or to improve the quality of the answers (or conclusions, decisions, etc.) provided by the systems. The strength of knowledge-based systems comes from two aspects: the inference power of the systems and the rich knowledge stored in the systems. The result of the marriage between creativity and expertise, or heuristic knowledge related to creativity, may contribute to such systems in both aspects: as an enrichment of the inference power, and/or as an extension of the knowledge possessed by the system.

8.5.2 STRATEGIC KNOWLEDGE AS KNOWLEDGE RELATED TO CREATIVITY

To make our discussion more focused, we will consider a kind of knowledge related to creativity which is the wisdom and heuristics as demonstrated in non-conventional problem solving processes. It is different from domain-dependent knowledge because it is not restricted to any specific application domain. It also differs from non-domain knowledge such as meta-knowledge (which is knowledge about knowledge, more discussion in Chapter 14) or commonsense knowledge (which is the knowledge and reasoning methods possessed by every school child, see Chapter 5). In order to make the study of creativity matchable with the intensive knowledge as used in knowledge-based systems, an innovated approach is needed to focus on knowledge related to creativity. However, this kind of knowledge will not be simply referred to as creativity knowledge, because possessing such knowledge does not guarantee creativity (since it consists of heuristic rules) and creativity is not a pure cognitive activity (for example, social factors may play an important role). In addition, since in most cases we are not pushed to invent new things or ideas, this kind of knowledge is of secondary importance (not as fundamental as domain knowledge which is important in solving various real-world applications in our daily life), but could be very useful.

Due to the lack of an appropriate term, we will use the term *strategic knowledge* to refer to the heuristic knowledge related to creativity. The creative knowledge demonstrated in unconventional problem solving in various creative activities usually presents good strategies to achieve the goals implied in the problem statements.

We now point out the need for studying a kind of creative knowledge concerning strategic heuristics. The issue of acquiring creative knowledge from folklore is discussed in some detail and is illustrated by some examples. The impact of such knowledge on the architecture of knowledge-based expert systems is also discussed.

Knowledge-based systems (particularly expert systems) have become very popular in various applications. A well-known project which is still in progress is the CYC project [Lenat and Guha 1990]. In addition, machine learning techniques have been incorporated for automated knowledge acquisition of knowledge-based systems [Michalski 1983].

Knowledge is an important aspect of intelligence; creativity is another one. However, although sometimes expert systems may produce unpredicted results, the basic philosophy is reusing existing knowledge rather than creating new knowledge. Expert systems are not necessarily creative, and in general, they are not. In fact, expert systems are aimed to reuse experts' knowledge and to reuse reasoning process as well. Reuse also exists at even higher levels; for example, by developing expert system shells. (This is not to say that the activity of reuse itself cannot be creative. But this is not an issue to be investigated here.)

Creativity has been studied in computational intelligence in decades, although in most cases, it was not studied in the context of knowledge-based systems. One possible reason is due to the complex nature of creativity. The recent discussion [Stefik and Smoliar 1995] around Margaret Boden's book *The Creative Mind* [Boden 1990] reveals how little we know about creativity, and how much is yet to be done.

We notice that there is a need to study a kind of knowledge which is closely related to creative activities. It is different from domain-dependent knowledge because it is not restricted to any specific application domain. It also differs from non-domain knowledge such as meta-knowledge, because it is not knowledge about knowledge. In addition, it is not commonsense knowledge because the latter is the common knowledge possessed by every school child and methods used to make obvious inference from this knowledge [Davis 1990]. The knowledge related to creativity is much more complicated than this. It is the wisdom and heuristics as demonstrated in unconventional problem-solving processes.

8.5.3 STUDYING STRATEGIC HEURISTICS OF CREATIVE KNOWLEDGE

However, heuristic knowledge itself may not necessarily imply creativity. In order to combine creativity with knowledge as used in knowledge-based systems, there is a need to study heuristics which are related to creative knowledge. Since creative knowledge involved in intelligent behavior is huge and diverse, to focus our study, we will examine a kind of creative heuristics which may provide us useful hints to achieve our goal in an unconventional way. Such knowledge can extend our domain knowledge, and enhance our reasoning ability. To distinguish this kind of heuristic knowledge from other forms of creative knowledge, due to the lack of an appropriate term, in this paper we will informally refer it as *strategic heuristics*. Note the meaning of the word "strategic" used here corresponds to the meaning of noun *strategy* which is "the art or skill of using stratagems as in politics or business," while a *stratagem* is "a scheme designed to obtain a goal" (both from *The American Heritage Dictionary*, 1983).

In addition to technical invention, creative ideas can also be found in other kinds of human intelligence activities, including the wisdom as spotted in folklores, proverbs, idioms, folk tales, legends, etc. in various cultures. In the rest of this paper we will examine some examples from folk tales. Following the lead of Weber and Perkins, we will examine some examples of folk tales and discuss how to obtain strategic heuristics from them. For example, how can you weigh an elephant without using a large size scale? How can you use a boat, a regular size scale, and a rich supply of rocks to measure the weight of an elephant? Folk tales like this reflect unconventional problem-solving techniques and provide a vivid source of creative knowledge.

In particular, in the following we will use an example taken from Chinese folk tales to illustrate why folklore is a resource for studying creativity. You want to know the weight of an elephant, but you do not have scales large enough to do the job. The solution provided by Cao Chong (the sun of a famous general at that time) can be sketched as the following informal algorithm. (Note that we cannot directly use the divide and conquer method, but we can apply a similar idea.)

Elephant weighing algorithm:
Input: an elephant, a boat (which is strong enough to hold the elephant), a river to hold the boat (along with the elephant), enough supply of rocks, and a scale which can weigh rocks.
Output: the weight of the elephant.
Method:

---

1. Put the elephant in the boat, make a notch at the waterline.
2. Remove the elephant from the boat.
3. Put rocks into the boat until they reach the notch made in Step 1.
4. Loop

- Each time remove a portion of rocks from the boat and weigh them in the scales;
- add up the weights

until all rocks are removed and weighed.

5. Return the final weight of the rocks, which is the weight of the elephant.

The method used in this algorithm employs the typical idea of divide and conquer , but other heuristics are also used. The heuristics learned here can be described at different levels. At one extreme, we may use direct variablization to replace the constant "elephant" by a variable "thing." This is a simple use of generalization in induction [Michalski 1983]. At a much higher level, generalization can be used in full scale for all constants, including the measurement itself (that is, measurement can be in any form, not restricted to weighing). From this discussion, we may have the following two heuristic rules.

- *Replacement heuristic (lower level abstraction)*: If a thing is too heavy to be weighed, you can put it in a boat, mark the waterline, replace the heavy thing by rocks, remove a portion of the rocks and weight, and take the sum.
- *Replacement heuristic (higher level abstraction)*: In case that you want to measure a thing A which is not in manageable size, if there is another thing B which is of same measurement as A (without actually measuring) but can be divided into manageable pieces or components, then you can replace A by B, measure these pieces separately and take the sum.

Other examples of strategic heuristics can be found in [Chen 1997b].

8.5.4 DIFFICULTIES AND PROBLEMS IN ACQUIRING STRATEGIC HEURISTICS

Based on what we have discussed in this section, it is time to point out some difficulties and problems in acquiring strategic heuristics.

- First of all, not every folk tale has strategic value; in fact, many of them may not. So, how to determine the heuristic value of a folk tale?
- The next problem is, suppose a folk tale is determined to have some strategic value; how do we actually extract the folk tale, and make it computationalized?

Just like the case of inductive learning, another problem is over-generalization (namely, over-simplification). That is, the heuristics extracted from the folk tale may be too abstract, and the vivid color of the original story is lost. In this case, the heuristics extracted may not be as useful as one might have expected. In addition, at the current stage, how to extract the heuristics from a given folk tale is largely an art. For the time being, these heuristics can be entered manually by the programmers. However, in the long run, this process should be automated. To avoid over-generalization and manual heuristic entry, an alternative is to store original folk tales in a separate knowledge base. But for making use of the stored tales, an on-line analysis and understanding of stored folk tales is required, which could pose a very challenging task in natural language processing.

The reader may have also noticed that the heuristics learned from folk tales may not be accurate enough. In order to store strategic heuristics so that they can be useful for inference, the basic requirement is to express those rules in a (at least somewhat) formal way.

There are still some other difficulties. Our selection of folklore as the source of creative knowledge seems to be somewhat arbitrary. The reader may wonder that there may be a large number of sources for strategic heuristic knowledge. This is a very interesting observation. It is true that there may be many other possible sources for the study of creativity (one of them could be {\em humor}, for example). However, this does not necessarily mean that the number of sources is endless, because although human intelligent behavior can be characterized into many categories (folklore is one of them), the number of such categories is finite. But how to identify these sources? Are all these sources useful to us at all? Can the knowledge acquired from these sources be computationalized or does it need to be computationalized? We may ask ourselves endless questions, simply because our understanding about creative knowledge is so little. However, various problems encountered in creative knowledge acquisition are no excuse for not studying strategic heuristics of creative knowledge at all. On the contrary, they provide an excellent challenge to researchers and practitioners in computational intelligence and cognitive science.

8.5.5 THE NATURE OF STRATEGIC HEURISTICS

Another important issue which must be addressed here is the nature of strategic heuristics and its relationship with the heuristics discussed earlier. Knowledge related to creativity can be acquired by an analysis of inventions in history, folklore, as well as other sources. However, we should keep in mind that possessing this kind of knowledge does not guarantee creativity (since it consists of heuristic rules). Besides, we should also remember that creativity is not a pure cognitive or mental activity, it is mixed with other factors (such as social factor). In addition, since in most cases we are not pushed to invent new things or ideas, this kind of knowledge is of secondary importance (not as fundamental as domain knowledge which are important in solving various real-world applications in our daily life), but could be very useful. Time has come to incorporate this kind of knowledge into knowledge-based systems.

Notice that this kind of creative knowledge is knowledge at the object level rather than the level of controlling the use of knowledge. If we follow the traditional separation of control knowledge used by the inference engine and the domain knowledge, then this kind of knowledge should not be placed with control knowledge. However, knowledge base usually stores domain knowledge, which is different from the creative knowledge discussed here. Such knowledge also differs from meta knowledge, which is related to control knowledge. Therefore as to be addressed in the next section, the incorporation of creative knowledge may have impact on the *architecture* of expert systems.

8.5.6 TOWARD KNOWLEDGE-BASED ARCHITECTURE COMBINING CREATIVITY AND EXPERTISE

If knowledge is power, and if there is a need to code encyclopedias into the computer to be stored as knowledge, then why not store strategic heuristics as well? Due to the unique nature of creative knowledge, it should be stored in a separate knowledge base (separate from domain knowledge, meta-knowledge, commonsense knowledge, etc.). Since acquiring such knowledge may be time consuming, the creative knowledge base can be constructed in an incremental manner. Introducing such a component will have some impact on the architecture of knowledge-based systems. Note that this perspective is complementary to the issue of experience-based creativity [Levinson 1994], which is concerned with establishing some medium by which experience can be combined to create the new form of information so that it will be deemed as creative. The combination rule should be based on simple principles, and the creative act can be implemented and viewed as syntactive, a largely domain-independent process.

The ultimate goal of acquiring strategic heuristics and to store such rules is to use them as an aid to enhance the functions of knowledge-based systems. They can be combined with domain knowledge in various application domains so that interesting and novel conclusions or suggestions can be made, or the quality of the answer produced by the system can be improved. In general, creative knowledge will be consulted only when it is needed. For example, in case domain knowledge is not available (thus no conclusion can be made), creative knowledge may be consulted. Creative knowledge can also be used to deal with conflict resolution (that is, several rules in a rule-based system competing to be fired). In some cases, creative knowledge may be combined with domain knowledge to improve the quality of the answer.

Experienced researchers in human creativity have warned us that none of the methods of invention described here, nor any of the related heuristics, will mechanically or computationally produce inventions. Human judgment is very much required [Weber 1992]. However, as pointed out by [Schank and Foster 1995], "(s)ome would argue that creativity is too broad and ill-defined to possibly hope for the development of a mechanistic theory. AI's standard reply is and has been: well, then, let's bite off a small chunk of it, come up with a simple theory (maybe even a rather stupid one), test it out, see where it breaks down, and try again."

Another aspect is how to incorporate creativity into the general task of the knowledge acquisition itself (which is generally considered as the bottleneck of knowledge engineering). Existing knowledge acquisition approaches typically provide users some existing tools for knowledge acquisition, leaving very little room to the users to do creative work. It would be interesting to bring creativity into knowledge acquisition. Since comparing with the task of acquiring creative knowledge, this task is better defined, we have started implementing a prototype system, a self-evolving tool which is able to improve its behavior over time. The tool allows the user (a domain expert) not only to enter new knowledge, but also to specify what kind of knowledge should be acquired and what kind of questions should be asked. By this way, an expert in a knowledge domain can always recast the tool for his own need so that "everybody gets whatever he wanted."

With the hope that creative knowledge can be used to enhance the reasoning ability of knowledge-based systems, an extended expert system model can be developed (to be described in Chapter 14).

SUMMARY

In this chapter we discussed two related issues of computer assisted intelligence and the relationship between creativity and expertise. Since the topic covered in this chapter usually cannot be found in textbooks, in the following we provide some additional issues which may be interesting to some readers.

- *Computation tricks.* One aspect of intelligence we have not discussed so far is intelligence with trick. Computational tricks reflect such human reasoning with trick as "make a feint to the east and attack in the west." One may wonder whether notorious things like tricks deserve any effort of computation at all. Nevertheless, computational tricks have been discussed in the computer world for decades, and the Turing test has been considered as the design of computers which are able to fool human beings. Computational tricks were discussed in [Mauldin 1994, Sun and Weber 1997a, b]. What is the nature of computation tricks? Are they "legal"? Is it possible to use them? These are the among the numerous questions need to be answered.

- *Computers as stimulant.* Computers are used as tools to enhance human creativity. Knowledge-based systems, inductive learning and other techniques are used by social scientists to analyze data and identify patterns of behavior. These techniques have complemented the way humans think and thereby extended their analytical abilities -- enabling social scientists not to work just faster but smarter [Mills 1994].

Emotional intelligence: Another interesting topic is emotional intelligence, which strongly depends on the cultural environment, and is thus very different from "conventional" intelligence. Emotion consists of anger, sadness, fear, enjoyment, love, surprise, disgust, shame, and others. For more details, see [Mayer and Salovey 1993, Mayer and Salovey 1997].

SELF-EXAMINATION QUESTIONS

1. In the beginning of this chapter we mentioned the different tasks of computational creativity and computer assisted human intelligence. Can you provide a brief summary about their relationship?
2. The Prolog program introduced in this chapter has some problems. Can you point out some undesirable features related to inheritance?
3.   Select one of your favorite folk stories and analyze the strategic knowledge implied by it.

REFERENCES

Boden, M., *Creative Mind: Myths & Mechanisms,* Weidenfield and Nicolson, London, 1990.
Boden, M., Creativity and computers, *Cybernetics and Systems,* 26, 267-293, 1995.
Chen, Z., Combining creativity and expertise, *Cybernetics and Systems,* 28, 327-336, 1997a.
Chen, Z., Acquiring creative knowledge for knowledge-based systems, *Journal of Intelligent Systems,* 6(3/4), 179-198, 1997b.
Chen, Z., Idea Processors, *Encyclopedia of Electrical and Electronics Eng.* (Webster, J. G. ed.), John Wiley, New York, Vol. 9, pp. 467-480, 1999a.
Chen, Z., Retrospective analysis for knowledge-based idea generation of new articrafts, *Knowledge-based systems,* 1999b (to appear).
Dartnall, T. (ed.), *Artificial Intelligence and Creativity: An Interdisciplinary Approach,* Kluwer, Boston, 1994.
Dasgupta, S., *Creativity in Invention and Design: Computational and Cognitive Explorations of Technological Originality,* Cambridge University Press, New York, 1994.
Davis, E., *Representations of Commonsense Knowledge,* Morgan Kaufmann, Palo Alto, CA, 1990.
Finke, R. A., Ward, T. B. and Smith, S. M., *Creative Cognition: Theory Research and Applications,* The MIT Press, Cambridge, MA, 1992.
Friedel, R., Perspiration in perspective: Changing perceptions of genius and expertise in American invention, in Weber, R. J. and Perkins, D. N. (eds.), *Inventive Minds,* 11-31, 1992.
Holsapple, C. W. and Whinston, A. B., *Decision Support Systems: A Knowledge-Based Approach,* West Publishing, Minneapolis/St. Paul, 1996.
Koestler, A., *The act of creation.* New York, Macmillan 1974.
Langley, P., Simon, H. A., Bradshaw, G. L. and Zytkow, J. M., *Scientific Discovery: Computational Explorations of Creative Process,* MIT Press, Cambridge, MA, 1987.

Lenat, D. B. and Guha, R. V., *Building Large Knowledge-Based Systems: Representation and Inference in the CYC Project,* Addison-Wesley, Reading, MA, 1990.

Levinson, R., Experience-based creativity, in *Artificial Intelligence and Creativity: An Interdisciplinary Approach* (T. Dartnall, ed.), 161-180, 1994.

Luger, G. F. and Stubblefield, W. A., *Artificial Intelligence: Structures and Strategies for Complex Problem Solving* (3rd ed.), Addison-Wesley Longman, Harlow, England, 1998.

Mauldin, M. L., Chatterbots, Tinymuds, and the Turing test: Entering the Loebner prize competion, *Proceedings AAAI-94,* 1994.

Mayer, J. D. and Salovey, P., The intelligence of emotional intelligence. *Intelligence,* 1993, 17(4), 433-442.

Mayer, J. D. and Salovey, P. What is emotional intelligence? In P. Salovey and D. Slyter (eds.) *Emotional Development and Emotional Intelligence: Implications for Educators,* Basic Books, New York, 1993.

Michalski, R. S., A theory and methodology of inductive learning, *Artificial Intelligence,* 20, 2, 111-161, 1983.

Mills, W. deB., Working smarter: Compuers as stimulants for human creativity, *Social Science Computer Review,* 12(2), 215-230, 1994.

Osborne, A., *Applied Imagination: Principles and Procedures of Creative Thinking* (3rd ed.), Scribner, New York, 1963.

Piatetsky-Shapiro, G., and Frawley, W. (eds.), *Knowledge Discovery in Databases.* AAAI/MIT Press, Menlo Park, CA, 1991.

Rawlinson, J. G., *Creative Thinking and Brainstorming,* Westmead, England: Gower, 1981.

Rothenberg, A., *The Emerging Goddess: The Creative Process in Art, Science, and Other Fields,* University of Chicago Press, Chicago, 1979.

Schank, R. C. and Foster, D. A., The engineering of creativity: a review of Boden's *The Creative Mind , Artifiical Intelligence,* 219, 129-143. 1995.

Schorr, J., Smart thinking: Eight programs that help you think creatively and plan effectively, *Macworld ,* 11 (5), 138 - 144. 1995.

Simonton, D. K., *Genius, Creativity, and Leadership: Historiometric Inquiries,* Harvard University Press, Cambridge, MA, 1984.

Stefik, M. and Smoliar, S. (eds.), *The Creative Mind: Myths and Mechanisms*: six reviews and a response, *Artificial Intelligence,* 79, 65-67, 1995.

Sun, Z. and Weber, K., Logic with trick, Paper presented at InfoSymp'97, Baden-Baden, Germany, Aug. 1997a.

Sun, Z. and Weber, K., Turing test and intelligence with trick, *Proceedings of 8th Ireland Conference of AI,* Sept. 1997b.

Weber R. J. and Perkins, D. N., How to invent artifacts and ideas, *New Ideas in Psychology,* 7, 49-72, 1989.

Weber, R. J. and Perkins, D. N. (eds.), *Inventive Minds: Creativity in technology,* Oxford, New York, 1992.

Weber, R. J., Toward a language of invention and synthetic thinking, *Creativity Research Journal ,* 9(4), 353-368, 1996.

Young, L. F., The Metaphor Machine: A Database Method for Creativity Support, *Decision Support Systems,* 3, 309-317, 1987.
Young, L. F., *Decision Support and Idea Processing Systems,* Wm. C. Brown, Dubuque, Iowa, 1988.

Chapter 9

CONCEPTUAL QUERIES AND INTENSIONAL ANSWERING

9.1 OVERVIEW

In Chapter 5 we have examined different kinds of basic retrieval systems. An intelligent agent should be able to perform interoperation among different types of retrieval. In addition, in order to support decision making, we may also wish an intelligent agent to demonstrate other desirable features such as handling non-exact retrieval (as illustrated in Section 7.2). In general, an intelligent agent should be able to answer queries in a flexible manner. For example, in a company database, a user may want to retrieve products with "high" profits. In a job application candidate database, a recruiter may want to retrieve candidates with "excellent" working experience. Note that in these examples "high" profits and "excellent" working experience are not part of the database schema, but (hopefully) can be converted into the actual database schema. In this chapter we will examine several issues related to this topic. We start with a brief review of question answering systems, focusing on conceptual query answering. It uses knowledge discovery techniques (to be discussed in Chapter 10 and Chapter 13).

9.2 A REVIEW OF QUESTION ANSWERING SYSTEMS

9.2.1 WHAT IS A QUESTION ANSWERING SYSTEM?

Since the days of Turing test, question answering (QA) has been an important topic in computational intelligence. Although the study of computational intelligence has diversified far beyond the notion of intelligent behavior proposed in the Turing test, QA remains a fundamental capability needed by a large class of systems. It is a methodological tool to structure a task and specify its scope using a question grammar. Note that an interesting aspect of QA is that it may not be necessarily associated with intelligent behavior. For example, QA has a parallel to query processing in database management systems. However, it goes far beyond what can be achieved using DBMS. Many analytical tasks that involve gathering, correlating and analyzing information can naturally be formulated as QA problems. With the recent explosion of information available on the World Wide Web, QA is becoming a compelling framework for finding information that closely matches user needs. Important research issues include the following [AAAI 1999]:

- Methods to rapidly construct the knowledge base of a QA system;
- Techniques to construct a KB by reuse and reformulation;
- A study of existing knowledge repositories;
- Techniques for interfacing inference techniques with DBMSs;
- Using information from external knowledge sources in QA;
- Measuring competence of a QA system;
- Answer summarization and explanation;
- Techniques for evaluating and benchmarking QA systems; and
- An evaluation of implemented QA systems.

9.2.2 SOME FEATURES OF QUESTION ANSWERING

At the beginning of Chapter 7 we briefly discussed non-exact retrieval. An example of a fuzzy query could be: "Find the towns in the heartland that have a low unemployment rate and have nice residence areas." This query can be viewed as at least two ways: as a conceptual query which involves attribute-oriented induction (see below), or as a fuzzy query, which is a query formulated in fuzzy terms and for any of the attributes a fuzzy proposition formed: x_i is A_{ij}. Fuzzy queries are possible to non-fuzzy databases if the fuzzy predicates used in the queries are represented in advance by their membership functions. A fuzzy query to a non-fuzzy database resembles matching a fuzzy rule against crisp data, which is opposite to the fuzzy inference methods in fuzzy systems.

In another study, a data warehouse set-up for providing approximate query answers is discussed in [Gibbons and Matias 1998], where a theory of information granulation and its relationship with attribute-oriented induction is presented. Summary statistics have been used for query answering.

The above examples have shown that query answering is a multi-facet issue. In this chapter, we will focus on the concept of query answering alone, and use techniques mainly based on knowledge discovery in database (or KDD). A brief introduction on knowledge discovery in databases (KDD) and data mining will be presented in this paper. A more detailed discussion on data mining will be continued in Chapter 10, and an examination of data warehousing will be given in Chapter 11. Fuzzy set theory will be discussed in Chapter 12.

9.3   INTENSIONAL ANSWERING AND CONCEPTUAL QUERY

Our discussion on intelligent query answering starts with some basic terminology. We will be focusing on two related terms: intensional answering and conceptual query.

9.3.1 MEANING OF INTENSIONAL ANSWERS

An *intensional answer* to a query is a set of characterizations of the set of database values that satisfy the query (the actual data retrieved are referred to as the extensional answer.) Intensional answers are derived entirely from the extensional information in the database. Intensional answers can be derived using KDD techniques. KDD is concerned with the overall process and specific techniques of the nontrivial extraction of implicit, previously unknown, and potentially useful information from data. A more detailed discussion on KDD and data mining will be given in Chapter 10.

An *intensional answer* to a query is a set of characterizations of the set of database values that satisfy the query (the actual data retrieved are referred to as the extensional answer.) Intensional answers are derived entirely from the extensional information in the database [Motro 1989, 1994; Han, Huang, Cercone and Fu 1996]). For example, for the query of finding excellent students, an intensional answer could be some common features (such as good GPA) shared by these students, rather than the names of these students.

Note that the intensional database as discussed in Chapter 4 is part of the database while intensional answers are generated from the database. So their relationship is somewhat similar to relations (which are stored tables) versus views (which are virtual tables) in relational databases. So you should not equate intensional database with intensional answers, although the word "intensional" means the same thing for both (namely, non-extensional, or, "not tuples.")

To focus our discussion, in this chapter we will only consider conceptual query answering using a popular technique, namely, attribute-oriented induction method for knowledge discovery in databases (KDD) [Han, Fu and Ng 1994]. A more detailed discussion on KDD and data mining is continued in the next chapter.

9.3.2 INTENSIONAL ANSWERING USING KNOWLEDGE DISCOVERY

In order to understand what is an intensional answer and how knowledge discovery can help, let us consider a student database. We want to know "the most important features of graduate students." Note that this is an intensional answer because we are not interested in any particular names of the students. The following process demonstrates how an intensional answer can be produced using a specific technique called characteristic rules. This example follows [Cai, Cercone and Han 1991].

A *characteristic rule* is an assertion that characterizes the concept satisfied by all the data stored in the database. This can be illustrated by the following example. Suppose we have a student relation in a sample university database consisting of the following attributes (fields): name, category, major, birthplace and GPA. In addition, we have a concept hierarchy table which is a concept tree organized as an IS-A hierarchy (for example, "music" and "history" can be generalized into "art," while "junior" and "senior" can be generalized into "undergraduate," etc.). Now we want to find out something interesting about graduate students. A four-step algorithm for learning a characteristic rule can be performed as follows.

- *Step 1 is the extraction of the task-relevant data by performing selection, projection, and join on the relevant relations* (such as dropping the student name attributes, since we are not interested in individual students).
- *Step 2 is the attribute-oriented induction process*; generalization should be performed on attributes by substituting each attribute value with its higher-level concept (such as replacing "physics" by "science").
- *Step 3 is the simplification of the generalized relation* (such as removal of duplication).
- *Step 4 is the transformation of the final relation into a logic formula.*

The following is a sample rule which may be produced by the discovery process and can be used to produce an intensional answer:

> a graduate student is either a citizen born in this conutry with an excellent GPA or a foreign student majoring in science with a good GPA.

Notice that this rule was not explicitly stated anywhere in the database. Rather, it is *derived* from the stored data. The most popular format of a database rule takes the format of "If C_1 then C_2," or $C_1 \rightarrow C_2$. In fact, a rule is not necessary to cover all instances. If a rule is almost always correct, then it is called a strong rule.

The algorithm described above illustrates the basic idea of knowledge discovery in databases. According to the definition cited in the beginning of this paper, knowledge discovery is the nontrivial extraction of implicit, previously unknown, and potentially useful information from data. Given a set of facts (data) F, a language L, and some measure of Certainty C , a *pattern* is defined as a statement S in L that describes relationships among a subset F_s of F with a certainty c , such that in some sense S is simpler than the enumeration of all facts in F_s. A pattern that is *interesting* and *certain* enough is referred to as *knowledge*; the output of a program that monitors the set of facts in a database and produces patterns in this sense is referred to as *discovered knowledge*.

A term closely related to KDD is *data mining*. Some people use these two terms interchangeably. However, recently a distinction has been made so that the KDD will be used to refer to the overall process of knowledge discovery while the term data mining refers to the actual algorithms used in the discovery process. A more detailed discussion on KDD and data mining is presented in Chapter 10.

9.3.3 CONCEPTUAL QUERY ANSWERING

Conceptual query answering is concerned with the following information need. DBMS users may want to ask general questions involving conceptual terms which may not match the database schema or data. For example, "What are expensive restaurants in the heartland which are frequently visited by senior people?" Here the italicized words illustrate different cases of conceptual terms in the user's mind. The stored data may not have an attribute "heartland," does not have values such as "expensive" or "senior" (although actual ages may be stored), and does not indicate frequency of visit directly (although date of visit may be stored). Conceptual query answering should handle these problems.

Conceptual queries are not exactly the same as intensional answers, but they share some similar concerns. Although conceptual query answering has been studied in the field of information retrieval, it has not been widely studied in DBMS.

The task of *conceptual* (or *intelligent*) query answering is to map users' conceptual queries to actual database queries and to produce answers for the users' queries. Conceptual queries have been extensively studied in the Information Retrieval (IR) community, and have drawn increasing attention from the database research community as well. An example of conceptual query is: What kind of people are first-time homebuyers who bought expensive houses in West Omaha? Note here the term "expensive houses" is not a database attribute nor an actual value, and thus need to be mapped to actual database values. Note also that the term "conceptual query answering" is closely related to some other terms (such as flexible query answering [Barklund, Dell'Acqua and Costantini 1996] or cooperative query answering [Cuppens and Demolombe 1988, Demolombe 1991, Gaasterland, Godfrey and Minker 1992], thus containing a very rich content. In addition, conceptual queries may also be concerned with user intention or behavior [Gaasterland 1997, Wu, Cercone and Ichikawa 1995].

As for the format of the answers for conceptual answers, we follow the proposal made by [Imielinski 1987]. In this research, the structure of an answer is identical to the structure of database itself, with an extensional part and an intensional part. Such answers have both conceptual and computational advantages. In the previous example of first time homebuyers, we may answer this query by retrieving all the actual tuples (which is the extensional answer) along with a set of characteristics of these people (which is the intensional answer). In fact, an answer could also be of a mixed format, as discussed in [Motro 1994]. For example, the query, "Who has high income in Company SuperInfo?" could be answered by "All the employees assigned to project P2 and Mary." The first part of this answer is intensional while the second part is extensional. Therefore, just like answers for conventional queries could be extensional or intensional, answers for conceptual queries may also fall in two categories: to find actual tuples, or to find descriptive features for the conceptual information needs the user requested. Some work in cooperative query answering using multiple layered databases (MLDBs) can be found in [Han, Fu and Ng 1994, Yoon, Song and Park 1997].

In the remainder of this chapter we examine the relationship between conceptual query answering and intensional answers using techniques developed from knowledge discovery in databases. We start with a critical review on why existing studies do not satisfy conceptual query answering in data warehouse environments. The issues of our investigation include: to study the relationship between intensional answers and materialized views in databases, to study the duality principle between conceptual query answering and intensional answers under the simple case where conceptual queries can be answered by intensional answers alone (using one or more intensional answers), and to investigate two practical approaches to deal with cases when some intensional answers are not available for answering conceptual queries. The first approach involves the use of a query-invoked process to produce necessary intensional answers to answer the conceptual query, thus combining both lazy and eager strategies. The second approach requires rewriting of the original conceptual query submitted by the user. Furthermore, as an application of conceptual query answering using intensional answers, we sketch the basic idea of constructing recommender systems using a data warehousing approach.

9.3.4 DUALITY BETWEEN CONCEPTUAL QUERIES AND INTENSIONAL ANSWERS

9.3.4.1 The duality principle

In this section, we consider conceptual queries through their connection with intensional answers under the simple case where conceptual queries are constructed in such a manner so that they can be answered by their corresponding intensional answers.

We assume intensional answers are expressed in English or Datalog-like rules. The conceptual queries are usually stated in English while its answers are expressed in Datalog-like rules. For example, suppose we have the following intensional answer for a query in a student database, which states that an excellent student is a young TA (note that "excellent" is not an attribute or a data value in the database; rather, it is in a concept hierarchy):

$$excellent(s) :- (s \in Student), (c \in Course), (c.TA = s.Sname),$$
$$(s.age = young).$$

(Remember a comma stands for "and.")

This intensional answer allows us to handle the following conceptual query: Who are the excellent students? This conceptual query can be answered by either (a) providing features of excellent students as stated in the body of the above rule, or (b) displaying tuples of the students which are TAs.

As illustrated in the above example, we are mainly interested in conceptual queries (CQs), but an important relationship between conceptual queries and intensional answers (IA) should be studied first. The duality between these two kinds of information activities can be informally stated as two properties, as shown below.

Property 1 of CQ-IA Duality:

> (i) A conceptual query C can be answered if there is an intensional answer in the form of a rule "C :- body" (here both C and body indicate valid form of left-hand side and right-hand side of a rule).

> (ii) If "head :- body" is an intensional answer for a conventional query, then the head can be used as a conceptual query.

Recall that from the same extensional answer, several different intensional answers can be formed. Similarly we may have the following property.

Property 2 of CQ-IA Duality:

> If a conceptual query C can be expressed in the form of the form C :- C_1, C_2,..., C_n (where each C_i is a conceptual sub-query), then each C_i can be connected to an IA in a manner of (i) or (ii) as stated in Property 1 of CQ-IA duality.

9.3.4.2 Constructing conceptual queries from intensional answers

A straightforward use of the Duality principle is that from each intensional answer we can identify a variety of potential conceptual queries it can answer. For example, consider the intensional answer:

> valued-customer(X) :- rich(X), willing-to-buy(X).

The following are some conceptual queries that can be answered from this intensional answer:

> (a) What are the characteristics of valued customers? (Answer: rich and willing to buy.)

> (b) What if a customer is rich? (Answer: She would be a valued customer if she is willing to buy.)

> (c) What if a customer is willing to buy? (Answer: She would be a valued customer if she is rich.)

Note that the issue of distinguishing sufficient and necessary conditions is omitted here due to space limitation. (We may also consider Quasi-answer and meta patterns.)

9.3.4.3 Query-invoked generation of intensional answers

For cases where some intensional answers are not available to answer a conceptual query, we propose two alternatives. In this section, we discuss how to use a query-invoked process to produce necessary intensional answers to answer the conceptual query. In the next section, we discuss a more general method which involves query rewriting.

Using the duality we can identify that at least four different approaches exist. Note that except for approach A, all the other approaches require query-invoked generation of intensional answers. Also note that these approaches described above subsume some approaches reviewed earlier.

Approach A: Apply data mining techniques to obtain intensional answers. Intensional answers obtained earlier will be used later to generate answers for conceptual queries. In this case, the extensional part attached with an intensional answer plays the role of a materialized view. Discussions provided in the previous section can be applied here.

Approach B: CQ serves as a trigger to activate an IA process. This approach assumes no preprocessing; instead, CQ activates a process so that intensional answers will be generated and then compared with the CQ. This approach may be interesting in theoretical perspectives (particularly those associated with CQ-IA duality), but it is also difficult to implement for several obvious reasons; for example, in order to activate an intensional answer, a conventional query should be generated, and this query should be as "close" to the conceptual query as possible. A kind of measure (or any criterion) needs to be established to determine this closeness.

Approach C: Generating answers on the fly. This approach also assumes no preprocessing; CQ will trigger a process to construct an answer on the fly. This may need the help of some pre-existing mechanism, for example, using the concept hierarchy. If the corresponding IA is to use generalization, then this process uses specialization. It may even spawn to subqueries of the original conceptual queries if necessary. Note that Approach C is similar to Approach B, but answers obtained in these two approaches may not be identical.

Approach D: Bi-directional search. Note that the CQ-IA duality implies that to process CQ and to find an IA can be considered as two opposite directions. Approach D utilizes this fact by combining approaches A and B or A and C, so that some "middle" ground can be found from two different directions.

In summary, these approaches combine both lazy and eager approaches for answering conceptual queries.

9.4   AN APPROACH FOR INTENSIONAL CONCEPTUAL QUERY ANSWERING

9.4.1 INTRODUCTION

The connections between conceptual queries and intensional answers in database management systems: Both of these concepts are closely related to knowledge discovery in databases (KDD) and data mining [Piatetsky-Shapiro and Frawley 1991, Fayyad, Smyth and Uthurusamy 1996], which are concerned with the overall process and specific techniques of the nontrivial extraction of implicit, previously unknown, and potentially useful information from data.

On the one hand, an intensional answer to a query is a set of characterizations of the set of database values that satisfy the query (the actual data retrieved are referred to as the extensional answer.) Intensional answers are derived from the extensional information in the database [Motro 1994, Han, Cercone and Fu 1996]. For example, for the query of finding excellent students, an intensional answer could be some common features (such as good

GPA) shared by these students, rather than the names of these students. On the other hand, the task of *conceptual* (or *intelligent*, or *cooperative*) query answering is to map users' conceptual queries to actual database queries and to produce answers for the users' queries [Imilienski 1987].

Studies in intensional answers and conceptual query answering have largely been done by researchers in different camps. Traditionally, conceptual query answering handles conceptual queries by providing extensional data, while intensional answers handle conventional queries by providing abstract data. Although some authors started investigating their connections, a general methodology that deals with *how* to provide intensional answers for conceptual answers has yet to be developed. For example, based on an attribute-oriented data mining technique, an outline of cooperative query answering using multiple layered databases (MLDBs) was proposed in [Han, Fu and Ng 1994].

Intensional answers for conceptual queries are particularly important for processing users' *ad hoc* decision support queries for On-Line Analytical Processing (OLAP) in data warehousing environments (see Chapter 5 and Chapter 11). Relaxation can be used to automatically identify new queries that are related to the user's original query [Gaasterland 1997]. A related but more radical concept is query-free information retrieval [Hart and Graham 1997].

In the following we focus on the cases where conceptual queries can be answered by intensional answers or can be answered through a query-invoked knowledge-reorganization process. The query-invoked process to produce necessary intensional answers for a conceptual query can be carried out in several different ways, including application of data mining techniques to obtain intensional answers so that they can be used later (an eager approach), or to have conceptual queries serve as a trigger to activate an intensional answer generation process (*a lazy approach*). We present an outline of a methodology which provides intensional answers for conceptual queries using attribute-oriented data mining techniques. In order to incorporate the eager approach, an abstract database should be constructed to handle frequently submitted queries. The process of generating intensional answers for conceptual queries are then outlined. The actual steps of generating intensional answers for conceptual queries are then discussed.

9.4.2 CONSTRUCTING AN ABSTRACT DATABASE FOR INTENSIONAL ANSWERS

The construction of an abstract database can be summarized as follows.

1. In frequently used relations, keep only those frequently referenced attributes.

2. Based on the given concept hierarchies and statistical information, generalize the values of the retained attributes level by level, from the most specific layer to the most general layer.

3. Merge identical tuples in each generalized relation and update the count or vote of the generalized tuples. (The purpose of using vote or

count is to control the quality of generalization using a predefined threshold.)

4. Based on the given information of query access patterns, some relations may be joined together to form a new relation. The join operation should be performed on primitive relation to avoid key removal. After the join operation, perform steps 1, 2, and 3.

5. Keep the record for every new schema for generalized relations, and also keep the record of different concept levels for every attribute in each relation.

As an example, let us consider a database consisting of information of house-buyers, along with the furniture purchased. Figure 9.1 depicts a concept hierarchy for family-income in relation House-buyer. Figure 9.2 depicts a concept hierarchy for household-appliances in relation Family-purchase. Table 9.1 is a portion of the generalized relation of House-buyer after the conceptual hierarchies are applied. Table 9.2 is a portion of the generalized relation after House-buyer and Family-purchase are joined [Lu and Chen 1998].

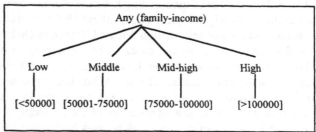

Figure 9.1 Income hierarchy

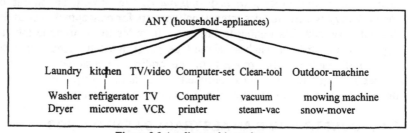

Figure 9.2 Appliances hierarchy

Table 9.1 House relation (Part)

Age	family-income	house-price	house-type	vote
young	high	expensive	two-story	12
middle	middle-high	mid-expensive	two-story	54
young	middle	medium	tri-level	88
young	low	medium	tri-level	40
old	low	low	ranch	
young	mid-high	expensive	two-story	33

Table 9.2 Family appliance (Part)

age	family-income	house price	furniture	f-price	household-appliances (h.a.)	h.a-price
young	high	Expensive	bedroom living-room dining-room	5400	TV/video kitchen laundry outdoor-machine	3400
middle	mid-high	mid-expensive	bedroom living-room	2200	laundry outdoor-machine	1700
young	mid-high	medium	dining-room living-room study-room	3750	computer-set TV/video	3000
...	...	...	...		...	...

9.4.3 GENERATING INTENSIONAL ANSWERS FOR CONCEPTUAL QUERIES

The general   process of generating   intensional answers for conceptual queries are sketched below. We assume the existence of related conceptual hierarchies, as well as a related abstracted database. Conceptual query answering consists of three steps [Lu and Chen 1998].

Step 1. Analyzing query type. Upon receiving a query, we analyze the conditions involved in the query and decide which type the query belongs to. In general, we distinguish three types of query: (a) simple conceptual query (which can be answered directly using the abstract database), (b) complex conceptual query (which should be mapped to abstract database), (c) mixed queries (which contains a part which can be directly answered by the abstract database and another part which needs to be mapped to the abstract database).

Step 2. Acquiring the extensional answer. For consideration related to efficiency, some attributes may be removed first. We then process the query and acquire the answer.

Step 3. Producing intensional answers.

The answers acquired in Step 2 may be of a different format. Although the result of simple queries might already be in the form of an intensional answer with high level concepts, the result of complex queries will still be in conventional form (namely, extensional answer). For extensional answers, further data mining is needed, which can be carried out using the steps such as removal of irrelevant attributes, with user's help, if necessary; generalization of each specific value to higher level (one level at a time); and generating an intensional answer from the generalized result.

9.4.4 METHOD FOR INTENSIONAL CONCEPTUAL QUERY ANSWERING

We now provide more detail on generating intensional conceptual query answers. In general, we can distinguish three cases:

Case 1: Queries can be answered directly by search-only abstract database. This is an extreme case and demonstrates the typical eager approach.

Case 2: Queries cannot be answered by the abstract database. This is another extreme case and demonstrates the typical lazy approach.

Case 3 is the combination of the above two cases, which combines the eager and lazy approaches.

Since Case 3 is the combination of Case 1 and Case 2, in the following we use the following example to illustrate Case 3. Consider a database containing information about the housing market in Omaha. The original relation schema is

House-sold (original-owner, address, location, house-price, house-type, floor-area, construction-data, school-area, distance-to-school, day-of-sale).

In addition, using conceptual hierarchies, a relation with the following schema is generated and is stored in an abstract database House-for-sale' (in general, an abstract relation for relation r is denoted as r'):

House-for-sale' (address, location house-price, house-type, floor-area, construction-date).

Note that although attributes in the abstract database may have the same name as those in the actual database, the domains of these attributes are usually different. For example, the values for the floor-area in the actual database are numerical values in square feet, while the values in the abstract database are qualitative values such as large, medium, small, and so on.

A user who just relocated in Omaha may want to submit the following query: "Find a house for sale at *west Omaha*, which should be located *near to a school*, and the price of the house is in the *middle range*, with *middle size* floor area, and the *average price* of the houses in this residential quarter has increased *mostly* in the past three years."

Note that in this query, some needed information (such as distance-to-school) is in the actual database while some other information (such as middle-size floor area) will make use of the abstract database. Therefore, to answer this query, both of the original and the abstract databases should be accessed. In addition, the conceptual hierarchies used for the construction of the abstract database may also be needed.

The following are the major steps involved in answering this query.

(1) Remove non-referenced attributes from relation House-sold.

(2) Select the tuples with the values of attribute day-for-sale equal to 1995, 1996 and 1997.

(3) Map the abstract terms "west Omaha," "middle," "near to school" to their corresponding primitive values and select these tuples satisfying the conditions in the query.

(4) Group the tuples by location.

(5) For tuples in each location, further group them by year.

(6) Calculate the average sales price of different years for every location.

(7) Create a new attribute increase-rate for every location and calculate the increase-rate based on the values of average sales price of different years.

(8) Select attributes location and increase-rate from the relation House-sold and join with the generalized relation House-for-sale' in the abstract database using key location.

(9) Find the location(s) with middle house price, middle size floor area, near to school, and with the largest value of increase-rate.

The final answer to the query contains one or few locations.

The above steps illustrate a general methodology for intensional conceptual query answering.

SUMMARY

In this chapter we examined the issue of conceptual query answering. Although it is a relatively short chapter, it has a close relationship with other chapters, particularly with materials to be presented in Chapters 10 and 11. We will get a chance to review the issue of conceptual query answering in Chapters 10 and 11.

SELF-EXAMINATION QUESTIONS

1. In the method presented in Section 9.4, we have assumed that the conceptual hierarchy is already constructed. Suppose no such hierarchy exists; how will you construct such a hierarchy which is useful for conceptual query answering?

2. Based on the description of the abstract database, give an example to show what the tuples in the abstract database would look like. You may first construct a few tuples in the original database, and use the conceptual hierarchy to generate tuples in the abstract database.

3. Using the database schema described in Section 9.4, make two examples of conceptual queries.

REFERENCES

AAAI 1999, Workshop of Question Answering Systems, AAAI 1999 Fall Symposium Series.

Barklund, J., Dell'Acqua, P. and Costantini, S., Multiple meta-reasoning agents for flexible query-answering systems, in 1996 Workshop on Flexible

Query-Answering Systems (FQAS '96), *Datalogiske Skrifter*, No. 62, 155-156, 1996.

Cai, Y., Cercone, N. and J. Han, J., Attribute-oriented induction in relational databases, Chaps. 12 in G. Piatetsky-Shapiro and W. J. Frawley (eds.), *Knowledge Discovery in Databases*, AAAI/MIT Press, Menlo Park, CA, 1991.

Cuppens, F. and Demolombe, R., Cooperative answering: a methodology to provide intelligent access to databases, *Proc. 2nd Int'l Conf. Expert Database Systems*, 621-643, 1988.

Demolombe, R., Cooperative access to data and knowledge bases, Proc. 7th Int'l Conf. VLDB, pp. 387, 1991.

Fayyad, U. M., Piatetsky-Shapiro, G., Smyth, P. and Uthurusamy, R. (eds.), *Advances in Knowledge Discovery and Data Mining*, AAAI/MIT Press, Menlo Park, CA, 1996.

Gaasterland, T., Godfrey, P. and Minker, J., An overview of cooperative query answering. *J. Intel. Info. Sys*, 1, 123-157, 1992.

Gaasterland, T., Cooperative answering through controlled query relaxation, *IEEE Expert*, 12(5), pp. 48-59, 1997.

Gibbons, P. B. and Matias, Y., New sampling-based statistics for improving approximate query answers, *Proc. SIGMOD '98*, 331-341, 1998.

Han, J., Fu, Y. and Ng, R., Cooperative query answering using multiple layered databases, *Proceedings of 2nd International Conference on Cooperative Info. Sys.*, 47-58, 1994.

Han, J., Huang, Y., Cercone, N. and Fu, Y., Intelligent query answering by knowledge discovery techniques, *IEEE Transactions on Knowledge and Data Engineering*, 8(3), June 1996, pp. 373-390.

Hart, P. and Graham, J., Query-free information retrieval, *IEEE Expert*, 12(5), pp. 32-37, 1997.

Imielinski, T., Intelligent query answering in rule based systems, *J. Logic Programming*, 4(3), 229-257, 1987.

Lu, P. and Chen, Z., Intensional conceptual query answering through data mining, *Proceedings 4th Joint Conference of Information Sciences*, Vol. III, pp. 479-482, 1998.

Motro, A., Using integrity constraints to provide intensional answers to relational queries. *Proceedings of 15th International Conference on VLDB*, 237-246, 1989.

Motro, A., Intensional answers to database queries. *IEEE Transactions on Knowledge and Data Engineering*, 6(3), 444-454, 1994.

Piatetsky-Shapiro, G. and Frawley, W. J. (eds.), *Knowledge Discovery in Databases*, AAAI/MIT Press, Menlo Park, CA, 1991.

Wu, X., Cercone, N. and Ichikawa, T., A knowledge-based system for generating informative responses to indirect database queries, *Journal of Intelligent Information Systems*, 5, 5-23, 1995.

Yoon, S. C., Song, I. Y. and Park, E. K., Intensional query processing using data mining approaches, *Proceedings CIKM '97*, 201-208, 1997.

Chapter 10

FROM MACHINE LEARNING TO DATA MINING

10.1 OVERVIEW

In this book we stay with a unified approach to discuss data and knowledge management. We started from what we called exact retrieval, and then moved to non-exact retrieval. We have seen knowledge retrieval as extended data retrieval through analogical reasoning. The next thing we want to focus on is how to *max out useful information from retrieval systems*. This leads to the discussion of two closely related issues: machine learning (which was briefly introduced in Chapter 9) and data mining.

The materials presented in this chapter are important, due to several reasons. First of all, the notion of machine learning is very useful. As already briefly explained earlier, machine learning, as a process of search and knowledge representation, serves as a re-examination of computational intelligence (Chapter 2), and provides an effective way for automated knowledge acquisition (Chapter 5). Machine learning is extremely important for building intelligent agents. When the designer has incomplete knowledge of the environment that the agent will live in, learning is the only way that the agent can acquire what it needs to know. Learning thus provides autonomy. It also provides a good way to build high-performance systems [Russell and Norvig 1995].

In addition, the topic covered in this chapter reveals an interesting connection between database management and knowledge-based systems. The two concepts, data and knowledge, can be connected through the notions of knowledge discovery in databases (KDD) and data mining. Knowledge discovery in databases (KDD) and data mining is a typical example of shared interest of computational intelligence and data/information retrieval. It is also a typical example of how their methods differ from each other. Computational intelligence techniques can be used to achieve agent-based data mining. Finally, we should also notice the interesting connection between uncertainty reasoning in knowledge-based systems and machine learning, because uncertain reasoning methods may contribute useful techniques to perform machine learning. Their relationship can also be examined from another perspective: machine learning methods intend to find regularity from data, and thus remove uncertainty from data, or maintain what is certain in the data.

Basic research has been carried out in the field of machine learning for many years. But in reality it is data mining which is rapidly gaining popularity, largely due to the ever-increasing information need from profit-making organizations. Machine learning and data mining share common concerns in philosophy: making implicit things (such as patterns hidden in the data) explicit. One frequently mentioned difference between machine learning and data mining is the problem related to scaling. The study of machine learning puts emphasis on the development of algorithms based on various inference mechanisms and usually assumes data are already residing on the main memory. On the other hand, data mining has been outgrowing from conventional database queries and is a natural extension of database management operations. Note that data mining is not just a database brand of machine learning; it combines work from other fields, including statistic inference. Because of these reasons, machine learning and data mining are studied under different disciplines and are seldom covered in the same book.

The unique perspective adopted by this book allows us to take an integrated approach to discuss both topics in the same chapter. In the following, we start with a discussion on the basics of machine learning (Sections 10.2-10.5), and extend our discussion to data mining (Sections 10.6-10.9).

10.2 BASICS OF MACHINE LEARNING

10.2.1 MACHINE LEARNING: DEFINITION AND APPROACHES

To understand what machine learning is, it is important to know what is learning. According to Herbert Simon, learning refers to any change in a system that allows it to perform better the second time on repetition of the same task or on another task drawn from the same population [Simon, 1983]. Therefore, learning is defined in terms of measurement of future performance. The best model for machine learning is human learning. Evidence from brain science has been used to establish various approaches for machine learning.

- Symbolic approaches build on the assumptions of knowledge-based systems. In these approaches, the primary influence on the behavior of the learning program is its base of explicitly represented domain knowledge.

- Sub-symbolic (artificial neural or connectionist networks) do not construct an explicit model of the world; rather, they are shaped by it. Neural networks do not learn by adding representations to their knowledge base; instead, they learn by modifying their overall structure in order to adapt to the contingencies of the world they inhabit.

- Other approaches: For example, according to social and emergent models of learning, learning algorithms patterned after the processes, underlying evolution: shaping a population of individuals through the survival of its most fit members. Emergent models of learning simulate nature's most elegant and powerful form of adaptation.

In order to carry out machine learning, *training examples* are often needed. Training examples refer to empirical data used to learn a specific concept. For example, in order to learn the concept of a "ball," we need to provide various examples of balls. Based on how training examples are used, machine learning algorithms can be categorized as either *supervised learning* (in which a teacher exists) and *unsupervised learning* (in which such teachers do not exist). Also, additional examples may be needed to test (or verify) the obtained result.

In this book we will only be able to discuss some selected features of machine learning, particularly those related to data mining.

10.3 INDUCTIVE LEARNING

10.3.1 GENERALIZATION FOR INDUCTION

We use inductive learning process to review the notion of machine learning as search and representation. Recall that in Chapter 3, we have discussed the basic notion of inductive reasoning, and pointed out that an important form of performing inductive reasoning is through *generalization*. There are several principles for generalization, such as:

1. Replacing constants by variables: For example, we can replace "student(mary)" by "student(X)."

2. Dropping conditions in conjunctive expressions so that less restriction will be imposed. For example, we can generalize from

"qualified(X) :- gpa(X,G), $G>3$, employment-year(X,Y), $Y>5$"

to

"qualified(X) :- gpa(X,G), $G>3$"

where employment history requirement is dropped.

3. Adding disjunct so that more alternatives will be allowed. For example, we can generalize

"qualified(X) :- gpa(X,G), $G>3$"

by adding another condition, so the rule would look like

"qualified(X) :- gpa(X,G), $G>3$; employment-year(X,Y), $Y>5$."

Note that here semicolon denotes "or."

4. Replacing a property by its parent in the class hierarchy. For example, consider a rule which says the qualification requires a graduate degree. If this requirement is replaced by a college degree, then the requirement is relaxed (namely, generalized).

We should be cautious about the problem of *overgeneralization*, due to the unsoundness of induction. For example, we may attempt to induce that any new car is fast. However, a new toy car is not fast. To avoid overgeneralization, we can simply perform generalization as little as possible (examples of hierarchies in Chapter 9 can provide some insight about this issue). A recent discussion on generalization and generalizability measures is provided by [Wah 1999].

10.3.2 CANDIDATE ELIMINATION ALGORITHM

We now introduce the basic idea of the well-known *candidate elimination algorithm* to illustrate the approach of *version space search*. Here the term candidate refers to candidate concepts, namely, the set of all concept descriptions consistent with the training examples. The algorithm maintains two sets, G and S. G contains maximally general candidates, it stands for the upper bound found so far; while S stands for maximally specific candidates, standing for lower bound found so far. Initially, G contains whole space or all candidate concepts while S is empty. During the execution of the algorithm, G shrinks to exclude negative instances (considering negative examples which were not aware in the past), while S expands to include new positive instances (considering positive examples which were not aware in the past). Any concept that is more general than some concept in G will cover negative instances, while any concept that is more specific than some concept in S will fail to cover some G positive instances. The algorithm terminates when $S = G$. This general process is illustrated in Figure 10.1.

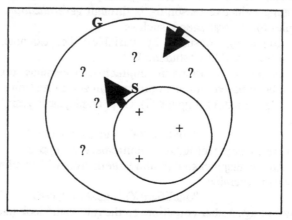

? -- potential target concepts;   +: positive examples

Figure 10.1 G and S in candidate elimination algorithm

10.3.3 ID3 ALGORITHM AND C4.5

As an introduction of a complete machine learning algorithm, let us take a look at ID3. It employs a process of constructing a *decision tree* in a top-down fashion. A decision tree is a hierarchical representation that can be used to determine the classification of an object by testing its values for certain properties. In a decision tree, a leaf node denotes a decision (or classification) while a non-leaf node denotes a property used for decision (such as color, size, etc.). We prefer the shortest path to reach a leaf, because it implies the fewest possible number of questions are needed. Note also that the role of examples is used to guide the construction of a decision tree.

The main algorithm is a recursive process. At each stage of this process, we select a property based on the *information gain* calculated from the training examples. The skeleton of the ID3 algorithm is shown below (following the presentation of [Luger and Stubblefield 1998]. A brief discussion on calculating the information gain will follow.

Algorithm ID3
Input: a set of examples
Output: a decision tree
Method:

ID3_tree (examples, properties)
  if all entries in examples are in the same category of decision variable
    return a leaf node labeled with that category
  else
    calculate information gain;
    select a property P with highest information gain;
    root of the current tree = P;
    properties = properties - P;
    for each value V of P
      create a branch of the tree labeled with V;
      examples_V = subset of examples with values V for property P;
      append ID3_tree (examples_V, properties) to branch V

The information gain is calculated based on the notion of information *entropy*; roughly speaking, it involves a formula of the form $\Sigma k \log k$ where k is the number of training examples pertaining to a particular property (such as color) or a particular value of the property (such as red).

To illustrate the ID3 algorithm, we consider the following set of training example. Our goal is to learn the concept of high or low profit.

Table 10.1 Training examples

ID	Color (C)	Size(S)	Made in (M)	On sale (O)	Profit?
1	Black (Bl)	M	US	Y	Low
2	Brown (Br)	L	US	N	High
3	Brown (Br)	M	US	Y	Low
4	Gray (G)	L	US	Y	High
5	Black (Bl)	S	Foreign	Y	High
6	Gray (G)	M	Foreign	Y	High
7	Black (Bl)	S	US	N	Low
8	White (W)	M	US	N	High

To illustrate how ID3 algorithm proceeds, we make use of a table format to show the steps of the ID3 algorithm. First, we calculate the entropy in regard to all the possible outcomes (regardless properties): high or low profit. We have the following simple calculation:

$$H = -3/8 * log\ 3/8 - 5/8 * log\ 5/8 = 0.955.$$

After the first three columns, there are 11 columns in the table for processing (note that if the classification variable has more than two outcomes, more columns are needed):

(1):c_{ik}: Total number of training examples with value k of the current property with the first classification outcome (i.e., profit is high);

(2) d_{jk}: Total number of training examples with value k of the current property with the second classification outcome (i.e., profit is low);

(3):$c_{jk} + d_{jk}$ = (1)+(2)

(4): f_{ik} = (1)/(3)

(5): g_{ik} = (2)/(3)

(6): $\log f_{ik} = \log(4)$

(7):$\log g_{ik} = \log(5)$

(8): H_{jk} = -(4)*(6) - (5)*(7)

(9): p_{jk} = (3)/n

(10)$H_p = E(H_j) = \Sigma_l^n$ (8) × (9) (Note that there is one H_p value per property. The result is recorded in the first row of the property).

(11): $G_p = H - H_p = H$ - (10) (Note that there is one G_p value per property. The result is recorded in the first row of the property. Note also that H needs to be calculated only once).

The process of computing can be captured using a table format, as illustrated in Table 10.2.

Table 10.2 Calculation of information gains

P	k	v	(1) c_{ik}	(2) d_{jk}	(3)	(4) f_{ik}	(5) g_{ik}	(6) $\log f_{ik}$	(7) $\log g_{ik}$	(8) H_{jk}	(9) p_{jk}	(10) H_p	(11) G_p
C	1	W	0	1	1	0	.5	--	-1	0	.13	.59	.36
	2	Bl	2	1	3	.67	.33	-.59	-1.6	.92	.38		
	3	Br	1	1	2	.5	.5	-1	-1	1	.25		
	4	G	0	2	2	0	1	--	--	0	.25		
S	1	M	2	2	4	.5	.5	-1	-1	1	.5	.75	.2
	2	S	1	1	2	.5	.5	-1	-1	1	.25		
	3	L	0	2	2	0	1	--	--	0	.25		
M	1	U	3	3	6	.5	.5	-1	-1	1	.75	.75	.2
	2	F	0	2	2	0	1	--	--	0	.25		
O	1	Y	3	2	5	.6	.4	-.74	-1.3	.97	.63	.60	.35
	2		0	3	3	0	1	--	1	0	.37		

Based on the calculation, property color with the largest information gain, is selected. The first level of ID3 tree is shown in Figure 10.2(a), with color as the root, and values of color as leafs. Identifiers of examples are attached with the leaf nodes.

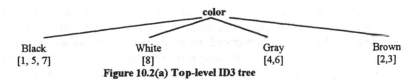

Figure 10.2(a) Top-level ID3 tree

The recursive process continues for a leaf with training examples with mixed results of profits. At the nodes of "black," we have three properties to choose: Size, Made-in and On-sale. The training set involved here contains only three elements, namely instances with ID 1, 5, and 7. Suppose the property "Made-in" was chosen after the information gain is calculated (please verify it). A subtree with root "made-in" is then constructed, as shown in Figure 10.2(b). Since both instances 1 and 7 are made in US·and both have low profit, we have reached the leaf nodes, and no more subtrees should be further considered. At the node "white," there is only one instance 8, so it is a leaf node, and no subtree construction is needed. Same is the case of node "Gray," where both instances 4 and 6 are in the same classification of profit "high." Finally, at the node "brown," the two instances 2 and 3 have different profit classifications, so a recursive process of subtree construction should be carried out. Suppose the property "Size" is chosen (please verify), the subtree can be constructed as shown in Figure 10.2(b). Since size M and L can distinguish the profit, we have reached leaf nodes, and no further construction is needed.

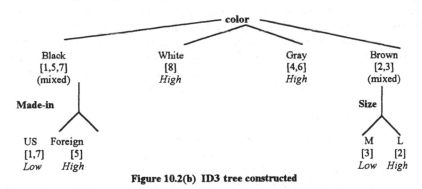

Figure 10.2(b) ID3 tree constructed

The table format shown above clearly indicates the step by step process of ID3 algorithm. Note that there are only two classifications (profit high or low) are involved in the classification. However, the table format calculation can be generalized to the case where more than two classifications exist. In this case, more columns are needed.

ID3 has been proven a very useful method, yet there are many restrictions which make this algorithm not applicable in many real-world situations. For example, the data could be bad (when two or more identical attribute sets give different results), missing data, showing a continuous variable, as well as others. C4.5 was developed to deal with these problems, and can be considered as an enhancement of ID3. Issues considered include bad or missing data, continuous variables, as well as large data size. Specific techniques have been introduced to deal with these issues. For example, bagging produces replicate training sets by sampling with replacement from the training instances, and boosting uses all instances at each replication, but maintains a weight for each instance in the training set [Quinlan 1993, 1996].

10.4   EFFICIENCY AND EFFECTIVENESS OF INDUCTIVE LEARNING

10.4.1 INDUCTIVE BIAS

Generalization provides a useful approach for induction, and empirical data can be used to guide generalization, as shown in ID3 as well as many other algorithms. In order to make induction successful and to improve efficiency, however, it is desirable for the user to provide some hint to guide the learning process. Prior knowledge and assumptions about the nature of the concepts being learned are important to successful learning. One way to incorporate prior knowledge is by providing inductive bias, which refers to any criterion (usually heuristics) a learner uses to constrain the concept space or to select concepts within that space (namely, to prune the search structure). For example, ID3 performs a hill-climbing search through the space of possible decision trees. The calculation of information gain represents a greedy approach: At each stage of the search, ID3 algorithm examines all the tests that could be used to extend the tree and chooses the test that gains the most information to reach a decision. In addition, inductive bias can also take advantage of domain-specific knowledge (even though many learning algorithms are not restricted to any specific domains).

10.4.2 THEORY OF LEARNABILITY

10.4.2.1 Why theory of learning is important

The goal of inductive bias is to restrict the set of target concepts in a way so that we may perform search efficiently and find concept definitions with high quality. This consideration leads to a discussion of quantifying the effectiveness of an inductive bias. The *theory of learnability* has been established for this purpose. Briefly, learnability is a property of concept spaces and is determined by the language required to represent concepts. The theory of learnability is important because it is concerned with two aspects which are both crucial for the success of learning:

- quality of concepts learned; and
- the size of the sample set.

10.4.2.2 PAC learning

Learnability can be measured in terms of probability as discussed in probability theory. Probability theory is concerned with how to handle randomness. (A brief discussion on probability theory will be provided in Chapter 12.) A class of concepts is considered as *learnable* if an algorithm exists that executes efficiently and has a high probability of finding an approximately correct concept. (Note that this definition does not guarantee the correctness of learning.) The theory based on this definition is referred to as PAC learning (i.e., Probably Approximately Correct learning). [Viliant 1984] provided the following definitions for this theory:

- A learned rule r will be called *approximately correct* with accuracy ε if and only if $P(\text{error}) \leq \varepsilon$, where P is the probability function and $0 < \varepsilon < 1$.
- A learning procedure L is *probably approximately correct* (*PAC*) with confidence δ if, given a sequence of randomly selected training examples, the probability that L learns a rule that is not approximately correct is at most δ $(0 < \sigma < 1)$. In other words, we require $P[P(\text{error}) > \varepsilon] < \delta$, here P is the probability function.

The notion of learnabiblity is important for inductive learning. However, a more detailed discussion on PAC learning is out of the scope of our discussion.

10.5 OTHER MACHINE LEARNING APPROACHES

We now take a brief look at some other machine learning techniques. Our purpose is to demonstrate the variety of the techniques available, rather than the detail of these techniques. It is important to understand the unique features of each approach, which is important for an integrated use of various techniques for decision making.

10.5.1 MACHINE LEARNING IN NEURAL NETWORKS

10.5.1.1 Review of neural networks

As briefly described in Chapter 2, the basic feature of neural networks is that they de-emphasize the use of symbols to denote objects and relations; intelligence is viewed as arising from the collective behavior of large numbers of simple, interacting components. The terms subsymbolism and connectionism are used to describe this basic feature. The nodes and weights in a neural network demonstrate a distributed knowledge representation. The architecture of neural networks make themselves suitable for machine learning. In fact, in a neural network, learning is carried out by adjusting weights.

Neural networks have been very useful for many applications. A rich literature exists. For example, using neural networks for business problems solving was discussed in [Bigus 1996]. In this book we will not provide a detailed discussion on neural networks. Instead, we will only summarize some important results which indicate the uniqueness of this approach.

10.5.1.2 Supervised learning

We start with supervised learning where a "teacher" (namely, the "correct" answer) exists in the training session. A type of single-layer network called a perceptron was proposed in late 1950s. A generalization of the perceptron learning algorithm called the *delta rule* is used in many neural network architectures. The delta rule is a mathematical formula to handle error used for training. (Note errors can be measured because of the existence of the teacher.) Intuitively, this delta rule is based on the idea of an error surface, which represents cumulative error over a data set as a function of network weights. Given a weight configuration, the learning algorithm should be able to find the direction on this surface which most rapidly reduces the error.

Multi-layered perceptrons (MLPs) were then proposed to overcome the limitations of single-layer perceptrons. A multilayer perceptron (MLP) consists of an input layer, at least one intermediate or hidden layer, and one ouptut layer. The neurons from each layer are usually fully connected to the neurons from the next layer. The MLPs were put into practice only when learning algorithms were developed for them, one of them being the error-propagation algorithm called *backpropagation*. Error propagation starts at the output layer and an error is propagated backwards through the hidden layers. Backpropagation uses generalized delta rule for training.

Regardless of the training algorithm used for an MLP, there are some common features of MLP architectures, including the following:

- *MLPs are universal approximators* (theorem): An MLP with one hidden function layer can approximate any continuous function to any desired accuracy, subject to a sufficient number of hidden nodes. Multilayered networks are computationally complete, namely, they are equivalent to the class of Turing machines. Note, however, this theorem only shows such an MLP exists without telling how to construct it.
- MLPs are multivariate non-linear regression models.
- MLPs can learn conditional probabilities.

More detailed discussion on MLP can be found in [Kasabov 1996].

10.5.1.3 Unsupervised learning

We now further consider learning in neural networks without a teacher. In this case, we cannot rely on the error rate, because we cannot measure it. In unsupervised learning, a critic is not available, and the weight is modified solely as a function of the input and output values of the neuron. Unsupervised learning is considered to be psychologically plausible, because humans tend to learn more about nature and life through their own experience, rather than by following the correction of a teacher. *Hebbian learning* (or Hebb's theory of learning) can be used as an example of unsupervised learning, although Hebbian learning can also be supervised. Hebb's theory is based on the observation that in biological systems when one neuron contributes to the firing of another neuron, the connection or pathway between the two neurons is strengthened. This theory is appealing because it establishes behavior-based reward concepts at the neuron level. In unsupervised Hebbian learning, the training of the network has the effect of strengthening the network's responses to patterns that it has already seen. Hebbian techniques can be used to model conditioned response learning, where an arbitrarily selected stimulus can be used as a condition for a desired response.

An important theory for unsupervised learning is *Adaptive resonance theory* (ART). It makes use of two terms used in the study of brain behavior: stability and plasticity. The stability/plasticity dilemma is the ability of a system to preserve the balance between retaining previously learned patterns and learning new patterns. The key element in Grossberg's realization of this dilemma is the control of the partial match between new feature vectors and ones already learned. Two layers of neurons are used in the architecture: a top layer (an output, concept layer) and a bottom layer (an input, feature layer). Two sets of weights between the neurons in the two layers are used. The top-down weights represent learned patterns or expectations. The bottom-up weights represent a scheme for new inputs to be accommodated in the network.

10.5.2 EVOLUTIONARY ALGORITHMS FOR MACHINE LEARNING

10.5.2.1 Basics of evolutionary algorithms

We now turn to another kind of learning algorithms which represent social and emergent models of learning [Luger and Stubblefield 1998]. *Evolutionary algorithms* refer to learning algorithms patterned after the processes underlying evolution: shaping a population of individuals through the survival of its most fit members. The power of selection across a population of varying individuals has been demonstrated in the emergence of species in natural evolution, as well as through the social processes underlying cultural change. Since the evolutionary process learns an agent function based on occasional rewards as supplied by the selection function, it can be seen as a form of *reinforcement learning*. However, there is no attempt to learn the relationship between the rewards and the actions taken by the agent or the states of the environment. A genetic algorithm searches directly in the space of individuals, with the goal of finding one that maximizes the fitness function. The search is carried out in parallel, because each individual in the population can be seen as a separate search. The search also employs the idea of hill climbing (Chapter 2), because we are making small genetic changes to the individuals and using the best resulting offspring [Russell and Norvig 1995].

10.5.2.2 Genetic algorithms

As an example of evolutionary algorihtms, let us take a look at genetic algorithms [Mitchell 1998; Luger and Stubblefield 1998; Pakath 1996]. A *genetic algorithm* (*GA*) is one that seeks to improve upon the quality of a problem solution through a process that mimics that of natural selection and adaptation of species in nature. The method begins with a set of initial solutions (called an *initial population*) to a complex problem. It then crosses and mutates selected solutions from this initial set to develop a new set of solutions. The procedure is repeated to create successive generations of solutions until a predefined stopping criterion is met. This criterion may be based on a threshold value for error expended, solution quality, or a combination.

The philosophy behind the method is that if we conduct a search for a better answer simultaneously from multiple locations within a complex space of solutions, we stand a better chance of locating the globally optimal solution. Consequently, the GA approach has generally been advocated for complex, multi-modal solution space where there is high likelihood of a search strategy being trapped at a local optima. The probability of entrapment is generally higher for methods that localize their search efforts to a specific region of the solution space.

The initial set of solutions is either entirely randomly chosen or determined through a deliberate strategy that involves both deterministic and random choice. The former approach is used when the decision maker has no particular reason for wanting to choose a starting set otherwise and is generally how a GA operates. In certain instances, however, it is worthwhile to seed the starting solution set with some carefully chosen set of initial solutions along with some randomly generated solutions, usually because the population of solutions is of fixed, limited size.

A problem that must be dealt with is that when the space is very large in relation to population size, it is likely that a random starting solution set may not be a representative of the entire space. The method prefers that the set be as diversified as possible to enable it to search for improved solutions from multiple, well-dispersed points in the space. Another reason is that the random starting population may be made up entirely of very poor quality solutions. This situation increases the likelihood of being trapped at a local optima. Another problem is that while it may at times be possible to wade through such solutions and ultimately locate the globally best answer, the effort required may be highly prohibitive. Deliberately seeding the starting population with some high-quality solutions may help accelerate the move toward the desired solution.

Given a starting population, a GA would start its processing by selecting a set of members from this set to populate a gene pool. New solutions are generated using members picked randomly from the gene pool. The general strategy is to associate selection probabilities with individual members of the current population that reflect the standing or strength (called the *fitness*) of each member in relation to other members in the set. Usually, we convert the quality measure of each solution in the population into a selection probability measure for that member by converting the fitness to *relative fitness*. Solutions of higher quality (i.e., highly fit solutions) have higher likelihood of being selected to participate in the gene pool.

Once the gene pool is determined, a GA begins the next phase of its operations by using members of the gene pool for procreation. That is, members from the pool are randomly selected to act as parents. Parents are either mutated or crossed with one another to generate new solutions. These new solutions replace existing solutions in the population. The general procedure is as follows. Associated with any GA is a set of genetic operators called mutation, crossover, and reproduction. Each of these has a predetermined probability of application. The GA selects two members at random from the gene pool.

Based on the crossover probability, it is first determined whether the two parents must be crossed. If the answer is yes, they are crossed with one another, yielding either one or two offspring solutions, depending on the type of crossover being applied. At this stage one is left with either the original parents (if the decision was not to cross them) or the offspring generated via crossover. A determination is then made on whether each of the currently available solutions should be mutated, based on the mutation probability.

The key idea of a generic algorithm is now summarized below.

Algorithm genetic

Input: a goal, a set of operators, an evaluation criterion;
Output: an offspring equal to the goal
Method:

---

round $t = 0$;
initialize the population $P(t)$;
while the termination condition is not met do
{evaluate the fitness of each member in $P(t)$;
if no member in $P(t)$ is better than the previous round
use mutation to change one member;
select the most fit members from $P(t)$ as parents for next round;
use crossover to produce the offspring of these pairs;
$t = t+1$;}

As an example of learning using genetic algorithm, let us consider how to solve the "mastermind" game. In this game one of two players thinks up a number and the other has to find it out with a minimal number of questions (following [Kasabov 1996]). There are two players, the first player has the key of a number to be guessed by the second player. At the beginning, the second player is asked to provide four answers (a 6-digit string of 0 and 1s), and each answer is evaluated based on its fitness. The best two answers are used to produce the offspring using crossover. Crossover can be done by dividing each parent string in a flexible manner (such as a 3-3 split, 1-5 split, and so on). This process continues until the correct answer is reached. In case this process does not converge, mutation can be used to alter certain characters. An example of applying genetic algorithm to the game "guess the number" is shown in Table 10.2. In this game, the first player picks a number (in binary form) and the second player is asked to guess what it is. Each time the second player is allowed to give four answers and these answers are evaluated by the first player according to their closeness to the guessed number. The top two answers will be used as the parents to produce offspring. In general, crossover will be used; however, in a case (which is rare) that such produced offspring does not have a better evaluation score, mutation may be used. The first player could be the computer. Table 10.2 shows the answers provided by the second player as well as their evaluations in each round of play. Suppose the number to be guessed is 110101. The first round of play is shown in Table 10.3(a) (no crossover is involved in this round).

Table 10.3(a) The initial answers

Candidate name	Candidate string	Evaluation Score
A	000010	1
B	101010	1
C	010011	3
D	100100	4

Using the criterion of 110101, the best ones are chosen, namely, C and D. The next step of play is shown in Table 10.3(b). The exact manner of crossover is described in comments column.

Table 10.3(b) The first round of play

Parent name	Parent string	Offspring name	Offspring generated	Evaluation score	Comments
C	01:0011	E	01:0100	4*	Divide a string with 2 to
D	10:0100	F	10:0011	3	4 characters
C	0100:11	G	0100:00	3	Divide a string with 4 to
D	1001:00	H	1001:11	4*	2 characters

Selecting E and H, the next round of play is shown in Table 10.3(c).

Table 10.3(c) The second round of play

Parent name	Parent string	Offspring name	Offspring generated	Evaluation score	Comments
E	0:10100	I	0:00111	3	Divide a string with 1 to
H	1:00111	J	1:10100	5*	5 characters
E	010:100	K	010:111	4*	Divide a string with 3 to
H	100:111	L	100:100	4(dropped))	3 characters

Selecting J and K, the fourth round of play is shown in Table 10.3(d). The game ends at this round because offspring N produces the right answer.

Table 10.3(d) The final round of play

Parent name	Parent string	Offspring name	Offspring generated	Evaluation score	Comments
J	1101:00	L	1101:11	4	Divide a string with 4 to
K	0101:11	M	0101:00	5	2 characters
J	11010:0	N	11010:1	6*	Divide a string with 5 to
K	01010:1	O	01010:0	4	1 characters

Let us summarize the different roles of the three classes of operators.
* Reproduction seeks to preserve what is good in the current generation in subsequent generations.

- Crossover seeks to mingle the attributes of two solutions to create a new solution that could possess the more desirable traits of each parent.
- Mutation seeks to inject some novelty into the population by attempting to generate offspring quite unlike any in existence. Its role is rejuvenation. Mutation is especially useful in jolting the process out of extrapment at a local optima.

Generally, crossover is most popular, with mutation being used only when crossover fails to bring about any improvement. Too high a mutation probability would reduce the process to a random walk. In the above example, mutation is not used at all. However, if no answer produced in the second round is better than those produced in the previous round, mutation may take over; for example, mutate 010100 to 010101 by changing one bit of one offspring.

10.5.3 SUMMARY OF MACHINE LEARNING METHODS

We have provided a brief sketch of several representative machine learning methods. There are still many other methods not mentioned above. For example, within the symbolic camp, machine learning can be carried out through learning by analogy (in which a new concept is learned by mapping from an old one), learning by examples (in which learning is carried out as a careful theoretical analysis of a given example), as well as many other more advanced techniques.

10.6 FEATURES OF DATA MINING

Having discussed some important features of several important machine learning techniques, we are now ready to turn to data mining. In the last chapter, we have already illustrated what is knowledge discovery in databases (KDD) and data mining. In this section, we discuss some important features of data mining (including its relationship with data mining). Several data mining techniques will then be examined in the rest of this chapter.

10.6.1 THE POPULARITY OF DATA MINING

The ever-increasing popularity of data mining is due to demands from various real-world applications in decision making. The following are some typical cases:

- *Business data mining*: *Ad hoc* techniques are no longer adequate for sifting through vast collections of data. They are giving way to data mining and knowledge discovery for turning corporate data into competitive business advantage.
- *Scientifc data mining*: Digesting millions of data points, each with tens or hundreds of measurements can be turned over to data mining techniques for data reduction, which functions as an interface between the scientist and large data sets. KDD applications in science may generally be easier

than applications in business or finance, mainly because science users typically know their data in intimate detail.

*   *Internet and data mining:* Some have advocated transforming the Web into a massive layered database to facilitate data mining, but the Web is too dynamic and chaotic to be tamed in this manner. As an alternative, a proposal has been made which is based on the structured Web hypothesis: information on the Web is sufficiently structured to facilitate effective Web mining [Etzioni 1996].

As an example, let us consider mutual funds which are a popular investment tool. It has been noted that among mutual fund winners, history seems to repeat itself. In a classic study of 728 stock funds done a few years ago, Yale professors Roger Ibbotson and William Goetzmann discovered that "funds ranked in the top one-fourth in 3-year performance had a 72 percent chance of making the top half over the next 3 years." And Morningstar Research also found that "almost half of the diversified stock funds it awarded 5-stars a decade ago still merited 4 or 5-stars in 1997. Only 20 percent fell to just one or two stars." (Paul B. Farrell, CBS MarketWatch: "Rule no. 9: Past performance counts," May 20, 1999).

As another example, if you access on-line book seller Amazon.com's web page, if you have searched for *Data Mining Techniques: For Marketing, Sales, and Customer Support* by Michael J. A. Berry, Gordon Linoff, you will also see the message:

> Customers who bought this book also bought: *Predictive Data Mining: A Practical Guide* by Sholom M. Weiss, Nitin Indurkhya (Contributor), etc.

This message reveals book-buyers' activities, and illustrates a primitive form of data mining.

In this book, we will focus on computational intelligence methods that may contribute to database-centric approaches for data mining.

10.6.2 KDD VERSUS DATA MINING

As mentioned in Chapter 9, knowledge discovery from databases (KDD) has caught great attention to many researchers and practitioners from various fields. According to [Piatetsky-Shapiro and Frawley 1991], *knowledge discovery* is the nontrivial extraction of implicit, previously unknown, and potentially useful information from data. Knowledge discovery differs from machine learning in that the task is more general and is concerned with issues specific to databases.

The term KDD was coined in 1989 to refer to the broad process of finding knowledge in data. It has been mostly used by computational intelligence and machine learning researchers. For several years, this term was used interchangeably with another term: data mining, which has been commonly used by statisticians, data analysts and the MIS community. Recently, a kind of consensus has been made. The term KDD is now viewed as the overall process of discovering useful knowledge from data, while data mining is viewed as the application of some particular algorithms for extracting patterns from data without the additional steps of the KDD process. These additional steps are essential to ensure that useful information is derived from the data. In other words, the task of KDD is to emphasize the "high-level" application of particular data mining methods. For convenience, in this book, we will use the term data mining to refer to both tasks.

Although the term KDD and data mining have been used interchangeably, there are different emphases in these two terms. KDD is more related to the overall process (is thus concerned about the infrastructure) while data mining is more concerned with the actual mining algorithms. In this book, we will mainly use the term data mining, although sometimes we will discuss the infrastructure of the mining process (particularly in Chapter 11).

Knowledge discovery in databases creates the context for developing the tools needed to control the flood of data. In practice, a large portion of the applications effort can go into properly formulating the problem (asking the right question) rather than optimizing the algorithmic details of a particular data mining method. [Fayyad, Piatetsky-Shapiro and Smyth 1996].

Knowledge discovery in databases has four main characteristics [Piatetsky-Shapiro and Frawley 1991]:

(i) the discovered knowledge is represented in a high-level language which can be understood by human users;
(ii) the discoveries accurately portray the contents of the database;
(iii) the discovered knowledge is interesting according to users; and
(iv) the discovery process is efficient.

Important issues in data mining include the following:

- human-centered;
- subjective measures of interestingness (e.g., unexpected and actionable);
- different types (automated or user-guided);
- visualization;
- enhancement from current non-mature, *ad-hoc* status (many algorithms, little systematic framework)

As a remark, [Silberschatz and Tuzhilin 1996] and [Dong and Li 1998] discussed the issue of interestingness. The notions of *distance* between rules and distance between neighborhoods of rules are proposed to reflect the "*interestingness*" of a discovered rule. The neighborhood-based interestingness of a rule is then defined in terms of the pattern of the fluctuation of confidences or the density of mined rules in some of its neighborhoods. The interesting rules can be ranked by combining some neighborhood-based characteristics, the support and confidence of the rules, and users' feedback [Dong and Li 1998].

It has been observed that there are three generation data mining systems [Piatetsky-Shapiro 1997]:

First generation: These systems usually performed classification or clustering, and relied upon a particular technique, such as decision trees or neural networks.

Second generation: These tools provided better support in knowledge discovery process.

Third generation: They differ from the previous two generations in that they deal with the business end user rather than providing power of data analysis. These shells have led to the development of customized tools oriented towards specific business problems.

Many algorithms have been proposed for data mining. Statistical or machine learning methods have been used to analyze the retrieved data. Most algorithms developed for data mining typically demonstrate the inductive learning process.

10.6.3 DATA MINING VERSUS MACHINE LEARNING

Statistics is obviously relevant to data mining because that field has always focused on construction of models from data. Databases, too, are clearly central because current applications of data mining can involve very large corpora of information that are not necessarily in flat file form. One may wonder what is left to be claimed by computational intelligence and, in particular, machine learning. [Quinlan 1999] offers a recent discussion on data mining from a computational perspective from a long-time machine learning researcher.

The idea of unsupervised learning from basic facts (axioms) or from data has fascinated researchers for decades (Ramakrishnan and Grama 1999]. Despite the similarities, however, one important factor we should bear in mind is that the size of data may make a big difference for machine learning and data mining. Finding an appropriate structure to conduct machine learning could be a task which is NP-hard [Dean, Allen and Aloimonos 1995]. In fact, computational learning theory has been developed for dealing with related computational problems. Though machine learning methods can be adopted for data mining purposes, it would also be desirable to explore new methods that directly address the need of decision support queries. Another difference is the objective. In fact, for machine learning, the emphasis of research has been on inference mechanisms involved in the learning process. Although much attention has been paid in developing efficient algorithms and even though researchers are aware of the importance of scaling up, algorithms developed usually assume the data are residing on the main memory. The driving force of machine learning research has been largely from academy, although many algorithms have found many applications (such as the case of ID3 or C4.5). In contrast, the driving force of data mining is mainly from business and industry. Some machine learning techniques are not of interest to data mining practitioners, such as learning by analogy or by examples. The data mining community has also initiated some new types of rules, such as association rules (to be discussed in Section 10.8), which can be effectively studied by incorporating computational intelligence techniques. Therefore, data mining and machine learning are different to each other, but may also benefit each other.

Authors in [Lin and Cercone 1997] discussed particular methods used to discover patterns (or knowledge) in ultra large data sets in the light of model representation and evaluation. In particular, it has been noticed that data dependencies (functional dependencies) in DBMSs are defined during the design of conceptual schema, whereas in machine learning they are induced from given data. Depending on how data dependencies are perceived, their use in these two disciplines is different. For example, data dependencies in DBMSs are used for normalizing relations and indexing relations, whereas in machine learning they are used as a preprocessing step of a knowledge discovery technique. The purpose of this preprocessing is to reduce the number of attributes in a given data set, to divide continuous values of an attribute into categories, for testing a hypothesis, or for constructing a data dependency graph.

Researchers have warned of several tricky issues in data mining. Inherited from machine learning methods, KDD may pursue a harmful equation of "knowledge = concepts." Research on automation of scientific discovery in natural sciences takes a broader perspective on knowledge. Since a narrow view of knowledge is accompanied by a narrow view of the discovery method, scientific discovery can shed some light on KDD with a broader vision of knowledge and discovery method [Zytkow 1997]. Another remark is from John McCarthy, who has warned that the main technical point of data mining is that functions and predicates involving the phenomena should be explicit in the logical sentences and not just present in the mind of the person doing the data mining [McCarthy 1996].

10.6.4 DATA MINING VERSUS EXTENDED RETRIEVAL

The organization of this book allows us to examine issues related to data mining from the perspective of retrieval systems. Indeed, in a sense data mining can be considered as extended retrieval in the sense discussed in Chapter 7, because it tries to max out the information stored there and tries to derive new knowledge which were not explicitly stored. However, it takes a form completely different from the approach presented in Chapter 7. The approach discussed there shares some concerns with machine learning using analogy, and is thus based on individual examples (which are retrieved and used as analogs). On the other hand, data mining is *only* interested in a flood of data. Although the extended retrieval (discussed in Chapter 7) and knowledge discovery both generate new knowledge, the *form* of generated knowledge is very different. In the case of data mining, the generated knowledge contains the condensed information extracted from structured databases, while in the case of extended retrieval, the generated knowledge is through the mapping of structure information (which is usually not considered in data mining). Therefore, extended retrieval as discussed in Chapter 7 and data mining techniques discussed in this chapter represent two complementary approaches of bridging data and knowledge.

10.6.5 DATA MINING VERSUS STATISTIC ANALYSIS AND INTELLIGENT DATA ANALYSIS

The relationship between data mining on one hand, and statistical analysis and other kinds of intelligent data analysis on the other hand, has been addressed by many authors, including [Elder and Pregibon 1995, Glymour, Madigan, Pregibon and Smyth 1996, Hosking, Pednault and Sudan 1996, Huber 1997, Hand 1997, 1998]. Some opinions of these authors are summarized below.

- *Different objectives*: To many statisticians, data mining is a term synonymous with *data dredging* or *data fishing*. The objective of data analysis is not to model the fleeting random patterns of the moment, but to model the *underlying structures* which give rise to consistent and replicable patterns. Compared with the traditional interest of computational intelligence, statistics may have little to offer the search architectures in a data mining search, but a great deal to offer in *evaluating hypotheses* used in the search and *evaluating the results* of the search, as well as in applying the results. Understanding causation is the hidden motivation behind the historical development of statistics [Glymour, Madigan, Pregibon and Smyth 1996].

- *Different kinds of problems*: To some extent, the differences between statistical and data mining approaches to modeling and inference are related to the different kinds of problems on which these approaches have been used. For example, statisticians tend to work with relatively simple models for which issues of computational speed have rarely been a concern.

- *Different kinds of data to be handled*: According to [Hand 1997, 1998], statistics might be described as being characterized by data sets that are small and clean, and permit straightforward answers via intensive analysis of single data sets. Data sets used in statistic analysis are static, often collected to answer the particular problem being addressed, and are solely numeric. In contrast, real-world database data are dirty, inconsistent, and may be mixed with different types. Some critics from statistics believe that scaling-up of data mining algorithms is problematic, because computational complexity of many procedures explodes with increasing data size. The available success stories suggest that the real function of data mining and KDD is not machine discovery of interesting structures by itself, but targeted extraction and reduction of data to a size and format suitable for human inspection [Huber 1997].

- *Different goals of inference*: Starting from the classical statistical inference, both statistical learning theory and computational learning theory have provided productive extensions as theoretical results

[Hosking, Pednault, and Sudan 1997]. It has been noticed that the inference procedures of classical statistics involve repeated sampling under a given statistical model and statistical learning theory bases its inferences on repeated sampling from an unknown distribution of the data. In contrast, the PAC-learning results from computational learning theory seek to identify modeling procedures that have a high probability of near-optimality over all possible distributions of data.

Nevertheless, some of the differences present opportunities for statisticians and data miners to learn from each other's approaches.

10.6.6 DATA MINING MECHANISM: DATA MINING FROM A DATABASE PERSPECTIVE

For researchers from the database management systems community, the focus has been on the concern of *database-centric* data mining, namely, studying data mining by staying with traditional issues related to DBMS. [Ullman 1998] believes that the term data mining has been a big umbrella covering several domains that bear little if any relationship. Data mining provides the opportunity to increase human capabilities, in particular the ability to get answers from very large bodies of information that were not created for the purpose of answering that query. Systems issues include scalability, usability, reusability, generality and efficiency. However, data mining is not really a new field. Though the task set for data mining itself may be far from straightforward, data mining is not a core technology. In fact, data mining can be considered as an extension of traditional DBMS querying process, as indicated in the two research programs proposed by [Imielinski and Mannila, 1996]. The *short term program* is concerned with developing efficient algorithms implementing data mining tools on the top of large databases and utilizing the existing DBMS support. The *long term program* is concerned with building optimizing compilers for *ad hoc* queries and embedding queries in application programming interfaces. A discussion of SQL-aware data mining systems can be found in [Chaudhuri 1998]. For simplicity, we will refer the database techniques needed for supporting data mining as *data mining mechanism*. Some specific issues related to the data mining mechanism are briefly discussed in Section 10.8.3.5.

10.6.7 SUMMARY OF FEATURES

In summary, we notice that data mining shares some common concerns with other research fields such as machine learning and statistics, but it also has its unique features, which are mainly driven from analyzing a huge size of data needed in decision support queries. From a database perspective, data mining has imposed new challenges for traditional database techniques. Nevertheless, data mining is not a new field within DBMS research. It may be more appropriately viewed as applying computational intelligence principles to databases. In the remaining part of this chapter (as well as in this book), we will stay with this perspective.

10.7   CATEGORIZING DATA MINING TECHNIQUES

We now provide an overview on various data mining techniques by categorizing them. Different criteria can be used for this purpose.

10.7.1 WHAT IS TO BE DISCOVERED

One criterion for categorizing data mining is based on what is to be discovered. The following are some typical cases.

- *Regularity:* In many cases we are interested in knowledge patterns or regularity of data. This is the most popular case and will be further examined in the next section.

- *Single datum:* In some other cases, we may be interested in some specific items of data or single pieces of information (singular datum). Note that this is not simply to discover the outliers. The purpose of such kind of analysis is to increase the efficiency of knowledge works. For example, such kind of data mining may be useful in the fight against criminality, in particular in domains such as drug trafficking or the theft, transport and sales of art objects or cars. Several cases will be analyzied, and even the so-called neighborhoods should be explored [Siklossy and Ayel 1997].

10.7.2 DISCOVERY OR PREDICTION

Data mining problems can also be divided into two general categories: prediction and knowledge discovery. Prediction is arguably the strongest goal of data mining, has the greatest potential payoff and has the most precise description. Knowledge discovery is an all-encompassing label for many topics related to decision support. Knowledge discovery problems usually describe a stage prior to prediction, where information is insufficient for prediction. Knowledge discovery is complementary to predictive mining, but is closer to decision support than decision making.

- Prediction (classification, regression, time series): The two central types of prediction problems are classification and regress. Time series is a specialized type of regression or occasionally a classification problem, where measurements are taken over time for the same features.

- Knowledge discovery: It includes deviation detection, database segmentation, clustering, association rules, summarization, visualization, text mining, as well as others.

Predictive data mining requires data modeling (which is different from data reduction). There is also a concern related to timelines in predictive data mining. From the perspective of database systems, the efficient storage and query of time-stamped information is a complex task. From a predictive data-mining perspective, the time-stamped data greatly increase the dimensions of problem solving in a completely different direction. Instead of cases with one measured value for each feature, cases have the same featured measured at different times. Predictive data-mining methods prefer the classical sample and case model of data but have difficulties reasoning with time and its greatly increased dimensions.

10.7.3 SYMBOLIC, CONNECTIONISM AND EVOLUTIONARY ALGORITHMS

As already discussed in Secion 10.6, many data mining techniques have a close relationship with machine learning. Just like machine learning algorithms, data mining techniques could be based on symbolic, connectionism, evolutionary, or some other forms. For example, there has been a growing interest in data mining using evolutionary algorithms. Research topics include the following [AAAI 99]:

- Evolutionary algorithms (EA) for classification, clustering, dependence modeling, regression, time series and other data mining tasks;
- Discovery of comprehensible, interesting knowledge with EA;
- Scaling up EA for very large databases;
- Comparison between EA and other data mining methods;
- Genetic operators tailored for data mining tasks;
- Incorporating domain knowledge in EA;
- Integrating EA with DBMSs;
- Data mining with evolutionary, intelligent agents;
- Hybrid (such as neural-genetic, rule induction-genetic) EA;
- Data pre-processing (such as data cleansing, attribute selection) with EA;
- Post-processing of the discovered knowledge with EA;
- Mining semi-structured or unstructured data (such as text mining) with EA.

10.7.4 CLASSIFYING DATA MINING METHODS

As pointed out by [Chen, Han and Yu 1996], data mining techniques can be classified by different criteria, such as the following:

- By what kinds of databases to work on (such as relational databases, object-oriented databases, etc.);
- By what kind of knowledge to be mined (such as association rules or characteristic rules); or
- By what kind of techniques to be utilized (such as data-driven, query-driven).

In the following, we take a look on what kind of knowledge to be mined, as discussed in [Chen, Han and Yu 1996]:

- *Association rules* (to be discussed in the next section);

- *Data generalization and summarization tools*: The most popularly used data mining and data analysis tools.
- *Data classification*: It is the process that finds the common properties among a set of objects in a database and classifies them into different classes, according to a classification model. The objective of the classification is to first analyze the training data and develop an accurate description or a model for each class using the features available in the data. Some machine learning techniques, such as ID3, are closely related to discovery of classification knowledge.
- *Data clustering*: It is the process of grouping physical or abstract objects into classes of similar objects. Clustering analysis helps construct meaningful partitioning of a large set of objects based on a divide and conquer methodology which decomposes a large scale system into smaller componets to simpify design and implementation. The task of clustering is maximizing the intraclass similarity and minimizing the interclass similarity. It has a close relationship with spatial data mining (see below);
- *Spatial/temporal data mining*: It is concerned with data mining involving spatial and/or temporal data. There is an interesting relationship between these spatial and temporal data mining (for example, the problem of temporal data mining can be converted to spatial data mining).
- *Mining path traversal patterns*: There is an interesting relationship between data mining and Internet. This relationship has several aspects. The Internet provides a huge resource for data mining. Note also that recently there have been various efforts to apply data mining for Web page analysis. [Chen, Han and Yu 1996] contains a brief summary on this topic.

In addition, the following types of knowledge discovery have also been identified:

- *Pattern-based similarity search,*
- *Data mining query languages and graphical user interface,* and
- *Sequential patterns.*

10.8   ASSOCIATION RULES

10.8.1 TERMINOLOGY

We now take a closer look at the association rules. Bar-code technology has made it possible for retail organizations to collect and store massive amounts of sales data, referred to as basket data. Here we talk about transaction databases; a *transaction database* is usually a relation consisting of transactions as tuples (each transaction is a list of items purchased by a customer in one shopping activity -- so just think about your receipt). (Note the term "transaction database" *is NOT same as "database transaction"!)*

Given a database of sales transactions (each transaction in the transaction databases has a transaction ID called TID), it is desirable to discover the important associations among items such that the presence of some items in a transaction will imply the presence of other items in the same transaction. (Note: Here we are not talking about transaction processing!) Association rules are statements of the form "70% of customers that purchase 2% milk will also purchase bread."   Finding customer purchase patterns is an important task for many organizations (such as for supermarkets to promote sales).

The constructed association rules take the format of "Head :- Body" (or equivalently: Body → Head), which means: *if a customer buys items in the Body, he also buys the Head.* It may also written as LHS → RHS (LHS: Left Hand Side, RHS: Right Hand Side).

Two important measures used to indicate the strength of association rules are support and confidence. The definitions of these two concepts are given below.

- *Support*: The support for a set is the percentage of transactions that contain all of these items. The support for a rule *LHS→RHS* (Or: *Body→Head)* is the support for the set of items *LHS ∪ RHS* ("LHS and RHS appear together"). The formula used for calculation is:

    s = (number of transactions involving all items in LHS and RHS of this rule)/
    (number of total transactions).

    The rule is satisfied in the set of transactions T with the support s if and only if at least s% of transactions in T contain all items appearing in either LHS or RHS. The support is the joint probability of finding LHS and RHS in the same transaction.

- *Confidence*: The confidence for a rule *LHS→RHS* is the percentage of such transactions that also contain all items in *RHS*. It indicates the degree of correlation between purchases of these sets of items. The formula used for calculation is:

    c = (number of transactions involving all items in LHS and RHS of the rule)/
    (number of transactions involving all items in LHS).

    The rule is satisfied in the set of transactions T with the confidence factor c if and only if at least c% of transactions in T that satisfy (contain) LHS also satisfy (contain) the RHS. The confidence is the conditional probability in the same transaction of finding RHS having found LHS.

Both support and confidence are represented by a number between 0 and 1 (the percentage involved in the calculation). A threshold (such as 0.1) is used as a cut-off point for support, and a (different) threshold (such as 0.2) is used as a cut-off point for confidence. Note some authors use the number of transactions as support, confidence and threshold. It is straightforward to convert from one way to another. For example, if threshold is 0.1 and total transactions are 1000, then the threshold can be converted to 100 (in terms of number of transactions.) A rule with support or confidence below threshold is considered as not strong enough to be accepted. The meaning of support and confidence can be studied from an example with initial transaction data shown in Table 10.4(a) (revised from [Meo, Psaila and Ceri 1996]).

Table 10.4(a) The purchase table for a big store

TID	customer	item	date	price	quantity
100	C1	ski pants	01/11/99	150	2
100	C1	hiking boots	01/11/99	180	1
200	C2	color shirts	01/12/99	28	3
200	C2	brown boots	01/12/99	160	2
200	C2	jackets	01/12/99	250	2
300	C3	jackets	01/14/99	260	1
400	C4	color shirts	01/14/99	28	2
400	C4	jackets	01/14/99	260	3

For convenience of use, the purchase table is grouped by transactions as shown in Table 10.3(b) (In a sense this is to perform denormalization as discussed in Chapter 4). In the following, we will just use this table.

Table 10.4(b) The purchase table grouped by transactions

TID	customer	item	date	price	quantity
100	C1	ski pants	01/11/99	150	2
		hiking boots	01/11/99	180	1
200	C2	color bags	01/12/99	28	3
		brown boots	01/12/99	160	2
		jackets	01/12/99	250	2
300	C3	jackets	01/14/99	260	1
400	C4	color bags	01/14/99	28	2
	C4	jackets	01/14/99	260	3

Some simple association rules can be found as shown in table 10.4(c). (S stands for support, C for confidence):

Table 10.4(c) Some association rules mined

Rule #	Body	Head	Support S	Confidence C
1	ski pants	hiking boots	.25	1
2	hiking boots	ski pants	.25	1
3	color bags	brown boots	.25	.5
4	color bags	jackets	.5	1
5	brown boots	color bags	.25	.5
6	brown boots	jackets	.25	1
7	jackets	color bags	.5	.66

Now let us verify S and C for rule 3: Item in LHS: "color bags" appears in TID=2, TID=4; Item in RHS: "brown boots" appears in TID=2. So only TID=2 involve all items in LHS and RHS. We have the following results (the vertical bars are used to indicate the cardinality of the set, or the number of elements in the set):

$$S = |\{TID\ 2\}| / |TID\ 1, 2, 3, 4\}| = 0.25,$$
$$C = |\{TID\ 2\}| / |\{TID\ 2, TID\ 4\}| = 0.5.$$

As another example, let us verify S and C for rule 7 (LHS "jackets" in TIDs 2, 3, 4; RHS "color bags" in TID 2, 4):

$$S = |\{TID\ 2, TID\ 4\}| / |\{TID\ 1, TID\ 2, TID\ 3, TID\ 4\}| = 0.5.$$
$$C = |\{TID\ 2, TID\ 4\}| / |\{TID\ 2, TID\ 3, TID\ 4\}| = 2/3 = 0.667$$

10.8.2 FINDING ASSOCIATION RULES USING APRIORI ALGORITHM

Algorithm *Apriori* constructs a candidate set of large itemsets, counts the number of occurrences of each candidate itemset, and then determines large itemsets based on a predetermined minimum support. The trick of the algorithm is the so-called the Apriori property: Every subset of a frequent itemset must also be a frequent itemset. The following are some basic terminology.

- *Itemset*: A set of items.
- *k-itemset*: An itemset having k items.
- *Large itemset*: itemsets with minimum support.
- L_k: Set of large k-itemsets
- c_k: Set of condidate k-itemsets

The following example illustrates the process of large item set generation (taken from [Chen, Han and Yu 1996] (assuming minimum transaction support required is two). Consider the transaction database shown in Table 10.5(a).

Table 10.5(a) Database D:

TID	ITEMS
1000	A C D
2000	B C E
3000	A B C E
4000	B E

We now illustrate how to process to generate candidate itemsets and large itemsets. Scanning D, we have the data mining process shown in Tables 10.5(b) to 10.5(d).

Table 10.5(b): First pass: C_1 and L_1

C_1

Itemset	Support
A	2
B	3
C	3
D	2
E	3

L_1

Itemset	Support
A	2
B	3
C	3
D	3

Table 10.5(c) Second pass: C_2 and L_2

C_2

Itemset	Support
A B	1
A C	2
A E	1
B C	2
B E	3
C E	2

L_2

Itemset	Support
A C	2
B C B E	2
C E	3
	2

Table 10.5(d) Third pass: C_2 and L_2

C_3

Itemset	Support
BCE	2

L_3

Itemset	Support
BCE	2

Note that the Apriori algorithm has a *prune* phase which is best illustrated in the last pass in the above example. (It is also used in previous passes, but to no significant effect.) Why do we not consider *ABC* or *ABE*? Because, for example, *AB* (the subset of *ABC*) is not a large 2-itemset, so ABC is not qualified in large 3-itemset. Now you should be able to answer the following question: Why should we stop at 3-itemset? Or: Why don't we consider 4-itemsets at all? For more discussion on the prune phase, see [Agrawal and Srikant 1994].

The *Apriori* algorithm is now sketched below.

```
L(1) = {large singular item sets};
for (k=2 ; L(k-1)  k++ ) do begin
   C(k) = Apriori-generation(L(k-1)); // new candidates
      for each transaction t  ∈ D begin
         C(t) = subset(C(k),t); // Candidates contained in t
            for each candidate c  ∈ C(t) do
                     c-count ++;
             end;
   L(k) = {c C(k) | c-count  ≥  minimum support}
   end
 ∪ₖ L(k)
return
```

The *Apriori*-generation function takes as argument L(k-1), the set of all large (k-1)-item sets. It returns a superset of the set of al large k-item sets. The function works as follows: First, in the join step, we join L(k-1) with L(k-1):

```
insert into C(k)
    select p-item(1), p-item(1),... p-item(k-1), q-item(k-1),
    from L(k-1) as p, L(k-1) as q
    where p-item(1) = q-item(1),...,
             p-item(k-2) = q-item(k-2),
             p-item(k-1) < q-item(k-1)
```

Next, in the prune step, we delete all the item sets c in C(k) such that some (k-1)-subset of c is not in L(k-1):

```
For each item sets c in C(k) do
    For each (k-1)-subsets s of c do
       If (s not in L(k-1)) then
             delete c from C(k);
```

The subset(C(k),t) function can be sketched as follows. Candidate item sets C(k) are stored in a hash-tree. A node of the hash-tree either contains a list of item sets (a leaf node) or a hash table (an interior node). In order to add to the c items set: The hash-tree is scanned from root to leaf. In an interior node of depth d, the branch to follow is the result of the hash function applied to $c[d]$. All nodes are initially created as leaf nodes. When the number of item sets in a leaf node exceeds a specified threshold, the leaf node is converted to an interior node.

In order to find all item sets contained in transaction t, the items sets contained in a leaf node are found and added to the answer set. In an interior node that has been reached by hashing on $t[j]$; all $t[k](kj)$ will be hashed and this procedure will be recursively applied to the node in the corresponding bucket. At the root node, every itemset is hashed.

10.8.3 MORE ADVANCED STUDIES OF ASSOCIATION RULES

Research activities in finding association rules have been quite active in the last few years. In this section, we provide a discussion on some advanced studies on this topic. Our discussion is not intended to be complete, but to be representative.

10.8.3.1 Extension of association rules

Association rules have been extended in many ways. [Agrawal, Imielinski and Swami 1993] is one of the earliest papers on mining association rules in transaction databases (databases containing transactions of customers' baskets). Also considers buffer management and pruning techniques. [Agrawal and Srikant 1994] proposed the well-known apriori algorithm to improve the efficiency of finding large itemsets. [Srikant and Agrawal 1995] further considers generalized association rules involving hierarchies. [Srikant and Agrawal 1996] extends association rules to handle intervals as well as categories. [Srikant, Vu and Agrawal 1997] discusses how to incorporate user-specified constraints to find rules containing a specific item or rules that contain children of a specific item in a hierarchy. [Bayardo Jr., Agrawal, and Gunopulos 1999] is a further study of using user-specified constraints for mining association rules. In addition, dense databases are considered; they are different from transaction databases which consist of itemsets that are "sparse" (as studied in earlier literature).

10.8.3.2 Sampling techniques in finding association rules

Sampling large databases in mining association rules is based on a portion of the database from the whole database in order to decrease the operation of disk I/O. The tradeoff for this method is the possibility of missing the real frequency sets. The following techniques can be used to avoid missing the frequency sets: decrease the frequency threshold during mining of the sample;

use negative border to further increase the supersets which are possible to be the real frequent sets; keep the sample size large enough to represent the whole database. [Toivonen 1996] is a well-known paper on the use of sampling techniques for association rules.

[Srikant and Agrawal 1996] extends association rules to handle intervals as well as categories. [Srikant, Vu and Agrawal 1997] discusses how to incorporate user-specified constraints to find rules containing a specific item or rules that contain children of a specific item in a hierarchy.

10.8.3.3 Variations of association rules

In addition to extensions, there are also various extensions which digress from the original studies as cited in 10.8.3.2. For example, [Carter, Hamilton and Cercone 1997] introduced measures share, concidence and dominance as alternatives to the standard itemset methodology mesure of support. [Lin and Kedem 1998] noticed discovering frequent itermsets typically takes a bottom-up breadth-first search and performance drastically decreases when some of the maximal frequent itemsets are relatively long. A new algorithm is proposed which is still bottom-up, but a restricted search is also conducted in the top-down direction. This search is used for mainitaining and updating a data structure called the maximum frequent candidate set.

Much of research work from J. Han's group is rooted in attribute-oriented induction. Mining association rules at multiple concept levels may lead to discovery of more specific and concrete knowledge from data, as is discussed in [Han and Fu 1995]. Relaxation of the rule conditions for finding "level-crossing" association rules is also discussed.

In a more recent study, [Hidber 1999] presents an algorithm to compute large itemsets online. The user is free to change the support threshold any time during the first scan of the transaction sequence. The algorithm maintains a superset of all large itemsets and for each itemset a shrinking, deterministic interval on its support. After at most two scans the algorithm terminates with the precise support for each large itemset.

10.8.3.4 Clustering and representative association rules

Since many association rules many be found in the same transaction database, it makes sense to ask where there are any most important findings shared by these rules. Different criteria have been developed. *Representative association rules* are defined as a least set of rules that covers all association rules satisfying certain user specified constraints. A user may be provided with a set of representative association rules instead of the whole set of association rules. The non-representative association rules may be generated on demand by means of the cover operator [Kryszkiewicz 1998]. [Lent, Swami and Widom 1997] discusses how to cluster two-dimensional association rules in large databases.

10.8.3.5 Association rules and data mining mechanism

Association rules discovery process has also spawned research work related to the basic data mining mechanism (as discussed in 10.6.6). For example, [Holsheimer, Kersten, Mannila and Toivonen 1995] discusses how general purpose database management systems can be used for data mining. [Meo, Psaila and Ceri 1996, Meo, Psaila and Ceri 1998a] proposes extending SQL for mining association rules. A more recent paper from the same author group [Meo, Psaila, and Ceri 1998b] discussed related issues in more depth. In [Agrawal and Shim 1996], issues related to loosely and tightly-coupled data mining techniques are discussed. Extending SQL. An extended study of [Agrawal and Shim 1996] can be found in [Sarawagi, Thomas, and Agrawal 1998].

SUMMARY

In this chapter we have provided an overview on machine learning and data mining, and discussed several basic data mining techniques. There are a number of directions which may require more in-depth research in the years to come [Han 1997]. We have already mentioned some important issues, such as support of data mining query languages and efficient, interactive, *ad-hoc* data mining (Section 10.6.6). In addition, Section 10.8.3 provides a long list of references for more advanced study on mining association rules. There are many other research issues that need to be examined, including (a) handling increasingly complex data (including semi-structured and unstructured data, hypertext, documents, spatial and multimedia data); (b) high performance data mining (efficient and scalable mining algorithms will be further enhanced by developing parallel, distributed and incremental data mining algorithms); (c) user interface (including visualization), and (d) integration of data mining techniques with data warehousing and OLAP technology. This last issue will be examined in the next chapter (Chapter 11). Chapter 12 is also related to data mining, but with a different focus. In Chapter 12 (and continued in Chapter 13), we study the issue of reasoning under uncertainty. A seemingly quite different issue, uncertain reasoning actually offers powerful techniques which can be used in data mining.

SELF-EXAMINATION QUESTIONS

1. Provide a brief discussion on knowledge generation, and compare knowledge generation using extended retrieval (as discussed in Chapter 7) versus knowledge discovery as discussed in this chapter.

2. Give an example to illustrate how genetic algorithms can be used for idea generation (as discussed in Chapter 8).
3. Consider the "mastermind" game discussed in Section 10.5.2. Suppose the number in the mind of the first player is "111111;" also assume current candidate solutions are A, B, C, D, as shown below.

   (A) 011001
   (B) 100111
   (C) 101010
   (D) 010111

   How will you solve this problem using a genetic algorithm? Show the steps of problem solving and briefly explain how crossover and mutation operators are used to solve the problem.
4. Give a brief discussion on two machine learning methods which may be useful for data mining. Also provide a brief discussion on one machine learning method which is not appropriate for data mining.
5. In the association rules discussed in Section 10.8, quantities of purchase are not considered. What is your opinion on the importance of quantities in discovery of association rules?
6. Collect 10 receipts of supermarket shopping from your friends. Construct a transaction database from these receipts. Use Apriori algorithm to find association rules.

REFERENCES

AAAI 99, Workshop of Data mining with evolutionary algorithms: Research directions, AAAI-99.

Agrawal, R., Imielinski, T. and Swami, A., Mining association rules between sets of items in large databases, *SIGMOD'93*, 1993.

Agrawal, R. and Shim, K., Developing tightly-coupled data mining applications on a relational database system, *Proceedings KDD'96*.

Agrawal, R. and Srikant, R., Fast algorithms for mining association rules, *Proceedings VLDB'94*, 1994.

Bayardo Jr., R. J., Agrawal, R. and Gunopulos, D., Constraint-based rule mining in large, dense databases, *Proceedings ICDE'99*, 1999.

Bigus, J. P., *Data Mining with Neural Networks: Solving Business Problems - From Application Development to Decision Support*, McGraw-Hill, New York, 1996.

Carter, C., Hamilton, H. J. and Cercone, N., Shared based measures for itemsets, *Proceedings PKDD'97*, pp, 14-24, 1997.

Chaudhuri, S., Data mining and database systems: Where is the intersection? *Data Engineering Bulletin*, 21(1), 4-8, 1998.

Chen, M. -S., Han, J., and Yu, P. S., Data Mining: An Overview from a Database Perspective, *IEEE transactions on knowledge and data engineering*, 8(6), 866-897, 1996.

Dong, G. and Li, J., Interestingness of discovered assocation rules in terms of neighborhood-based unexpectedness, *Proceedings PAKDD'98*, 1998.

Elder IV, J. F. and D. Pregibon, D., A statistical perspective on KDD, *Proceedings KDD 95*, pp. 87-93, 1995. (A longer version is in *Advances in Knowledge Discovery and Data Mining*, 1995.)

Etzioni, P., The World-Wide Web: Quagmire or gold mine? *Communications of the ACM*, 39(11), pp. 65-68, 1996.

Fayyad, U. M., Piatetsky-Shapiro, G., Smyth, P. and Uthurusamy, R. (eds.), *Advances in Knowledge Discovery and Data Mining*, AAAI/MIT Press, Menlo Park, CA, 1996.

Fayyad, U., Piatetsky-Shapiro, G. and Smyth, P., The KDD process of extracting useful knowledge from volumes of data, *Communications of the ACM*, 39(11), 27-34, 1996.

Glymour, G. Madigan, D., Pregibon, D. and Smyth, P., Statistical inference and data mining, *Communications of the ACM*, 39 (11), 35-41, 1996.

Han, J., Data mining: Where is it heading? *Proceedings of 1997 International Conference on Data Engineering (ICDE'97)*, Birmingham, England, p. 508, 1997.

Han, J. and Fu, Y., Discovery of multiple-level association rules from large databases, *Proc. VLDB '95*, 420-431, 1995.

Hand, D. J., Intelligent data analysis: Issues and opportunities, in Liu, X., Cohen, P. and Bertholds, M. (eds.), *Advances in Intelligent Data Analysis (IDA-97)* (LNCS 1280), 1-14, 1997.

Hand, D. J., Data mining: Statistics and more? *American Statistician*, 52(2), 112-118, 1998.

Hidber, C., Online Association Rule Mining, *Proceedings SIGMOD*, 1999.

Holsheimer, M., Kersten, M., Mannila, H. and Toivonen, H., A perspective on databases and data mining, *Proceedings Knowledge Discovery in Databases (KDD'95)*, 1995.

Hosking, J. R. M., Pednault, E. P. D. and Sudan, M. A statistical perspective on data mining, *Future Generation Computer Systems*, 13, 117-134, 1997.

Huber, P. J. From large to huge: A statistician's reactions to KDD & DM, *Proceedings KDD-97*, 304-308, 1997.

Imielinski, T. and Mannila, H., A database perspective on knowledge discovery, *Communications of the ACM*, 39(11), 58-64, 1996.

Kasabov, N. K., *Foundations of Neural Networks, Fuzzy Systems, and Knowledge Engineering*, MIT Press, Cambridge, MA, 1996.

Kryszkiewicz, M., Representative association rules, *Proceedings PAKDD'98*, 1998.

Lent, B., Swami, A. and Widom, J., Clustering association rules, *Proceedings ICDE'97*, 1997.

Lin D.-I. and Kedem, Z. M., Pincer-search: A new algorithm for discovering the maximum frequent set, *Proceedings 6th EDBT*, pp. 105-119, 1998.

Lin, T. Y. and Cercone, N. (eds.), *Rough Sets and Data Mining: Analysis for Imprecise Data*, Kluwer Academic, Boston, MA, 1997.

Luger, G. and Stubblefield, W., *Artificial Intelligence: Structures and Strategies for Complex Problem Solving* (3rd ed.), Addison-Wesley Longman, Harlow, England, 1998.

McCarthy, J., Phenomenal data mining: From observations to phenomena, 1996, available at: http://www-formal.stanford.edu/jmc/data-mining/data-mining.html.

Meo, R., Psaila, G. and Ceri, S., A new SQL-like operator for mining association rules, *Proceedings Conference on Very Large Data Bases* (*VLDB'96*), 1996.

Meo, R., Psaila, G. and Ceri, S. , An Extension to SQL for Mining Association Rules, *Data Mining and Knowledge Discovery*, 2(2), 195-224, 1998a.

Meo, R., Psaila, G. and Ceri, S., A tightly-coupled architecture for data mining, *Proceedings ICDE* 1998, pp. 316-323, 1998b.

Mitchell, M., *Introduction to Genetic Algorithms*, MIT Press, Cambridge, MA, 1998.

Pakath, R., Genetic algorithms, Chapter 41 in Holsapple, C. W. and Whinston, A. B (eds.)., *Decision Support Systems: A Knowledge-Based Approach*, West Publishing Company, Minneapolis/St. Paul, 1996.

Piatetsky-Shapiro, G., Data mining and knowledge discovery: The third generation, in Z. W. Ras and A. Skowron (eds.), *Foundations of Intelligent Systems* (LNAI 1325), pp. 48-49, 1997.

Piatetsky-Shapiro, G. and Frawley, W. (eds.), *Knowledge Discovery in Databases*. AAAI/MIT Press, Menlo Park, CA, 1991.

Quinlan, J. R., C4.5: *Programs for Machine Learning*, Morgan Kaufmann, San Mateo, CA, 1993.

Quinlan, J. R., Bagging, boosting and CN4.5, *Proceedings AAAI 1996*, AAAI Press, Menlo Park, CA, 1996.

Quinlan, R., Data Mining from an AI Perspective (Keynote speech), *Proceedings of the 15th International Conference on Data Engineering*, 1999.

Ramakrishnan, N. and Ggrama, A. Y. (eds.), Special issue: Data mining: from serendipity to science, *IEEE Computer*, 32(8), 34-75, 1999.

Russell, S. and Norvig, P., *Artificial Intelligence: A Modern Approach*, Prentice Hall, Englewood Cliffs, NJ, 1995.

Sarawagi, S., Thomas, S. and Agrawal, R., Integrating association rule mining with relational database systems: Alternatives and implications, *Proc. SIGMOD'98*, 1998.

Siklossy, L. and Ayel, M., Data discovery, in Liu, X., Cohen, P. and Berthold, M. (eds.), *Advances in Intelligent Data Analysis* (*IDA '97*), LNCS 1280, pp. 459-463, 1997.

Silberschatz, A. and Tuzhilin, A., What makes patterns interesting in knowledge discovery systems. *IEEE Transactions on Knowledge and Data Engineering*, 8(6), 970-974, 1996.

Simon, H. A., Why should machines learn? In R. S. Michalski, J. G. Carbonell and T. M. Mitchell (eds.), *Machine Learning: An Artificial Intelligence Approach*, Vol. I., Tioga, Palo Alto, CA, 1983.

Srikant, R. and Agrawal, R., Mining generalized association rules, *Proceedings VLDB'95,* 1995.

Srikant, R. and Agrawal, R., Mining quantitative association rules in large relational tables, *Proceedings SIGMOD'96,* 1996.

Srikant, R., Vu, Q. and Agrawal, R., Mining association rules with item constraints, *Proc. KDD'97,* 1997.

Toivonen, H., Sampling large databases for association rules, *Proceedings VLDB'96,* 1996.

Ullman, J. D., Abstract of a talk given at University of Washington/Microsoft workshop on data mining, 1998. Available at http://www-db.stanford.edu/~ullman/pub/mining.txt.

Viliant, L. G., A theory of Learnable. *Communications of the ACM,* 27, 1134-1142, 1984.

Wah, B., Generalization and generalizability measures, *IEEE Transactions on Knowledge and Data Engineering,* 11(1), 175-186, 1999.

Zytkow, J., Knowledge = concepts: a harmful equation, *Proeedings KDD 97,* pp. 104-109, 1997.

Chapter 11

DATA WAREHOUSING , OLAP AND DATA MINING

11.1 OVERVIEW

In the previous chapter we discussed useful data mining techniques for decision support. It is important to keep in mind that data mining is not an isolated phenomenon. Data mining is only a portion of the larger picture concerning decision support queries, and is closely related to the task of holistic analysis of organization data, usually referred to as On-Line Analytical Processing, or OLAP (which was briefly introduced in Chapter 5). A data warehouse (also introduced in Chapter 5) provides an ideal environment where intelligent agents can fully utilize all the needed resources for discovery of useful knowledge patterns. In this chapter, we examine the issue of agent-based data mining in data warehouses. Starting from a discussion on practical concerns related to decision support queries, we examine data warehouses from a database perspective, with a focus on maintenance of materialized views, as well as related indexing techniques. The semantics of data mining on aggregating data are analyzed, and the gap between OLAP and data mining is then examined. This discussion allows us to introduce an integrated architecture for combined OLAP and data mining.

In the rest of this chapter, we first take a look at the issue of data mining in data warehousing environment. The reason of why data mining is preferable in data warehousing environment to non-warehousing environment is examined from two aspects: the concerns from database management systems proper, as well as the relationship between data mining and other activities in a data warehousing environment. The first aspect leads us to an in-depth examination of data warehousing from the perspective of materialized views and indexing. The second aspect leads us to a discussion of decision support queries and OLAP. The discussion allows us to consider an integrated architecture which combines data mining and OLAP at the end of this chapter.

11.2 DATA MINING IN DATA WAREHOUSES

Data warehouses provide an excellent environment for database-centric data mining. In this section, we examine several issues of database support for data mining.

Data mining and query processing. [Imielinski 1996] discussed data mining as a querying process, and proposed two research programs. The short-term program calls for efficient algorithms implementing data mining tools on the top of large databases and utilizing the existing DBMS support. The long-term calls for building optimizing compilers for *ad-hoc* queries and embedding queries in application programming interfaces.

There is a need to focus on generic scalability requirements rather than on features tuned to specific algorithms where possible, and furthermore, there is a need to build "SQL-aware." A lot of ongoing projects in the data mining area have focused on inventing new data analysis techniques. Less work has been done on scaling data analysis techniques over large data sets. In designing the scalable implementations, some of the algorithms have made assumptions that ignore the fact that a data warehouse will serve not just data mining, but also traditional query processing [Chaudhuri 1998].

Data warehouses are deploying relational database technology for storing and maintaining data. For pragmatic reasons, the data mining utilities should assume a relational backend.

Today's data mining algorithms are invoked on a materialized disk-resident data set. If data mining were to succeed, data mining must evolve to *ad-hoc* data mining, where the data set which is minded is specified on-the-fly. In other words, mining may be invoked on a data set that has been created on-the-fly by the powerful query tools. Therefore, there is a need for building SQL-aware data mining systems. Effectively using an SQL backend for data mining applications is a nontrivial problem, because using the SQL backend as much as possible in an obvious way may hurt performance. As we implement mining algorithms that generate SQL efficiently, we also will identify primitives that need to be incorporated in SQL. Again we draw similarities with the OLAP world. Generation of SQL queries against the backend clearly benefits from the CUBE construct. We can identify two goals for studying possible extensions to SQL, extensions that:

- Strongly interact with core SQL primitives and can result in significant performance improvement;
- Encapsulate a set of useful data mining primitives.

Data mining and meta-data. In a data warehouse, views which are materialized or partially materialized contain valuable information such as value distributions and other statistical information that are much more accurate than those views which are run once in a while. A smarter system can extract this valuable meta-data and, with a query feedback mecahnism, maintain precise statistics [Roussopoulos 1998].

Performance issues. The on-going research program is concerned with an efficient algorithm implementing machine learning tools (such as C4.5) on the top of large databases and utilizing the existing DBMS support. For example, training a classifier on a large training set stor. a database may require multiple passes through the data using different ⸲erings between attributes. This can be implemented by utilizing DBMS support for aggregate operations, indexes and database sorting (using ORDER BY clause in SQL).

11.2.1.1 Research issues

However, in the long run, database mining should learn from the general experience of DBMS field and follow one of the key DBMS paradigms: building optimizing compilers for *ad-hoc* queries and embedding queries in application programming interfaces. Query languages, query optimization, and transaction processing were the driving ideas behind the tremendous growth of the database field since the 1960s. The focus should be on increasing programmer productivity for KDD application development, and a sort of Knowledge and Data Discovery Management Systems (KDDMS) should be developed. To be more specific, first a KDD query language has to be formally defined then query optimization tools would be developed to compile queries into reasonably efficient execution plans. These execution plans will include existing inductive learning and statistical data analysis algorithms and may include new inductive tools as well. This process essentially mirrors the development of query languages and query optimization in relational databases. However, KDD query optimization will be more challenging than relational query optimization due to the higher expressive power of KDD queries. Another difficulty is that *the border between querying and discovery is blurred.* Discovery is just a matter of the expressive power of a query language (see remarks given in Chapter 7).

11.3 DECISION SUPPORT QUERIES, DATA WAREHOUSE AND OLAP

11.3.1 DECISION SUPPORT QUERIES

The need for data warehouses is justified by the concerns behind decision support queries, such as OLAP and data mining. An agent-based data mining process prefers tightly-coupled environments so that data mining becomes part of the database management process. Data warehouses provide such support.

Decision support queries are *ad hoc* user queries in various business applications. In these applications, current and historical data are comprehensively analyzed and explored, identifying useful trends and creating summaries of the data, in order to support high-level decision making in data warehousing environment [Widom 1995]. A class of stylized queries typically involve group-by and aggregation operators. Applications dominated by such queries are referred to as On-Line Analysis Processing (OLAP) [Chaudhuri and Dayal 1997].

Recently the importance of integrating OLAP and data mining have been widely addressed by database practitioners from industry's perspectives [Parsaye 1997]. As a reply from academia for this practical need, studies on multiple-level data mining [Han, Fu and Ng 1994] can be viewed as a step closer to the goal of this integration. The various ways of mining knowledge at multiple concept levels, such as progressive deepening, progressive generalization, and interactive up-and-down, bear significant similarities with OLAP operations (such as roll-up and drill-down). More recently, research papers on integrated OLAP and data mining started emerging, particularly from Han and his research group who investigated the issue of incorporating data cubes into data mining techniques [Han 1997, 1998]

In the following, rather than presenting new algorithms for integrated OLAP and data mining, we focus on the different and complementary roles of OLAP and data mining in the overall *process* of intelligent data analysis in data warehousing environments; that is, we examine how to put together different aspects of OLAP and data mining.

We introduced the notion of *decision support queries* in Chapter 1. In order to better understand the function of data warehouses, here we provide a little more discussion on decision support queries These queries are intended to comprehensively analyze/explore current and historical data, identify useful trends and create summaries of data to support high-level decision making for knowledge workers (executives, managers, analysts) [Chaudhuri and Dayal 1997]. There are three classes of data analysis tools [Ramakrishnam 1998]. In addition to data mining, the other two are:

> (1) Complex queries: Tools that support traditional SQL-style queries, but designed to *support complex ueries* efficiently. Relational DBMSs optimized for decision support applications.
>
> (2) *OLAP* : Tools that support a class of stylized queries that typically involve group-by and aggregation operators. Applications dominated by such queries are called *On-Line Analytic Processing*, or OLAP. These systems support a query style in which the data is best thought of as a multidimensional array, and are influenced by end-user tools such as spreadsheets, in addition to database query languages. OLAP systems work in a mostly-read environment.

11.3.2 ARCHITECTURE OF DATA WAREHOUSES
11.3.2.1 Components in data warehouses

The data warehouse is integrated (containing integrated data, detailed and summarized data, historical data and meta-data) so the data miner can concentrate on mining data rather than cleansing and integrating data.

Data warehousing provides an effective approach to deal with complex decision support queries over data from multiple sites. A data warehouse is a subject-oriented, integrated, time-varying, non-volatile collection of data that is used primarily in organizational decision making [Inmon 1996]. The key to the data warehousing approach is to create a copy of all the data at some one location, and to use the copy rather than going to the individual sources. Data warehouses contain consolidated data from many sources (different business units), spanning long time periods, and augmented with summary information. Warehouses are much larger than other kinds of databases, sizes are much larger, typical workloads involve *ad hoc*, fairly complex queries, and fast response times are important. Since decision support often is the goal of data warehousing, clearly warehouses may be tuned for decision support, and perhaps vice versa.

A typical data warehousing architecture consists of the following:

- A relational database for data storage;
- *Data marts,* which are departmental subsets focused on selected subjects;
- *Back end* and *front end* tools and utilities;
- *Metadata:* The system catalogs associated with a warehouse are very large, and are often stored and managed in a separate database called a metadata repository;
- Other components (depending on the design methods and the specific needs of the organizations).

Figure 11.1 (on next page) depicts the architecture of a data warehouse. A recent discussion on data warehouse creation, along with a comparison with data integration is given in [Srivastava and Chen 1999].

11.3.2.2 Relationship between data warehousing and OLAP

Having described the basic architecture of data warehouses, we may further examine the relationship between data warehousing and OLAP, which can be elaborated as follows. Decision-support functions in a data warehouse involve hundreds of complex aggregate queries over large volumes of data. To meet the performance demands so that fast answers can be provided, virtually all OLAP products resort to some degree of these aggregates. According to a popular opinion from OLAP Council [Forsman, 1997], a data warehouse is usually based on relational technology, while OLAP uses a multidimensional view of aggregate data to provide quick access to strategic information for further analysis. A data warehouse stores tactical information that answers "who?" and "what?" questions about past events. OLAP systems go beyond those questions; they are able to answer "what if?" and "why?" questions. A typical OLAP calculation is more complex than simply summarizing data.

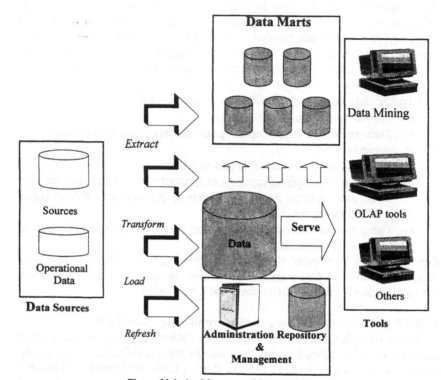

Figure 11.1 Architecture of data warehouse

11.3.3 BASICS OF OLAP

11.3.3.1 Terminology

We now describe the basics of OLAP. OLAP or multi-dimensional analysis is a method of viewing aggregate data called measurements (e.g., sales, expenses, etc.) along a set of dimensions such as product, brand, stored, month, city and state, etc. An OLAP typically consists of three conceptual tokens:

- *Dimension:* Each dimension is described by a set of attributes.
- *Measure:* Each of the numeric measures depends on a set of dimensions, which provide the context for the measure. The dimensions together are assumed to uniquely determine the measure. Therefore, the multidimensional data views a measure as a *value* in the multidimensional space of dimensions.
- *Domain hierarchy*: For example, "country," "state" and "city" form a domain hierarchy.

There are several basic approaches to implementing an OLAP:

- *ROLAP (Relational OLAP)*: OLAP systems that store all information (including fact tables) as relations. Note that the aggregations are stored with the relational system itself.
- *MOLAP (Mulitdimensional OLAP)*: OLAP systems that use arrays to store multidimensional datasets.

In general, ROLAP is more flexible than MOLAP, but has more computational overhead for managing many tables. One advantage of using ROLAP is that sparse data sets may be stored more compactly in tables than in arrays. Since ROLAP is an extension of the matured relational database technique, we can take advantage of using SQL. In addition, ROLAP is very scalable. However, one major advantage is its slow response time. In contrast, MOLAP abandons the relational structure and uses a sparse matrix file representation to store the aggregations efficiently. This gains efficiency, but lacks flexibility, restricts the number of dimensions (7 to 10), and is limited to small databases. (Remark on dimension: a relation can be viewed as a *2D* table or *n-D* table (each attribute represents a dimension). One advantage of using MOLAP is that dense arrays are stored more compactly in the array format than in tables. In addition, array lookups are simple arithmetic operations which results in an instant response. A disadvantage of MOLAP is long load times. Besides, MOLAP design becomes very massive very quickly with the addition of multiple dimensions.

To get the best of both worlds, we can combine MOLAP with ROLAP. Other approaches also exist. For example, LowLAP tools function so similarly to MOLAP that they rely on a proprietary data set for their OLAP capabilities. They offer advantages of an integrated user environment with a common GUI and a feature-rich work space; but provide limited processing capabilities.

11.3.3.2 OLAP operations
The two most well-known operations for OLAP queries are:

- *Roll-up*: This operation takes the current data object and does a further group-by on one of the dimensions. For example, given total sale by day, we can ask for total sale by month.
- *Drill-down*: As the converse of rule-up, this operation tries to get more detailed presentation. For example, given total sale by model, we can ask for total sale by model by year.

Other operations include:

- *Pivot* (Its result is called a cross-*tabulation*),
- *Slice* (It is an equality selection, reducing the dimensionality of data),
- *Dice* (It is the range selection), and
- *Others*.

In the following we illustrate the motivation behind the operation of pivot. This example also illustrates the basic idea of the roll-up operator. Consider a relational database on auto sales. The database is assumed to be in 3NF. Being more specific, let us consider a relation in this database with schema (Model, Year, Color, Dealer, Sales date). Now we want to have data aggregated by Model, then by Year, and finally, by Color. Suppose the result is shown in Table 11.1.

Table 11.1 Sales roll up

Model	Year	Color	Sales by model by year by color	Sales by model by year	Sales by model
Toyota	1998	black	100		
		light	120		
				220	
Toyota	1999	black	130		
		light	110		
				240	
					460

....Table 11.1 is not in first normal form (see Chapter 4 for a discussion on no-first normal form relations). There are many null values. In addition, the number of columns grows as the power set of the number of aggregated attributes. A better way of presenting the needed information is shown in Table 11.2, where a dummy value "ALL" is used to indicate the aggregation data regardless of the actual value of a particular attribute (such as color) [Gray, Bosworth, Layman and Pirahesh 1996].

If you examine Table 11.2 carefully, you may notice that it does not aggregate the sales by year; that is, there are no rows aggregating sales by color. For example, you will not be able to find that the total sales of black Toyota is 230. This observation suggests a more symmetrical presentation is needed. This results in the *cross tabulation* as shown in Table 11.3. The operation involved here is called the *pivot*. Note how the cross tabulation table can be obtained in a systematic way: when pivot is performed, *the values that appear in columns of the original presentation* (such as "black," "light" for Color, and "1998," "1999" for Year) now *become labels of axes in the result presentation*.

Table 11.2 Sales summary in 1NF

Model	Year	Color	Units
Toyota	1998	black	100
Toyota	1998	light	120
Toyota	1998	ALL	220
Toyota	1999	black	130
Toyota	1999	light	110
Toyota	1999	ALL	240
Toyota	ALL	ALL	460

Table 11.3 Toyota sales cross tabulation

Toyota	1998	1999	Total (ALL)
Black	100	130	230
Light	120	110	230
Total (ALL)	220	240	460

The cross tabulation in this example is a 2D (two dimensional) aggregation. But this is just a special case. For example, if other automobile models (such as Dodge, Ford, etc.) are added, it becomes a 3D aggregation. Generally speaking, the traditional GROUP BY clause in SQL can be used to generate the core of the N-dimensional *data cube*. The N-1 lower-dimensional aggregates appear as points, lines, plains, cubes or hyper-cubes in the original data cube. For this reason, a data CUBE operator was proposed [Gray, Bosworth, Layman and Pirahesh 1996].

11.3.3.4 Star schema and snowflake schema

Most data warehouses use *star schemas* to represent the multidimensional data model. In a star schema, there is a single fact table (which is at the center of a star schema) and a single table for each dimension (dimension table). [Chaudhuri and Dayal, 1997]. For convenience of discussion, we will use the star schema shown in Figure 11.2, which is slightly revised from the example appearing in many recent publications (e.g. [Chaudhuri and Dayal 1997]).

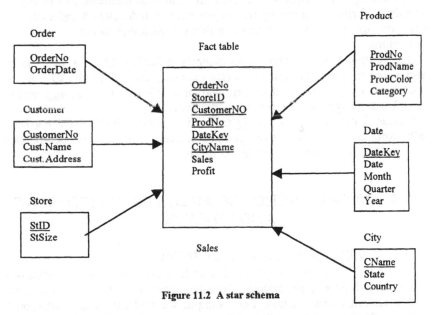

Figure 11.2 A star schema

Join operations in a star schema may be performed only between the fact table and any of its dimensions. Data mining has frequently been carried out on a view that is joined by the fact table with one or more dimension tables, followed by possible project and select operations. In addition, to facilitate data mining, such a kind of view is usually materialized.

Table 11.4 is revised from [Parsaye 1997], which can be considered as a materialized view obtained by join operations on the star schema shown in Figure 11.2. OrderID can be treated as TID in association rules. Both Figure

11.1 and Table 11.4 will be frequently cited by examples in the rest of this chapter.

Table 11.4 A materialized view for sales profit

RID	Product	Color	Store	Size	Profit ($1000s)
0	Jacket	Blue	S1	Small	-200
1	Jacket	Blue	S2	Medium	-100
2	Jacket	Blue	S3	Large	7000
3	Hat	Green	S1	Small	300
4	Hat	Green	S2	Medium	-1000
5	Hat	Green	S3	Large	-100
6	Glove	Green	S1	Small	2000
7	Glove	Blue	S2	Medium	-300
8	Glove	Green	S3	Large	200

11.3.3.5 Granularity and aggregation levels

In OLAP, data can be examined at different levels.

Granularity level: Data at this level are individual elements and served as base data. Various data mining techniques have been developed and applied at this level, including those discussions that can be found in other chapters of this volume.

Aggregation level: As shown in examples in Section 11.3.3.3, data can be aggregated in many different ways (for example, sales by model by year, or sales by model). Each level of aggregation is referred to as an aggregation level. Data at aggregation levels are summary data.

Unique features of data mining techniques at these levels have not been fully explored. The existence of aggregation levels provides new opportunities for data mining carried out at different levels:

11.4   DATA WAREHOUSE AS MATERIALIZED VIEWS AND INDEXING

11.4.1 REVIEW OF A POPULAR DEFINITION

Earlier in Chapter 4, we provided a brief discussion on data warehouses based on a business perspective. However, this discussion requires some further technical clarification. For example, we said that a data warehouse consists of a copy of data acquired from the source data. What does this copy look like? In fact, we may need to distinguish between a "true" copy (duplicate), a derived copy, approximate duplicate, or something else. For this reason, we need to examine the concept of data warehouse in more depth. In fact, a data warehouse can be characterized using materialized views and indexing. In the following, we will examine these two issues.

The WHIPS prototype developed at Stanford University is an interesting research project for data warehouse creation and maintenance [Hammer, Garcia-Molina, Widom, Labio, Zhuge 1995].

11.4.2 MATERIALIZED VIEWS

11.4.2.1 The necessity of using materialized views

Views are the most important asset of the relational model. Recall that we have the following basic concepts in relational databases:

Relation (base table): It is a stored table;

External view (virtual view, or simply view): It is a virtual table (derived relation defined in terms of base relations)

Materialized view: A view is materialized when it is stored in the database, rather than computed from the base relations in response to queries.

The general idea of the approach is to materialize certain expensive computations that are frequently inquired, especially those involving aggregate functions, such as count, sum, average, max, etc., and to store such materialized views in a multidimensional database (called a *data cube*) for decision support, knowledge discovery, and many other applications.

Commercial relational database products are used to discard views immediately after they are delivered to the user or to a subsequent execution phase. The cost for generating the views is for one-time-use only instead of being amortized over multiple and/or shared results. Caching query results or intermediate results for speeding up intra- and inter-query processing has been studied widely. All these techniques share one basic idea: the reuse of views to save cost.

In a data warehouse where query execution and I/O are magnified, the mandate for reuse cannot be ignored. In addition, in an OLAP environment, updates come in bulk rather than in small numbers, making incremental update techniques more effectively amortized. Therefore, query optimizers based on materialized view fragments are a necessity. Note that amortization and reuse of views can only be possible if they can be discovered by the query optimizer that decides to invoke those views which reduce the cost of the query. The most common techniques for discovering views (in any of its forms) in its most general form is an undecidable problem, but for the most common queries can be reduced to an NP-complete problem. Furthermore, for simple conjunctive query views, the time complexity is reduced to polynomial-time and very efficient algorithms.

The benefit of using materialized views is significant. Index structures can be built on the materialized view. Consequently, database access to the materialized view can be much faster than recomputing the view. A materialized view is just like a cache, which is a copy of the data that can be accessed quickly.

Materialized views are useful in new applications such as data warehousing, replication servers, chronicle or data recording systems, data visualization, and mobile systems. Integrity constraint checking and query optimization can also benefit from materialized views, but will not be emphasized in our current context.

11.4.2.2 The many facets of materialized views

It is interesting to note the multifaceted form of relational views (virtual or materialized), ranging from pure program to pure data (which is not maintainable). Relational views are used both as a specification technique and as an execution plan for the derivation of the warehouse data [Roussopoulos 1998].

- *Pure program (derivation procedure):* A *virtual (unmaterialized)* view is a program specification, or the *intension* (in terms of deductive database terminology) that generates data.
- *Derived data:* A *materialized* view can be considered as the *extension* (again in terms of deductive database terminology) of the pure program form. Therefore, it is derived data.
- *Pure data:* When we focus on the contents of the materialized views, they are the result of executing the procedure used to derive them. The derivation procedure is detached, so the views become pure data (i.e., converted from derived data to instances -- at least from the perspective of users).
- *Pure Index:* When materialized views are implemented in certain ways, such as through view indexes or view caches, their extension has only pointers to the underlying data, which are dereferenced when the values are needed. Therefore, materialized views are treated as pure indices.
- *Hybrid data and index:* A *partially materialized* view stores some attributes as data while the rest are referenced through pointers, thus combining data and indexes.
- *OLAP aggregate/indexing:* A very useful viewpoint of materialized views in decision making is that they play the role of data cubes in OLAP. A *data cube* contains data values aggregated from a collection of underlying relation values. It corresponds to project operations in relational algebra (Chapter 4) of the multi-dimensional space data to lesser dimensionality subspaces and stores aggregate values in it. For example, a data cube may provide aggregate values of sales data per month per product. A data cube can be obtained as *a set of materialized views or indexed views* derived from aggregation.

A discussion on these different forms gives us a better understanding on the nature of relational views, and their roles in data warehousing environment. In addition, these forms help us to deal with various issues related *to processing of views*, which involves *view scanning* and *maintenance* (usually through *incremental update*). For example, view scanning in the pure program view form is typically the same as re-execution of the query that created view and is no performance benefit for non-materialized views. Incremental update of materialized views can be done in either real-time during the query execution (along with scanning) or can be done at times other than scanning.

11.4.2.3 Materialized views and data warehousing

A data warehouse can be defined as a collection of materialized views derived from data that may not reside at the warehouse. It is a redundant collection of data replicated from several possibly distributed and loosely coupled source databases, organized to answer OLAP queries. One can view the problem of data warehousing as the problem of maintaining, in the warehouse, a materialized view or views of the relevant data stored in the original information sources. Challenges in exploiting materialized views include:

- *identify* which views should be materialized;
- *exploit* the materialized views to answer queries;
- *keep consistency* of the warehouse data from multiple data sources;
- *efficiently update* the materialized views during load and refresh;
- *predict* the amount of *storage* for a specified precomputations will require without actually performing the precomputation (or, given a certain amount of storage, determine which aggregates are best to precompute).

There are several important issues in regard to view management.

- *View maintenance*: A materialized view becomes dirty whenever the underlying base relations are modified. The process of updating a materialized view in response to changes to the underlying data is called view maintenance.
- *Incremental view maintenance*: Algorithms that compute changes to a view in response to changes to the base relations.

Discussion on materialized views and data warehousing can be found in [Widom 1995].

11.4.2.4 Integrated data and knowledge management in data warehouses

Data warehouses provide an excellent environment for integrated data and knowledge management [Baader, Jeusfeld and Nutt 1997; Borgida, Chaudhri, and Staudt 1998]. Specific questions need to be answered for integration including the following:

(1) The adequate languages to describe a user's information needs,
(2) Type of the reasoning needed,
(3) Background knowledge about application domain,
(4) Access views,
(5) Adequate representation and querying of meta-data,
(6) Dealing with incompleteness and other forms of uncertainty,
(7) Suitable formalisms to represent data quality, and more.

11.4.3 MAINTENANCE OF MATERIALIZED VIEWS

Due to the importance of view maintenance, we take a look at some recent studies related to maintenance of materialized views.

- *Maintaining the consistency of warehouse data*: A data warehouse is a repository containing integrated information for efficient querying and analysis. Data warehouse maintenance requires maintaining the consistency of warehouse data. Data sources are autonomous, views of the data at the warehouse may span multiple sources, and multiple updates may occur at one or more sources. [Zhuge, Garcia-Molina and Wiener 1998] discussed this problem, and presented the Strobe family of algorithms.

- *View self-maintenance:* Warehouse views need to be maintained in response to changes to the base data in the sources. In data warehousing environments where maintenance is performed locally at the warehouse, an important incremental view maintenance issue is how to minimize external base data access. [Quass, Gupta, Mumick and Widom 1996] discusses the problem of *view self-maintenance,* where the views are maintained without using all the base data. It is shown that by using key and referential integrity constraints, one often can maintain a select-project-join view when there are insertions, deletions, and updates to the base relations without going to the data sources or replicating the base relations in their entirety in the warehouse. [Huyn 1997] further discussed this problem in the presence of multiple views.

- *Maintenance of discovered rules:* The issue of data mining in a data warehousing environment will be discussed later in this chapter. Nevertheless, here we can briefly point out that a further issue of view maintenance is the maintenance of rules discovered using materialized views. When the materialized views are updated, the discovered rules should be updated as well. For example, in the task of maintaining discovered association rules, support and confidence of the rules may change, and a previously discovered rule may no longer be significant, while some other rules may have their support and confidence improved. [Cheung, Han, Ng and Wong 1996] discuss the issue of maintenance of the discovered rules, which is concerned with the situation when the database has been updated. Such updates may not only invalidate some existing strong association rules but also turn some weak rules into strong ones. An incremental updating technique is proposed to handle the case when new transaction data are added.

11.4.4 NORMALIZATION AND DENORMALIZATION OF MATERIALIZED VIEWS

11.4.4.1 Normalization versus denormalization

We now discuss the issue of what materialized views look like. The traditional relational database design (as discussed in Chapter 4) has put emphasis on normalization. However, data warehouse design cannot be simply reduced to relational database design. In fact, frequently materialized views involve join operation, and they are no longer in 3NF or BCNF (even though the data sources are in these normal forms).

First, we want to comment on the pros and cons of normalized data from a business perspective. In the business community, it is not uncommon for people to feel that normalized designs are hard to comprehend; denormalized designs tend to be more self-explanatory, even though denormalized tables have longer records. Typical multi-attribute search-and-scan performance is better on denormalized data because fewer tables are involved than in normalized designs. Denormalization data provide an intuitive productive environment for users who need to be trained or re-trained. On the other hand, denormalization is the greatest cultural hurdle for most incremental data mart design teams, because they are used to deal with OLTP. A result of denormalization is the redundancy of data. For example, two relations along with the joined result co-exist.

Another remark we want to make here is on the impact of ER modeling to data warehouse design. There are two schools of thought in enterprise data warehouse design. The ER normalized school [Inmen 1996] still starts from the fundamentally normalized tables and then spawning off subset data marts that are denormalized. In contrast, Ralph Kimball and his school [Kimball 1996] endorse a consistent, denormalized star schema environment across the entire enterprise data warehouses.

11.4.4.2 Physical implementation of materialized views

So, what is the reality of implementation? At the physical level of a data warehouse, data could be highly denormalized and heavily replicated across the data warehouse and data mart systems.

On the other hand, further decomposition may be needed even for a normalized relation: Suppose we have $r(ABCD)$ with the functional dependency $F = A \rightarrow BCD$. Apparently relation r is normalized (in which normal form?) However, suppose attribute C is not frequently accessed, then the relation may be further decomposed into $r_1(ABD)$ and $r_2(AC)$ so that the two relations r_1 and r_2 will be maintained in different ways.

There is a need to deal with non-normalized data: A hierarchy may be use in dimension tables, so dimension tables may not necessarily be normalized. This will be more appropriate for browsing the dimensions. In fact, dimensional tables are usually not normalized. The rationale is that a database used for OLAP is static; update, insertion and deletion anomalies are not important. Further, because the size of the database is dominated by the fact table, the space saved by normalizing dimension tables is negligible. Therefore, minimizing the computation time for combining facts in the fact table with dimension information is the main design criterion, and the use of denormalized dimension tables may avoid additional joins.

11.4.5 INDEXING TECHNIQUES FOR IMPLEMENTATION

Due to the close relationship between materialized views and indexing, here we provide a brief examination on the issue of indexing. Traditional indexing techniques (as briefly mentioned in Chapter 4) can be used, but there are also additional issues which are unique in a data warehousing environment.

The mostly-read environment of OLAP systems makes the CPU overhead of maintaining indices negligible, and the requirement of interactive response times for queries over very large datasets makes the availability of suitable indices very important.

> *Bitmap index:* The idea is to record values for sparse columns as a sequence of bits, one for each possible value. For example, the biological gender of a customer (male or female) can be represented using bitmap index. This method supports efficient index operations such as union and intersection; more efficient than hash index and tree index.
>
> *Join index:* This method is used to speed up specific join queries. A join index maintains the relationships between a foreign key with its matching primary keys. The specialized nature of star schemas makes join indices especially attractive for decision support.

We use the following example (taken from [Widom 1995]) to illustrate the join index. Let us consider the two relations "Sale" and "Product" shown in Table 11.5(a) and (b).

Table 11.5 (a) The sale table

Rid	Prod-id	Store-id	date	amount
R1	P1	C1	1	12
R2	P2	C1	1	11
R3	P1	C3	1	50
R4	P2	C2	1	8
R5	P1	C1	2	44
R6	P1	C2	2	4

Table 11.5 (b) The product table

id	name	price
P1	Bolt	10
P2	nut	5

If we perform join on sale.prod-id = prod-id, and precompute the result, we can obtain the *join index* as shown in Table 11.6.

Table 11.6 Example of join index

Product.id	Sale.prod-id
P1	R1, R3, R5, R6
P2	R2, R4

In addition, we can give the following two remarks.

Relationship between join index and materialized views. If we do not use join index, we can compute the join of two relations "sale" and "product", and store the result. In this case, we have a materialized view shown below, which has the same effect of using join index (namely, avoid recomputation). The result is shown in Table 11.7 (columns are re-ordered for clarity.) Notice that the result of join is usually a denormalized relation.

Table 11.7 A materialized view

Rid	Prod-id	name	price	Store-id	date	amount
R1	P1	Bolt	10	C1	1	12
R2	P2	Nut	5	C1	1	11
R3	P1	Bolt	10	C3	1	50
R4	P2	Nut	5	C2	1	8
R5	P1	Bolt	10	C1	2	44
R6	P1	Bolt	10	C2	2	4

Combining join index and bitmap index. Suppose we have very few products to consider, then the bitmap can be used for products. (This is a very important condition to check. It is not appropriate if there are many products.) The join index table after bitmap technique is incorporated is shown in Table 11.8.

Table 11.8 Combined join/bitmap indexing

P1	P2	Sale.prod-id
1	0	R1, R3, R5, R6
0	1	R2, R4

Indexing is important to materialized views for two reasons: Indexes for a materialized view reduce the cost of computation to execute an operation (analogous to the use of an index on the key of a relation to decrease the time needed to locate a specified tuple); indexing reduces the cost of maintenance of the materialized views. One important problem in data warehousing is the maintenance of materialized views due to changes made in the source data. Maintenance of materialized views can be a very time consuming process. There need to be some methods developed to reduce this time (one method is use of supporting views and/or the meterializing of indexes).

11.5 REMARKS ON PHYSICAL DESIGN OF DATA WAREHOUSES

Although the goal of this book is not on physical data warehouse design, it is still important for us to understand some basics of this process. An excellent overview on this issue can be found in [Labio, Quass and Adelberg 1997]. Another discussion with focus on distributed and parallel computing issues in data warehousing can be found in [Garcia-Molina, Labio, Wiener and Zhuge 1999]. In the remaining part of this short section, we give a brief example to illustrate how basic computational intelligence techniques can be applied to physical data warehouse design process.

The problem considered here is that a data warehouse is often kept only loosely consistent with the sources, because it is periodically refreshed with changes sent from the source. When this happens, the warehouse is taken off-line until the local relations and materialized views can be updated. An important issue is how to select the sets of supporting views and of indexes to materialize so that the down time can be minimized. This problem is referred to as the *view index selection (VIS) problem*. As described in [Labio, Quass and Adelberg 1997], an algorithm takes as input the set of all possible views and indexes to materialize, M. M does not include the base relations B nor the primary view V but includes indexes that can be defined on them. (V and B are constrained to be materialized.) The goal of the algorithm is to choose a subset M' of M to materialize such that the total cost C is minimized. The solution is built incrementally using the A* search (see Chapter 2 for a discussion). It begins with an empty materialization set ($M' = \emptyset$) and then considers adding single views or indexes. The intermediate steps reached in the algorithm were referred to as *partial states*. The exact cost of the best solution given a partial state can be decomposed as $C = g + h$, where g is the maintenance cost for the features chosen so far and h is the maintenance cost for the features in M'_u (which is the unconsidered features that would be chosen). A partial order < is imposed upon M such that if a feature m_1 can be used in a query plan for propagating insertions to view m_2, then $m_1 < m_2$ (so in this section < does not represent the conventional meaning less than). Also, for an index m_1 on a view m_2, we have $m_2 < m_1$.,

11.6 SEMANTIC DIFFERENCES BETWEEN DATA MINING AND OLAP

Although both OLAP and data mining deal with analysis of data, the focus and methodology are quite different. In this section, we provide a much-needed discussion on this issue and use several examples to illustrate these differences. We point out the difference of data mining carried out at different levels, including how different types of queries can be handled, how different semantics of knowledge can be discovered at different levels, as well as how different heuristics may be used.

11.6.1 DIFFERENT TYPES OF QUERIES CAN BE ANSWERED AT DIFFERENT LEVELS

We first point out that different kinds of analysis can be carried out at different levels: What are the features of products purchased along with promotional items? The answer for this query could be association rule(s) at the granularity level, because we need to analyze actual purchase data for each transaction which is involved in promotional items (we assume information about promotional items can be found in product price).

- What kinds of products are most profitable? This query involves aggregation, and can be answered by OLAP alone.
- What kinds of customers bought the most profitable products? This query can be answered by different ways. One way is to analyze individual transactions and obtain association rules between products and customers at the granularity level. An alternative way is to select all most profitable products, project the whole set of customers who purchased these products, and then find out the characteristics of these customers. In this case we are trying to answer the query by discovering characteristic rules

at an aggregation level. (For example, customers can be characterized by their addresses.)

11.6.2 AGGREGATION SEMANTICS

The above discussion further suggests that data mining at different levels may have different semantics. Since most people are familiar with semantics of knowledge discovered at the granularity level, here we will provide a discussion emphasizing what kind of difference is made by the semantics of knowledge discovered at aggregation levels (which will be referred to as aggregation semantics).

11.6.2.1 Aggregation semantics for classification rules

Take a look at a simple sales table shown in Table 11.9(a). In order to obtain rules to characterize what kinds of products are profitable, we may first map the value of profit to a Boolean function Yes or No. (Of course we may also use a more sophisticated multiple classification; eg. profit 10000 < profit < 20000 will be classified as "low" profit).

Table 11.9(a) A simple sales table

RID	Quarter	Product	Product Color	Quantity	Profit
1	1st	Hat	Red	62	-100
2	1st	Scarf	Blue	125	300
3	1st	Glove	Blue	270	1000
4	2nd	Hat	Red	116	100
5	2nd	Scarf	Blue	34	-200
6	2nd	Glove	Red	52	-100
7	3rd	Hat	Blue	10	-400
8	3rd	Scarf	Red	37	-300
9	3rd	Glove	Blue	48	-200
10	4th	Hat	Red	412	6000
11	4th	Scarf	Blue	206	200
12	4th	Glove	Blue	149	300

Classification rules can be discovered at the granularity level as usual. For example, we may have the following rule [Parsaye 1997]:

Rule 1:

If ProdColor = Blue

then Profitable = No

with confidence 0.75

Alternatively, we may apply aggregate functions on each particular kind of product, and then at aggregation level, there is only one result (tuple) per each particular aggregation, so confidence will no longer make any sense. For example, if we apply the aggregation operations as supported by DATA CUBE operator [Gray, Bosworth, Layman and Pirahesh 1996], we will get the following summary data as shown in Table 11.9(b):

Table 11.9(b): A summary sales table

Quarter	Product	Product Color	Quantity	Profit
ALL	ALL	Blue	ALL	640
...	....	...	...	...

The following rule can be obtained:
  Rule 1':
        If ProdColor = Blue
        then Profitable = Yes
Note that Rule 1 and Rule 1' are contradictory to each other. There is   an inconsistency of knowledge discovered at the aggregation levels and at the granularity level. This is just an example of "anomalies" which may occur for data mining involving aggregation: Knowledge discovered at the granularity level may not (and usually not) be able to correctly derive results obtained at aggregation level. Since knowledge discovered at different levels have different semantics, there is no general answer to the question of "which one is correct" when a kind of inconsistency exists.

11.6.2.2 Aggregation semantics for association rules
Do association rules still make sense at aggregation levels? May be, but with different semantics. Consider the summary table in Table 11.10.

Table 11.10 A summary table

Year	Month	Sum (OrderID)	Sum (Milk)	Sum (Bread)	Sum (Cigarette)	Sum (Beer)
1998	01	18000	7000	8000	900	1000
1998	07	21000	8500	9200	1700	5000

The primary key at the granularity level (OrderId) disappeared. We may be interested in how the sales data are related to the new primary key (year and month). Although at the granularity level TID serves only the purpose of the identifier (i.e., surrogate), the primary key in the summary table may bear more meaning, and may be used for explanation purposes. For example, the sale of beer is much higher in July than in January, because there were more outdoor social events in July than in January due to the weather.
    The association between the sum of milk and the sum of bread is now examined in the orders involved in whole month, not in each individual orders (namely, transactions). Therefore, in an extreme case, 7000 orders of milk may be from the same 8000 transactions which ordered bread, while in another extreme case, the purchase of milk and bread may be from completely disjoint 15000 transactions.
    But this is not to say that association rules will not make any sense at aggregation levels. The summary data obtained from different states may reveal some connections of attributes which can only be found at the aggregation level of the state. For example, we may have the following (hypocritical) rule discovered:

Rule 2. States which have high amount of sales in milk and eggs are likely to have high amount of cheese sales in Winter.

Note that what this rule said is different from saying that the same customer who purchased milk and eggs is likely to purchase cheese in Winter. Therefore, association rules have different semantics between granularity and aggregation levels.

11.6.2.3 Sensitivity analysis

Related to the issue of inconsistency discussed above is the need for carrying out a kind of sensitivity analysis for knowledge discovered at aggregation levels. In fact, the change of a single value at the granularity level may significantly change the rules discovered at aggregation levels. Suppose we change the profit of RID 2 from 700 to 10; the overall evaluation for blue products will be changed significantly. Rule 1 remains true, if we can tolerate confidence at a lowered level (0.50). However, since the total profit as in Table 1 is now changed to -50, Rule 1' is no longer true. One well-known lesson learned from this kind of example is to keep the numerical data as long as possible (namely, defer the mapping from numerical data to classifications) [Parsaye 1997]. However, the problem of *how* to determine the change of the numerical data will affect the resulting classification is an issue yet to be studied.

11.6.2.4 Different assumptions or heuristics may be needed at different levels

Assumptions and heuristics are frequently needed to make the data mining process more effective. For example, in order to discover rules characterizing graduate students at the granularity level, the names of students can be dropped. Assumptions and heuristics are also important for data mining at aggregation levels, but they may be quite different from those at the granularity level.

Consider association rules at aggregation levels. We may compute the rate (percentage) of total orders for one product over some other products in each month. The following heuristic may be used:

> If for two products, the rate of orders is relatively stable over time, it may imply some kind of association between them; on the other hand, if the rate highly fluctuates, it may indicate little or no association between two products.

For example, applying this heuristic to Table 11.10, we may find out that the total purchase of milk and total sale of bread is associated more closely than the total purchase of milk and total purchase of beer, because the total orders of milk changed very little from January to July (7000 to 8000), which is not proportional to the change of total orders for beer (from 1000 to 5000).

11.7 NONMONOTONIC REASONING IN DATA WAREHOUSING ENVIRONMENT

Basic concepts of computational intelligence as discussed in early chapters of this book play an important role in decision making in data warehousing environments. As a brief remark, in this section we revisit the concept of nonmonotonic reasoning in data warehousing environments. Roughly speaking, nonmonotonic reasoning refers to the withdrawal of previous conclusions when new knowledge has been acquired. Nonmonotonic reasoning is an important mechanism of uncertain reasoning. As mentioned in Chapter 3, when probabilistic reasoning (and not just the axiomatic basis of probability theory) has been fully formalized, it will be formally nonmonotonic [McCarthy 1980].

We continue our discussion on integrated OLAP and data mining in the last section, but this time from the perspective of nonmonotonic reasoning. Recall that the granularity level and the aggregation level are different concept levels for mining rules over multiple dimensions. Data at the granularity level are detailed elements and served as base data, while data at the aggregation level are summary data. Knowledge discovered at these levels may have different semantics, and the semantics may be inconsistent with each other. When we roll-up from the granularity level to an aggregating level, the conclusion made at the granularity level may have to be withdrawn. Similarly, when we drill-down from an aggregating level to the granularity level, the conclusion made at the aggregating level may have to be withdrawn. Obviously, reasoning at these levels has to be nonmonotonic.

The examples given in the previous section are quite simple. Nevertheless, they reveal the nonmonotonic nature of reasoning involved in integrated OLAP and data mining: When we drill down or roll up, the conclusion we made at the previous level may have to be withdrawn. It is important to realize that rules mined at different levels have different semantics, and these rules are not isolated to each other. Understanding the nonmonotonic nature of reasoning from one level to another level (such as moving from the granularity level to an aggregating level, and vice versa) is important for us to establish a comprehensive picture of data analysis, and thus has a great business value.

In summary, a methodology should be developed to analyze summary data guided by nonmonotonic reasoning. Although previous studies in nonmonotonic reasoning have taken a logic-based approach, this current study should focus on pragmatics so that knowledge workers will be able to use this methodology. There are many issues that should be addressed by this methodology, including the following:

(1) A set of guidelines involving the infrastructure of the data mining process. Knowledge workers should carefully study the semantics and the schema of the data to be analyzed, understand various issues such as what kind of knowledge is needed by their organizations, which factors they

should look at, which existing tools are available, as well as other related aspects. This kind of knowledge will guide the direction of nonmonotonic reasoning.

(2) A method for preparing summary data for nonmonotonic data mining. For example, frequently numeric data need to be categorized into meaningful groups so that summary data can be obtained and used for analysis.

(3) A method or a set of algorithms that can be used to actually carry out nonmonotonic reasoning for data mining. The method or the algorithms should identify the most effective directions to analyze the data, such as roll up or drill down according to a specific set of attributes.

11.8 COMBINING DATA MINING AND OLAP

11.8.1 AN ARCHITECTURE COMBINING OLAP AND DATA MINING

The discussion of Section 11.6 leads to an integrated architecture for combined OLAP/data mining in data warehousing environment as depicted in Figure 11.3. This architecture is proposed in data warehousing environments.

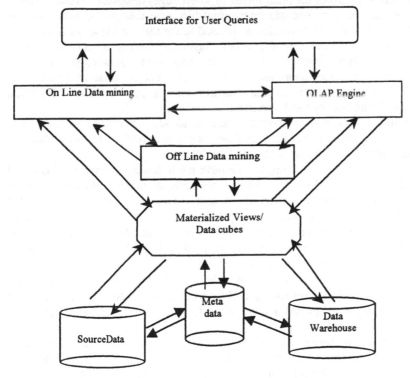

Figure 11.3 Integrated OLAP and data mining

We focus on the different and complementary roles of OLAP and data mining in the overall *process* of intelligent data analysis in data warehousing environments; that is, how to put together different aspects of OLAP and data mining. Note that at the center of this architecture are the materialized views (with an emphasis of *data cubes*, which are a special form of materialized views -- see Section 11.4.2.2 for a discussion on the multi-facet features of materialized views).

11.8.2 SOME SPECIFIC ISSUES

Using the integrated architecture as a guideline, we now discuss three specific issues related to combined OLAP/data mining. These three issues are: how to use and reuse of intensional historical data, how benefit OLAP using data mining, and how to enrich data mining using concepts related to OLAP.

11.8.2.1 On the use and reuse of intensional historical data

First, we provide some remarks on the use of reuse of discovered rules. In many cases, the rules (or other forms of knowledge) discovered from previous data are stored; they become intensional historical data and can be used or reused. Here the term "intensional" is used in the same sense as in intensional databases. Also note that the word "historical" refers to the knowledge discovered from previous data. The discovered knowledge (i.e., the intensional historical data) itself may or may not be time-sensitive. This feature (or the absence of the feature) may affect how the intensional historical data may be used or reused.

To use a previously discovered rule is to apply that rule directly. The following are some examples to indicate how a previously discovered rule can be used in the case of non time-sensitive data:

- *Provide prediction.* Suppose we have the following intensional historical data available: "*Rule 6.* In September 1998, the number of orders for blue products whose price marked x% down increased 1.5x% (10 < x < 20)." If a user wants to know in September 1999, when the price of a blue jacket is to be marked down 20%, how the number of orders will be affected; using the above rule a predicted increase of 30% will be provided to the user as a quick response.

- *Offer suggestions.* The above rule can also be used to guide users' decision making. For example, Rule 6 can also be used to suggest users to mark down the price for blue products if they want to have a significant increase of orders.

- *Perform inference.* The above examples already indicated the use of inference (for example, modus ponens was used in prediction). Furthermore, the inference process can be carried out so that inference chains can be constructed. Suppose from the combined historical and current data, the following rule is discovered: "*Rule 7.* For whatever product, the number of orders increased 15% or above will always bring significant profit." Rule 6 and Rule 7 can be used together to infer that "If we mark down the price for blue jacket in September 1999 by 12%, then significant profit may be made." In addition, time-sensitive intensional historical data can also be used for future data analysis and data mining, as exemplified in the following case:

- *Perform second order data mining.* Generalization or other forms of induction can be used to perform further data mining on intensional historical data. For example, consider the summary table in Table 11.11 which was constructed from intensional historical data (i.e., each tuple is a rule discovered from previous sales):

Table 11.11 Another summary table

year	Product color	Store size	Profitable
1996	Blue	Large	Low
1997	...Yellow	Small	High
...	...	...	...
1998	Yellow	Large	Very high

In this summary table, we may perform further data mining on various directions, such as the impact of the color or store size without considering years, or the general trend of color or store size over years. Since this kind of analysis is to perform data mining on the intensional historical data, it will be referred to as the *second-order data mining.* Second-order data mining provides an approach to derive rules at aggregation levels .

- *Reuse* of a previously discovered rule differs from direct use of a rule in that some adaptation or revision is needed before the discovered knowledge can be used. Just like reuse of a piece of a previously developed software component, reuse of a rule requires necessary changes of some parameters. A kind of mapping may occur, which may take the form of analogical reasoning. The result of reusing a rule may be a derived *candidate* rule whose validity should be carefully checked. For example, consider the following intensional historical data Rule 8, which is an association rule with certain support and confidence: "*Rule 8.* In states where there is a significant increase on the sale of sweet candies, there is also a moderate increase on the sale of iced tea." An example of reusing this rule may result in following a somewhat speculative rule: "*Rule 8'.* For states where there is a significant increase on the sale of salty peanuts, there may be a moderate increase on the sale of ginger-ale." Rule 8' is produced by using the following analogy:

sweet solid food : mild sweet liquid :: salt solid food : mild salt liquid

Of course rules derived in this way should be validated carefully before they can actually be used (sometimes revision may be necessary). Since checking the validity of a candidate rule may incur less overhead than deriving a new rule, reuse may be an interesting technique deserving further exploration.

11.8.2.2 How data mining can benefit OLAP

In the following we outline several sample cases in which data mining may benefit OLAP. A more detailed discussion can be found in [Chen 1999].

- *Construction and maintenance of materialized views:* Many data mining techniques have already implicitly assumed the use of some basic functions of OLAP techniques; for example, the materialized view constructed from the star schema to be used for data mining. However, OLAP alone cannot decide which attributes should be used to form the schema of the view to be used for data mining. The feedback of data mining can be used to identify most important attributes (that is, to determine schema for constructing materialized views), as well as the most important conditions for selecting the data to be included in the materialized views. Data mining may also provide help to handle indexing issues in evolving databases in data warehouse environment.

- *Data mining guided aggregation for OLAP:* In order to determine which view should be materialized (precomputed), the common interests of *ad hoc* queries from existing and potential users should be studied. Data mining on historical data may also provide a kind of guide for aggregation (namely, what to aggregate, and how to aggregate).

- *Instructed construction of materialized views for data mining.* Furthermore, the need for data mining can instruct OLAP aggregation so that various materialized views can be constructed which can be used to discover rules at aggregation levels. By placing the group-by operator at different attributes, various materialized views can be constructed for data mining at aggregation levels or at mixed granularity-aggregation levels. In general, knowledge discovered earlier can always provide refined instructions for the construction of materialized views.

11.8.2.3 OLAP-enriched data mining

There is another direction of connection between OLAP and data mining, namely, OLAP can benefit data mining. We use drill-down data mining as an example to illustrate how OLAP may provide a useful guide for data mining. First we note that summary data shows the general picture but lack of detail. For example, during a certain period, the sale of milk in Nebraska increased 10% while during the same period, the sale of milk dropped 5% in neighboring Iowa. This could be due to several reasons. If we know during the same period, the sales of all kinds of goods had dropped in Iowa but increased in Nebraska, then we may not need to pursue further analysis. On the other hand, if no convincing explanation exists, then we may have to perform some kind of data mining. In this case, the data mining process is drill-down in nature, because we should examine several dimensions in more detail.

We illustrate how the OLAP-related concerns can enrich the study of data mining by studying a variation of association patterns. This study addresses some concerns related to aggregation semantics as discussed in Section 11.6.2. Given a transaction database, where each transaction is a set of items, an association rule is an expression of the form $X \rightarrow Y$, where X and Y are sets of items. However, association patterns may be limited to basket data. For instance, in a sales database, the query "how does product color affect profits?" promotes "color" and "profit" to be the objects of analysis. The data domain of color or profit is not the same as of basket items, such as hat or glove. Moreover, the association between color and profit (which is a numeric measure) suggests a new type of pattern -- an influence pattern, which has not been covered by conventional association rules. The major purpose of influence patterns is to describe the influences of one set of objects called influencing factors on another set of objects called influence objects. Algorithms have been proposed for discovery of influential association rules. Moreover, when conflicts exist for rules discovered at granularity and aggregation levels, a rule-refinement process is invoked to resolve the conflicts. This refinement process resembles the drill-down operation of OLAP. For example, when we consider the effect of product color alone to the total sales, the rules obtained at the aggregation level may not agree with the rules obtained at the granularity level. The refined process may drill-down to some other dimension (such as the time dimension), and resolve the difference by generating the following rule where two dimension attributes are involved:

<Product Color, Red> => <Sales, High> with average value = 140, much of the Sales come from <Quarter, 4th> and <Product, Hat>.

A set of algorithms for discovery and maintenance of influential association rules have been developed and a prototype system has been implemented. A very brief outline of the main algorithm for rule discovery is shown below. The terminology involved in the algorithm skeleton as well as a much more detailed discussion of this approach can be found in [Chen, Chen and Zhu 1999].

Algorithm Influence analysis

Input: A relational view that contains a set of records and the questions for influence analysis.

Output: An influential association rule

Method:

(1) Specify the dimension attribute and the measure attribute.
(2) Identify the dimension item sets and calculate support counts.
(3) Identify the measure item sets and calculate support counts.
(4) Construct sets of candidate rules, compute the confidence and aggregate value.
(5) Form a rule at the granularity level with greatest confidence, and form a rule at the aggregation level with largest abstract value of the measure attribute.
(6) Compare the assertions at different levels, exit if comparable (i.e., there is no inconsistency found in semantics at different levels).
(7) For the case where the discovered rules are not comparable, derive the refined measure item set and the framework of the rule.
(8) If the value of the measure consists of both negative and positive values, form a rule indicating the summary value; otherwise, form a rule concerning average value.
(9) Construct the final rule.

11.9   CONCEPTUAL QUERY ANSWERING IN DATA WAREHOUSES

11.9.1 MATERIALIZED VIEWS AND INTENSIONAL ANSWERING

We discussed conceptual query answering and intensional answers in Chapter 9. In order to understand the role of intensional answers for conceptual query answering, it would be advantageous to briefly examine how materialized views may be used for intensional query answering in data warehousing environments. Intensional answers resemble materialized views in that, as discovered rules, they are stored for future use. Intensional answers are much smaller in size (usually one or few tuples per rule) than "conventional" materialized views. However, since both intensional answers and their extensional parts may be requested by users' conceptual queries, the extensional parts of the answers may also be stored. In general, when concept hierarchies are used, answers in layers can be organized according to their level of detail, and present to the user only the most general answers [Pirotte and Roelants 1989]. If the user rejects an answer, it will be used in the generation of additional, more specific answers; when the user approves an answer, the particular avenue will not be pursued any further. This kind of consideration justifies the choice of storing extensional answers along with intensional answers. When extensional answers are stored with intensional answers, we have *materialized intensional answers*. For instance, consider the "excellent" student example in Chapter 9 (Section 9.3.4.1). If the actual tuples for excellent students are stored along with the discovered rule, we have the materialized intensional answer for "excellent" students.

The advantage of using materialized intensional answers is same as using materialized views, namely, for fast response. In order to take this advantage, just like materialized views, several problems need to be dealt with for materialized intensional answers. In the following we briefly consider two problems:

(1) what to materialize;

(2) how to incrementally maintain these materialized views and how conceptual query answering can take advantage of incremental maintenance.

The first question was already illustrated by the "excellent" students example. As a little more sophisticated example, let us consider the following rule (an intensional answer):

$$q :- b, c, d.$$

Several strategies exist to answer the query q. At one extreme is the lazy approach, where no precomputation is performed. The other extreme is an eager approach which performs join on b, c, d at the body of the rule and stores the result (which is similar to what we have seen in the student example). Between these two extremes are some mixed approaches, such as to precompute the join of b and c and store the result or recompute the join of c and d and store the result.

For the second question, we have the following observations. The idea of incremental maintenance (similar to what is used for materialized views) has been incorporated in the work of [Pirotte and Roelants 1989] for maintenance of intensional answers. For example, the closure of the constraints is generated a priori and stored. The checks for redundancy are not performed anew for each new answer, but the outcome of the checking of an answer is used in the checking of answers generated from it. In general, the problem of incremental maintenance for materialized intensional answers has not been studied on its own right. However, methods for incremental maintenance for materialized views can be adopted for maintaining materialized intensional answers.

11.9.2 REWRITING CONCEPTUAL QUERY USING MATERIALIZED VIEWS

We now turn to more general cases where conceptual queries need to be rewritten so that materialized views can be used to answer queries. [Levy, Mendelzon, Sagiv and Srivastava 1995] discussed issues related to answering query using materialized views, including the problem of finding a rewriting of a query that uses the (materialized) views, the problem of finding minimal rewritings, and finding complete rewritings (i.e., rewriting that uses only the views). Although their work does not consider conceptual queries, some important methods and results may be extended to solve our problem. For example, possible rewritings of a query can be obtained by considering containment mappings form the bodies of the views to the body of the query as introduced by [Levy, Mendelzon, Sagiv and Srivastava 1995], but here containment mappings should incorporate concept hierarchy using the so-called *watermark* technique as proposed in [Han, Fu and Ng 1994]. In a multilevel database (MLDB), a database layer L is consistent on an attribute A_i with a query q if the constants of attribute A_i in query q can absorb (i.e, level-wise higher than) the concept(s) (level) of the attribute in the layer. The watermark of a (non-join) attribute A_i for query q is the topmost database layer which is consistent with the concept level of query constants/inquiries of attribute A_i in query q.

Consider the following conceptual query Q and materialized intensional answer V:

Q: booming(Area,Profit) :- isa (Area, MSA),
             consists(MSA,WestCoast), produce(Area, ComputerProduct),
             totalSale(ComputerProduct, Profit).

The query asks for booming areas in the west coast which should be in some MSA (Metropolitan Statistical Areas), producing computer products and the total sale profit. Suppose we have a materialized view V for good sales in Pacific states as shown below, where Region is a descendent of Area in a concept hierarchy:

V: goodSales(Region, PacificStates) :-
             isa(Region, MSA), consists(MSA, PacificStates),
             produce(Region, PCproduct).

Following the basic rewriting technique introduced in Example 2.2 of [Levy, Mendelzon, Sagiv and Srivastava 1995] and combining with the concept hierarchy, Q can be rewritten as Q' using V as shown below. Note that Area has now absorbed Region, and this rewriting is thus not a straightforward application of the basic technique as described in [Levy, Mendelzon, Sagiv and Srivastava, 1995].

> Q': booming(Region,Profit) :-
> goodSales(Region,   WestCoast),   produce(Region,
> ComputerProduct), totalProfit(ComputerProduct, Profit).

Suppose in the view goodSales , the join of isa and Consists materialized, then it can be used directly to further compute Q'. On the other hand, if the needed materialized view does not exist, then the query may need to be rewritten into some other form.

In large data warehousing environments, it is often advantageous to provide fast, approximate answers to queries based on summaries of the full data. However, the difficulty of providing good approximate answers for join-queries using only statistics (in particular, samples) from the base relations, significantly limits the scope of the current approaches for approximate query answering. [Acharya, Gibbons and Poosala 1999] proposed using join synopses as an effective solution for this problem. Details of these approaches will not be further discussed here.

11.10   WEB MINING

11.10.1 BASIC APPROACHES FOR WEB MINING

Web mining is a good example of an integrated use of various methods discussed in this chapter. Recent work has shown that the analysis needs of Web usage data have much in common with those of a data warehouse, and hence OLAP techniques are quite applicable. In the following we briefly examine this topic by following the presentation of [Cooley, Mobasher and Srivastava 1997].

Web mining can be broadly defined as the discovery and analysis of useful information from the World Wide Web. This broad definition on the one hand describes the automatic search and retrieval of information and resources available from millions of sites and on-line databases, i.e., *Web content mining*, and on the other hand, the discovery and analysis of user access patterns from one or more Web servers or on-line services, i.e., *Web usage mining*.

In recent years these factors have prompted researchers to develop more intelligent tools for information retrieval, such as intelligent Web agents, as well as to extend database and data mining techniques to provide a higher level of organization for semi-structured data available on the Web. In Chapter 5 we have already described the basic architecture of Web search. In the following we further summarize some efforts for Web mining conducted in this basic architecture.

- *Agent-Based Approach.* The agent-based approach to Web mining involves the development of sophisticated computational intelligence systems that can act autonomously or semi-autonomously on behalf of a particular user, to discover and organize Web-based information. Generally, the agent-based Web mining systems can be placed into the following three categories:
  - ◆ *Intelligent Search Agents*;
  - ◆ *Information Filtering/Categorization*; and
  - ◆ *Personalized Web Agents.*
- *Database Approach.* The database approaches to Web mining have generally focused on techniques for integrating and organizing the heterogeneous and semi-structured data on the Web into more structured and high-level collections of resources, such as in relational databases, and using standard database querying mechanisms and data mining techniques to access and analyze this information.
  - ◆ *Multilevel Databases.* Several researchers have proposed a multilevel database approach to organizing Web-based information. The main idea behind these proposals is that the lowest level of the database contains primitive semi-structured information stored in various Web repositories, such as hypertext documents. At the higher level(s) meta-data or generalizations are extracted from lower levels and organized in structured collections such as relational or object-oriented databases. A discussion on meta-database will be given in Chapter 14.
  - ◆ *Web Query Systems.* There have been many Web-base query systems and languages developed recently that attempt to utilize standard database query languages such as SQL, structural information about Web documents, and even natural language processing for accommodating the types of queries that are used in Web searches. Some Web-based query systems are summarized in [Florescu, Levy and Mendelzon 1998].

11.10.2 DISCOVERY TECHNIQUES ON WEB TRANSACTIONS

As already introduced earlier, *web usage mining* is the type of Web mining activity that involves the automatic discovery of user access patterns from one or more Web servers. Organizations often generate and collect large volumes of data in their daily operations. Most of this information is usually generated automatically by Web servers and collected in server access logs. Analyzing such data can help these organizations to determine the lifetime value of customers, cross marketing strategies across products, and effectiveness of promotional campaigns, among other things. Analysis of server access logs and user registration data can also provide valuable information on how to better structure a Web site in order to create a more effective presence for the organization.

Web usage mining employs many important ideas of basic data mining techniques as summarized in [Chen, Han and Yu 1996]. There are several types of access pattern mining that can be performed depending on the needs of the analyst. Below we briefly discuss these types and illustrate them using simple examples.

- *Path analysis.* Using path analysis may be able to discover that "50% of new investors who accessed /fund-family/products/purchase.html did so by starting at /fund-family, and proceeding through /fund-family/top-performance, and /fund-family/products/minimum-investment.html."

- *Association rule discovery.* For example, using association rule discovery techniques we can find correlations such as "20% of clients who accessed /SuperStar.com/announcements/promotion-item.html, placed an online order in /SuperStar.com/products/fancy-computer. "

- *Sequential Patterns.* The problem of discovering sequential patterns is to find inter-transaction patterns such that the presence of a set of items is followed by another item in the time-stamp ordered transaction set. By analyzing this information, the Web mining system can determine temporal relationships among data items such as "35% of clients who placed an online order in /SuperStar/products/fancy-computer.html, also placed an online order in /SuperStar/products/digitalTV within 30 days."

- *Clustering and Classification.* Discovering classification rules allows one to develop a profile of items belonging to a particular group according to their common attributes. For example, "50% of clients who placed an online order in /SuperStar/products/fancy-computer, were in the 25-28 age group with income in high 5-digits." Clustering analysis allows one to group together clients or data items that have similar characteristics.

After the patterns are discovered, the next task is the analysis of discovered patterns. Web site administrators are extremely interested in questions like "How are people using the site?", "Which pages are being accessed most frequently?", etc. Techniques and tools for enabling the analysis of discovered patterns are expected to draw upon a number of fields, including visualization techniques, data warehousing and OLAP techniques, usability analysis as well as data and knowledge querying. Given the large number of patterns that may be mined, there is a need for a mechanism to specify the focus of the analysis. A query mechanism will allow the user (usually, an analyst) to provide more control over the discovery process by specifying various constraints. The user may provide control by placing constraints on the database to restrict the portion of the database to be mined for, or by querying the knowledge that has been extracted by the mining process.

SUMMARY

In this chapter we discussed the data warehousing infrastructure for OLAP, data mining and their integration. It is important to keep in mind that data mining is not a phenomenon isolated from the functionality of the DBMS, and data warehouses are just an extension of the basic structure of DBMS. Though the emphasis of this chapter has been on DBMS aspects, we have also seen the role of computational intelligence in the implementation of data warehouses, as illustrated in the view index selection problem (Section 11.5). More discussion related to data mining will continue in the next two chapters, where different aspects of computational intelligence will be presented.

SELF-EXAMINATION QUESTIONS

1. Give an example of conceptual query answering involving aggregation data (you may use the tables and examples available in this chapter). How many different answers can be found? Can you compare these answers?
2. In the example discussed in Section 11.3.3.2, we described how roll-up operations can be performed, but without a detailed discussion on drill-down. Could you illustrate how a drill-down operation is performed on the data set used in this example?
3. In Section 11.6.2, we discussed aggregation semantics, and in Section 11.8.3.3, we provided a skeleton of the influence analysis algorithm which takes care of some concerns raised in Section 11.6.2. Note that in Step 6 of the algorithm, we exit if no semantic inconsistency is found. Is there any need to revise the algorithm so that Step 7 will be executed even if there is no inconsistency found in Step 6? Justify your answer.
4. In Chapter 10 we discussed discovery of association rules. How is it that the intensional historical data may aid the process of association rule discovery? Give an example.

REFERENCES

Acharya, S., Gibbons, P. B. and Poosala, V., Join Synopses for Approximate Query Answering, *Proceedings SIGMOD* 1999.
Baader, F., Jeusfeld, M. A. and Nutt, W., Intelligent access to heterogeneous information sources: Report on the 4th workshop on knowledge representation meets databases, *SIGMOD Record*, 26(4), pp. 44-48, 1997.
Borgida, A., Chaudhri, V. K. and Staudt, M., Report on the 5th workshop on knowledge representation meets databases (KRDB'98), *SIGMOD Record*, 27(3), 10-15, 1998.

Chaudhuri, S., Data mining and database systems: Where is the intersection? *Data Engineering Bulletin,* 21 (1), pp. 4-8, 1998.

Chaudhuri, S. and Dayal, U., An Overview of Data Warehousing and OLAP Technology, *SIGMOD Record,* 26(1), 65-74, 1997.

Chen, M. -S., Han, J., and Yu, P. S., Data Mining: An Overview from a Database Perspective, *IEEE transactions on knowledge and data engineering,* 8(6), 866-897, 1996.

Chen, X., Chen, Z. and Zhu, Q., From OLAP to data mining: An analytical influential association approach, *Journal of Information Management and Computer Science,* 1999 (to appear).

Chen, Z., An integrated architecutre for OLAP and data mining, pp. 114-136 in M. Bramer (ed.), *Knowledge Discovery and Data Mining: Theory and Practice,* 1999.

Cheung, D. W., Han, J., Ng, V. T. and Wong, C. Y., Maintenance of discovered association rules in large databases: An incremental updating technique, *Proceedings ICDE '96,* 1996.

Cooley, R., Mobasher, B. and Srivastava, J. , Web Mining: Information and Pattern Discovery on the World Wide Web. 1997. Document is available at the following URL:
http://www-users.cs.umn.edu/~mobasher/webminer/survey/survey.html.

Florescu, D., Levy, A. and Mendelzon, A., Database techniques for the World-Wide Web: A survey, *SIGMOD Record,* 27(3), 59-74, Sept. 1998.

Forsman, S., OLAP Council white paper, 1997, available at http://www.pin.co.za/software/miniolap/faq/olap.htm.

Garcia-Molina, H., Labio, W. J., Wiener, J. L. and Zhuge, Y., Distributed and parallel computing issues in data warehousing (invited talk), *Proceedings ACM Principles of Distributed Computing Conference,* 1999.

Gray, J., Bosworth, A., Layman, A. and Pirahesh, H., Data cube: A relational aggregation operator generalizing group-by, cross-tab, and sub-totals, *Proceedings Of International Conference on Data Engineering (ICDE 96),* 1996.

Hammer, J., Garcia-Molina, H., Widom, J., Labio, W. J., and Zhuge, Y., The Stanford Data Warehousing Project, *Data Engineering Bulletin,* 18(2), 41-48, 1995.

Han, J., Towards On-Line Analytical Mining in large databases, *SIGMOD Record,* 27(1), 97-107, 1998.

Han, J., Fu, Y., and Ng, R., Cooperative query answering using multiple layered databases, *Proceedings 2nd International Conference on Cooperative Information Systems,* 47-58, 1994.

Huyn, N., Multiple-view self-maintenance in data warehousing environments, *Proceedings 23rd VLDB Conference,* 1997.

Imielinski, T. and Mannila, H., A Database Perspective on Knowledge Discovery, *Communications of the ACM,* 39(11), 58-65, 1996.

Inmon,W. H., *Building the Data Warehous,.* John Wiley, New York, 1996.

Kimball, R., *The Data Warehouse Toolkit,* Wiley, New York, 1996.

Labio, W. J., Quass, D. and Adelberg, B., Physical database design for data warehousing, in *Proceedings of the International Conference on Data Engineering*, 1997.

Levy, A. Y., Mendelzon, A. O., Sagiv Y. and Srivastava, D., Answering queries using views, *Proceedings PODS*, 95-104, 1995.

McCarthy, J., Circumscription - A form of nonmonotonic reasoning, *Artificial Intelligence*, 13 (1 & 2), 1980.

Parsaye, K., OLAP & data mining: Bridging the gap, *Database Programming & Design*, 10(2), 30-37, 1997.

Pirotte, A. and Roelants, D., Constraints for improving the generation of intensional answers in a deductive database, *Proceedings 5th Data Eng.* 652-659, 1989.

Quass, D., Gupta, A., Mumick, I. and Widom, J., Making views self-maintainable for data warehousing, *Proc. of the Conference on Parallel and Distributed Information Systems*, 1996.

Ramakrishnam, R., *Database Management Systems*, WCB McGraw-Hill, Boston, 1998.

Roussopoulos, N., Materialized views and data warehouses, *SIGMOD Record*, 27(1), 21-25, 1998.

Srivastava, J., and Chen, P.-Y., Warehouse creation -- a potential roadblock to data warehousing, IEEE Transactions on Knowledge and Data Engineering, 11(1), 118-126, 1999.

Widom, J. (ed.), Special issue on materialized views and data warehousing, *Data Engineering Bulletin*, 18(2), 3-48, 1995.

Zhuge, Y., Garcia-Molina, H. and Wiener, J. L., Consistency algorithms for multi-source warehouse view maintenance, *Journal of Distributed and Parallel Databases*, 6(1), 7-40, 1998.

Chapter 12

REASONING UNDER UNCERTAINTY

12.1 OVERVIEW

In Chapter 1, we described the relationship among data, information and knowledge (as indicated in Figure 1.1). At that time, we did not focus on the role of uncertainty in this overall picture (although we did briefly mention the existence of noise). Now it is time for us to deal with this issue. From a business perspective, we can view *information* as that which resolves uncertainty, and *decision making* is the progressive resolution of *uncertainty* and is a key to a purposeful behavior by any mechanism (or organism) [Berson and Smith 1998].

Uncertainty is everywhere in our daily life. We are used to see fluctuations in stock markets. There are a lot of words in our daily language concerning uncertainty, such as "probably," "more or less," as well as others. An intelligent agent should demonstrate an ability to perform reasoning and support decision making under uncertainty. The discussion on reasoning under uncertainty is deferred until now, mainly due to pedagogical concerns. One concern is that since search and representation have been the main theme of symbolic computational intelligence, the discussion made so far has been largely around these two topics. Uncertain reasoning (or reasoning under uncertainty), due to the subject nature, requires some methods of its own, and is better to be discussed at a later time. The second reason of postponing the discussion of uncertain reasoning is due to the following concern. As already briefly mentioned in Chapter 10, uncertain reasoning is related to machine learning (and data mining). Since machine learning is more directly related to search and representation, it is better to discuss machine learning and related materials first. Now that we have discussed machine learning, it is time to discuss uncertain reasoning. In a sense we expand our discussion made in the last chapter to intelligent data analysis in a broader sense. We will first discuss approaches based on probability theory, including Bayesian networks. The second half of this chapter is mainly devoted to uncertain reasoning using fuzzy set theory. Reasoning based on probability and reasoning based on fuzzy logic are the two most popular approaches used in uncertainty reasoning. Note that due to space limitation and the wide availability of uncertain reasoning literature, our purpose is to introduce some key ideas only so that we can present an integrated perspective of uncertain reasoning. Having learned basic ideas of these approaches from this chapter, interested readers can dig into more technical details by following the references provided at the end of this chapter. Based on the same consideration, in the next chapter we will continue to present key ideas of some other approaches in uncertain reasoning.

12.2 GENERAL REMARKS ON UNCERTAIN REASONING

12.2.1 LOGIC AND UNCERTAINTY

As to be explained in a later section, there are several different forms of uncertainty. One important form is *randomness*: If you toss a coin, the chance of seeing head or tail is about half-half. Probability theory (to be outlined in the next section) has been developed for dealing with uncertainty. We now use probability reasoning as an example to illustrate the difference between logic and uncertainty. Probabilistic reasoning systems have several important properties different from logical reasoning systems [Russell and Norvig 1995]:

* *Nonmonontonicity.* As indicated by McCarthy in the earlier age of nonmonotonic reasoning, when probabilistic reasoning (and not just the axiomatic basis of probability theory) has been fully formalized, it will be formally nonmonotonic [McCarthy 1980]. As briefly discussed in Section 3.5, first order predicate logic exhibits strict monotonicity, although commonsense reasoning exhibits nonmonotonicity. In contrast, in a probability reasoning system we can add or withdraw beliefs, which makes it nonmonotonic.

* *Non-locality.* In logical systems, when we have a rule of the form $A \rightarrow B$, we can conclude B given evidence A, without worrying about any other rules. In contrast, probabilistic systems demonstrate a global feature, because we need to consider all of the available evidences.

* *Non-detachment.* In dealing with probabilities, the source of the evidence for a belief is important for subsequent reasoning. In contrast, in a logical system, when we have a rule of the form $A \rightarrow B$, once a logical proof is found for a proposition B, the proposition can be used regardless of how it was derived; in this sense, it is detached from its justification.

* *Non-additive*: In general, probability combination is a complex process, except under strong independence assumptions. This is quite different from logic, where the truth of complex sentences can be computed from the truth of the components.

Both first order predicate logic and uncertain reasoning are concerned with reasoning properly, but unlike first-order logic, where proper reasoning means that conclusions follow from premises, in probability, we are dealing with *beliefs*, not with the state of the world.

Note that the above discussion is concerned with one particular form of reasoning under uncertainty: probability reasoning. As we are going to discuss in Section 12.2.2, there are different types of uncertain reasoning, and the relationship between logic and uncertainly as discussed above may not hold for other types of reasoning. Nevertheless, the above discussion revealed the very different nature of reasoning using logic (without considering uncertainty) and reasoning under uncertainty.

12.2.2 DIFFERENT TYPES OF UNCERTAINTY AND ONTOLOGIES OF UNCERTAINTY

There are different kinds of uncertainty. Uncertainty may be caused due to the reasoning mechanism (such as using abductive reasoning as briefly discussed in Chapter 3), or due to the problems encountered by the data used, such as missing, incomplete, or incorrect information. A discussion on this topic leads us to the topic of ontological commitment. Recall that in Chapter 5 we discussed ontology as explicit, knowledge-based specifications of conceptualizations. (Review Section 5.9.2 for more detail.) Randomness and vagueness are two examples of different types of uncertainty. Different theories have been developed to deal with different types of uncertainty; for example, probability theory has been developed to deal with randomness while fuzzy set theory is intended to deal with vagueness. In addition, different approaches can be combined. In the following we follow [Russell and Norvig 1995] to give a brief discussion on this issue. Though probability theory has enjoyed a long history of extensive studies, due to the scaling-up problem, probabilistic approaches fell out of favor from roughly 1975 to 1988, and several alternatives have been proposed. Some of them are summarized below.

- *Extension of logical rule-based approaches*: These approaches extend logical rule-based systems by affiliating some numerical values to accommodate uncertainty. These methods were developed in the 1970s.
- *Extending probability theory*: For example, the Dempster-Shafer theory (see Section 12.3.6) uses interval-valued degrees of belief to represent an agent's knowledge of the probability of a proposition. At the heart of this approach is the notion of ignorance, which was not considered in classical probability theory. Other methods using second-order probabilities were also proposed.
- *Qualitative judgmental reasoning*: A more radical approach is to handle the critical problem faced by probability theory: probability theory is essentially quantitative, and does not match human judgmental reasoning which is more qualitative. This approach is largely carried out under the umbrella of default reasoning. Qualitative reasoning mechanisms can also be built on the top of probability theory.
- *Shifting ontology:* Probability makes the same ontological commitment as logic: that events are true or false in the world, even if the agent is uncertain as to which is the case. Fuzzy set logic has marked a major shift away from this tradition. In fact, fuzzy set theory proposed an ontology that allows vagueness so that an event can be "somewhat" true. Fuzzy set theory is a means of specifying how well an object satisfies a vague description. For example, consider the statement "Tom is tall." What can

we say if Tom is 5'11"? A reasonable answer would be "a sort of." Note that this is not a question of uncertainty about the external world; rather it is a case of vagueness or uncertainty about the meaning of the linguistic term "tall." Note also that the ontology behind fuzzy set theory is not necessarily in conflict with the traditional one: Take, for example, a statement concerning "nice weather." It involves vagueness on the term "nice," but also involves probability concerning the chance of weather being nice.

The ontological shift as mentioned above has turned out a very controversial issue. From the perspective of computational intelligence as a science, "most authors say that fuzzy set theory is not a method for uncertain reasoning at all" [Russell and Norvig 1995]. Nevertheless, fuzzy set theory has been proven very successful in engineering problem solving. Much of the remaining part of this chapter will be devoted to uncertain reasoning using probability and fuzzy set approaches.

12.2.3 UNCERTAINTY AND SEARCH

In order to build practical computational intelligence systems, one has to deal with issues related to uncertainty and incomplete information. The search methods for problem solving discussed in earlier chapters did not take uncertainty into concern. However, searching with uncertainty is a reality in all kinds of problem solving. Therefore, it is worth examining uncertain reasoning from the classical perspective of search. Many related issues should be addressed, including the following [AAAI 1999]:

- When the traditional search techniques can be appropriately applied;
- How uncertain and incomplete information can be exploited to control search processes;
- Whether there is a difference in principle between reasoning with deterministic and probabilistic representations of uncertain and incomplete information (for example, comparison between constraint networks or belief networks);
- How the level of uncertainty affects problem complexity;
- How different search paradigm (such as heuristic search and dynamic programming) can be combined to provide additional pruning power;
- How the structure of search spaces can be exploited to speed up search;
- Search strategies that can be applied across domains and application areas; and
- New search strategies.

Exploring these issues would give us a comprehensive view of reasoning with or without considering uncertainty. However, due to space limitation, we will only focus on practical aspects (rather than theoretical aspects) of uncertain reasoning.

12.3 UNCERTAINTY BASED ON PROBABILITY THEORY

Probability theory is a very important theory on its own. In this section, we will only be able to sketch some of the most key ideas related to uncertain reasoning.

12.3.1 BASICS OF PROBABILITY THEORY

The basic properties of probability theory can be described as follows. Let A and B be two events (such as tossing a coin or running out of gas) and P be the probability. The following are the basic properties of probability theory:

(i)   If $A \subseteq B$ then $p(A) \leq p(B)$.

(ii) $P(\neg A) = 1 - p(A)$.

(iii) $P(A \cup B) = p(A) + p(B) - p(A \cap B)$.

Note that Property iii can be generalized to more than two events. In addition, in case that A and B are independent events, property (iii) is simplified to

(iii') $P(A \cup B) = p(A) + p(B)$.

In general, the assumption of independence may largely simplify the calculation related to probability. However, in many cases, independence assumption is not realistic. Independence assumption is a major hurdle of applying probability theory in some real-world assumptions.

Another basic concept is *conditional probability*. For example, $P(A|B)$ indicates the probability of A given B. For example,

$$P(\text{brain tumor} \mid \text{headache}) = 0.01$$

indicates that when headache occurs, the chance of having a brain tumor is 0.01. This is different from the following formula,

$$P(\text{headache} \mid \text{brain tumor}) = 0.2,$$

which indicates that when brain tumor presents, the chance of having a headache is 0.3. These two formulas have different meanings, but they are closely related. How to derive one from the other is an example of *statistical inference*. We will briefly examine this issue in the next subsection. But before that, we give some remarks on the nature of probability theory.

Probability theory can be defined as the study of *how knowledge affects belief*. Belief in some proposition, *f*, can be measured in terms of a number between 0 and 1. The probability f is 0 means that f is believed to be definitely false (no new evidence will shift that belief), and a probability of 1 means that f is believed to be definitely true. Statistics of what has happened in the past is knowledge that be conditioned on and used to update belief [Poole, Mackworth and Goebel 1998].

There are different interpretations of statements involving probabilities. In the frequentist interpretation, a probability is a property of a set of similar events. In subjective interpretation, a subjective probability is a probability expressing a person's degree of belief in a proposition or the occurrence of an event. In this text, we will stay with the latter [Dean, Allen and Aloimonos 1995]. We assume that the uncertainty is *epistemological* (pertaining to our knowledge of the world) rather than *ontological* (how the world is). We assume that our knowledge of the truth of propositions is uncertain, not that there are degrees of truth.

Much reasoning in computational intelligence can be seen as *evidential reasoning*, going from observations to a theory about what is inside the system, followed by causal reasoning, going from a theory about the mechanism of a system to predicting output of the system. Evidential reasoning is also called diagnosis, while diseases or malfunctions are hypothesized to explain symptoms. These diagnoses make predictions which lead to tests being performed. Evidential reasoning can also be considered as perception, where an agent hypothesizes what is in the world to account for what is perceived by the agent. Based on its hypothesis about what is in the world, the agent acts and then receives further percepts [Poole, Mackworth and Goebel 1998].

12.3.2 BAYESIAN APPROACH

The conditional probability $P(A|B)$ states the probability of event A given that event B occurred. The inverse problem is to find the inverse probability that states the probability of an earlier event given that a later one occurred. This type of probability occurs very often. For example, in medical diagnosis or various troubleshooting problems, we want to find the most likely cause for the observed symptoms. The solution for this problem is stated as Bayes' theorem (or Bayes rule), which serves as the basis of a well-known approach in probability theory called Bayesian approach.

Bayes' theorem: This theorem provides a way of computing the probability of a hypothesis H_i, following from a particular piece of evidence, given only the probabilities with which the evidence follows from actual causes (hypotheses).

$$P(Hi|E) = \frac{P(E|H_i)\, P(H_i)}{\sum_{k=1}^{n} P(E \mid H_k)\, P(H_k)}$$

where $P(H_i|E)$ is the probability that H_i is true given evidence E; $P(H_i)$ is the probability that H_i is true overall; $P(E|H_i)$ is the probability of observing evidence E when H_i is true; n is the number of possible hypotheses. The formula can be further simplified to

$$P(H_i \mid E) = P(E \mid H_i) \times P(H_i) / P(E).$$

As a simple example, we can now get back to the issue of computing the conditional probability involving headache and brain tumor. Suppose from experience we have learned that $P(H_i)$ = (headache) = 0.3, $P(E)$ = P(brain tumor) = 0.015, and P(brain tumor | headache) = 0.01. Then according to Bayes' theorem we have

P(headache | brain tumor)
= P(brain tumor | headache) × P(headache) / P(brain tumor)
= 0.01 × 0.3 / 0.015 = 0.2.

Bayesian reasoning is based in formal probability theory. Bayesian theory supports the calculation of more complex probabilities from previously known results. The method of Bayesian decision making was used in an early expert system called PROSPECTOR to decide favorable sites for mineral exploration. Each model for PROSPECTOR is encoded as a network (called "*inference net*") of connections or relations between evidence and hypotheses.

12.3.3 BAYESIAN NETWORKS

12.3.3.1 Assumptions

Bayesian networks (also called *belief networks* or *causal networks*) [Cooper and Herskovits 1994] relax several constraints of the full Bayesian approach. These networks are also referred to as *causal networks*. This approach takes advantage of three assumptions:

(a) The modularity of a problem domain makes many of the dependence/independence constraints required for Bayes approach be relaxed.

(b) The links between the nodes of the belief network are represented by conditioned probabilities. For example, the link between two nodes A and B, denoted $A \rightarrow B(c)$, reflects evidence A's support for the belief in B with confidence c, sometimes referred to as a causal influence measure.

(c) Coherent patterns of reasoning may be reflected as paths through cause/symptom relationships. The cause/symptom relationships of the problem domain will be reflected in a network. Paths within this network represent the use of different possible arguments.

A directed acyclic graph can be used to reflect the argument path through the cause/symptom network. Note that causes can influence the likelihood of their symptoms and the presence of a symptom can affect the likelihood of all its possible causes. To create a Bayesian belief network we must make a clear distinction between these two kinds of potential influence, and then select the path our reasoning will take through the network.

In the general case, exact inference in Bayesian networks is known to be NP-hard (for a brief discussion on NP-hard, see [Weiss 1998]). This is because a general belief network can represent any propositional logic problems are known to be NP-complete [Russell and Norvig 1995].

12.3.3.2 Some key concepts in Bayesian networks

For convenience of discussion, we now describe some key concepts in Bayesian belief networks. A *random variable* is a variable that can take on values from a set of mutually exclusive and exhaustive values referred to as the sample space of the random variable.

A probabilistic network employs an intuitive representation which can be formalized to capture both qualitative and quantitative relationships. The formal model will allow us to reason forward from causes to effects and backward from effects to causes. The former is called *predictive reasoning* while the latter is called *diagnostic reasoning*. We can gain additional insight into probabilistic networks by re-characterizing independence relationships in terms of paths through the underlying graph. We say that X is dependent on Y given a set of variables S if and only if there exists some dependency-connecting path from X to Y in G.

The notion of *conditional independence* can be used to give a concise representation of mainly domains. The idea is that given a random variable v, there may be a small set of variables that directly affect the variable's value in the sense that every other variable is independent of v given values for the directly affecting variables. This locality is exploited in Bayesian belief networks. A Bayesian belief network is thus a graphical representation of conditional independence. The independence allows us to depict direct effects within the graph and prescribes which probabilities need to be specified. Arbitrary posterior probabilities can be derived from the network.

Formally, a Bayesian network [Pearl 1991] is a *directed acyclic graph* ($\mathcal{DAG}$) with nodes labeled with random variables, together with a domain for each random variable and a set of conditional probability tables for each variable given its parents. These conditional probability tables include prior probabilities for nodes with no parents. The independence assumption embedded in a belief network is: Each random variable is independent of its non-descendants given its parents [Poole, Mackworth and Goebel 1998]. The number of probabilities that needs to be specified for each variable is exponential in the number of parents of variable. The independence assumption is useful insofar as the number of variables that directly affect another variable is small. As part of a Bayesian network, we provide a set of conditional probability tables that gives the probability of each value of a variable for each value of the variable's parents.

Bayesian networks have often been called causal networks, and claimed to be a representation of causality. Although this is controversial, there is a good motivation for this. A causal model in our mind is expected to obey the independence assumption of the belief network. The model is also expected to be acyclic. In general, a belief network itself has nothing to say about causation, and it can represent non-causal independence, but it seems particularly appropriate when there is causality and locality in a domain. The notion of causality makes it very natural to build a belief network. The idea is to determine what variables are relevant to the domain we want to represent, and add arcs that represent the local causality [Poole, Mackworth and Goebel 1998].

Changes of probabilities are propagated in a Bayesian network. If some values of a variable have been changed, we would expect that only the variable's descendants would be affected. Causality in belief networks relates to causal and evidential reasoning. A Bayesian belief network can be seen as a way of axiomatizing in one direction, abducing to causes, and then predicting from there.

Finally, let us get back to a remark on probabilistic theory and logic. A direct mapping exists between the logic-based abductive view and belief networks: Belief networks can be modeled as logic programs with probabilities over possible hypotheses.

12.3.3.3 Constructing a Bayesian network

To represent a domain in a Bayesian network, various issues should be considered, as indicated below [Poole, Mackworth and Goebel 1998]:

- What are the relevant variables?
- What is the relationship between them? This should be expressed in terms of local influence.
- What values should these variables take? This involves considering the level of detail at which we want to reason.

How does the value of one variable depend on the variables that locally influence it (its parents)? This is expressed in terms of the conditional probability tables.

12.3.3.4 Implementing Bayesian networks

Approaches of implementing Bayesian networks can be divided into several categories [Poole, Mackworth and Goebel 1998]. The problem of determining posterior distributions (the problem of computing conditional probabilities given the evidence) is one that has been widely researched. The problem of estimating the posterior probability in a belief network within an absolute error (of less than 0.5), or within a constant factor, is NP-hard, so general efficient implementations will not be available.

Approaches for implementation of belief networks fall in three categories:

- Exploiting the structure of the network. This approach is typified by the clique tree propagation method, where the network is transformed into a tree with nodes labeled with sets of variables.
- Search based approaches. These approaches enumerate some of the possible worlds, and estimate posterior probabilities from the worlds generated. These approaches work well when the distributions are extreme (all probabilities are close to either 0 or 1).
- Stochastic simulation. Random cases are generated according to the probability distributions and are treated as a set of samples. These cases are then used to estimate the marginal distribution on any combination of variables.

Algorithms have been developed for the different conditions of Bayesian networks [Dean, Allen and Aloimonos 1995]:

- *Exact inference in tree-structured networks* which are networks in which each node has at most one parent.
- *Exact inference in singly connected networks* which are networks in which nodes have more than one parent, but there is exactly one undirected path between any two nodes.
- *Approximate inference using stochastic simulation in multiply connected networks* in which there are two or more undirected paths between some nodes.

The *belief network inference problem* is the problem of computing the posterior distribution of a variable given some evidence. The problem of computing posterior probabilities can be reduced to the problem of computing the probability of conjunctions. In real-world applications, this algorithm faces the problem of how to speed up. This can be done by using preprocessing as much as possible and by using a secondary structure to save intermediate results so that evidence can be incrementally added and each variable's probability can be derived after each addition of evidence. The algorithm can be speeded up also by pruning the irrelevant nodes from the network before the query starts. Roughly speaking, relevant nodes include the following: The query node, ancestors of relevant nodes, and observed descendants of relevant nodes. All other nodes are irrelevant. However, extensive preprocessing would allow arbitrary sequences of observations and derive the posterior on each variable, and thus preclude pruning the network. A kind of trade-off must be made. Note that the philosophy of preprocessing can be compared with constructing an abstract database in conceptual query answering as discussed in Chapter 9 and Chapter 11. This provides another example of cross-domain similarity.

12.3.3.5 The notion of d-separation

A detailed discussion on probability propagation in Bayesian networks is beyond the scope of this book. Here we will only briefly introduce an important property which shaped the recent studies of Bayesian network, namely, d-separation. Two nodes (variables) A and B in a Bayesian belief or qualitative probabilistic network are *d-separated* if for all paths between A and B, there is an intermediate node (variable) V such that one of the following is true:

(i)   The connection is *serial* or *diverging* and the state of V is known;

(ii)   The connection is *converging* and neither V nor any of V's children have evidence.

The meaning of three connections mentioned above is illustrated in the following figure which represents the relationships between subgraphs of a Bayesian network. The directions of the arrows linking states indicate how states can probabilistically influence each other.

(a) There is a possible *serial* relationship of A on B and B on C, with $A \rightarrow B(c_1)$ and $B \rightarrow C(c_2)$, where c1 and c2 are the causal influence measures. If there is no evidence supporting B then A and C are d-separated and independent. If there is evidence of B then C cannot support A, but evidence for B can still support A.

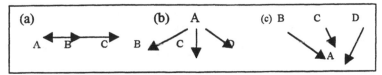

Figure 12.1 Cases of d-seperation

(b) The diverging connections B, C, ..., E are not independent, because there exists a single event A that can make them all true. If we do know that A does not occur, then B, C, ..., E are d-separated and independent.

(c) The converging connection occurs. If A is known to be true then B, C, ..., E are not independent; if A is unknown then B, C, ..., E are d-separated and independent.

The notion of d-separation is important in formalizing the evidence propagation in a Bayesian belief network (namely, how the evidence for a node in a belief network can affect an argument). For a more detailed discussion on this issue, see [Neapolitan 1990; Pearl 1991].

12.3.4 BAYESIAN NETWORK APPROACH FOR DATA MINING

12.3.4.1 Introduction

As indicated in the first section of this chapter, machine learning and uncertain reasoning are closely related. We have already explained how Bayesian networks can be used for uncertain reasoning. In fact, they can be used for data mining as well [Heckerman 1997]. In this section, we study the problems in control and attention of a knowledge discovery process, where control is a process of activating information sources and attention is a process of extracting knowledge patterns from the sources activated. Built upon the use of a belief network structure, the goal-driven technique represents a knowledge pattern in terms of a sequence of goals and sub-goals, and moderates the control and attention processes under the guidance of domain knowledge. The technique eases the burden of knowledge management and reduces the complexity of the control and attention processes in knowledge discovery.

12.3.4.2 An agent-based model for data mining using Bayesian networks

A high-level agent-based model for data mining using Bayesian networks has been developed in Figure 12.2, where G denotes the goal, B (or BN) denotes the Bayesian network, A denotes the agents, D denotes the database, and K denotes the knowledge discovered. In the following we provide a brief discussion of this model. More details can be found in [Chen and Zhu 1998].

In this model, a knowledge pattern is defined as a construct consisting of the goals, the relations among the goals, and the functions defined on them. A causal network can be used to represent the knowledge patterns that are explored at the initial, intermediate and final stages of a knowledge discovery process.

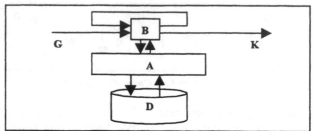

Figure 12.2 A data mining model

In a knowledge discovery process, new nodes and links associated with the relevant data attributes in exploration could be added to the BN conveniently. A structural analysis that traces the nodes and links of the whole or partial BN identifies the dependency relations and the network structure to be updated. The BN could thus serve as a control mechanism to guide the generation and evaluation of the subsequent sub-goals, as well as a representation of the intermediate and final knowledge patterns. In this sense, the belief network is used as both a reasoning tool and a memory structure for the knowledge applied and deducted.

A knowledge discovery process performed in the above model would start from the construction of an *initial BN* that consists of the following:
(1) An ultimate goal, g_0, which is the objective of a KDD process and serves as the starting point of the BN construction;
(2) A set of sub-goals, $\{G_I\}$ that may have certain probabilistic or logic dependencies (directly or indirectly) with g_0; and
(3) A set of hypothetical inference rules $\{\pi[g_0 \mid G_I]\}$ that may be defined in terms of probability dependence functions on the connection between g_0 and the sub-goals.

Figure 12.3 depicts an example of this initial BN. Note that the arrows linking the nodes indicate the direction of probability propagation (for example, from a child node to a parent node).

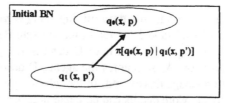

Figure 12.3 An initial Belief Network

Given an initial BN, variables of relevant objects that pertain to the goal and sub-goals will be acquired from the data sources under exploration. The goal and sub-goal sets are to be expanded in the exploration process thereafter. An evaluation of the goal and the sub-goal relations in this process detects data changes and recognizes the need for network revisions subsequently. The task is conducted by propagating the probability dependence values along the network links. After certain process and manipulation, a portion of the network will be updated by adding and/or modifying the nodes and links. The process of propagating and refining the BN will then lead to the generation of useful knowledge patterns.

In the following, we use an example to show that the above approach is able to direct the control and attention of a knowledge discovery process that is tailored to a particular instance by applying certain domain knowledge. The agent-based system will develop, revise, and refine the sub-goals dynamically with respect to the intermediate results at different stages of the knowledge discovery process.

12.3.4.3 An example

To illustrate the role of causal network in this model, consider a database consisting of employee information including the educational background and employment history. Let $Q(x, p)$ be a goal for a KDD process, where x = "profit," and p = "high." The proposition $Q(x, p)$ intends to find a knowledge pattern that gives a qualitative and/or quantitative description of *"Profitable"* for a "profit" to be "high." Given such a request, we have an initial BN as Figure 12.4.

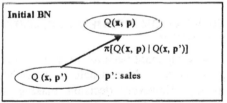

Figure 12.4 An initial BN with one sub-goal

Expanding the initial network by incorporating the sub-goal $Q(x, p')$ with the database contents to be explored, we have a new BN of Figure 12.5 , where the goal $Q(x, p')$ has links to two sub-goals.

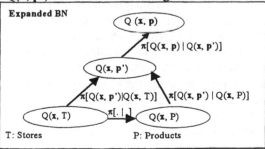

Figure 12.5 An expansion of initial BN

It is the task of KDD to establish the necessary probability dependency functions on the links of the above network. According to this expanded BN, we have two sub-goals; one is related to "*stores*" and the other to "*locations*." In these cases, the involved nodes can be further expanded.

In summary, in order to generate useful knowledge patterns from the information retrieved from databases, it is necessary to focus properly on the goals and sub-goals of the knowledge discovery process. This paper presents a goal-driven approach for regulating the control and attention activities. The knowledge discovery process is built upon the deposition of a set of goals and sub-goals on which the control and attention of the process can be specified. The approach uses a belief network structure to represent the knowledge patterns in the forms of goals and sub-goals relations, and moderates the propagation of domain knowledge in a dynamic process. An initial BN records possible relations between the ultimate goal and a set of sub-goals. One purpose for the use of this structure is to reduce the complexity involved in the dependency representations for the goal and sub-goals. The network serves as an underlying structure to regulate the operations in the control and attention of a knowledge discovery process. The approach is suitable to generate knowledge patterns that start from a coarse description and then refined in a step by-step process.

12.3.5 A BRIEF REMARK ON INFLUENCE DIAGRAM AND DECISION THEORY

Uncertain reasoning is important because we want to deal with uncertainty in decision making. Belief networks can help us in prediction and diagnosis involved in uncertainty. However, decision making still means more, including planning (a brief introduction of planning was given in Chapter 3). Decision theory is a discipline concerned with mathematical theories of decision making. Ideas from decision theory are adapted for use in automated decision-making systems. In the following, we give a quick remark on decision theory.

The consequences of decision making are represented by a set of *outcomes* Ω that represent all aspects of the world that the decision maker cares about. In case there is more than one outcome, we assign to each outcome a number, called the *utility* of the outcome, that provides a measure of the value of a given outcome. A utility function U maps outcomes to the real numbers. We can also compute the *expected utility* for a plan π, $E_\pi(U) = \Sigma P(\omega) U(\omega)$ for all $\omega \in \Omega$ A decision tree method can then be used for representing decision problems and computing a plan that maximizes expected utility.

An *influence diagram* represents all the information necessary to compute a plan that maximizes expected utility. Influence diagrams are extensions of belief networks to include decision variables and utility. A *decision variable* is like a random variable, with a domain, but it does not have an associated probability distribution. Instead, an agent chooses a value for each decision variable. An influence diagram is a DAG with three types of nodes:

- *Chance nodes* (ellipses) are the same nodes that are in a belief network.
- *Decision nodes* (rectangles) are labeled with decision variables whose values can be set by the decision maker.
- A *value node* (diamond) represents the utility. There is only one such node.

The notion of *utility* is a reflection of relative worth to the agent of different decision outcomes. Utilities are defined in terms of *lotteries*. More details of inference diagram can be found in [Russell and Norvig 1995].

12.3.6 PROBABILITY THEORY WITH MEASURED BELIEF AND DISBELIEF

12.3.6.1 Certainty factors

An early *ad hoc* approach for uncertain reasoning employs the concept of *certainty factors* as used in an expert system called MYCIN. This approach starts from the basic notion of probability, but does not stay with the whole theory. The certainty factor is used to indicate the degree of confirmation, and is calculated in terms of measure of belief and measure of disbelief. A certainty factor (CF) is defined as

$$CF(H, E) = MB(H,E) - MD(H,E),$$

where CF is the certainty factor in the hypothesis H due to evidence E, MB is the measure of increased belief in H due to E, MD is the measure of increased disbelief in H due to E. In addition, combination function has been defined to combine two certainty factors. The major advantage of CF was the simple computations by which uncertainty could be propagated in the system. However, the simple computations have conflict with conditional probabilities and is thus lacking of a theoretical foundation.

12.3.6.2 Dempster-Shafer Theory

The concepts of belief and disbelief are also used in Dempster-Shafer theory. But in addition to belief and disbelief, a third concept, *nonbelief*, is also introduced. Unlike the approach of certainty factors, Dempster-Shafer theory has a sound theoretical foundation based on probability theory. The irony is, in practice, very few applications are based on this theory, due to the problems to be discussed at the end of this section. Nevertheless, it is an important theoretical development, and has connections with other uncertain reasoning methods.

The Dempster-Shafer theory is based on two ideas:

- the idea of obtaining degrees of belief for one question from subjective probabilities for related questions;
- the use of a rule about combining these degrees of belief when they are based on independent items of evidence.

Dempster's rule produces a new mass that represents a consensus of the original, possibly conflicting evidence (in favor of agreement). An important feature of Dempster-Shafer theory is that it considers *ignorance*: there is a fundamental distinction between lack of certainty and ignorance; belief and disbelief are no longer viewed as functional opposites.

The following are some basic terminology used by this theory.

- *Frame of discernment* Θ (a finite nonempty set) is an environment (i.e., universe of discourse) where its elements may be interpreted as possible answers, and only one answer is correct.

- *Mass* (also called *basic probability assignment*) is an evidence measure. Formally, it is a function m: $2^{\Theta} \rightarrow [0,1]$ such that
  (1) $m(\varnothing) = 0$ (no belief is committed to the empty set)
  (2) $\Sigma_{A \subseteq \Theta}$ m (A) = 1 (total belief is equal to 1)}

  Note that $m(\Theta) \neq 1$. Note also that the term "mass" is due to an analogy: degree of belief in evidence is similar to mass of physical object.

- *Belief* (denoted as Bel) is also called the *belief function*, belief function over Θ, belief measure, or *support*. Belief (a number between 0 and 1) is defined in terms of *mass* (m): $\text{Bel}(X) = \Sigma_{Y \subset X} m(Y)$. It is the *total* belief of a set and all its subsets. In contrast, mass is the *local* belief, the belief in a set and not any of its subsets.

- *Focal element of a belief function over* Θ is a subset A of the frame of discernment Θ which satisfies m(A) > 0 (a subset with non-empty mass),where m is the basic probability assignment associated with Bel (mass). The union of all the focal elements of a belief function is called the *core*.

- *Plausibility (Pls)* is defined as $\text{Pls}(A) = 1 - \text{Bel}(\bar{A})$ (a number between 0 and 1). It is thus not disbelief.

We can now introduce the *principle of indifference*: a fundamental difference with probability theory is the treatment of *ignorance*. Ignorance is neither belief nor disbelief. *Nonbelief* (no belief) is any belief that is not assigned to a specific subset. Therefore, nonbelief $\neq$ disbelief.

The following are some important properties of belief and plausibility functions:

$$\text{Bel}(\varnothing) = \text{Pls}(\varnothing) = 0$$
$$\text{Bel}(\Theta) = \text{Pls}(\Theta) = 1$$
$$\text{Bel}(A) \leq \text{Pl}(A)$$
$$\text{Bel}(A) + \text{Bel}(\bar{A}) \leq 1$$
$$\text{Pls}(A) + \text{Pls}(\bar{A}) \geq 1$$
$$A \subseteq B \Rightarrow \text{Bel}(A) \leq \text{Bel}(B)$$
$$A \subseteq B \Rightarrow \text{Pls}(A) \leq \text{Pls}(B)$$

Instead of restricting belief to a single value, there is a range of belief in the evidence. This range is referred to as *evidence interval (EI)*. EI is bounded by support and plausibility:

- lower bound: support (Spt) or Bel; minimum belief based on the evidence.
- upper bound: plausibility (Pls); maximum belief.

As an example, let us think about event A: "it will snow tonight" (with degree of belief 0.3); and $\bar{A}$ ("Not snow tonight" with degree of belief 0.4). Then we have the evidence interval as depicted in Figure 12.6.

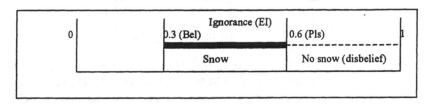

Figure 12.6 An example of evidence interval

The following are some important properties concerning Bel, Pls and EI:

$0 \leq Bel \leq Pls \leq 1$

$EI = [Bel\ (S),\ 1 - Bel(\ \bar{S})]$

$EI = [total\ belief,\ plausibility]$

$= [evidence\ for\ support,\ evidence\ for\ support + ignorance]$

We can also define *Doubt* (or *Dbt*):

$Dbt(X) = Bel\ (X') = 1 - Pls\ (X) = Igr(X) = Pls(X) - Bel(X)$

$Pls\ (X) = 1 - Bel(X') = 1 - Dbt(X)$

$= 1 - \Sigma_{Y \subseteq X}\ m(X')$

$= \Sigma_{B \subseteq A}\ m(B) - \Sigma_{B \subseteq A}\ m(B) = \Sigma_{B \cap A \neq \varnothing}\ m(B)$

As we mentioned earlier, a strength of Dempster-Schafer theory is the ability of combining evidence. Note the assumption used here is that both pieces of evidence are independent; therefore, the purpose is to combining independent evidences.

We may use Dempster's rule of combination to yield the combined mass:

$m_1 \oplus m_2\ (Z) = \Sigma_{X \cap Y = Z}\ m_1(X)m_2(Y)$

(where $\oplus$ denotes the *orthogonal sum*, also called *direct sum*).

As an example, consider the frame of discernment $\Omega = \{A,B,C,D\}$. Assuming we have two independent measures: in m1, we have 0.6 for ABD, 0.4 for Ω; in m2, we have 0.7 for ABD and 0.3 for Ω. Combining m1 and m2, we obtain m3, as shown in Table 12.1(a). Note that all measures for m3 add up to 1.

Table 12.1(a) Combining m1 and m2

m3 m2 / m1	ABC (0.7)	Ω(0.3)
ABD (0.6)	AB(0.42)	ABD(0.18)
Ω(0.4)	ABC(0.28)	Ω(0.12)

In addition, suppose we have a third independent opinion m4: 0.8 for D and 0.2 for Ω. We can further combine m4 with m3, as shown in Table 12.1(b).

Table 12.1 (b) Combining m3 and m4

m3 \ m5 \ m4	D(0.8)	Ω(0.2)
AB(042)	∅(0.336)	AB(0.084)
Ω(0.12)	D(0.096)	Ω(0.024)
ABC(0.28)	∅(0.224)	ABC(0.056)
ABD(0.18)	D(0.144)	ABD(0.036)

Note that all measures for m5 add up to 1. However, since empty sets do not represent any real meaning, they should be removed. The process of removing empty sets and re-distributing the measure is called normalization. In this example, the empty sets ∅ has measure 0.336 + 0.224 = 0.56. Measures for non-empty sets are divided by denominator (1 - 0.56 = 0.44). Note also the measure for D (which appears twice in the table) is combined ((0.096 + 0.144) / 0.44 = 0.545). (Measure for empty set is dropped to 0.)

The main difficulty of Dempster-Shafer theory is that in order to use this approach, we have to consider all subsets and assign probabilities. This has posed a very serious restriction to real-world applications. The problem with normalization is that it ignores the belief that the object being considered does not exist.

12.4 FUZZY SET THEORY

12.4.1 FUZZY SETS

In order to illustrate different considerations in uncertain reasoning for decision making, we now turn to reasoning using fuzzy set theory. Due to the existing rich literature in this area and the wide scope of this topic, we will only provide a brief overview on fuzzy set theory. Our discussion is restricted to the unique features presented in fuzzy reasoning, rather than a detailed discussion of fuzzy reasoning itself.

There is a brief remark on the terminology. The term fuzzy logic was originally coined to refer to multivalued logic (in contrast to standard logic as discussed in Chapter 2, which is two valued -- true or false, nothing else). In this sense, fuzzy logic is not the alias of fuzzy set theory. However, later development in this area has changed the meaning of the term "fuzzy logic." It is now widely used to refer to reasoning with fuzzy sets or with sets of fuzzy rules. This makes the term "fuzzy logic" somewhat redundant. In the rest of this book, we will not distinguish these two terms, and will use the term "fuzzy set theory" to refer to materials related to both issues.

12.4.1.1 Probability reasoning versus fuzzy reasoning

Probability is concerned with occurrence of well-defined events. It can be distinguished into subjective one and objective one. On the other hand, fuzzy sets deal with *graduality* of concepts and describe their boundaries and have nothing to do with frequencies (repetition) of an event.   Consider an experiment whose outcome (O) can eventually occur. Only before the experiment can one think of the probability of O, P(O). Once the experiment is over, the probability facet of uncertainty vanishes. The outcome is unambiguously known: A has happened or not. In contrast, let O be a fuzzy set; after the experiment, the idea is still valid and fully intact. The conceptual difference between these two notions of uncertainty makes the mathematical frameworks of fuzzy sets and probability also very different. While approaches based on probability hinge on the concepts of (additive) measure theory, fuzzy set approaches rely on set theory and logic [Kasabov 1996].

Fuzzy set theory provides a very flexible theoretical framework and an ocean of related literature exists. We will only provide an overview on some selected notions of fuzzy set theory to illustrate the basic concerns of fuzzy set theory.

12.4.1.2 Conceptualization in fuzzy terms using linguistic variables

A *linguistic variable* is a variable which takes fuzzy values and has a linguistic meaning. A linguistic variable has *linguistic values* (or *fuzzy labels*). Linguistic variables can be quantitative (for example, time early or late) or qualitative (for example, certainty or belief). The process of representing a linguistic variable into a set of linguistic values is called *fuzzy quantization*. Two parameters must be defined for this procedure: the number of fuzzy labels and the form of the membership functions for each of the fuzzy labels. Note that fuzzy discretization does not lead to loss of information if the fuzzy labels are correctly chosen (this is not the case with interval discretization). Zadeh noted that the use of linguistic values may be viewed as a form of data compression. It is suggestive to refer to this form of data compression as granulation. We also need to consider fuzzy qualifier and fuzzy quantifier: a *fuzzy qualifier* indicates true to some degree, such as "somewhat true" or "fairly tall." A *fuzzy quantifier* indicates true to some extent, such as "most" or "usually."

12.4.1.3 Characteristic functions of fuzzy sets

According to Zadeh, a fuzzy set may be regarded as a class in which there is a graduality of progression from membership to non-membership or, more precisely, in which an object may have a grade of membership intermediate between unity (full membership) and zero (non-membership).

The concept of fuzzy set is defined as follows. Consider a classical set A' of the universe U. A fuzzy set A is defined by a set of ordered pairs, a binary relation,

$$A = \{(x, \mu_A(x)) \mid x \in A', \mu_A \in [0,1]\},$$

where $\mu_A(x)$ is a function called membership function and it specifies the grade or degreee to which any element x in A belongs to the fuzzy set A.

The *S function* (so called because it is shaped like English character S) is a mathematical function that is often used in fuzzy sets as a membership function. It is defined for continuous variable X as follows (with parameters α, β, γ):

$$S(X; \alpha, \beta, \gamma) = \begin{cases} 0 & \text{for } X \leq \alpha \\ 2((X - \alpha)/(\gamma - \alpha))^2 & \text{for } \alpha \text{ in} \leq X \leq \beta \\ 1 - 2((X - \gamma)/(\gamma - \alpha))^2 & \text{for } \beta \leq X \leq \gamma \\ 1 & \text{otherwise} \end{cases}$$

Using S-function we can conveniently define fuzzy membership functions such as "tall." In fact, "tall" can be defined as S(X; 5, 6, 7). In addition, for easy of use, S-function can be discretized. For example, by plugging in X = 5, 5.5, 6, 6.5 and 7, we can obtain the Table 12.2 as a discrete membership function for "tall."

Table 12.2 Fuzzy membership function Tall

5	5.5	6	6.5	7
0	0.125	0.5	0.875	1

This table can be written in a shorthand form as
Tall = {0/5, 0.125/5.5, 0.5/6, 0.875/6.5, 1/7}

Another useful function is called Π function. It consists of two S-functions (as shown in the following definition). Since it is symmetrical, it can be used to define fuzzy proposition such as "X is close to γ." This function is defined as:

$$\Pi(X; \beta, \gamma) = \begin{cases} S(X; \gamma - \beta, \gamma - \beta/2, \gamma) & \text{for } x \leq \gamma \\ S(X; \gamma, \gamma + \beta/2, \gamma + \beta) & \text{otherwise} \end{cases}$$

Yet another useful function is called Z function, because it shapes like the letter Z. But the formula will not be presented at here. Examples of using these three functions will be presented in the section on FuzzyCLIPS where these functions will be plotted.

Finally, the *support* of a fuzzy set, F, is a subset of the universe set, X, defined as
$$\text{Support}(F) = \{x \mid x \in X \text{ and } \mu_F(X) > 0\}$$

12.4.1.4 Fuzzy decision making systems

Fuzzy logic, when applied to decision-making problems, provides formal methodology for problem solving, and incorporates human consistency, which are important characteristics required by fuzzy decision-making systems. Such systems should possess the following functionality:
(a) Explain the solution to the user.
(b) Keep a rigorous and fair way of reasoning.
(c) Accommodate subjective knowledge.
(d) Account for "grayness" in the solution process.

Fuzzy reasoning particularly suits modeling a group decision-making process. There are a group of individuals (experts) x_i involved in this process, there are a set of options s_j, and there are parameters describing the experts' opinions and preferences. The task is to find some option on which there is a consensus among the experts. The task can be handled by using fuzzy preference relations or using linguistic quantified propositions of the form "QBX are F." For example, Q denotes "most," B denotes "stock," x denotes "prices," F denotes "up."

12.4.2 FUZZY SET OPERATIONS

12.4.2.1 Basic operations

There are many ways to define fuzzy set operations. The following are some popular ones. They are defined on two fuzzy sets μ_A and μ_B. Examples for some operations are also included.

- *Set equality A=B*, if and only if $\mu_A(x) = \mu_B(x)$ for all $x \in X$
- *Set complement A'*: $\mu_A(x) = 1 - \mu_A(x)$
- *Set containment A $\subseteq$ B* if and only if $\mu_A(x) \le \mu_A(x)$
- *Set union A $\cup$ B*: $\mu_{A \cup B}(x) = \vee (\mu_A(x), \mu_B(x)) = \max(\mu_A(x), \mu_B(x))$
  For example, suppose $\mu_A(x)$ = {0.2/3, 0.5/4, 0.8/5) and $\mu_B(x)$ = {0.3/3, 0.6/4, 0.7/5}, we have $\mu_{A \cup B}(x)$ = {0.3/3, 0.6/4, 0.8/5}.
- *Set intersection A $\cap$ B*: $\mu_{A \cap B}(x) = \wedge(\mu_A(x), \mu_B(x)) = \min (\mu_A(x), \mu_D(x))$
  For example, for the same two sets defined above, we have $\mu_{A \cap B}(x)$ = {0.2/3, 0.5/4, 0.7/5}.
- *Set product AB*: $\mu_{AB}(x) = \mu_A(x) \mu_B(x)$
- *Power of a set A^N*: $\mu_{AN}(x) = (\mu_A(x))$
- *Bounded sum (bold union) A $\oplus$ B*: $\mu_{A \oplus B} = \wedge(1, \mu_A(x) + \mu_B(x))$
- *Concentration CON(A)*: $\mu_{CON(A)} = (\mu_{A(x)})^2$
  Concentration can be used to define concepts modified by the word "very." For example, from the "tall" function defined earlier, we can define "very tall" using concentration:
  Very Tall = {0/5, 0.015/5.5, 0.25/6, 0.77/6.5, 1/7}
  Comparing with the original Tall function, we can see the effect of the concentration operation: For example, 6 foot was considered as "tall" with degree 0.5, but is considered as "very tall" with a much reduced degree of 0.25.
- *Dilation DIL(A)*: $\mu_{DIL(A)} = (\mu_{A(x)})^{0.5}$. This is the inverse operation of concentration.
- *Intensification INT(A)*: $\mu_{INT(A)}(x)$ is defined as
  $2(\mu_A(x))^2$ for $0 \le \mu_A(x) \le 0.5$
  $1 - 2(1 - \mu_A(x))^2$ for $0.5 < \mu_A(x) \le 1$
- *Normalization NORM(A)*: $\mu_{NORM(A)}(x) = \mu_A(x) / \max\{\mu_A(x)\}$
  Normalization actually requires the largest fuzzy set function value be equal to one. So for $\mu_A(x)$ = {0.2/3, 0.5/4, 0.8/5), its normalization is $\mu_A(x)$ = {0.25/3, 0.63/4, 1/5).

318   Reasoning under uncertainty

12.4.2.2 Triangular norms

We now take a look at the fuzzy set operations from a broader perspective. Since characteristic functions are equivalent representations of sets, the basic intersection, union and complement operations are conveniently represented by taking the minimum, maximum and one-complement of the corresponding characteristic functions for all $x \in X$:

$$(A \cap B)(x) = \min(A(x), B(x)) = A(x) \wedge B(x),$$
$$(A \cup B)(x) = \max(A(x), B(x)) = A(x) \vee B(x),$$
$$A(x) = 1 - A(x),$$

where A and B are sets defined in a universe X, and $(A \cap B)(x)$ and $(A \cup B)(x)$ denote the membership functions of the sets resulting from the intersection and union of A and B, respectively. The use of max and min operators is very common in fuzzy set applications. Moreover, they can be generalized into triangular norms which are the models of operations on fuzzy sets.

Triangular norm (t-norm). It is a binary operation t: $[0,1]^2 \rightarrow [0,1]$ satisfying the following requirements:

- Commutativity: $xty = ytx$
- Accociativity: $xt(ytz) = (zty)tz$
- Monontonicity: If $x \leq y$ and $w \leq z$, then $xtw \leq ytz$
- Boundary conditions: $0tx = 0$, $1tx = x$.

Apparently, the min operator $\wedge$ is a t-norm. Therefore, the concept of t-norm extends the concept of set intersection operation. As another simple example, arithmetic multiplication can be used as "t": $xty = xy$. We may easily verify all the above four requirements are satisfied.

Triangular co-norm (s-norm). It is a binary operation t: $[0,1]^2 \rightarrow [0,1]$ satisfying the following requirements:

- Commutativity: $xsy = ysx$
- Accociativity: $xs(ysz) = (zsy)sz$
- Monontonicity: If $x \leq y$ and $w \leq z$, then $xsw \leq ysz$
- Boundary conditions: $xs0 = x$, $xs1 = 1$.

Apparently, the min operator $\vee$ is an s-norm. Therefore, the concept of s-norm extends the concept of set union operation. As another simple example, the following formula defines an s-norm: $xsy = x + y - xy$. We may easily verify all the above four requirements are satisfied.

For each t-norm there exists a dual s-norm, this means

$$xsy = 1-(1-x) \, t \, (1-y),$$
$$xty = 1 - (1-x) \, s \, (1-y).$$

The above two formulas can be written as

$$1-xsy = (1-x) + (1-y),$$
$$1-xty = (1-x) \, s \, (1-y).$$

Apparently, these two relationships are just de Morgan laws (s and t are corresponding to $\cup$ and $\cap$, respectively):

$$\neg(A \cup B) = \neg A \cap \neg B$$
$$\neg(A \cap B) = \neg A \cup \neg B$$

12.4.3 RESOLUTION IN POSSIBILISTIC LOGIC

12.4.3.1 Possibility and necessity

In order to demonstrate how fuzzy set theory can be combined with traditional interest of computational intelligence, we provide a brief discussion on possibility and necessity. In particular, we want to show that the theoretical result derived from fuzzy set theory can be used to enhance resolution proof as discussed in Chapter 3. The measures of possibility and necessity are among the most commonly used mechanisms of expressing matching between two fuzzy sets (and more generally, fuzzy relations). For example, the possibility measure $Poss(X,A)$ describes a degree of overlap between X and A. The *confidence parameter* $g(E)$ is defined as $0 \leq g(E) \leq 1$, $E \subseteq U$, where E is an event from a domain U of all possible events. The following axioms are valid for $g(E)$:

A1. $E1 \subseteq E2 \Rightarrow g(E1) \leq g(E2)$.

A2. $\forall A, B \subseteq U, g(A \cup B) \geq max(g(A), g(B))$.

A3. $\forall A, B \subseteq U, g(A \cap B) \leq min(g(A), g(B))$.

When a measure for the confidence parameters of A and B makes A2 an equality, it is called *possibility*:

$$\forall A, B \subseteq U, g(A \cup B) = max(g(A), g(B)).$$

When a measure for the confidence parameters of A and B makes A3 an equality, it is called *necessity*:

$$\forall A, B \subseteq U, g(A \cap B) = min(g(A), g(B)).$$

Possibility is the degree to which an expert considers a hypothesis H to be feasible or simply possible. Possibility is non-statistical; rather, it is capacity or capability. It refers to allowed values.

12.4.3.2 Remark on possibilistic logic

The resolution rules presented in this section are in possibilistic logic which is closer to classic logic than fuzzy logic. But we will not focus on possibilistic logic itself. Our purpose is to use possibilistic logic to demonstrate how resolution proof can be done when an inexact match is used. [Dubois, Lang and Prade 1991] provides an example. The proof entails the existence of "optimal refutations," i.e., derivations of an empty clause with a maximal valuation, the valuations being ordered by:

$(N\,\alpha) \leq (N\,\beta)$ if and only if $\alpha \leq \beta$

$(\Pi\,\alpha) \leq (\Pi\,\beta)$ if and only if $\alpha \leq \beta$

$(\Pi\,\alpha) \leq (N\,\beta)$ for any $(\alpha, \beta) \in [0,1] \times [0,1]$

12.4.3.3 An example

Consider an example with the following knowledge base.

K1. If Alan attends a meeting, then Bob does not.

K2. Alan comes to the meeting tomorrow.

K3. If Cindy attends a meeting, then it is likely that the meeting will not be quiet.

K4. It is highly possible that Cindy comes to the meeting tomorrow.

K5. If Don comes tomorrow and Bob does not, then it is almost certain that the meeting will not be quiet.

K6. It is likely that Bob or Elvis will come tomorrow.

K7. If Elvis comes tomorrow, it is rather likely that Don will come.

K8. If Elvis does not come tomorrow, it is almost certain that the meeting will be quiet.

The knowledge can be represented in following clauses:

C1. $\neg$ attends(alan) $\vee \neg$ attends(bob)   (N 1)

C2. attends(alan).   (N 1)

C3. $\neg$ attends(cindy) $\vee \neg$ quiet(meeting).   (N 0.7)

C4. attends(cindy).   (P 0.8)

C5. attends(don) $\vee \neg$attends(elvis) $\vee \neg$quiet(meeting). (N 0.8)

C6. attends(bob) $\vee$ attends(elvis).   (N 0.7)

C7. $\neg$ attends(elvis) $\vee$ attends(albert)   (N 0.6)

C8. attends(elvis) $\vee$ quiet(meeting).   (N 0.8)

In addition, we have the negated goal: C0. quiet(meeting). The process of fuzzy resolution is shown in Figure 12.7.

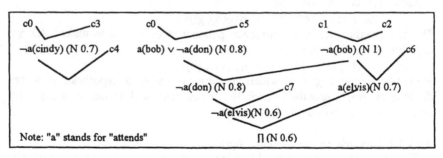

Figure 12.7 Resolution in possibility logic

12.5 FUZZY RULES AND FUZZY EXPERT SYSTEMS

In this section we examine some most of the important concepts related to fuzzy inference. We start our discussion on fuzzy relations.

12.5.1 FUZZY RELATIONS

Fuzzy relations link two fuzzy sets in a predefined manner. A fuzzy relation is fundamentally a fuzzy subset in the Cartesian product universe. The fuzzy relation for N sets is defined as

$$R = \{\mu_R (x_1, x_2, ... \ x_N) \ / \ (x_1, x_2, ... \ x_N) \ | \ x_i \in X_i, \ I = 1, 2, ... \ N)\}$$

which associates the membership grade of each N-tuple.

A fuzzy relation can be represented by a matrix or a fuzzy graph. In this chapter, we will use matrix form only.

A *composition relation* (or simply *composition*) of fuzzy relations $R_1(A,B)$ and $R_2(B, C)$ is a relation obtained after applying relations R_1 and R_2 one after another. A typical composition is the Max-min composition. The *composition of relations* is the net effect of applying one relation after another. For the case of two binary relations P and Q, the composition of their relations is the binary relation R,

$$R(A,C) = Q(A, B) \circ P(B,C),$$

where A, B, C are sets, and $R(A,C)$ is a relation between A and C, $Q(A,B)$ is a relation between A and B, $P(B,C)$ is a relation between B and C, and $\circ$ is the *composition operator*. In terms of membership grades, $R = \{\mu_R (a,c) / (a, c) \mid a \in A, c \in C\}$, where μ_R is defined as follows:

$$\mu_R(a, c) = \vee_{b \in B} [\mu_Q(a,b) \wedge \mu_P(b,c)] = \max_{b \in B} [\min (\mu_Q(a,b) \mu_P(b,c))]$$

A fuzzy relation usually is expressed in the form as exemplified in Table 12.3(a), where the entries are fuzzy membership function values.

Table 12.3(a) A fuzzy relation

	Y1	y2	y3
X1	0.2	0.1	0.2
X2	0.2	0.3	0.4

This table can be expressed in the form of conventional relation (as discussed in Chapter 3) in Table 12.3(a).

Table 12.3(b) Fuzzy relation in conventional format

X	Y	Membership grade
X_1	Y_1	0.2
X_1	Y_2	0.1
X_1	Y_3	0.2
X_2	Y_1	0.2
X_2	Y_2	0.3
X_2	Y_3	0.4

The advantage of representing a fuzzy relation in the form of Table 12.3(a) is that it clearly indicates the fuzzy membership function values and certain operations (such as projections) [Giarritano and Riley 1998] can be easily applied.

The reason we are interested in fuzzy relations is that they are closely related to fuzzy inference using fuzzy rules.

12.5.2 SYNTAX AND SEMANTICS OF FUZZY RULES

12.5.2.1 Fuzzy system components

A fuzzy system consists of three parts: fuzzy input and output variables and their fuzzy values; fuzzy rules; and fuzzy inference methods, which may include *fuzzification* and *defuzzification*. This is because the outcome of the fuzzy inference process is a fuzzy set, specifying a fuzzy distribution of a conclusion. However, in control applications, only a single discrete action may be applied, so a single point that reflects the most appropriate value of the set needs to be selected. The process of reducing a fuzzy set to a single point is known as defuzzification.

There are several types of fuzzy rules. For example, Zadeh-Mamdani's fuzzy rules have the following format:

$$\text{If } x \text{ is } A, \text{ then } y \text{ is B,}$$

where

"x is A" and "y is B" are two fuzzy propositions;

x and y are fuzzy variables defined over universes of discourse U and V respectively;

A and B are fuzzy sets defined by their fuzzy membership functions.

12.5.2.2 Syntax of fuzzy rules

Fuzzy rules are conditioned fuzzy propositions. When the proposition in the consequent of the first statement (If A then B) is also an antecedent of the second (If B then C), the rules are said to be *chained*. Otherwise, they are *parallel rules*. Parallel rules are most commonly interpreted by viewing each rule as inducing a fuzzy relation R_i, and the set of rules as a fuzzy relation that is an "aggregation" of the individual relations.

Fuzzy rules typically involve qualified or quantified propositions.

- *Qualified propositions.* Fuzzy propositions can be qualified by associating with the proposition's modal or intensional operators leading to *possibility qualification* (as in "If the temperature is low, then the good product is *impossible*") and *probability qualification* (as in " If the temperature is low, then valve opening is low is *unlikely*"). Propositions may be more generally qualified (with the word "usually").
- *Quantified propositions.* Propositions can be quantified by fuzzy quantifiers such as *most, frequently, many, several, about ten,* etc.

We also note that there are some special types of rules:

Unless rules: Rule may have exceptions;

Gradual rules: Rules with the format of "The more...the more" or "The less...the less..."

Compound propositions can be constructed through *conjunctions* and/or *disjunctions* of propositions to form new propositions.

12.5.2.3 Fuzzy inference and fuzzy relations

Essentially, statements of the form "If X is A, then Y is B" describe a relation between the fuzzy variables X and Y. This suggests that a fuzzy rule can be defined as a fuzzy relation R, with the membership grade $R(x,y)$ representing the degree to which $(x, y) \in \mathbf{X} \times \mathbf{Y}$ is compatible with the relation between the variables X and Y involved in the given rule. If A and B are fuzzy sets of $\mathbf{X}$ and $\mathbf{Y}$, then the relation R on $\mathbf{X} \times \mathbf{Y}$ can be determined by the relational assignment equation

$$R(x, y) = f(A(x), B(y)), \ \forall (x, y) \in \mathbf{X} \times \mathbf{Y},$$

where f is a function of the form $f: [0,1]^2 \rightarrow [0,1]$. In general, the fuzzy relations induced are derived from three main classes of f functions: fuzzy conjunction, fuzzy disjunction and fuzzy implication.

A fuzzy relation can be represented by a matrix or a fuzzy graph. The Rc implication relation "heavy smoker" (in terms of number of packs of cigarettes consumed) → "high risk of cancer" can be represented in a matrix form shown in Table 12.4 (following [Kasabov 1996]). (Here the relation can be considered as representing a rule: "if heavy smoker then risk".)

Table 12.4 A relation used to represent a rule

Cigarette packs	Low risk	Medium risk	High risk
0	0	0	0
5	.2	.5	.5
10	0	.7	1

A composition relation of fuzzy relations $R1(AB)$ and $R2(BC)$ is a relation $R(AC)$ obtained after applying relations $R1$ and $R2$ one after another. A typical composition is the Max-Min composition:

$$R(AC): \quad \mu_{R(ac)} = \vee\{\mu_{R1(ab)} \wedge \mu_{R2(bc)}\},$$

where $\vee$ denotes Max and $\wedge$ denotes Min, $a \in A$, $b \in B$, $c \in C$.

12.5.2.4 Fuzzy implication

When we are given a statement of the form "x is A," from (x,y) is F (here $A \subseteq X$ and F is a relation, $F \subset X \times Y$), we can infer that y is B, $B \subseteq Y$. The computing scheme involves sets and retains the symbolic form

$$X \text{ is } A$$
$$\underline{(x,y) \text{ is } F}$$
$$y \text{ is } B.$$

In the more general case when a collection of fuzzy rules is interpreted as a functional dependency F^* between the fuzzy variables X and Y, the problem of computing the value of Y given a value of X can be expressed as the inference scheme

$$X \text{ is } A$$
$$\underline{(x,y) \text{ is } F^*}$$
$$y \text{ is } B.$$

The compositional rule of inference also applies when interpreting each fuzzy rule of a given collection as a fuzzy relation R_i, $I = 1, ..., N$, induced by any of the fuzzy implication functions. Therefore, for (X,Y) is R, using the compositional rule of inference we have

$$X \text{ is } A$$
$$\underline{(X, Y) \text{ is } R}$$
$$y \text{ is } B,$$

which implies

$$X \text{ is } A$$
$$\underline{(X, Y) \text{ is } R}$$
$$y \text{ is } A \circ R.$$

12.5.3 FUZZY INFERENCE METHODS

12.5.3.1 Fuzzy inference laws

Fuzzy inference refers to an inference method that uses fuzzy implication relations, fuzzy composition operators, and an operator to link the fuzzy rules. The result of the inference process is some new facts based on the fuzzy rules and the input information supplied. A popular reasoning strategy is generalized modus ponens. When this law is applied over a simple fuzzy rule, it works in the following manner:

$$\text{If } x \text{ is } A, \quad \text{then } y \text{ is } B,$$
$$\underline{\text{Now } x \text{ is } A'}$$
$$\text{so } y \text{ is } B'.$$

The compositional rule of inference can be used to implement the generalized modus ponens:

$$B' = A' \lozenge (A \rightarrow B) = A' R_{ab},$$

where $\rightarrow$ is a compositional operator, and R_{ab} is a fuzzy relational matrix representing the implication relation between the fuzzy concepts A and B.

12.5.3.2 Combining inference results

In a fuzzy production system, within a recognize-act cycle, all the rules are fired at every cycle (due to inexact matching) and they all contribute to the final result. There are so-called *else-links* to combine these results.

Rules of inference in fuzzy systems

One way of defining generalized modus ponens is throught the following formula:

$$X \text{ is } F$$
$$\underline{Y \text{ is } G \text{ if } X \text{ is } H}$$
$$Y \text{ is } F \circ (H' \oplus G)$$

where H' is the fuzzy negation of H and the bounded sum is defined as

$$\mu_{H' \oplus G}(x, y) = 1 \wedge (1 - \mu_H(x) + \mu_G(y)).$$

12.5.3.3 Fuzzy rule evaluation

The most important difference between the fuzzy logic and the conventional two state logic must be their inference techniques. Consider the simple rule of form:

if A then C	A is the antecedent of the rule
A'	A' is the matching fact in the fact database
----------------	C is the consequent of the rule
C'	C' is the actual consequent calculated

In the two state logic, the antecedent A and fact A' have to be exactly the same to issue the conclusion C' referring to consequent C. On the other hand, in the fuzzy logic, the rule can issue the actual consequent C' as long as the matching fact A' is somewhat belongs to the antecedent A. Four types of rules can be considered, as shown in Table 12.5.

Table 12.5 Types of Inference Rules

Antecedent	Consequent	Type of Rule
CRISP	CRISP	CRISP – CRISP
CRISP	FUZZY	CRISP - CRISP
FUZZY	CRISP	FUZZY – CRISP
FUZZY	FUZZY	FUZZY - FUZZY

Various evaluation methods have been proposed by different authors. In the following we describe one approach to deal with the following two cases:
- Rules with single proposition in the antecedent and multiple conjunctive proposition in the consequence; and
- Rules with multiple proposition in the antecedent and single proposition in the consequence:

Case 1. Rules with single proposition in the antecedent and simple proposition in the consequence

We illustrate this case by considering the following two sub-cases in a rule with the form "If A then C." We use CF to indicate the certainty factor (which reflects the degree of vagueness) associated with consequence C.

a. *A is nonfuzzy and C is fuzzy.* Consider the following example.

Rule: If visibility (A) is 16 miles (V_1),

then expected average traffic speed (C) is high (V_2) (CF1 = 0.7)

Suppose the case-specific fact is: visibility is 16 miles (CF2 = 0.9), we can calculate CF3 = 0.7 * 0.9 = 0.63. Our conclusion is that the expected average traffic speed (C) is high (V_2') (CF = 0.63).

b. *A and C are fuzzy objects:* In this case, it is needed to form a relation R_G which maps A to C. Example of using R_G is shown below

Rule: if visibility (A) is poor (V_1),
then traffic speed is low (C)

The fuzziness of A and C is given as

poor visibility: $\mu_{F1} = 0.9/0.5 + 0.5/5$
low speed: $\mu_{F2} = 0.8/5 + 0.7/15 + 0.4/25$

Suppose the case-specific fact is visibility (A) is poor' (V_1'), where

$\mu_{F1}' = 0.8/0.5 + 0.6/5$

In addition, we are given a relation $R_G: \mu_{F1} \rightarrow \mu_{F2}$ (v) which is a 2 * 3 table as shown in Table 12.6.

Table 12.6 Relation R_G

F_1 \ F_2	5	15	25
0.5	0.8	0.7	0.4
5	1	1	0.4

We can calculate $F_{2'} = F_{1'}$ o $R_G = 0.8/5 + 0.7/15 + 0.4/25$.

Case 2. Rules with single proposition in the antecedent and multiple conjunctive proposition in the consequence.

In this case, we can split the consequence to form separate rules, with each conjunct as the sole consequence in a rule. Each rule is then evaluated by applying Case 1.

Case 3.   Rules with multiple proposition in the antecedent and single proposition in the consequence.
We consider rules with the following format:

Rule: If A_1 AND A_2 THEN C is V_3
facts: A_1', A_2'
conclusion: C is V_3'

We use the logic inference laws to change the form of the rule (this is an example how predicate logic can aid production rule development):

$$A_1 \wedge A_2 \rightarrow C$$
$$= \neg(A_1 \wedge A_2) \vee C$$
$$= (\neg A_1 \vee \neg A_2) \vee C$$
$$= (\neg A_1 \vee C) \vee (\neg A_2 \vee C)$$
$$= (A_1 \rightarrow C) \vee (A_2 \rightarrow C)$$

Consider the following rule as an example.

Rule: If visibility (A_1) is poor (V_1) and weather (A_2) is bad (V_2),
then traffic speed (C) is low (V_3).

Suppose we are given case-specific facts: visibility (A_1) is poor' (V_1'), weather (A_2) is bad' (V_2') (here we use poor' and bad' to denote the degree of "poor" and "bad" associated with a given fact). How can we handle the conclusion: traffic speed (C) is slow' (V_3)?. (Here we use slow' to denote the degree of "slow" derived from the given facts.)
In order to process this, the rule is split into two rules.

Rule 1:   If visibility (A_1) is poor (V_1) then traffic speed (C) is low (V_3).

facts: visibility (A_1) is poor' (V_1')
conclusion: traffic speed (C) is slow' (V_3)

Rule 2:   If weather (A_2) is bad (V_2) then traffic speed (C) is low (V_3).

facts: weather (A_2) is bad' (V_2')
conclusion: traffic speed (C) is slow' (V_3)

Suppose from rule 1, $F_{12}' = 0.6/5 + 0.6/15 + 0.4/25$ and from rule 2, we have $F_{22}' = 0.7/5 + 0.5/15 + 0.3/25 + 0.1/35$. Performing a union operation (as introduced in Section 12.4.1) on these two fuzzy sets we obtain the resulting fuzzy membership function $F_2' = 0.7/5 + 0.6/15 + 0.4/25 + 0.1/35$.

Note that suppose in rule (2) *AND* is changed to *OR*. In this case, we should still perform the split first, and then take the set intersection (instead of set union).

12.6   USING FUZZYCLIPS

As a concrete example of incorporating fuzzy set theory into expert systems development, let us take a brief look at *FuzzyCLIPS*, an extended version of the CLIPS rule-based shell for representing and manipulating fuzzy facts and rules. In addition to the CLIPS functionality, FuzzyCLIPS can deal with exact, fuzzy, and combined reasoning, allowing fuzzy and normal terms to be freely mixed in the rules and facts of an expert system. When FuzzyCLIPS is used, all fuzzy variables must be predefined before using the *deftemplate* statement. A fuzzy *deftemplate* describes a fuzzy variable. One may use these *deftemplates* to describe fuzzy facts in patterns and assert commands. In addition, FuzzyCLIPS has a set of predefined modifiers that can be used at any time to describe fuzzy concepts when fuzzy terms are described in fuzzy *deftemplates*, fuzzy rule patterns are written, or fuzzy facts or fuzzy slots are asserted. The user may also define modifiers that can be used in exactly the same manner as the predefined ones. FuzzyCLIPS commands and functions include the following [Orchard 1998]:

- Accessing the universe of discourse;
- Accessing the fuzzy set;
- Accessing the certainty factor;
- Accessing the threshold certainty factor;
- Setting the rule CF evaluation behavior;
- Controlling the fuzzy set display precision;
- Controlling the fuzzy inference method;
- Setting the fuzzy pattern matching threshold;
- Establishing fuzzy value predicate function;
- Creating and operating on fuzzy values;
- Accessing a fuzzy slot in a fact;
- Displaying a fuzzy value in a format function;
- Plotting a fuzzy value; and
- Controlling the result of defuzzification.

The conventional two state logic has been used for the various types of applications. However, the two state logic is not appropriate for the applications that need to handle the real world because of its lack of the capability to process the uncertain information. Expert systems are expected to perform like a human in the real environment. Therefore, the data handling methods in the expert systems should be able to well process the uncertain information as human beings do. In the following we introduce techniques employed in FuzzyCLIPS Version 6.04A by implementing simple codes. FuzzyCLIPS Version 6.04A was released by Institute for Information Technology National Research Council Canada in 1998. FuzzyCLIPS is an extended version of the CLIPS rule-based shell for representing and manipulating fuzzy facts and rules. A fuzzy expert system shell is implemented on top of the conventional CLIPS. (Some relevant materials can be found at http://ai.iit.nrc.ca/fuzzy/fuzzy.html).

We now give an example which expresses a linguistic expression, "cold," "warm," and "hot" of *deftemplate* "temp" ("temp" itself is not fuzzified). These three variables are expressed using Z, π (or PI) and S functions, respectively (as discussed in 12.4.1.3). Temperature ranges from 5 to 40 Celsius. For the Z function, when temp is 10, its value is 0 and when temp is 24, its value is 1 (as shown in the template). For the PI and S functions, the corresponding numbers are shown in the template definition. Figure 12.8 depicts these three functions.

```
(deftemplate temp
  5 40 Celsius
  (
   (cold (z 10 24))
   (warm (PI 2 24))
   (hot (s 26 31))
  )
)

Fuzzy Value: temp
Linguistic Value: cold (c), warm (w), hot (h)

1.00cccccccccc                  w            hhhhhhhhhhhhh
0.95          c                 w          h
0.90            cc
0.85
0.80              c                 w       h
0.75                c
0.70                 c
0.65                              w
0.60                  c                    h
0.55
0.50                    c
0.45                     c
0.40
0.35                       c             h
0.30                                 w
0.25                        c
0.20                         c
0.15                          c        h
0.10                         c w
0.05                          cc       h
0.00hhhhhhhhhhhhhhhhhhhhhhhhhhhhhhhhhhhhhwwwwwwwwwwwwwwwwwww
    |----|----|----|----|----|----|----|----|----|----|
    5.00     12.00     19.00     26.00     33.00     40.00
Universe of Discourse:  From   5.00  to   40.00
```

Figure 12.8 Plots of linguistic values with standard function representation

12.7 FUZZY CONTROLLERS

12.7.1 BASICS OF FUZZY CONTROLLER

As a typical example of fuzzy expert systems, we take a look of *fuzzy controllers*. A fuzzy controller's underlying structure comes from its rule-based organization. Its key premise is that control knowledge is available to specify a control strategy represented by a collection of if-then rules. Thus the control strategy is structured into control protocols linking the system's current state with the corresponding control action. Fuzzy controller design is thus concerned with the calculus of fuzzy rules, and its computing procedures are governed by rule-based computations.

The architecture of a fuzzy logic controller is shown in Figure 12.9. The fuzzy logic controller contains three components, the fuzzification, the fuzzy inference engine, and the defuzzification.

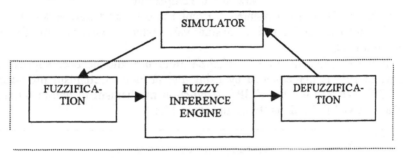

Figure 12.9 Fuzzy controller architecture

12.7.2 BUILDING FUZZY CONTROLLER USING FUZZYCLIPS

As an example, let us consider a simple simulation of the room temperature and an electrical heater. The controller acquires the room temperature from the sensor and sends the power setting to the electrical heater. The process repeats until the desired temperature is achieved.

The feature of the electrical heater is governed by the physics formulas as shown below:

Where:

$P = E^2 / R$ P: Power[w]

or   E: Control Voltage [V]

$P = I^2 * R$ R: Resistance of the heater circuit [Ω]

     I: Control Current [A]

The voltage level is often used to control the performance of the electrical devices It is reasonable to assume that the rise of room temperature is linear against the control voltage, Power Setting:

When Power Setting is equal to 0, no temperature rises.

When Power Setting is equal to 1, the maximum rise of the temperature.

A simple formula to imitate the electrical heater has been employed:

New Room Temperature
= Current Room Temperature + Room Factor * Heater Temperature * Heater Power Setting

where Room Factor and Heater Temperature are constant values which are governed by the room environment such as size, the material of walls etc. and the maximum temperature of the heater, respectively. Also, we assume the outside temperature is always 0°C so that we can ignore the relative temperature and the change of the outside temperature.

Next, we have to consider the drop of the temperature caused by the outside low temperature, 0°C. The room temperature should drop little by little if the heater is off at the high room temperature. A simple formula has been developed:

New Room Temperature
= Current Room Temperature – Current Temperature * Refrigerator Factor

where Refrigerator Factor is a constant value which is governed by the room environment.

In this example, the FUZZY–FUZZY inference rule has been applied. This type of rule is implemented by using the *defrule* mechanism provided by CLIPS. We also use the CLIPS *deffunction* mechanism to define functions. The FuzzyCLIPS code is shown in Figure 12.10.

```
; conf.clp
; This demonstrates the fuzzy logic controller.
; Always adjust the room temperature to 24 degree.
;;;;;;;;;;;;;;;;;;;;;;;;;;;;;;;;;;;;;;;;;;;;;;;;;;;;;;;;;;;;;;

(defglobal
 ?*HEATER-TEMP* = 40.0
 ?*ROOM-FACTOR* = 0.05
 ?*COUNTER* = 0
 ?*ROOM-TEMP* = 0
 ?*REFRIG-FACTOR* = 0.05
)
(deftemplate Crisp-Value
 (slot HeaterPower)
 (slot RoomTemp)
)
(deftemplate Fuzzy-RoomTemp
 -1 28 Celsius
 (
   (cold (z 10 23))
 )
)
 (deftemplate Fuzzy-HeaterPower
 0 1
 (
   (strong (s 0.25 0.75))
 )
)
;;;;;;;;;;;;;;;;;;;;;;;;;;;;;;;;;;; Simulation
(deffunction Simulator(?HeaterPower)
 ;----------------------------------------;
 ; Room temp.  Adjusted by HeaterPower  ;
 ;----------------------------------------;
 (bind ?*ROOM-TEMP* (+ ?*ROOM-TEMP* (* ?*ROOM-FACTOR*
                                   (* ?*HEATER-TEMP*
?HeaterPower)))))
 ;----------------------------------------------------------;
 ; Room temp.  Decreases 10 % of current room temperature ;
 ; due to the refrigeration by outside temperature.       ;
```

```
;-----------------------------------------------------------;
(bind ?*ROOM-TEMP* (- ?*ROOM-TEMP* (* ?*ROOM-TEMP* ?*REFRIG-
FACTOR*)))
(printout t " New room temperature: " ?*ROOM-TEMP* crlf)
(assert (RoomTemp ?*ROOM-TEMP*))
)
;;;;;;;;;;;;;;;;;;;;;;;;;; Fuzzification
(defrule Fuzzification
?f1 <- (RoomTemp ?)
=>
  (retract ?f1)
  (assert (Fuzzy-RoomTemp (pi 1 ?*ROOM-TEMP*)))
  (printout t " Fuzzified temperature is asserted."crlf)
)

;;;;;;;;;;;;;;;;;;;;;;;;; Fuzzy Inference
(defrule Cold-PowerStrong
 (Fuzzy-RoomTemp cold)
 =>
  (assert(Fuzzy-HeaterPower strong))
)
;;;;;;;;;;;;;;;;;;;;;;;;; Defuzzification
(defrule Defuzzify-HearterPower
?f1 <- (Fuzzy-HeaterPower ?)
=>
  (bind ?HeaterPower (moment-defuzzify ?f1))
  (assert (HeaterPower ?HeaterPower))
  (retract ?f1)
)
;;;;;;;;;;;;;;;;;;;;;;;;; Call Simulator
(defrule Call-Simulator
?f2 <- (Fuzzy-RoomTemp ?)
(HeaterPower ?HeaterPower)
=>
  (retract ?f2)
  (printout t " Heater power set " ?HeaterPower crlf)
  (bind ?*COUNTER* (+ ?*COUNTER* 1))
  (printout t ?*COUNTER* " Calling Simulator()" crlf)
  (Simulator ?HeaterPower)
)
;;;;;;;;;;;;;;;;;;;;;;;;;;;;;;;; Start Program
 (defrule Start
 =>
  (assert (HeaterPower 0))
  (assert (RoomTemp 0))
)
```

Figure 12.10 FuzzyCLIPS code for the heater

A portion of the output is shown in Figure 12.11.

```
CLIPS> (run)
  Heater power set 0.7389322916666667
1 Calling Simulator()
  New room temperature: 1.403971354166667
  Fuzzified temperature is asserted.
```

```
Heater power set 0.7389322916666667
2 Calling Simulator()
   New room temperature: 2.737744140625001
   Fuzzified temperature is asserted.
   Heater power set 0.7389322916666667
...
15  Calling Simulator()
   New room temperature: 14.34680654100141
   Fuzzified temperature is asserted.
   Heater power set 0.7252339145874244
15 Calling Simulator()
   New room temperature: 15.00741065166745
   Fuzzified temperature is asserted.
   Heater power set 0.7211679617832571
```

Figure 12.11 Part of the output

The output is collected up to 100 minutes (100 repetitions) and plotted using spreadsheet (not shown here). The line shows a slower achievement of the desired temperature 24°C. However, the time to achieve the desired temperature should be adjustable. The fuzzy logic control does not show it has unstable period. It produced a very smooth and flat temperature line.

12.7.3 FUZZY CONTROLLER DESIGN PROCESS

We now present an example which describes the application of fuzzy rule-based systems applied to automatic control. The major objective is to show how fuzzy rule-based control algorithms could be used for developing controller.

The control problem can be stated trivially as a mapping between inputs and outputs: $y = f(x)$, the control law. Traditionally, control laws are derived from integral-differential equation models of the system dynamics, i.e., leading to the computation of forcing values that will cause the system state to tend to the desired set-point. In control theory, the dynamic nature of a controlled system is preeminent while in the other two problems we would normally think of static states; nevertheless, the integrity of the analogy is not affected. Traditional control theory concentrates on mathematical model building: the input-output control function is expressed as a closed-form -- with only a few parameters needing to be specified, e.g., related to the coefficients of the system differential equation.

Fuzzy logic and the method of approximate reasoning led to new concepts in control theory and in the design of expert systems. These concepts imitate human thought processes better than conventional methods. The major characteristic of fuzzy control is the incorporation of a knowledge-based expert system somewhere in the controller. In fuzzy controller, the control law is model-free, i.e., design does not consist of putting values on a few parameters that complete the specification of an input-output function; rather, the input-output function can be of any form and highly non-linear. Rule-based fuzzy systems can be used if human expert knowledge is available which can be expressed in the form of if-then rules.

Fuzzy control has advantages especially in the cases that the mathematical model of the control process may not exist or may be too expansive in term of computing time.

In the following we describe how to implement a fuzzy control algorithm using FuzzyCLIPS. We show the steps needed to design and implement a fuzzy logic-based expert system based on the following seven tasks needed to build fuzzy logic expert systems.

In order to build a fuzzy logic expert system, there are seven major tasks typically performed when developing a fuzzy logic expert system, as described below.

Task 1: Define the problem. Like all expert system projects, we need to first obtain a source of knowledge. In this example, the fuzzy rule-based expert system will be used to Navigate the Golf Cart from initial position to the location of the golf ball. The problem is depicted in Figure 12.12. In order to accomplish these tasks, we will need provide the fuzzy system with control over both the direction and speed of the cart. The cart must initially steer toward the ball by nullifying the error between the angular direction of the cart and the direction toward the ball. The cart should also accelerate to some maximum allowable speed, then slow down and eventually stop when it is close to the ball.

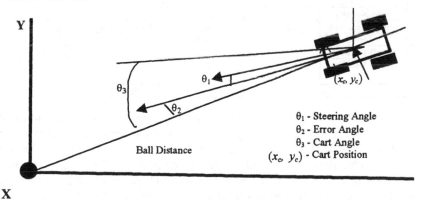

Figure 12.12 Cart navigation geometry

Task 2: Define the linguistic variables. We accomplish this task by listening to experts and then abstract the knowledge of experts. We want to uncover the variables that will represent our universes of discourse and the fuzzy sets that will be defined on each. For our example, from task 1, we know that our fuzzy system must contend with two basic problems: control steering of cart to direct it toward the ball, and control the cart's speed. We need to ask experts to discuss in general how each of these problems is solved. For example, for the first problem, we can follow common sense strategy for steering the cart toward the ball which is "When the direction of the cart is

away from the ball, make the cart's direction toward the ball." In a similar fashion we obtain the expert's strategies for controlling the cart's speed:
"When the cart is far from the ball, make the cart's speed fast. Otherwise, make the cart's speed slow."

From this discussion we can define the following linguistic variables – the universe of discourses, and define their ranges, as shown in Table 12.7.

Table 12.7 Linguistic variables

Linguistic Variable	Range
Error angle	-60 to 60
Steering angle	-45 to 45
Speed	0 to 5 yd/s
Acceleration	-2 to 1 yd/s/s
Ball distance	0 to 600 yd/s

Task 3: Define the fuzzy sets. This includes defined member functions for every linguistic variable and their associated adjectives. In our example, in order to accomplish this task we need to know a list of typical adjectives used with each linguistic variable. Our assumptions are summarized in Table 12.8.

Table 12.8 Assumptions used

Error angle	Steering angle	Speed	Acceleration	Ball Distance
Large Negative	Hard Right	Zero	Brake Hard	Zero
Small Negative	Slight Right	Real Slow	Brake Light	Real Close
Zero	Zero	Slow	Coast	Close
Small Positive	Slight Left	Medium	Zero	Medium
Large Positive	Hard Left	Fast	Slight Acceleration	Far
			Floor it	

The next step we need to know is the information that will allow us to define the fuzzy sets for each adjective given in the above table. That is, we can define at what degree the experts believe each fuzzy value will be, for example, what degree do we believe the speed is slow? These fuzzy mapping or membership functions can have a variety of shapes depending on how the expert relates different domain values to belief values. In practice, a piecewise linear function, such as triangular or trapezoidal shape, provides an adequate capture of the expert's belief and simplifies the computation.

Task 4: Define the fuzzy rules. The fuzzy rules come from the domain knowledge of experts. In our example, we can consider two primary problems to define the fuzzy rules: steering the cart to the ball and controlling the cart's speed. The following rule is an example.

Maintain steering direction

```
IF error_angle is Zero
THEN make steering_angle zero
     (defrule maint_steering
        (ErrorAngle Zero)
```

```
=>
    (assert (SteeringAngle Zero))
)
```

Task 5: Build the fuzzy expert system. This task involved the coding of the fuzzy sets, and rules and procedures for performing fuzzy logic functions such as fuzzy inference. There are two ways to accomplish this task: (a) to build the system from scratch using a basic programming language; or (b) rely on a fuzzy logic development shell. If we choose the second method, which is FuzzyCLIPS. Since we have already shown the FuzzyCLIPS file for the previous example (i.e., the heater problem), no code will be shown at here.

Task 6: Test the system. After you have built the system, you will want to test it to see if it meets the specifications defined during task. There are several useful commands, such as *using Batch, dribble-on, clear, load* and *halt* commands.

Task 7: Tune the system. This step tunes the fuzzy system to achieve better performance. In general, tuning a fuzzy logic system involves one or more of the following:

(a)   **Rules**
- Adding rules for special situations
- Adding premises for other linguistic variable

(b)   **Fuzzy Sets**
- Adding sets on a defined linguistic variable
- Broadening or narrowing existing sets
- Shifting laterally existing sets
- Shape adjustment of existing sets

In summary, when fuzzy logic is used, vague terms or rules can be represented and manipulated numerically to provide results that are consistent with the expert. By fuzzy control, an application of fuzzy logic to control problems is meant. Fuzzy control is different from standard control, mainly in three respects:

- The use of *linguistically described concepts,* rather than formulas
- The use of *commonsense knowledge,* rather than mathematical knowledge
- The use of *methods of fuzzy logic.*

12.8 THE NATURE OF FUZZY LOGIC

In the last section of this chapter, we provide an important and interesting philosophical review on the nature of fuzzy logic.

12.8.1 THE INCONSISTENCY OF FUZZY LOGIC

We start with basic notations in fuzzy logic. Let A denote an assertion. It is assigned the degree of truth $t(A)$, which is a numerical value between 0 and 1. For a sentence composed from simple assertions and logical connectives "and", "or", and "not", the degree of truth is defined as follows (which can be viewed as axiomatizing degree of membership for fuzzy set intersections, unions, and completeness):

(1) $t(A \cap B) = \min\{t(A), t(B)\}$

(2) $t(A \cup B) = \max\{t(A), t(B)\}$

(3) $t(\neg A) = 1 - A$

(4) $t(A) = t(B)$ if A and B are two assertions equivalent according to the rules of classical two-valued propositional calculus.

The following important result has been proved by [Elkan 1993] for any general formal system satisfying the four postulates listed above:

Theorem. For any two assertions A and B, either $t(B) = t(A)$ or $t(B) = 1 - t(A)$.

The importance of this theorem is that it revealed the intrinsic inconsistency of fuzzy logic. Although fuzzy logic is intended to allow an indefinite variety of numerical truth values, the result has proved that only two truth values are possible inside a standard fuzzy system employing the above four postulates.

12.8.2 WHY FUZZY LOGIC HAS BEEN SUCCESSFUL IN EXPERT SYSTEMS

Fuzzy logic is an attempt to capture valid patterns of reasoning about uncertainty. However, there is a lack of common consensus on what types of uncertainty are captured by fuzzy logic. From practical experience in the construction of expert systems [Elkan 1993] concluded that fuzzy logic is not uniformly suitable for reasoning about uncertain evidence.

So where does the magic power of making fuzzy logic a seemingly successful approach for building expert systems come from? Since heuristic control is the area of application in which fuzzy logic has been the most successful (in fact, fuzzy controllers can be implemented by embedded specialized microprocessors), a careful examination of successful fuzzy controllers would reveal some secrets of this kind of success. [Elkan 1993] noticed that there are five important aspects shared by these systems. One aspect is that they all use the operators of fuzzy logic, such as minimum and maximum, explicit possibility distributions, and some fuzzy implication operators (we would point out that one such operator is generalized modus ponens). However, the use of fuzzy logic is not essential to the success of fuzzy controllers. The other four properties have nothing to do with the fuzzy logic but they are vital to practical success, because they make the celebrated credit assignment problem solvable:

(1) The knowledge base of a typical fuzzy controller consists of less than 100 rules (often no more than 20 rules are used).

(2) The knowledge entering into fuzzy controllers is structurally shallow, both statistically and dynamically. It is not the case that some rules produce conclusions which are then used as premises in other rules. Statically, rules are organized as a one-level list. Dynamically, there is no run-time chaining of inferences, which is very different from most non-fuzzy expert systems.

(3) The knowledge stored in the knowledge base typically reflects immediate correlations between the inputs and outputs of the system to be controlled, as opposed to a deep, causal model of the system.

(4) The numerical parameters of their rules and of their qualitative input and output modules are tuned in a learning process. The algorithms used are gradient-descent "hill-climbing" ones that learn by local optimization.

12.8.3 IMPLICATION TO MAINSTREAM COMPUTATIONAL INTELLIGENCE

Under the section title of "Recapitulating mainstream AI," [Elkan 1993] pointed out that the designers of larger systems based on fuzzy logic are encountering all the problems of scale already identified in traditional knowledge-based systems. However, this is not to say building fuzzy expert systems has made no contribution to the main interests of computational intelligence itself. As demonstrated in some fuzzy expert systems reported in the early 1990's, the aim of the knowledge engineering process may no longer be simply to acquire knowledge from human experts. Rather, the aim is to develop a theory of the situated performance of the experts: knowledge bases are constructed to model the beliefs and practices of experts and not any "objective" truth about underlying physical processes. Thus the expert's beliefs provide an implicit organization of knowledge about the external process with which the knowledge-based system is intended to interact. This sophisticated view provides some new insight on the nature of knowledge engineering.

SUMMARY

In this chapter we summarized the two most popular approaches of uncertain reasoning. Bayesian techniques have drawn increasing attention from researchers and practitioners alike [Haddawy 1999]. A theoretical inquiry on probabilistic reasoning, including Bayesian belief networks, can be found in [Gammerman 1996]. Fuzzy set approaches can be considered as a kind of perturbation around a "standard" situation. A recent discussion on fuzzy logic is given in [Yen 1999], which introduces the "modern" perspective of viewing fuzzy logic as an approximation theory. Interesting applications of fuzzy logic in business, finance and management can be found in [Bojadziev and Bojadziev 1997], including a discussion on fuzzy queries from databases. Integration of fuzzy logic with other approaches, including an integration of probability theory and fuzzy set theory, has been studied by various researchers. Another interesting issue is to incorporate fuzzy set theory into Prolog programming [van Le 1994]. Other techniques related to fuzzy set theory can be found in [Pedrycz and Gomide 1998, Schneider, Kandel, Langholz and Chew 1996].

In this chapter we have mainly emphasized some practical issues, although we have also introduced some theoretical results such as those related to resolution proof. There are other important results as well. Here we briefly mention one of them. A family of systems are considered as *universal function approximators* if for any function there exists a system from this family that approximates it to any degree of accuracy. Fuzzy systems are universal approximators. There is an existence theorem, but it does not reveal how to construct such a system [Kasabov 1996].

SELF-EXAMINATION QUESTIONS

1. Consider the data mining model described in Section 12.3.4. Whatdoes the causal network look like if the original goal is affected from another subgoal "state-from?"
2. Write the fuzzy membership function for "fast car."
3. Recall the examples used in Section 12.5.3.3.
   (a) Suppose the fact for poor visibility poor' is an S -function 1 - S(1, 2.5, 4) . Write the actual function.
   (b) Suppose we use the generalized modus ponens as defined in Section 12.5.3.2, and $\mu_{H' \otimes G}$ *(x, y)* is defined as
   $$(1\ 0.7\ 0.5\ 0.2$$
   $$1\ 0.725\ 0.525\ 0.225$$
   $$1\ 0.799\ 0.599\ 0.299$$
   $$1\ 0.922\ 0.722\ 0.422$$
   $$1\ 1\ 1\ 1)$$
   Calculate the resulting membership function.
4. Give a brief summary on the differences between probability-based approaches and fuzzy set approaches.

REFERENCES

AAAI 99, Workshop of Search techniques for problem solving under uncertainty and incomplete information, AAAI 1999 Spring Symposium Series.

Berson, A. and Smith, S. J., *Data Warehousing, Data Mining, & OLAP*, McGraw-Hill, New York, 1998.

Bojadziev, G. and Bojadziev, M., *Fuzzy Logic for Business, Finance, and Management*, World Scientific, Singapore, 1997.

Chen, Z. and Zhu, Q., Query construction for user-guided knowledge discovery in databases, *Information Sciences,* 109, 49-64, 1998.

Cooper, G. F. and Herskovits, E., A Bayesian method for the induction of probabilistic networks from data, *Machine Learning,* 9(4), 309-348, 1994.

Dean, T., Allen, J. and Aloimonos, Y., *Artificial Intelligence: Theory and Practice,* Benjamin/Cummings, Redwood City, CA, 1995.

Dubois, C., Lang, J. and Prade, H., Advances in automated reasoning using possibilistic logic, in Kandel, A. (ed.), *Fuzzy Expert Systems,* CRC Press, Boca Raton, FL, pp. 125-134, 1991.

Durkin, J. *Expert Systems: Design and Development,* Macmillan Publishing Company, New York, 1994.

Elkan, C., The paradoxical success of fuzzy logic, *Proceedings 11th AAAI (AAAI '93),* 698-703, 1993.

Gammerman, A. (ed.), *Computational Learning and Probabilistic Reasoning,* John Wiley, Chichester, UK, 1996.

Giarratano J. and Riley, G., *Expert Systems: Principles and Programming* (3rd ed.), PWS Publisher, Boston, 1998.

Haddawy, P., An overview of some recent developments in Bayesian problem-solving techniques, *AI Magazine,* 20(2), 11-20, 1999.

Heckerman, D., Bayesian networks for data mining, *Data Mining and Knowledge Discovery,* 1, 79-119, 1997.

Kasabov, N. K., *Foundation of Neural Networks, Fuzzy Systems, and Knowledge Engineering,* MIT Press, Cambridge, MA, 1996.

McCarthy, J., Circumscription -- A form of nonmonotonic reasoing, *Artificial Intelligence,* 13, 1980.

Neapolitan, R. E., *Probabilistic Reasoning in Expert Systems: Theory and Algorithms,* Wiley, New York, 1990.

Orchard, R. A., *FuzzyCLIPS Version 6.04A User's Guide,* Integrated Reasoning Institute for Information Technology, National Research Council Canada, 1998.

Pearl, J., *Probabilistic Reasoning in Intelligent System* (2nd printing), Morgan Kaufmann, San Francisco, 1991.

Pedrycz W. and Gomide, F., *An Introduction to Fuzzy Sets,* MIT Press, Cambridge, MA, 1998.

Poole, D., Mackworth, A., and Goebel, R., *Computational Intelligence: A Logical Approach,* Oxford University Press, New York, 1998.

Russell, S. and Norvig, P., *Artificial Intelligence: A Modern Approach,* Prentice Hall, Englewood Cliffs, NJ, 1995.

Schneider, M., Kandel, A. Langholz, G. and Chew, G., *Fuzzy Expert System Tools,* John Wiley, New York, 1996.

Van Le, T., Fuzzy programming in Prolog, *AI Expert,* 31-36, July 1994.

Weiss, M. A., *Data Structures and Algorithm Analysis in C++* (2nd ed.), Benjamin/Cummings, Redwood City, CA, 1998.

Yen, J., Fuzzy logic -- a modern perspective, *IEEE Transactions on Knowledge and Data Engineering,* 11(1), 153-165, 1999.

Chapter 13

REDUCTION AND RECONSTRUCTION APPROACHES FOR UNCERTAIN REASONING AND DATA MINING

13.1 OVERVIEW

Continuing our discussion on uncertain reasoning, in this chapter we provide a brief introduction to several alternative approaches not presented in the last chapter. These methods illustrate the variety involved in uncertain reasoning. This chapter is motivated from the relationship between uncertainty and data mining. We examine two aspects related to uncertainty, namely, the reconstruction-reduction duality. Since this duality is rooted in fuzzy set theory, our discussion will start from a brief review of fuzzy set theory (as presented in Chapter 12) from this perspective. We then present the reduction-reconstruction duality in a more general form. These two approaches are illustrated by K-systems theory and rough set theory. Due to the increasing popularity of rough set theory, we discuss this approach in some detail.

13.2 THE REDUCTION-RECONSTRUCTION DUALITY

13.2.1 REDUCTION AND RECONSTRUCTION ASPECTS IN FUZZY SET THEORY

First, we take a look on the reductive and reconstructive feature of fuzzy set theory itself. On the one hand, linguistic variables and their values as discussed in Chapter 12 clearly indicate how information can be *reduced* by using the concept of fuzziness. For example, persons with different heights can be concisely represented using the same fuzzy membership function "tall." On the other hand, fuzzy set theory is also *reconstructive*, although people usually do not emphasize this. [Zadeh 1997] defined the *type hierarchy of fuzzy sets*. At the bottom of this hierarchy, the elementary type 1 fuzzy subset F of a universe X is defined by giving numeric values for its membership function in the closed interval of real numbers from 0 to 1:

$$\mu_F: X \to [0, 1].$$

For $N > 1$, a type N fuzzy subset is recursively defined by a mapping for μ_F from a universe to the set of fuzzy subsets of type N-1. This kind of hierarchy can be combined with the theory of information granulation as emphasized recently by [Zadeh 1997]. He noticed the hierarchical levels involved in information: object, granule, and attribute. For example, one may notice the following hierarchy:

head → nose + hair + ...
hair → length + color + texture + ...
length → long + short + ...

We have the following comments in regard to these two hierarchies. When these two hierarchies are put together, they provide a constructive power. This is because the fuzziness captured in lower type (starting from the ground level of type 1) can be propagated to higher level in the type hierarchy, and from small granule (i.e., attribute) to higher granule (e.g., object) in the granularity hierarchy. This process can continue forever or stop at any time using any stopping rule or criterion (e.g., as soon as the goal is reached or the user satisfaction is met). Furthermore, if we view this constructive process to reveal the existing uncertainty of a given problem (or system), then in this sense we can say that the fuzzy set approach is reconstructive.

Next, we take a look at reduction and reconstruction in fuzzy expert systems. In the context of rule-based fuzzy expert systems, [Di Nola, Pedrycz and Sessa 1991] noticed that certain antecedents in the rules are difficult to evaluate by the user and/or the reliability of this information is rather low. It is reasonable to reduce the condition space by taking only a few conditions (features) to form a condition subspace. These are the most significant ones considered for an action point of view. Such a procedure of reduction may lead to a slight modification of fuzzy actions, but it is an essential price to pay. The main point, while the most irrelevant conditions are eliminated, is to achieve a certain balance between imposed changes of the action parts and an achieved reasonable size of the condition space. Notice, however, that the fuzzy relation equation of the reasoning scheme should be modified with regard to the original one, where the entire original condition space has been utilized. This problem will be called a *reduction problem* of the knowledge base. Consequently, there is a reconstruction problem which is concerned with an overall picture of how the information coming from the reduced knowledge base can be combined, bearing in mind the influence of different levels of difficulty to get reliable results.

In summary, reduction and reconstruction are a pair of closely related aspects in fuzzy set theory. In the next two subsections, we will take a look at how these aspects are interrelated in different approaches to data mining.

13.2.2 RECONSTRUCTION AND DATA MINING

In order to understand reconstruction-driven approaches to data mining, we should first take a look at a general discussion on reconstruction from a system theoretic perspective. System reconstruction [Klir 1985] refers to the following problem: given a behavior system, viewed as an overall system, determine which sets of its subsystems are adequate for reconstructing the given system with an acceptable degree of approximation, solely from the information contained in the subsystems.

The problem of data mining can be re-examined from a system-theoretic perspective. In fact, the collection of data stored in a database describes a system. The task of system reconstruction and the task of knowledge discovery from databases (which can be viewed as systems) are of course quite different. The relationship between these two seems to be recovery of existing system versus discovery of previously unknown knowledge. However, discovery of something which was unknown does not necessarily mean that thing did not exist before it was discovered. Take a look at the case of archeology. Being the science of reconstructing an ancient society, archeology does not create any thing that is physically new, but breakthroughs made in archeology do bring new knowledge to modern society. Similarly, system reconstruction may reveal important, interesting and previously hidden features of the system. It is thus reasonable for us to hope that reconstruction of the system could be an effective process for the discovery of new knowledge.

System reconstruction and data mining share some common concerns, as well as some techniques utilized, such as statistics and information theory. Significant differences also exist between them. For example, reconstructability analysis requires that subsystems should adequately reconstruct the given system with an acceptable degree of approximation; this requirement is much more rigorous than the criteria used for determining an acceptable result in data mining, where heuristic rules are often deemed as sufficient. The theory developed for system reconstruction may not always be useful to data mining, and some data mining problems may not (or need not) be treated as reconstruction problems. Nevertheless, reconstructability analysis can benefit data mining due to some common interests and common techniques. Since reconstructability analysis is usually more rigorous than data mining, it may help to alleviate some problems faced by the data mining community as mentioned in the beginning of the next section.

13.3 SOME KEY IDEAS OF K-SYSTEMS THEORY AND ROUGH SET THEORY

13.3.1 RECONSTRUCTABILITY ANALYSIS USING K-SYSTEMS THEORY

A direct descendent of the general reconstructability analysis theory is Klir-Systems theory or K-systems theory [Jones 1985,1986], which makes use of information theory to carry out reconstructability analysis of general multivariate data. Although K-systems theory is not very well-known, it employs the very idea of reconstruction to recover the nature of the system using a reduced set of variables with their qualitative values [Chen 1997a, 1997b]. If we visualize the original data set as a huge flat table including attributes as columns and all instances as rows containing concrete data in various domains, an interactive execution of the K-systems analysis will result in sub-tables each consisting of much fewer number of columns and rows. The number of columns is reduced because less important attributes have been removed. The number of rows is reduced because only "typical" tuples remain and also because individual values in the tuples are replaced by intervals of the values representing the quality of data (for example, temperatures falling in -40°C to -200°C will be considered as very low, -20°C to 0°C as low, etc.). As a consequence of this process, the tuples in the original data set have lost their identity; in other words, although each factor can be considered as a representative of a cluster (or a subset) of the original data elements, we do not know (and we do not need to know) which data elements go to which cluster (namely, represented by which factor). Using this way, K-system analysis finds the factors that control and describe the behavior of the data (a factor, also called a substate, is a subset of variables each having its own values), thus reconstructing systems at the factor level. Since an emphasis of K-systems theory is on the interaction of variables, it has the potential of being a powerful tool for data mining.

13.3.2 REDUCTION-DRIVEN APPROACH IN ROUGH SET THEORY

As already indicated earlier, K-systems theory is mainly driven by considerations from system reconstruction: the system is reconstructed by factors representing reduced information. In contrast, the rough set theory approach [Pawlak 1991] is mainly driven by considerations more directly related to reduction. Some key ideas of this approach, as well as the way these ideas are used for data mining (or more generally, for machine learning), are sketched below (following the presentation of [Ziarko 1991]).

Due to its reduction nature, rough set theory sets an emphasis on studying decision tables (which are flat tables containing attributes and decisions as columns and actual data elements as rows). For the rows, the rough set theory employs the notion of indiscernibility class to group similar tuples (rows) together; while for the columns, it employs the notion of indispensable attributes to identify the significance of attributes.

The bottom line of this approach is the analysis of limits of discernibility of a subset of objects belonging to the domain. For any set X, we define its lower approximation (which is a union of X's all *containing* subsets) and upper approximation (which is a union of all subsets in which X is contained. Furthermore, based on these concepts, the dependency of attributes can also be defined. An issue in the analysis of dependencies among attributes is the identification and information-preserving reduction of redundant conditions. The next important concept is the minimal set of attributes: each minimal set can be   perceived as an alternative group of attributes that could be used to replace all available attributes. The main challenge is thus how to select an optimal reduct. In some practical problems, it is often necessary to find the subset of attributes contained in all reducts, if one exits. The attributes contained in all reducts are also contained in the reduct that represents the real cause of a cause-effect relationship. The intersection of all minimal sets is called the core.

When the rough set approach is used in data mining, production rules (of the "if...then" format) can be induced from the reduced set of condition and decision attributes. A unique feature (and a particular strength) of rough set approach is that unlike many other approaches in machine learning, it allows inconsistency and can deal with inconsistency in a very natural way. Roughly speaking, the computation involved in the lower approximation will produce certain rules while the computation involved in the upper approximation will produce possible rules.

13.3.3 K-SYSTEMS THEORY VERSUS ROUGH SET THEORY

The reconstruction-driven approach and the reduction-driven approach as exemplified by K-systems theory and rough set theory have different features, but they also share some common concerns. For example, the factors in K-system analysis play the similar role of reducts as in rough set theory. As a brief summary of our comparison, some features are shown in Table 13.1.

Table 13.1 Comparison of two approaches

Feature	K-systems theory	Rough sets
Key idea used	Reconstruction	Reduction
Sets are constructed By set operations only?	No	Yes
Sets are constructed using Information theory?	Yes	No
Key notions used for Knowledge discovery	Control factors	Reducts/Core

Understanding different features in these approaches are important because they can help us to determine when (i.e., under which conditions) to use which approach. For example, if measures as required in information theory are not available, a reconstructive approach such as K-systems theory may not be appropriate. In some other cases, when constructing equivalence classes are not a natural choice, a reductive approach (such as rough set theory) may not be suitable, and a reconstructive approach can be tried.

Having provided this general picture of the two approaches, in the next two sections, we will take a closer look at each of them.

13.4 ROUGH SETS APPROACH

13.4.1 BASIC IDEA OF ROUGH SETS

The starting point of using rough sets to perform uncertain reasoning is somewhat different from what we have seen in reasoning using probability theory or fuzzy set theory. Both of these two approaches are intended to deal with a certain kind of uncertainty: probability theory deals with randomness while fuzzy set theory deals with vagueness. For rough sets, the uncertainty is due to its own *method* used: Suppose we are interested in set X; instead of investing X itself, we invest its two sets called *approximations* and use these approximations to characterize X. Here an analogy may be helpful. Consider a circle with radius r. We know the area A bounded by this circle can be calculated using the formula $A = \pi r^2$. But at the ancient time, this formula was not known. How to calculate the area? We can use two polygons; one is enclosed in the circle while the other bounds the circle from the outside. Since areas of polygons are much easier to calculate, we can use the area of enclosed polygon A_{in} and the area of the polygon bounded from outside A_{out} to approximate the area in the circle. Apparently we have $A_{in} < A < A_{out}$. Here A_{in} serves as the *lower approximation* of A (since it is smaller than A), while A_{out} serves as the *upper approximation* of A. Of course using approximations would introduce some kind of error (which is a kind of uncertainty), but this uncertainty is compensated by the well-known features of the approximations. In addition, using approximations makes rough set approach very flexible in handling *inconsistent* data. So far we have assumed knowledge bases contain only consistent data (in fact, detecting inconsistency has been used as the basis of resolution proof). Rough sets approach thus has widely broadened the horizon of reasoning under uncertainty.

13.4.2 TERMINOLOGY

We give the following working definitions. Examples for these definitions are provided in 13.2.2, as well as in the remaining part of Section 13.2.

First, we introduce a popular concept: A *decision table* is a flat table containing attributes and decisions as columns, and actual data elements as rows. A decision table consists of several condition attributes, as well as one or more decision variables. An important issue in decision tables is to determine how the condition attributes affect the decision attributes. A relation as discussed in Chapter 4 can be considered as a decision table, but these two concepts are concerned with different aspects of a flat table.

Next, we introduce two important concepts related to reduction, one is related to reduction of rows, and the other one is related to reduction of columns.

- *Indiscernibility class*: Tuples (rows) with certain properties grouped together.
- *Indispensable attribute*: It is a significant attribute.

The next group of definitions are related to the concept of *approximation space* A, which is an ordered pair $A = (U, R)$, where U is the *universe* (a nonempty set), while R an *indiscernibility relation* (which is an equivalence relation) on U. Rough set theory employs the concept of equivalent class to reduce the information. The following definitions are related to this:

- $[x]_R$: for any element of U, the equivalence class of R in which x is contained.
- *Elementary sets* in A: equivalence classes of R.
- *Definable set* in A: any finite union of elementary sets in A.

The following two concepts of rough sets theory have already been introduced before, and here are more formal definitions:

- *Lower approximation* of X in A is the greatest definable set in A that is contained in X: $\underline{R}X = \{x \in U \mid [x]_R \subseteq X\}$.
- *Upper approximation* of X in A is the least definable set in A containing X: $\overline{R}X = \{x \in U \mid [x]_R \cap X \neq \varnothing\}$.

Note that for a set X, it is defined in terms of definable sets in A by using $\underline{R}X$ and $\overline{R}X$. Thus we can decide if x is in X on the basis of a definable set in A rather than on the basis of X; we deal with and $\underline{R}X$ and $\overline{R}X$ instead of X.) From the above definitions, we may define a *rough set* as the family of all subsets of U having the same lower and upper approximations in A.

From the definitions of lower approximation and upper approximation, we can also define the notions of *certainly in*, and *possibly in*: If $x \in U$, then:

$$x \text{ is } certainly \text{ in } X \Leftrightarrow x \in \underline{R}X$$
$$x \text{ is } possibly \text{ in } X \Leftrightarrow x \in \overline{R}X$$

We can also define the following *rough measures of a set:*

Quality of lower approximation of X by P: $\gamma_P(X) = |\underline{P}X| / |U|$

Quality of upper approximation of X by P: $\gamma_P(X) = |\overline{P}X| / |U|$.

Each kind of quality can be considered as a kind of relative frequency.

The following are some important properties of rough sets:

$$\underline{R}X \subseteq X \subseteq \overline{R}X$$
$$\underline{R}U = U = \overline{R}U$$
$$\underline{R}\varnothing = \varnothing = \overline{R}\varnothing$$
$$\underline{R}(X \cup Y) \supseteq \underline{R}(X) \cup \underline{R}(Y)$$
$$\overline{R}(X \cup Y) \supseteq \overline{R}(X) \cup \overline{R}(Y)$$
$$\underline{R}(X \cap Y) \supseteq \underline{R}(X) \cap \underline{R}(Y)$$
$$\overline{R}(X \cap Y) \supseteq \overline{R}(X) \cap \overline{R}(Y)$$
$$\underline{R}(X - Y) \supseteq \underline{R}(X) - \underline{R}(Y)$$
$$\overline{R}(X - Y) \supseteq \overline{R}(X) - \overline{R}(Y)$$

13.4.3 AN EXAMPLE

We use an example to illustrate the basics of rough set approach. Consider the decision table in Table 13.2 where a, b, c are attributes while d is the decision variable.

Table 13.2 A decision table

Row id	a	b	c	d
x1	0	3	0	0
x2	0	4	1	0
x3	0	4	1	0
x4	1	4	1	1
x5	1	4	1	0
x6	2	4	1	1
x7	2	4	1	0
x8	2	5	2	1

Let

$$Q = \{a, b, c, d\}$$
$$P = \{a, b, c\}$$

The tuples in the decision table are labeled as $x_1, x_2, x_3, x_4, x_5, x_6, x_7, x_8$, and we have

$$U = \{x_1, x_2, x_3, x_4, x_5, x_6, x_7, x_8\}$$

Partition induced from equivalence relation P is:

$$P* = \{\{x_1\}, \{x_2, x_3\}, \{x_4, x_5\}, \{x_6, x_7\}, \{x_8\}\}$$

Note that x_2 and x_3 are in the same equivalent class, because they have the same values in all attributes a, b, c.

Now consider $X = \{x_1, x_2, x_3, x_5, x_7\}$.   The lower approximation of X in $A = (U, R)$ is $\underline{R}X = \{x_1, x_2, x_3\}$. One rough measure is $\underline{y}_P(X) = 3/8$.   The upper approximation of X in $A = (U, R)$ is $\overline{R}X = \{x_1, x_2, x_3, x_4, x_5, x_6, x_7\}$. Another rough measure is $\overline{y}_P(X) = 7/8$.

Figure 13.1 explains the meaning of these two approximations. The elements in set X are in **bold face**. The figure indicates that the lower approximation consists of subsets with all their elements in X, while the upper approximation consists of subsets with any elements in X.

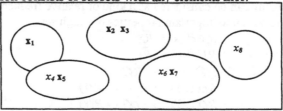

Figure 13.1 A simple example

The rough set is:

$$\{\{x_1, x_2, x_3, x_4, x_6\}, \{x_1, x_2, x_3, x_4, x_7\}, \{x_1, x_2, x_3, x_5, x_6\}, \{x_1, x_2, x_3, x_5, x_7\}\}.$$

We now use a different example to present another way to view a rough set. Consider a 30-element universe $U = \{x_1, \ldots x_{30}\}$ as shown in Figure 13.2.

x_{15} x_{16}	x_{17} x_{18}	x_{19}	x_{20}
x_{21}	x_1 x_2	x_9 x_3 x_4	x_{11} x_{10}
x_{22}	x_5 x_6 x_8	x_7 x_{13}	x_{12} x_{14}
x_{23} x_{24}	x_{25} x_{26} x_{27}	x_{28} x_{29}	x_{30}

Figure 13.2 Another simple example

Suppose each equivalent class in the partition induced from equivalence relation P is depicted as a cell in the figure. For example, $\{x_1, x_2\}$ is an equivalent class, and $\{x_7, x_{13}\}$ is another equivalent class. Now consider $X = \{x_2, x_3, x_4, x_6, x_7, x_{10}, x_{12}, x_{13}, x_{14}\}$. In Figure 13.2, all the elements involved in X are circled in a big oval. The lower approximation of X consists of all $\{x_7, x_{13}\}$ and $\{x_{12}, x_{14}\}$.

13.4.4 RULE INDUCTION USING ROUGH SET APPROACH

We use the following example to illustrate rule induction using rough set approach. Suppose we are given the decision table as shown in Table 13.3.

Table 13.3 A decision table

#	T	D	M	H	I
0	n	a	a	a	a
1	n	a	b	b	a
2	s	a	b	b	b
3	s	b	a	a	a
4	s	b	a	a	b
5	h	a	a	a	a
6	h	b	a	a	a
7	h	b	a	a	b
8	h	b	b	b	b
9	h	b	b	b	b

Partition generated *by decision* (I) is:
$$X - \{\{0, 1, 3, 5, 6\}, \{2, 4, 7, 8, 9\}\}$$
Partition generated *by attributes* is:
$$\{T, D, H, M\} = \{T, D, H\} = \{\{0\}, \{1\}, \{2\}, \{3,4\}, \{5\}, \{6,7\}, \{8,9\}\}$$
The set P of attributes is the *reduct* (or *covering*) of another set Q of attributes if P is minimal and the indiscernibility relations, defined by P and Q are the same. Here the set $\{T, D, H\}$ is a reduct by removing M, which has no effect on the partition.

For $X_1 = \{0, 1, 3, 5, 6\}$:

Since $\{0\} \subseteq X_1$, $\{1\} \subseteq X_1$, $\{5\} \subseteq X_1$, we have $\underline{P}X_1 = \{0\} \cup \{1\} \cup \{5\} = \{0, 1, 5\}$

Since $X_1 \subseteq \{0\} \cup 1\} \cup \{3,4\} \cup \{5\} \cup \{6,7\} = \{0, 1, 3, 4, 5, 6, 7\}$, we have $\overline{P}X_1 = \{0, 1, 3, 4, 5, 6, 7\}$.

For $X_2 = \{2, 4, 7, 8, 9\}$:

Since $\{0\} \subseteq X_2$, $\{8, 9\} \subseteq X_2$, we have $\underline{P}X_2 = \{2\} \cup \{8,9\} = \{2, 8, 9\}$.

Since $X_2 \subseteq \{2\} \cup \{3, 4\} \cup \{6, 7\} \cup \{8,9\} = \{2, 3, 4, 6, 7, 8, 9\}$, we have $\overline{P}X_2 = \{2, 3, 4, 6, 7, 8, 9\}$.

Certain rules from set $\underline{P}X_1 = \{0, 1, 5\}$ are:

$(T = n) \wedge (D = a) \wedge (H = a) \rightarrow I = a$
$(T = n) \wedge (D = b) \wedge (H = a) \rightarrow I = a$
$(T = n) \wedge (D = b) \wedge (H = a) \rightarrow I = a$
$(T = h) \wedge (D = a) \wedge (H = a) \rightarrow I = a$

After simplification, the first two rules become:
$$(T = n) \wedge (H = a) \rightarrow I = a$$
Certain rules after simplification from set $\underline{P}X_2 = \{2, 8, 9\}$ are:
$$(T = n) \wedge (H = b) \rightarrow I = b$$
Possible rules after simplification from $\overline{P}X_1 = \{0, 1, 3, 4, 5, 6, 7\}$ are:
$$T = n \; \rightarrow \; I = a$$
$$H = a \; \rightarrow \; I = a$$
Possible rules after simplification from $\overline{P}X_2 = \{2, 3, 4, 5, 6, 7, 8, 9\}$ are:
$$T = s \rightarrow \; I = b$$
$$D = b \; \rightarrow \; I = b$$

13.4.5 APPLICATIONS OF ROUGH SETS

We consider the case of generating multiple knowledge bases using reducts and decision matrix. We use this example to illustrate the unique way rough sets theory can contribute to knowledge discovery, particularly its strength of dealing with inconsistency -- an ability which is usually lacking in many approaches (including logic-based approaches). Technical details can be found in the reference [Lin and Cercone 1997]. Adding a novice is probably counterproductive and adding an expert whose knowledge is too similar to some other members only gives more importance to the previous expert. The multiple knowledge bases concept matches the concept of reducts in rough set theory. One reduct table can be obtained from a knowledge representation system by removing those attributes witch are not in the reduct without losing any essential information, thus simplifying the knowledge representation scheme. Using different reducts of the knowledge, we can derive different knowledge bases, thus forming multiple knowledge bases. The need for multiple knowledge bases is well-justified. For example, a patient may want to consider the second opinion from physicians about her health problem.

The skeleton of the main algorithm of generating multiple knowledge bases can be stated as follows.
1. Remove superfluous attributes from the decision table;
2. Compute the minimal decision rules through decision matrices;
3. Compute a set of reducts which cover all the indispensable attributes in the decision table (see below);
4. Group the minimal decision rules to the corresponding reducts to form a multiple knowledge base.

The algorithm for computing multiple reducts can be stated as follows. It starts with the core attribute (CO). The core is defined as the intersection of all reducts and can be computed from the discernibility matrix (which is similar to the decision matrix with certain details removed). The core attributes are those entries in the discernibility matrix which have only one attribute.

13.5 K-SYSTEMS THEORY

In Section 13.3 we briefly introduced K-systems theory as a tool for reconstructability analysis. In this section we provide some more detail of this approach.

We now take a look at the methodological implication of the K-systems theory. One interesting aspect we can point out is related to the way of discretizing data. We will not compare different discretization methods here; rather, we want to point out the underlying thought used to discretize data, and surprisingly, there is a striking similarity between K-systems theory and Lebesgue integral.

In the realm of system reconstruction, Klir-systems theory or K-system theory [Jones 1985, 1986] makes use of information theory to carry out reconstructability analysis of general multivariate data. It finds the factors that control and describe the behavior of the data, thus reconstructing systems at the factor level. (A factor, also called a substate, is a subset of variables each having its own values.) Since an emphasis of K-systems theory is on the interaction of variables, it has the potential of being a powerful tool for data mining.

Consider the variable Y and other variables x_1, x_2, ..., x_n which are associated through the parameter t

$$Y = y(t),$$
$$x_1 = x_1 (t),$$

$$x_n = x_n(t).$$

Observational data have been collected to form the data set to be used for data mining. The system function Y will be referred to as a variable dependent on x_1, x_2, ..., x_n, but this kind of dependency does not necessarily imply causal relationship. Another note to be made here is that we do not assume all x_i's ($i = 1, 2, ..., n$) are independent to each other.

In the problem presented above, the user's intention is to find the relationship between Y and one or more x_i' s, rather than the interaction among x_i s. K-systems theory is suitable for goal-driven data mining because of its flexibility in dealing with interaction of data. The concept of goal-driven can be realized through *Lebesgue discretization* as described below (for a more detailed discussion, see [Chen 1994]). For the function $Y = y(t)$ as defined above, instead of discretizing t into subsections, we discretize Y into subsections. All x_i' s are also dissected according to the intervals of t determined by Lebesgue discretization on Y. An intuitive explanation of performing discretization in this manner is that, starting from the values of the dependent variable (which is similar to the decision attribute in the rough set approach), we look for explanations of these values in terms of other variables (namely, condition variables). K-systems theory can then be applied to analyze the relationship between subsections of y values with corresponding values of x_i' s. Note that the name of Lebesgue discretization is from Lebesgue integral, where a similar discretization technique was used. Therefore, the concept of Lebesgue discretization is another example indicating the benefit of cross-domain analysis. We are interested in mining the knowledge about intrinsic relationships between variables implied from the data rather than the quantitative information itself. A natural way of representing intrinsic relationships of data is providing explanation by associating the quality (instead of the quantity) of the dependent variable and the quality (instead of the quantity) of other variables. This consideration has led to the concept of qualitative production rules. In other words, we apply the idea of qualitative reasoning as discussed in artificial intelligence. The basic idea is to convert continuous data into discrete data (e.g., through clustering) so that qualitative rules can be constructed.

The main steps involved in applying K-systems theory can be found in [Chen 1994]. Briefly, the algorithm starts with some initial variable combinations chosen by using some domain-specific heuristics. K-systems analysis is then carried out and is used to refine the variable combination.

A case study of using K-systems analysis was also reported and analyzed in [Chen 1994]. The task of that study was to examine the relationship between the catch number (the dependent variable or system function) for brown shrimp and various environmental variables. Values for more than 20 variables were collected with time (which is treated as parameter t); the purpose of the study was to find how the most influential environment variables affect the value of catch (the system function). Three variables have been determined for retention: lunar, level, and rain. The controlling factors that capture the most important features of the system indicate the importance of qualities of each variable. Two clusters sufficiently captured the information contained in variable rain while both lunar and level required three clusters; overall, there are $3 * 3 * 2 = 18$ factors representing the quality of variable combinations. Applying K-systems analysis is able to provide results whose meaning is equivalent to the following heuristic rules:

> If lunar = High and rain = Low and level = High
> then Predicted catch = rank-2 (the second highest catch).
> If lunar = Middle and rain = Low and level = Low
> then Predicted catch = rank-18 (the lowest catch).

We have discussed the relationship between reconstructability analysis and data mining. From an epistemological perspective, a common base for both data mining and reconstructability analysis is the role of induction. [Klir 1989] discussed inductive modeling in system science. He also felt that one of his contributions to inductive modeling is the set of procedures he developed for the reconstruction problem (including the discovery of the "reconstruction principle of novelty production").

A good understanding on the nature of uncertainty will benefit the development of decision support systems. For this purpose, we take a unique perspective by examining the relationship between uncertainty and data mining. We study the dual features in dealing with uncertainty, namely, reconstruction and reduction. Furthermore, the reconstruction-driven approach for data mining is illustrated by K-systems theory, and the reduction-driven approach is illustrated by rough set theory. Some differences between these two approaches are addressed, and their implication on applications is also briefly discussed.

In other words, the study of uncertainty can be viewed as a study of discovering hidden "true" systems. The study of data mining will thus enhance our understanding of uncertainty, which in turn will benefit the development of decision support systems.

SUMMARY

Uncertainty in knowledge-based systems can be studied at different levels:
- at the level of domain knowledge,
- at the level of control knowledge,
- at the level of control knowledge combined with user-system interaction, as well as
- other levels.

In this chapter we mainly address uncertainty at the level of domain knowledge. Started with the recent progress in data mining, we have examined some basic issues related to the nature of uncertainty. This discussion will benefit the construction of decision support systems. In particular, we have made our contributions in the following two issues:
- A new way of studying uncertainty. The starting point is that the task of data mining in a system and the task of dealing with uncertainty of the system, in a large degree, can be viewed as two sides of the same coin; therefore, studying one of these two issues should benefit the other.
- The duality of reconstruction and reduction approaches in uncertainty as exemplified by K-systems theory and rough set theory. In addition to connection between uncertainty and data mining, two approaches in dealing with uncertainty can be distinguished. Fuzzy set theory takes a reconstruction approach, while the more recent rough set theory takes a reduction approach. We also connect reconstruction approach with the reconstruction analysis of system theory, pointing out how k-systems theory can contribute to both the study of uncertainty and data mining.

To summarize our discussion in Chapters 12 and 13, we notice there is a close relationship between uncertain reasoning on the one hand, and machine learning/data mining on the other. Therefore, studying uncertain reasoning techniques not only gives us a chance of learning useful techniques for decision making, but also encourages an integrated way of thinking. A more systematic discussion on integrated problem solving and decision making is to be presented in the next chapter.

SELF-EXAMINATION QUESTIONS

1. Consider the set of data shown in Table 13.4. Perform a conventional discretization (namely, discretize independent variable X) using interval size = 10 (namely, from 1 to 10, then 11 to 20, etc.) Then perform a Lebesgue discretization also with interval size = 10. You may then change the size of the interval. What is your observation? What kind of knowledge pattern can be "discovered?" Compare Lebesgue discretization and regular discretization in this discovery process. (You may plot the data first.)

Table 13.4 Data set for discretization

X	Y
1	63
5	43
12	33
17	61
24	28
25	57
33	55
38	27
41	42
48	28

2. Suppose all values in Table 13.2 are increased by 10.
   (a) If we apply the rough set approach as described in Section 13.4.3, will the participation obtained there be changed? Why or why not?
   (b) Find certain rules and possible rules from Table 13.2 (after the revision indicated in part a).

REFERENCES

Chen, Z., Qualitative reasoning for system reconstruction using Lebesgue discretization, *International Journal of System Sciences*, 25(12), 2329-2337, 1994.

Chen, Z., Understanding uncertainty through data mining: reconstruction versus reduction, *Proceedings of 5th European Congress on Intelligent Techniques and Soft Computing (EUFIT '97)*, pp. 1611-1615, 1997a.

Chen, Z., K-systems theory for goal-driven data mining, *Advances in Systems Science and Applications*, 40-43, Special issue, 1997b.

Di Nola, A., Pedrycz, W. and Sessa, S., Reduction procedures for rule-based expert systems as a tool for studies of properties of expert's knowledge, Chap. 5 in Kandel, A. (ed.), *Fuzzy Expert Systems*, pp. 69-79, 1991.

Jones, B. Reconstructability considerations with arbitrary data, *Int. J. General Sys*, 11, 143-151, 1985.

Jones, B. K-systems versus classical multivariate systems. *Int. J. General Sys.*, 12, 1-6, 1986.

Klir, G., *Architecture of General Systems Problem Solving*, Plenum, New York, 1985.

Klir, G., System profile: The emergence of systems science, *Systems Research*, 5(2), 145-156, 1989.

Lin, T. Y. and Cercone, N. (eds.), *Rough Sets and Data Mining: analysis for Imprecise Data*, Kluwer, Boston, MA, 1997.

Pawlak, Z. *Rough Sets*, Kluwer, Dordrecht, 1991.

Piatetsky-Shapiro, G. and Frawley, W. (eds.), *Knowledge Discovery in Databases*. AAAI/MIT Press, Menlo Park, CA, 1991.

Zadeh, L., Fuzzy sets. in Belzer, J. (ed.), *Encyclopedia of Computer Science and Technology*, Marcel Dekker, New York, 1977.

Zadeh, L., Invited talk given in the Second IIGSS Workshop, San Marcos, TX, Jan. 10, 1997.

Ziarko, W., The discovery, analysis, and representation of data dependencies in databases. Chap. 11 in Piatetsky-Shapiro, G. and Frawley, W. (eds.) *Knowledge Discovery in Databases*. AAAI/MIT Press, Menlo Park, CA, pp. 195-209, 1991.

Chapter 14

TOWARD INTEGRATED HEURISTIC DECISION MAKING

14.1 OVERVIEW

In this book we have discussed various computational intelligence methods for decision making. It is important to keep in mind that intelligent agents should use these methods in an integrated manner. In this last chapter, we summarize the whole book from two perspectives. In Sections 14.2 and 14.3, we summarize materials presented in this book, with emphasis on integration. A discussion of these issues provides a cross-domain analysis of various technical methods; here the term *cross-domain analysis* refers to analyze two or more knowledge domains to find some commonality among these domains. In Section 14.4 we discuss integrated problem solving techniques by examining several "meta" issues in decision support. The actual meaning of the prefix "meta" varies in different contexts, but in general "meta-X" refers to "X about X" (for example, a meta-rule refers to a rule about rules). Therefore, meta-X, as the second order of X, implies some kind of control over the use of X. This kind of control knowledge provides the power of an effective use of the underlying knowledge.

14.2 INTEGRATED PROBLEM SOLVING

As indicated in the Preface and Chapter 1, this book is aimed to present some of the most important techniques of computational intelligence which are useful for decision support. Materials are selected to be representative in this field. Rather than a miscellaneous collection of a "technique show," materials are presented in a manner to foster an integrated way of scientific thinking. Users are reminded to compare these techniques as well as different perspectives behind these techniques. To understand where these approaches are from is important to reveal some important common features behind scientific thinking. Although it is difficult to predict where future techniques will go, an in-depth study of existing techniques will help readers be prepared to deal with technical challenges to be encountered in the future. Some techniques may fade away (or absorbed into newer techniques), but many key ideas will still last. It is thus important to understand the underlying philosophy.

This last chapter (Chapter 14) complements earlier chapters in that it provides a "cross-domain" study of some specific features of computational intelligence that are important to decision support. The emphasis here is *integration* in the problem solving process. Note that we do not intend to provide a philosophical discussion nor a complete overview of this topic; the reader is encouraged to apply (or revise, or criticize) what is discussed below to analyze his or her own problems. Also be cautious: we use the term "integration" in a positive feeling. Integration is distinguished from simple combination, which is not always good (because different methods may conflict each other).

As for integration of problem solving, there are several levels of the integration itself:

- *Integrated tools:* Here integration is taken care by the commercial tools themselves. This level of integration is convenient for the users, but it offers little flexibility and controllability to the users. This kind of integration is important, but is not the focus of this book.

- *Integrated use of existing methods:* Here the methods have been developed, but the task of integration is left to the user. So a user may have a combined use of, say, probability theory and rough set theory, so long as these techniques are appropriate for the problem solving. For example, the first stage of the problem solving can be carried by incorporating probability theory, while the result is further processed using rough set theory to identify useful rules.

- *Integrated thinking:* This is the most advanced level of integration, and is the most important idea deserving endorsement. *Integrated thinking* refers to an ability of problem solving guided by appropriate heuristics to employ existing techniques or to develop new methods. Integrated thinking thus requires a good understanding of existing techniques, but does not stop there. [Bienkowski 1998] characterized an agent as "rethink thinking: autonomy, environmental interaction, and reaction." Integrated thinking is the most important aspect of this rethinking.

Below we summarize the relationship of some major categories of techniques presented in this book, which is depicted in Figure 14.1. The figure is produced following the criteria given in [Raeth 1998]: perfect knowledge, accurate results, using algorithms or heuristics, and well-structured problems. Overall, these criteria characterize how adaptive a technique is for decision support. At the low end of this spectrum are numerical methods (we do not count rounding errors), as well as data and information retrieval techniques. Expert systems signal a main departure from these traditional methods, and reasoning using probability theory or fuzzy logic has further enhanced the adaptive problem solving ability. Closely related to fuzzy logic are neural networks, which have promoted unstructured problem solving abilities. Finally, at the high end of this spectrum are evolutionary programming, with genetic algorithms as a major sub-category. (Note that in Figure 14.1 we do not treat symbolic reasoning or any specific knowledge representation scheme as categories, because they are viewed as primitive methods underlying many techniques.) An integrated use of these methods (along with other methods not shown here due to space limitations in the figure, such as rough sets and K-

Systems theory, as well as new methods to be developed in the future) would be the key to successful decision making processes.

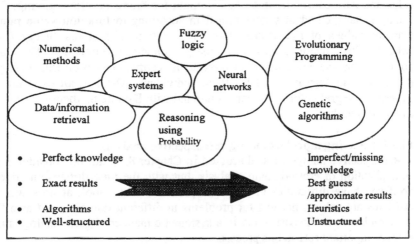

Figure 14.1 Adaptive automation spectrum

14.3 HIGH LEVEL HEURISTICS FOR PROBLEM SOLVING AND DECISION SUPPORT

14.3.1 A RETURN TO GENERAL PROBLEM SOLVER

An intelligent agent needs well-organized knowledge for problem solving and decision making. How to organize the thoughts? There is a need to find the invariant (namely, shared features) which can be used to serve as high level heuristics, a tradition started from G. Polya's *How to Solve It* [Polya 1957]. This means that we are returning to the general problem solver (as discussed in Chapter 3), but at a much higher level: They are not aimed to solve any individual problems, but do shed some light in problem solving methodology in general. In the remaining part of this section, we will discuss some of the heuristics while reviewing the materials presented earlier. Note that the heuristics discussed here are just for illustration purpose only.

14.3.2 SOME HIGH LEVEL HEURISTICS

14.3.2.1 Solving problems by analogical reasoning

In Chapters 7 and 8 we have discussed analogical reasoning. The reason we review it here is because of its close relationship with cross-domain analysis. In fact, frequently analogs can be acquired by performing a cross-domain analysis. In fact, analogical reasoning may be more pervasive than we realized. Chances are that we may have applied some analogy without noticing it. Situations also exist when analogical reasoning was not part of the original problem solving process but was developed later. This may sound weird, but an "after-thought" analogical thinking may have some pedagogical value and may contribute important thought for future problem solving. For example, the method of segmenting data according to function value rather than the values of independent variables used in K-systems theory (i.e., Lebesgue discretization) resembles Lebesgue integral (Chapter 13). This does not imply that the development of K-systems theory is based on this analogy. Rather, this analogy is useful for those individuals who had an exposure of Lebesgue integral before they got acquainted with K-systems theory (as in the case of this author).

14.3.2.2 Solving a problem using retrospective analysis

Retrospective analysis was discussed in Chapter 8. It can be considered as an application of cross-domain analysis, but with the *time* dimension added. So if you have difficulties in solving a problem, take a look at how similar problems are solved, not just for problems in different domains, but also for those problems in the past -- and in a systematic manner. Again, analogy may play an important role in this process.

14.3.2.3 Cartesian product

In a loose sense, Cartesian product approach for problem solving is just to combine appropriate elements of problem solving to form one solution. For example, in recent studies of association rules, [Kuok, Fu and Wong 1998] discussed mining fuzzy association rules in databases, which is an example of incorporating fuzzy set theory into data mining. Cartesian products can be used in a wider sense, however. In most cases of problem solving, the problem itself is given (although may not be defined accurately). From time to time, however, there may be some need to identify the problem itself. There are many advantages of identifying a problem beforehand rather than waiting it to happen. One way to "generate" a problem is to perform a Cartesian product, which could be done based on a retrospective analysis. An analysis of practical needs of course may help to identify problems, but sometimes future needs can also be identified by examining the functionality of the system. For example, research problems in expert systems can be studied by enhancing the functionality of individual components, or consider the interconnections among these components [Chen 1992b].

14.3.2.4 Solving a problem directly using perturbation

Perturbation is a notion studied in natural science, particularly physics. Roughly speaking, perturbation in problem solving refers to solving a problem around a standard. The difference between the current situation and the standard will be used to modify the solution. The basic idea of problem solving using fuzzy set theory can be explained using perturbation. Consider the example used in Chapter 12: "If visibility is poor then driving speed is slow." The evaluation of this rule is around the standard of "poor," and the degree of slow is determined by how far the actual degree of "poor" perturbs away from the standard "poor." Fuzzy logic is of course not the only example of using perturbation. For example, we may consider the issue of user modeling (as briefly discussed in Chapter 6). One interesting concept is perturbation model. In a *perturbation model*, the user model is assumed to be similar to the domain model, differing only in certain perturbations to the domain model. Such a theory may be useful in enhancing system adaptability [Kass and Finin 1989].

14.3.2.5 Solving a problem indirectly by using approximation

In case a problem is not easy to solve, it can be converted to some other forms. Sometimes we would like to use some known features of a solved problem in the same knowledge domain to deal with a new problem. This means we can solve a problem indirectly by using approximation. Note that approximation may take different forms. For example, it could be done through reduction as in the case of the rough set approach. Alternatively, the concept of a universal approximizer could be useful.

14.3.2.6 Using abstraction as problem solving infrastructure

Abstraction may be used as an effective vehicle for problem solving. Abstraction already plays an important role in some heuristics studied so far (such as in analogical reasoning, although there are different opinions on the exact role of abstraction in the process of analogical reasoning). Various aspects in computational intelligence for decision making, such as modeling, also rely on abstraction. In addition, abstraction is used in Hierarchical problem solving, where two worlds (a macro one and a micro one) work at different levels. This is sometimes referred to as *Brownian phenonmenon:* The macro level phenomenon may be the cumulative result of numerous underlying hidden processes. From this discussion has also outgrown the concept of *continuous* computational intelligence, where a conjecture is made which views intelligence as a continuous spectrum evolving from biological or mental levels [Chen 1993b, 1996c].

14.3.2.7 Inverse problems

In Chapter 8, when we examined useful heuristics in technical invention, we discussed *inverse operators*. In addition, some data structures can be constructed by incorporation of inverse; for example, an *inverse graph* can be constructed by having the direction of arcs in a graph reversed [Weiss 1998; Poole, Mackworth and Goebel 1998]. However, the importance of inverse goes far beyond individual operators or data structures. In fact, in many cases, we need to consider *inverse problems:* In many situations, if we examine a problem from an opposite direction, we may encounter a seemingly brand new problem. Solving this new problem may not necessarily provide a straightforward solution of the original problem. However, with the better insight of the background information (which is shared by the original problem and the inverse problem) revealed by the study of the inverse problem, we may be able to handle the original problem in a better way. In the following, we briefly examine two inverse problems related to data warehouses.

First, let use recall that a data warehouse stores consolidated data (usually materialized views with possible local relations). In order to build a data warehouse, we need to load and refresh data from various data sources. The *view data lineage problem* in a warehousing environment can be considered as an inverse of this loading/refreshing process. Rather than using known data sources to build a data warehouse, for a given data item in a materialized warehouse view, we want to identify the set of source data items that produced the view item. [Cui, Widom and Wiener 1997] studied this problem and developed a tool which allows analysts to browse warehouse data, select view tuples of interest, then "drill-down" to examine the source data that produced them.

As another example of inverse problem, [Faloutsos, Jagadish and Sidiropoulos 1997] studied how to estimate the original detail data from the stored summary. This task has been formulated as an inverse problem of summary data computation, and a well-defined cost function to be optimized under constraints has been specified. The rationale of this study is that the data are summarized over discrete ranges to create a database of manageable size for storage, manipulation, and display. Often, there is a need to respond to queries that can be answered accurately only from the base data, but that must be answered quickly from the summarized data. The task is then to reconstruct as good an estimate of the original base data as possible. The idea of an application in data warehousing is that the central site will have meta-data and condensed information (e.g., summary data) from each participating site which has detailed information. Accessing the remote site might be slow and/or expensive; therefore, a cheap, accurate estimate of the missing information is thus very attractive.

14.3.2.8 Storage versus recomputation

In many cases, the resources (such as time or memory storage) available to the problem solving process may present a significant factor of restriction. By emphasizing different restrictions, a problem may be solved in very different fashions. Unlike many other heuristics discussed so far, these restrictions do not serve as part of the solutions. Nevertheless, they are an indispensable part of the problem solving process. In the following we examine several examples.

- *Iterative deepening DFS versus dynamic programming:* In Chapter 2 we examined depth first search (DFS). Although DFS has some merits of space efficiency, it suffers from problems such as failing to find an optimal solution. Iterative deepening DFS (IDDFS) combines the space efficiency of DFS with the optimality of breadth-first search. The idea is to recompute the elements of the visited nodes rather than storing them. Each recomputation is conducted in DFS, thus saving space. IDDFS can be compared with *dynamic programming*, another improvement of DFS, in their different ways of dealing with the two different resources (time and storage). One intuition behind dynamic programming is to construct the "perfect" heuristic function so that heuristic depth-first search is guaranteed to find a solution without ever backtracking. The heuristic function constructed represents the exact costs of a minimal cost path from each node to the goal [Poole, Mackworth and Goebel 1998]. This is achieved by storing intermediate result calculated from a recursion into a table.

- *Eager learning versus lazy learning:* Another interesting area demonstrating the tradeoff between time and space is concerned with different strategies of machine learning. In Chapter 10 we have already discussed several different learning algorithms. Recent progress on lazy learning (and its comparison with eager learning) illustrates another dimension of categorization of machine learning algorithms. Eager learning algorithms greedily compile their inputs into an intensional concept description (such as a rule set, a decision tree, a neural network, etc.), and in this process discard the inputs. They reply to information requests using this a priori induced description, and retain it for future requests. In contrast, lazy learning algorithms simply store their inputs for future use, and thus defer processing of their inputs until they receive requests for information. Lazy learning algorithms reply to information requests by combining their stored data (such as data used for training). These algorithms also discard the constructed answer and any intermediate results. This eager/lazy distinction exhibits many interesting tradeoffs. For example, lazy algorithms typically have greater storage requirements and often have higher computational costs when answering requests, but what have gained are the lower computational costs than eager algorithms during training [Aha 1997].
- *Materialized views versus conventional (namely, virtual) views:* The comparison between them has been discussed in Chapter 11, and will not be repeated at here.

14.3.2.9 Step-wise refinement and manipulation of changes

In addition to what we described above, more conventional problem solving wisdom also plays important roles in integrated decision making, even they are less dramatical or exciting than heuristics studied above. For example, step-wise refinement helps solving problems in a step-by-step manner. Another example is solving problem by manipulating changes: For the same problem to be solved, if some parameters or variables have changed their values, instead of recomputing a new solution, we revise the old solution by reflecting the effect of these changes. The problem can thus be solved in a more efficient manner. For example, RETE algorithm developed in production systems model reflects this philosophy (Chapter 5). Another example is the semi-naïve method in deductive query evaluation (Chapter 4). Yet another example is incremental view maintenance (Chapter 4 and Chapter 11), which has made materialized views more manageable. However, we should note that the power of problem solving by manipulating changes may be somewhat limited, as shown in the case of semi-naïve method of deductive query evaluation, and that is why a more radical approach using magic sets was proposed (Chapter 4).

14.3.3 SUMMARY OF HEURISTICS

In summary, heuristics presented in this section suggest we find common features behind various problem solving methods, thus resembling considerations of *science of science* [Price 1963; Chen 1970, 1993a], or *Meta science*. In the next section, we will take a more systematic look at some important meta issues.

14.4   META-ISSUES FOR DECISION MAKING

In this section we examine several issues associated with the prefix "meta," including the use of meta-data and meta-knowledge for meta-reasoning. In general, this examination allows us a deeper understanding of subject materials, because although the exact meaning of "meta" varies, the discussed issues are all concerned with better control by taking advantage of broader knowledge.

14.4.1 META-ISSUES IN DATABASES AND DATA WAREHOUSES

14.4.1.1 Meta-data

We start our discussion of meta-issues in logical data modeling. In a database management system, the result of the compilation of the Data Definition Language (DDL) is a set of tables stored in special files collectively called *the system catalog* (Also called *data dictionary,* although the latter term usually refers to a more general software system). An important feature of the system catalog is that it integrates the *meta-data,* which are data about data, or the data describing objects in the database, and facilitating database access and manipulation. Meta-data play an important role in data warehouse integration. The major purpose of meta-data in a data warehouse (usually by employing a *repository*) is to show the pathway back to where the data began, so that the warehouse administrators know the history of any item in the warehouse. Meta-data have several functions with the data warehouse that relate to the processes associated with data transformation and loading, date warehouse management and query generation [Connolly, Begg and Strachan 1998].

14.4.1.2 Meta-databases

Note that meta-data as discussed above are used for guiding the access and manipulation of the database which usually stores the original (namely, non-meta) data. From meta-data we can further discuss *meta-databases,* whose contents themselves are meta-data. *Multilevel databases* are a good example of meta-databases. At the higher level(s) meta-data or generalizations are extracted from lower levels and organized in structured collections such as relational or object-oriented databases. For example, [Zaiane and Han 1995] uses a multi-layered database where each layer is obtained via generalization and transformation operations performed on the lower layers. [Khosla Kuhn and Soparkar 1996] proposes the creation and maintenance of meta-databases at each information providing domain and the use of a global schema for the meta-database. [King and Novak 1996] proposes the incremental integration of a portion of the schema from each information source, rather than relying on a global heterogeneous database schema.

14.4.1.3 Meta-searching in the Internet

Another aspect which shows the power of using meta-knowledge is meta-search on the Internet. We described the basic search architecture in Chapter 5. The complexity of Web search demands more effective Web search methods, and several approaches have been developed. In particular, [Gravano and Papakonstantinou 1998] compared meta-searching versus mediating on the Internet. Internet users can benefit from *mediators* and *meta-searchers* which provide users with a virtual integrated view of heterogeneous sources. They have shared goals and architecture. In both cases, wrappers export a common data model view of each source's data. Wrappers also provide a common query interface. After receiving a query, a wrapper translates it into a source-specific query or command, hence giving interface transparency to the user. The wrapper then translates the query results from the underlying source into the common data model or format. To evaluate a user query over multiple heterogeneous databases, both mediators and meta-searchers will typically perform three main tasks:

- *Database selection*: Choose the databases that have data relevant to the user query.
- *Query translation*: Find the query fragment to be evaluated at each of the databases chosen in the previous step, translate these fragments so that they can be executed at their corresponding databases, and retrieve the query results from the databases.
- *Result merging*: Combine the query results from the above databases into the final query answer.

Nevertheless, the focus of the research on meta-searchers has been quite different from that of the research on mediators. The following two key issues illustrate this difference, and indicate the strength of the meta-approach.

- *View complexity:* Mediators usually integrate multiple relations or objects with *complementary* information. Therefore, fusion of objects from several databases is not uncommon when defining mediator views. The higher complexity the mediator view requires, the more powerful view definition languages are needed, along with more powerful languages to query the integrated view. In contrast, meta-searchers typically operate on the top of document databases, and the view that meta-searchers export to users is generally some kind of *union* of the underlying databases.

- *Query matches and result completeness*: The interaction of a user with a mediator is very similar to the interaction of a user with a relational database system. In this process, the user sends a query and the mediator typically returns the complete answer to the query. In effect, mediators generally operate over databases where query results are well-defined sets of objects, as in the relational model discussed in Chapter 4. In contrast, meta-searchers usually deal with collections of unstructured text documents that return document ranks as the answer to a query, where the ranks are computed using undisclosed algorithms. Inexact matches are used between queries and documents, as in the vector-space model of information retrieval (IR) described in Chapter 5. Furthermore, these sources might return only the best matches for the query. Hence, meta-searchers have to handle query results that have been computed using unknown matching algorithms. Meta-searchers also are aware that partial answers to queries are usually acceptable on the Internet, thus abandoning the goal of producing complete answers. Therefore, meta-searchers are a natural blend of traditional database search and IR search engines.

Meta-search engines reduce the user burden by dispatching queries to multiple search engines in parallel and introduced a kind of adaptability into the search mechanism. As a concrete example of metasearch research, we can mention the SavvySearch meta-search engine [Howe and Dreilinger 1998], which is designed to efficiently query other search engines by carefully selecting those search engines likely to return useful results and responding to fluctuating load demands on the web. SavvySearch learns to identify which search engines are most appropriate for particular queries, reasons about resource demands, and represents an iterative parallel search strategy as a simple plan.

14.4.2 META-KNOWLEDGE AND META-REASONING

14.4.2.1 General remarks

In Chapter 3 we discussed logical properties of knowledge and belief. In fact, the *process* of inference can be formalized. This is an example of reasoning about reasoning, or *meta-reasoning*, and is discussed in the context of *modal logic* [Genesereth and Nilsson 1986]. At a more practical side, various aspects related to *meta-knowledge* (namely, knowledge about knowledge) in computational intelligence is discussed in [Chen 1993]. A particular form of meta-knowledge is a meta-rule, which provides some guide in using domain-specific rules. An example of constructing meta-rules is fuzzy meta-rules in genetic computing [Pedrycz 1996], which combines fuzzy set theory, genetic algorithms, and abstraction. The reason is that there is a need for some additional adjustment and tuning of parameters to perform genetic efficiency in a given environment. In order to determine parameters such as mutation rate or crossover rate, simply relying on experiments is not sufficient. Rule bases have been developed to contain rules describing the selection of suitable crossover and mutation rates.

In the following we take a look at two specific issues related to meta-reasoning in knowledge-based systems: meta-level reasoning for flexible inference control using fuzzy logic and combining creativity and expertise using a meta-level interpreter.

14.4.2.2 Meta-level reasoning for flexible inference control using fuzzy logic

In Chapter 6 we discussed the issue of flexible inference control in knowledge-based systems. In this chapter we take a closer look at a specific issue of flexible inference control, namely, inference control using meta-level reasoning. The history of using meta-knowledge for flexible inference control can be traced back to early expert systems such as Meta-DENDRAL and TEIRESIAS. Strategies were viewed as a means of controlling invocation in situations where traditional selection mechanisms become ineffective.

In order to understand the role of meta-knowledge in flexible inference control, we note that the terms "domain knowledge" and "control knowledge" are often used to distinguish *what* a system knows from *how* the system uses what it knows. One problem with this terminology is that it suggests that control knowledge is domain independent. However, in real-world applications, control knowledge can be either domain dependent or domain independent, depending on whether it refers to the contents of particular elements of domain knowledge. For example, the meta-knowledge "use rules that mention cheap blood tests before rules that mention expensive blood tests" is domain-dependent, while the meta-knowledge "use cheap rules before expensive rules" is not, because it only refers to the general form of the domain knowledge, without referring to its domain-specific contents.

In Chapter 5 we discussed the architecture of expert systems and in Chapter 12 we discussed fuzzy expert systems, with fuzzy controllers as an example. Note that a fuzzy controller uses fuzzy rules to control behavior, but the inference engine itself is not fuzzified. Below we describe an extended expert system architecture which incorporates a *flexible fuzzy inference controller* where the inference engine can demonstrate flexible behavior. Fuzzy inference control is achieved using meta-rules.

The discussion on the need for flexible inference control and the employment of meta-level reasoning to realizing flexible inference control can be traced back to early expert systems such as Meta-DENDRAL and TEIRESIAS (the preprocessor of MYCIN). Strategies were viewed as a means of controlling invocation in situations where traditional selection mechanisms become ineffective. Several ways of effecting such control were discussed; in particular, meta-rules were used as a means of specifying strategies which offer a number of advantages.

It is important to note that terms "domain knowledge" and "control knowledge" are often used to distinguish *what* a system knows from *how* the system uses what it knows. One problem with this terminology is that it suggests that control knowledge is domain independent. However, control knowledge can be either domain dependent or domain independent, depending on whether it refers to the contents of particular elements of domain knowledge, as in "use rules that mention cheap blood-tests before rules that mention expensive blood-tests," or whether it only refers to the general form of the domain knowledge, without referring to its domain-specific contents, as in "use cheap rules before expensive rules".

Meta-level reasoning thus plays an important role between the domain knowledge in the knowledge base and the control knowledge used by the inference engine. If reasoning is fuzzy in nature, then the inference procedure itself should be fuzzified. The fuzziness of inference can be achieved by using meta-level reasoning in an extended expert system model as depicted in Figure 14.2.

Meta rules can be used in the following ways.

(1) Instead of attaching a single number to indicate the priority of a rule, each rule in the domain knowledge base is associated with a *fuzzy priority vector with k factors* (namely, a *k*-dimensional vector) to indicate *k* different ways of firing rules (so that flexible inference control can be realized).

(2) Meta reasoning is achieved through meta-rules fired by the inference engine. Meta-rules are stored in the flexible inference controller; they provide instructions on how to activate the rules stored in the domain knowledge base. Each meta-rule takes the following format:

> if condition
>> then fire rules in knowledge domain with certain features.

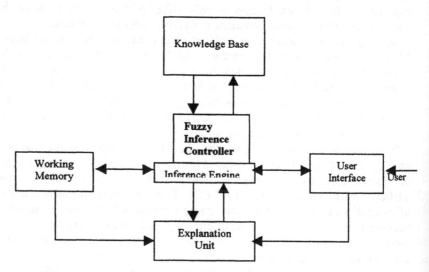

Figure 14.2 Extended expert system model with fuzzy inference control

Fuzzy inference controller stores various meta-rules which indicate how to employ fuzzy operators. Various fuzzy operators exist; for example, the *concentration* operator (CON) as described in Chapter 12. When the fuzzy priority vectors are used, a meta-rule can take a more concrete form such as

if the ith factor is involved in current request

then form a meta-level vector whose ith dimension is CON

and all the other dimensions take the value of 0.

For instance, meta-rules may use concentration CON(A), where $\lambda_{CON(A)}(x) = (\lambda_A(x))^2$. Note that the use of concentration operator will not change the relative relationship (namely, relative priority), but will increase the difference between priorities. If cutoff threshold remains unchanged, the number of rules in the conflict set will be reduced. For instance, suppose we use α-cut = 0.5, and the original conflict set consists of three rules with fuzzy priority numbers 0.5, 0.6, and 0.8, respectively. After the concentration operator is applied, the fuzzy priority numbers associated with these three rules become 0.25, 0.36, and 0.64, respectively; if α-cut remains unchanged, then only the last rule (with fuzzy priority number 0.64) will remain in the conflict set.

Another useful operator is intensification INT(A). The INT operation is like contrast intensification of a picture: it raise the membership grade of those elements within the crossover points and reduces the membership grade of those outside the crossover points, thus increasing the contrast grade between two kinds of elements. In our case, since each element represents a priority, the INT operation as specified in the meta-rules will increase the differences between the priority values associated with different rules, thus reducing the number of rules in the conflict rule set.

A top-level algorithm for fuzzy flexible inference control is shown below. This algorithm uses meta-rules to deal with conflict resolution by incorporating user environments or stereotypes.

While request from user do
1. categorize the user environment or stereotype;
2. fire a meta-rule;
3. perform fuzzy operations indicated by the meta-inference rule on domain rules;
4. perform backward chaining using activated domain rules;
5. display results to the user;

In the above algorithm, step 1 takes place in the user interface component U, step 2 takes place in the inference engine I and fuzzy inference controller C, step 3 takes place in fuzzy inference controller C and knowledge base K, step 4 takes place in inference engine I, knowledge base K and working memory W, and finally, step 5 again takes place in the user interface component U.

We use a fuzzy inference controller to reduce the size of the conflict set. The form of the meta-rules provided by the fuzzy inference controller follow what was described in the previous section; the following is an example:

if user belongs to ith type,

then form a meta-level reasoning vector

$(0, 0, ..., CON, ..., 0)$.

(namely, a vector with ith dimension set to fuzzy concentration operator, while all the other dimensions set to 0).

The vector as specified by the meta-level rule operates on rules (denoted as r_{KB}'s) in the knowledge base. This can be denoted as

$$max\ (\mathbf{r}_{meta}(r_{Kbi}))$$

(here we use bold face to emphasize that meta-rule $\mathbf{r}_{meta}$ is an operator). The specified operator is then further carried out through vector multiplication:

$$max\ (V_{meta} * V'_{KBi}),$$

where V_{meta} and V_{KBi} are two fuzzy priority vectors associated with the meta-rule and a rule in domain knowledge base, respectively; and a symbol ' is used to denote vector transposition.

To illustrate the idea of this approach, we use the following simple example. Consider an expert system which mimics a travel agency which selects appropriate trip packages for the users. Different users types have been defined. A sample rule defined in the knowledge base would be "If destination = Orlando and cost = Luxury then package = 1 with fuzzy priority vector (0.8, 0.8, 0.4)." To see how the fuzzy inference controller is used, consider a user of type family vacationer. A meta-rule stored in the fuzzy inference controller will be fired, which forms a fuzzy priority vector Vmeta = (0, 0, CON), because family vacationer is the third dimension in the vector. The result of vector mulitplication gives

$$max(0\ 0\ 1)(0.8\ 0.8\ 0.4)' = 0.4.$$

For more detail, see [Chen 1996a].

Flexible inference control is not necessarily be carried out in the context of fuzzy logic. A discussion (without specific concern over fuzzy logic) on user modeling for flexible inference control and its relevance to decision making in economics and management is provided in [Chen 1992b]. A more general discussion can be found in [Chen 1996b], where we discuss the issue of applying inductive reasoning on the different types of user so that the system behavior can be adapted to various situations.

14.4.2.3 Combining creativity and expertise using a meta-level interpreter

In Chapter 5 we discussed the basic architecture of rule-based expert systems, and in Chapter 6 we discussed the issue of knowledge modeling. In addition, in Chapter 8 we further discussed the need for combining creativity with expertise. How can we put all these things together? With the hope that creative knowledge can be used to enhance the reasoning ability of knowledge-based systems, in the following we sketch an extended expert system model where creative knowledge could be incorporated into knowledge-based systems and its impact on the architecture of these systems. We follow the discussion from [van Harmelen 1991] who distinguished three types of knowledge-based systems which are mixed up with object-level inference and meta-level inference:

- *Reflect-and-act systems*: the meta-level interpreter is called very frequently, before or after every object-level step.
- *Crisis-management systems*: the meta-level is called only if a crisis or an impasse occurs in the object level computation, for example when too many or not enough steps are possible at the object-level.
- *Subtask-management systems*: the meta-level knowledge is used to partition the object-level task into a number of subtasks.

Creative knowledge can be handled in a way similar to crisis-management systems, and an extended expert system architecture is depicted in Figure 14.2. In this extended model, the creative knowledge is consulted only if there is a need to do so. By this way, expertise and creativity thoughts can be used in a combined manner. For more detail of this approach, see [Chen 1997].

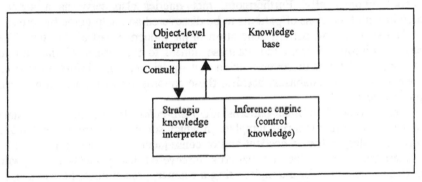

Figure 14.3 Extended expert system model

14.4.3 META-KNOWLEDGE AND META-PATTERNS IN DATA MINING

14.4.3.1 Meta-queries and meta rules

We now revisit the issue of data mining with emphasis on the role of meta knowledge. The discussion will mainly follow [Shen, Ong, Mitbander and Zaniolo 1996]. Meta-queries have been used to integrate inductive learning methods with deductive database technologies in the context of knowledge discovery from databases. Meta-queries are second-order predicates or templates. For example, let P, Q, and R be variables for predicates, then the following expression

$$P(X,Y) \wedge Q(Y,Z) \Rightarrow R(X, Z)$$

is an example of meta-query, which specifies that the patterns to be discovered are transitivity relations $p(X,Y) \wedge q(Y,Z) \Rightarrow r(X, Z)$, where p, q, and r are specific predicates. One possible result of this meta-query is the pattern

$$sales\ (X,Y) \wedge profitable\ (Y,Z) \Rightarrow making\text{-}money\ (X, Z)$$

with a probability (0.7)

where *sales, profitable* and *making-money* are relations that bind to P, Q, and R, respectively, in the current database.

Meta-queries are used for guiding deductive data collection, focusing attention for inductive learning, and assisting human analysts in the discovery loop. A system based on a framework has been developed which utilizes this idea to unify a Bayesian Data Cluster with the Logical Data Language (LDL++). According to this framework, meta-queries serve as the link between the inductive and deductive aspects of knowledge discovery, thus facilitating a deductive-inductive-human discovery loop. Meta-queries outline the data collecting strategy for the deductive part of the loop; they serve as the basis for the generation of specific queries, which are obtained by instantiating the variables in the meta-queries with values representing relations and attributes in the relational database of interest. These instantiated queries are then run against the database to collect relevant data. Users can either type their meta-queries directly, or have the system generate some initial meta-queries automatically. Furthermore, meta-queries also serve as a generic description of the class of patterns to be discovered and help guide the process of data analysis and pattern generation in the inductive part of the loop. The patterns discovered from the database adhere to the format of the current meta-query. Patterns discovered using meta-queries can link information from many relations in databases; besides, these patterns are relational (rather than propositional).

Closely related to meta-patterns are *meta-rules*. In the context of data mining, a meta-rule is a rule template in which some of the predicates (and/or their variables) in the antecedent and/or consequent of the meta-rule could be instantiated. Meta rules are patterns discovered using meta-queries with degree of certainty (for example, using a counter, probabilities, percentage, or something else). These rules can link information from many tables in databases, and they can be stored persistently for multiple purposes, including error detection, integrity constraints, or generation of more complex meta-queries.

According to [Shen, Ong, Mitbander and Zaniolo 1996], meta-queries can be specified by human experts or can be autoamtically generated from the database schema. They serve as an important interface between human discoverers and the discovery system. Using meta-queries, human experts can focus the discovery process onto more profitable areas of the database and the system generated meta-queries may provide valuable clues to the human experts.

14.3.3.2 Template design for mining association rules

Motivated from utilizing meta-knowledge for data mining, *templates* have been used more and more. For example, [Fu and Han 1995] employs a rule template to describe what forms of rules are expected to be found from the database, and such a rule template is used as a guidance or constraint in the data mining process. A classification of association rule types has been proposed in [Baralis and Psaila 1997], which provides a general framework for the design of association rule mining applications. Dimensions of rule types include mining condition, clustering condition, and filtering condition. Based on the identified association rule types, predefined templates can be introduced as a means to capture the user specification of mining applications. A general language to design templates has also been proposed for the extraction of arbitrary association rule types.

14.4.4 META-LEARNING

As already discussed in Chapter 10, closely related to data mining is the concept of machine learning, but these two have quite different focuses. Machine learning is more concerned with inference mechanisms involved in the overall process. For this purpose, it would be beneficial to examine the learning process itself, and meta-learning makes big sense. The following is a definition of *learning to learn*.

Given (a) a family of tasks, (b) training experience for each of these tasks, and (c) a family of performance measure (e.g., one for each task), an algorithm is capable of *learning to learn* if its performance at each task improves with experience *and* with a number of tasks.

In other words, a learning algorithm whose performance does not depend on the number of learning tasks, which hence would not benefit from the presence of other learning tasks, is not considered to fall in the category of learning to learn. For an algorithm to fit this definition, some kind of cognitive *transfer* must occur between multiple tasks that must have a positive impact on expected task performance.

As with traditional inductive machine learning methods, algorithms that learn to learn induce general functions from examples. However, learning to learn methods include an additional feature, which is that their learning bias is chosen based on learning experience in other tasks. Humans often generalize correctly after a small number of training examples by transferring knowledge acquired in other tasks; systems that learn to learn mimic this ability. Algorithms that learn to learn often outperform other learning algorithms [Thrun and Pratt 1998].

Other aspects of meta-learning also exist. For example, a discussion on meta learning and fuzzy sets can be found in [Pedrycz 1998].

14.4.5 SUMMARY AND REMARK ON META-ISSUES

In this section we examined several aspects of meta-issues. In general, when we talk about a meta-issue, there are always two levels involved: one is at the object level ("X"), the other is the second order ("X about X"). Examining different aspects of meta-issues in different contexts gives us a better understanding on how computational intelligence techniques can be used for decision making. There are many other meta issues not discussed here, and sometimes the prefix "meta" may have a meaning different from what we have seen so far. For example, we may take a brief look at *meta-talk*, which refers to meanings behind human beings' ordinary talk [Nierenberg and Calero 1974]. Talk exists on at least three levels of meaning:

(i)   What the speaker is saying;

(ii)   What the speaker thinks he is saying;

(iii)   What the listener thinks the speaker is saying.

The second and third levels require much more consideration than the first. Meta-talk is aimed to find hidden meanings in conversations.

Note that here meta-talk does not refer to "talk about talk;" rather, it refers to an analysis of talk. In this sense, meta-talk is related to modal logic and thus has some different concerns than those discussed in this section. Nevertheless, by analyzing the intention of the speaker, meta-talk may play an interesting role in decision support when conversations are an important part of a decision making process.

SUMMARY

In the last chapter, we have reviewed some important materials presented earlier in this book. The need for integrated heuristic decision making is discussed. We examined some important problem solving heuristics, which play the role of "invariant" for integrated decision making. Several meta-issues have been discussed, which illustrate the importance of control knowledge in problem solving. Various techniques summarized in this chapter are all important to creating intelligent agents for decision making. An important issue related to building intelligent agents is the development of self-adaptive software [Laddaga 1999].

To wrap up the whole book, we give the following final remarks. Technology keeps on changing, and it is essential to understand the important aspects underneath the surface. Studying high level heuristics or invariant behind these methods will help us to establish an integrated perspective of these techniques. It is important to keep in mind that learning existing techniques is an important aspect for intelligent decision making, but far from enough. More importantly, we should equip ourselves to deal with future challenges. This means that instead of having a piece of bread, we need the hunting gun. An intelligent agent is able to use a hunting gun that is powerful and flexible enough to get whatever he or she wants.

SELF-EXAMINATION QUESTIONS

1. In this chapter we discussed several high-level heuristics for integrated decision making. However, this discussion is far from complete; for example, other heuristics also exist. Try to identify at least one of them. (Hint: If you cannot think about anything else, consider the relationship between part and whole.)

2. Heuristics are rule of thumb; they are fallible. Give an example to illustrate how high-level heuristics may not work in some circumstances.

REFERENCES

Aha, D. W., *Lazy Learning*, Kluwer, Dordrecht, 1997.

Baralis, E. and Psaila, G., Design templates for mining association rules, *J. Intelligent Inf. Systems*, 9, 7-32, 1997.

Bienkowski, M.A., A reader's guide to agent literacy, *SIGART Bulletin*, 23-28, Fall 1998.

Chen, Z., *Comedy of Life* (in Chinese), unpublished manuscript, 1970.

Chen, Z., A conceptual framework for expert system description, *Computers and Education*, 18(4), 259-266, 1992a.

Chen, Z., User modeling for flexible inference control and its relevance to decision making in economics and management, *Computational Economics*, 6, 163-175, 1992b.

Chen, Z., Intelligence and discovery in an information society: An essay in memory of Derek de Solla Price, *The Information Society*, 9, 277-280, 1993a.

Chen, Z., On continuous AI and meta-knowledge, *Kybernetes*, 22(4), 78-84, 1993b.

Chen., Z., Using meta-rules for fuzzy inference control, *Fuzzy Sets and Systems*, 79(2), 163-173, 1996a.

Chen, Z., Users and system adaptivity: A GSPS perspective, *Int. J. General Systems*, 24 (1-2), 33-42, 1996b.

Chen, Z., Cybernetics and creativity: the metaphor of Brownian motions, *Kybernetes*, 25(5), 60-62, 1996c.

Chen, Z., Acquiring creative knowledge for knowledge-based systems, *Journal of Intelligent Systems*, 6(3/4), 179-198, 1997.

Connolly, T., Begg, C. and Strachan, A., *Database Systems: A practical Approach to Design, Implementation, and Management* (2nd ed.), Addison-Wesley, Harlow, England, 1998.

Cui, Y., Widom, J. and Wiener, J. L., Tracing the lineage of view data in a warehousing environment, Technical Note, Stanford University, 1997.

Faloutsos, C., Jagadish, H. V. and Sidiropoulos, N. D., Recovering information from summary data, *Proceedings of 23rd Conference of Very Large Data Bases (VLDB 97)*, pp. 36-45, 1997.

Fu, Y. and Han, J., Meta-rule-guided mining of association rules in relational databases, *Proceedings of International Workshop. on Knowledge Discovery and Deductive and Object-Oriented Databases (KDOOD'95)*, 1995.

Genesereth, M. R. and Nilsson, N. J., Logical Foundations of Artificial Intelligence, Morgan Kaufmann, Los Altos, CA, 1986.

Gravano, L. and Papakonstantinou, Y., Mediating and metasearching on the Internet, *Data Engineering Bulletin*, pp. 28-36, 21(2), 1998.

Howe, A. E. and Dreilinger, D., SavvySearch: A metasearch engine that learns which search engines to query, *Data Engineering Bulletin,* 21(2), 1998.

Kass, R. and Finin, T., The role of user models in cooperative interactive systems, *International Journal of Intelligent Systems,* 4, 81-112, 1989.

Khosla, I., Kuhn, B. and Soparkar, N., Database search using information mining, *Proceedings of 1996 ACM-SIGMOD International Conference on Management of Data,* 1996.

King, R. and Novak, M., Supporting information infrastructure for distributed, heterogeneous knowledge discovery, *Proceedings of SIGMOD 1996 Workshop on Research Issues on Data Mining and Knowledge Discovery,* Montreal, Canada, 1996.

Kuok, C. M., Fu, A. and Wong, M. H., Mining fuzzy association rules in databases, *SIGMOD Record,* 27(1), 41-46, 1998.

Laddaga, R. (guest ed.), Special issue: Creating robust software through self-adaptation, *IEEE Intelligent Systems & Their Applications,* 14(3), 26-62, 1999.

Nierenberg, G. I. and Calero, H. H., *Meta-talk: Guide to hidden meanings in conversations,* Trident Press, New York, 1974.

Pedrycz, W., *Computational Intelligence: An Introduction,* CRC Press, Boca Raton, FL, 1996.

Polya, G., *How to Solve it,* Princeton University Press, Princeton, NJ, 1957.

Poole, D., Mackworth, A. and Goebel, R., *Computational Intelligence: A Logical Approach,* Oxford University Press, New York, 1998.

Price, D., de S., *Little Science, Big Science,* Columbia University Press, New York, 1963.

Raeth, P., Fuzzy Engineering by Bart Kosko (book review), *SIGART Bulletin,* 39-41, Summer 1998.

Shen, W. M., Ong, K., Mitbander, B. and Zaniolo, C., Metaqueries for data mining, *Advances in Knowledge Discovery and Data Mining,* Chap. 15, 375-421, 1996.

Thrun, S. and Pratt, L. (eds.), *Learning to Learn,* Kluwer, Boston, 1998.

van Harmelen, F., *Meta-Level Inference Systems,* Morgan Kaufmann, San Mateo, CA, 1991.

Weiss, M. A., *Data Structures and Algorithm Analysis in C++* (2nd ed.), Benjamin/Cummings, Redwood City, CA, 1998.

Zaiane, O. R. and Han, J., Resource and knowledge discovery in global information systems: A preliminary design and experiment, *Proceedings of the First International Conference on Knowledge Discovery and Data Mining,* pp. 331--336, Montreal, Quebec, 1995.

INDEX